DATE DUE

NOV - 1 1994	
NOV 15 1994	
NOV 2 9 1994	
DEC 1 3 1994	
FEB 27 1995	
APR - 6 1996	
OCT - 8 1997	
OCT 22 1997	
NOV 1 2 1997	
NOV 27 1997	
OCT 27 1998	
OCT 11 1999	
NOV - 1 2001	
OCT 2 9 2002	

Festivals and Legends:
The Formation of Greek Cities
in the Light of Public Ritual

Public festivals are an important but neglected source of evidence for the physical and social development of Greek cities. Each city had a calendar of festivals that reflected the practical needs of the whole community. As the community grew and changed, so did the festival calendar and the program of a given festival. But though much was added, little was dropped; for ritual is by definition unchanging. Indeed the Greek cities, while originating a new form of society for the Western world, were strikingly conservative in their attachment to age-old ritual.

The festivals also gave rise to certain notions of the past that were cherished by the Greeks and still persist in conventional histories. The strange and solemn actions of ritual were inevitably understood as a re-enactment of momentary actions of long ago, actions that deserved to be commemorated. The action of long ago was deduced from the ritual and became a mythical adventure or a legendary battle. This is aetiology, the habit of explaining present customs from past events.

Ten festivals, and also a battlefield custom, have been selected for study. Five of the festivals belong to Athens, the city we know best; the others to Sparta, Argos, Messene, and Phigaleia. The festivals are mostly those addressed to the deities who preside over political organization and warfare, namely Apollo, Athena, and Zeus.

NOEL ROBERTSON is professor of Classics at Brock University. He has written and lectured on many topics of ancient, especially Greek, history and religion.

PHOENIX

Journal of the Classical Association of Canada
Revue de la Société canadienne des études classiques
Supplementary Volume XXXI
Tome supplémentaire XXXI

NOEL ROBERTSON

Festivals and Legends:
The Formation of Greek Cities
in the Light of
Public Ritual

UNIVERSITY OF TORONTO PRESS
Toronto Buffalo London

© University of Toronto Press 1992
Toronto Buffalo London
Printed in Canada

ISBN 0-8020-5988-0

Printed on acid-free paper

Canadian Cataloguing in Publication Data

Robertson, Noel
Festivals and legends : the formation of Greek cities
in the light of public ritual

(Phoenix. Supplementary volume ; 31 = Phoenix.
Tome supplémentaire, ISSN 0079-1784 ; 31)
ISBN 0-8020-5988-0

1. Festivals – Greece. 2. Legends – Greece. 3. Rites and
ceremonies – Greece. 4. Cities and towns, Ancient –
Greece. 5. War – Mythology. I. Title. II. Series: Phoenix.
Supplementary volume (Toronto, Ont.) ; 31.

DF123.R62 1993   394.2′6938   C92-094545-7

This book has been published with the help of a grant
from the Canadian Federation for the Humanities,
using funds provided by the Social Sciences and
Humanities Research Council of Canada.

For Laura

CONTENTS

ix Contents

MAPS

INDEXES

ABBREVIATIONS

Most abbreviations for ancient authors and standard works will be explicable from the lists in *The Oxford Classical Dictionary*[2] or in Liddell and Scott, *A Greek-English Lexicon*[9]. Periodical abbreviations follow *L'Année philologique*, unless they are fuller. These are additional:

CEG s. viii–v	P.A. Hansen, *Carmina Epigraphica Graeca saeculorum viii–v a. Chr. n.*, Berlin 1983
EGF	M. Davies, *Epicorum Graecorum Fragmenta*, Göttingen 1988
FGE	D.L. Page, *Further Greek Epigrams*, Cambridge 1981
GP	A.S.F. Gow and D.L. Page, *The Garland of Philip*, Cambridge 1968
HCT	A.W. Gomme *et al.*, *A Historical Commentary on Thucydides*, Oxford 1956–81
HE	A.S.F. Gow and D.L. Page, *Hellenistic Epigrams*, Cambridge 1965
LIMC	*Lexicon Iconographicum Mythologiae Classicae*, Zurich 1974–
LSAM	F. Sokolowski, *Lois sacrées de l'Asie Mineure*, Paris 1955
LSCG	F. Sokolowski, *Lois sacrées des cités grecques*, Paris 1969
LSCG Suppl.	F. Sokolowski, *Lois sacrées des cités grecques: Supplément*, Paris 1962
PEG	A. Bernabé, *Poetae Epici Graeci*, Leipzig 1987–
PMG	D.L. Page, *Poetae Melici Graeci*, Oxford 1962
Suppl. Hell.	H. Lloyd-Jones and P. Parsons, *Supplementum Hellenisticum*, Berlin 1983

The following are cited throughout by short title. For all other works, the full title and details of publication are given at the first occurrence in each chapter; thereafter a short title is used.

Bourriot, F., *Recherches sur la nature du genos*, Lille 1976

Camp, J.M., *The Athenian Agora*, London 1986

Carlier, P., *La Royauté en Grèce avant Alexandre*, Strasbourg 1984

Chantraine, P., *Dictionnaire étymologique de la langue grecque*, Paris 1968–80

Davies, J.K., *Athenian Propertied Families 600–300 BC*, Oxford 1971

Deubner, L., *Attische Feste*, Berlin 1932

Follet, S., *Athènes au IIe et au IIIe siècle*, Paris 1976

Frisk, H.J., *Griechisches etymologisches Wörterbuch*, Heidelberg 1960–72

Judeich, W., *Topographie von Athen²*, Munich 1931

Kolb, F., *Agora und Theater, Volks- und Festversammlung*, Berlin 1981

Kron, U., *Die zehn attischen Phylenheroen*, Berlin 1976

Kyle, D.G., *Athletics in Ancient Athens*, Leiden 1987

Martin, R., *Recherches sur l'agora grecque*, Paris 1951

Mommsen, A., *Feste der Stadt Athen*, Leipzig 1898

Nilsson, M.P., *Geschichte der griechischen Religion²*, Munich 1955–61

– *Griechische Feste*, Leipzig 1906

Parke, H.W., *Festivals of the Athenians*, London 1977

Pélékidis, C., *Histoire de l'éphébie attique des origines à 31 avant J.-C.*, Paris 1962

Rhodes, P.J., *A Commentary on the Aristotelian* Athenaion Politeia, Oxford 1981

Robert, C., *Die griechische Heldensage*, Berlin 1920–26

Robert, L., *Opera Minora Selecta*, Amsterdam 1969–89

Simon, E., *Festivals of Attica*, Madison 1983

Thompson, H.A., *The Athenian Agora: A Guide to the Excavation and Museum³*, Athens 1976

Thompson, H.A., and R.E. Wycherley, *The Athenian Agora XIV: The Agora of Athens*, Princeton 1972

Toepffer, J., *Attische Genealogie*, Berlin 1889

Travlos, J., *Pictorial Dictionary of Ancient Athens*, New York 1971

– *Poleodomikē exelixis tōn Athēnōn*, Athens 1960

Wilamowitz-Moellendorff, U. von, *Der Glaube der Hellenen*, Berlin 1931–2 (but I cite perforce *Glaube²*, Basel 1955, a pseudo-edition with slightly different paging)

Wycherley, R.E., *The Athenian Agora III: Literary and Epigraphical Testimonia*, Princeton 1957

– *The Stones of Athens*, Princeton 1978

INTRODUCTION

This book is meant to show that public festivals, a large part of life in every Greek city, can tell us much about secular history that is of general interest. They do so in two ways, positive and negative.

An old festival that has continued without change provides evidence for an early stage of society, evidence which is otherwise scarce. The setting, the facilities, the officiants, the festival business are all as of long ago. An old festival may be partly superseded by a later one, or a festival program may be enlarged; in such cases we can discern successive stages of society. And the details are concrete. Nowadays it is the fashion to interpret festivals and other ritual as a figurative language for expressing the more abstract values and attitudes of a given set of people. Every fashion has an element of truth, but in this one it is relatively small. Festivals are bound up with practical needs, and not only in Greece. They are a distinctive feature of every community, ancient or mediaeval or non-Western, that depends on a constant seasonal routine of farming and pasturing, of warfare and navigation. The Greek cities were such communities, but more tightly organized than most; their festivals were more frequent and elaborate than most. Athens, the leading city, also led in the number and variety of her festivals. Every ordinary concern is reflected. Here we shall focus on political organization and warfare.

In quite another way, the festivals bear on the narrative history of war and government. The Greeks themselves were much inclined to read off their past from the large impressive actions of public ritual, which they thought of as commemorating great men and great deeds. As a rule, the ritual is said to be a re-enactment or solemn mimicry of what was done on one memorable occasion. This is aetiology, i.e., the habit of explaining present customs by past events. The habit is deeply ingrained in Greek historical writing, and has larger consequences than scholars commonly admit. Much that is presented as a literal narrative of the past is not to be taken as literally true. Sometimes a real event, a battle or a coup, has been embroidered beyond recognition; sometimes the event itself is fictitious. Narrative history thus succeeds and perpetuates earlier myth and legend, for myth and legend are typically linked with existing customs. It will happen that the same custom is imprinted both in myth and in a quasi-historical episode.

At first sight these are different undertakings: to reconstruct social history, and to discount or re-evaluate narrative history. But in truth they are mostly inseparable. Take some great events of early Athenian history. Theseus 'synoecizes' Attica, concentrating settlement and power at Athens: though Theseus is a mythical figure, many accept the 'synoecism' as a real event, or a real process. Peisistratus drives into Athens in a chariot, with a pretended Athena beside him, and soon afterwards musters the people under arms, only to disarm them: many think that he really did thus and so. We shall find that all these events are quite straightforwardly deduced from festival actions. Negative conclusions, to be sure; though it is interesting to see how still other events are deduced from the same actions; as history loses, historiography gains. More importantly, once the 'synoecism,' the chariot, and the muster have been restored to their proper context, the festivals in question prove to be highly significant for the physical and social development of early Athens. From the festival sites, we see how the city grew, from southeast Athens to the old agora, then to the new Agora and the northwest sector. From the facilities and the officiants, we see how the citizen body was extended from a small Dark-Age community to phratry lodges throughout Attica.

Or consider some early battles and wars: Hysiae, Thyrea, the Messenian wars, the ordeal of Phigaleia. Each is generally accepted, and all are usually combined as the history of unfolding relations between Sparta, Argos, and other places. Yet these are local legends of independent origin; behind each is a local festival. The several stories changed with time, from myth or legend to a more chauvinistic episode. Local conditions changed as well, for these festivals were all conducted in border areas. By tracing the changes, we can reach a truer understanding of the early Peloponnesus.

If festivals have been seldom used for the purposes we envisage, the reason is that for most of them the detailed program is not understood. This, however, is due more to neglect than to lack of evidence. Festivals, like any matter of custom, are referred to quite offhandedly in our sources, literary or documentary. Many small, scattered indications must be brought together. The aetiology of the festival is itself a prime source of evidence. Often the festival action is but thinly disguised; often it emerges

as the common factor in different versions of a story. There is a great deal
to be done. Many festivals will prove informative when examined sensibly.
Here the choice falls on a few festivals of related interest, ten in all, and
on another Spartan custom for good measure.

Five are Athenian festivals. Three of them – the Hecatombaea, the
Synoecia, and the Panathenaea – come round in the first month of the
year, and all summon the citizen body to gather in strength – or did
so once, for these festivals clearly derive from different stages of Athens'
growth. The Hecatombaea and the Synoecia are both carried back in legend
to Theseus, but to Theseus young and old. Whereas the Hecatombaea
lapsed, the Synoecia were still celebrated long after the festival lost all
importance; for it is a festival of phratries, and they too were cherished even
when superseded. This ancient ceremony accordingly survived to inspire
a different sort of aetiology, the schematic delineation of early Attica by
[Aristotle] and Philochorus. Finally, the Panathenaea, as an ancient festival
of the Acropolis, received a new dimension at the hands of Peisistratus, as
did the actual city. The Panathenaea also signalize certain social changes
which the tyrant introduced, and which outlasted him.

Many other Athenian festivals suggest themselves for study; but two
may serve. The Oschophoria and other rites of the season throw further
light on early Athens. The Olympieia are another ancient festival refash-
ioned by Peisistratus, so that he vies with legendary heroes in the aetiology.

At Sparta the festival Gymnopaediae is again a general reunion of citizens at the beginning of the year. The program is chiefly of song and
dance, as handed down from early days. They had a warlike flavour, en-
hanced by some later innovations; but the modern view of this festival,
as a kind of military exercise, is far astray. Together with our festivals, it
seems worthwhile to consider a Spartan custom, the mass burial of fallen
soldiers on the field. It differs from the usual custom of Greek cities, but
goes far back: it is celebrated in myth and is even acknowledged in epic
poetry.

The other four festivals treated here belong to places round Sparta: the
Thyreatis, Argive Cenchreae, Mount Ithome, and Phigaleia. They have
this in common, that the aetiology turns on fighting with Sparta. It is
indeed a theme common to still other festivals of Argos and Arcadia.
These four are also similar in kind. Three of them are agonistic: the
Parparonia of the Thyreatis, a festival of Cenchreae for which we lack
a name, and the Ithomaea. At Phigaleia, the main festival action is a huge
blood-offering in the agora. Now agonistic festivals everywhere are traced
back to some mythical combat, death, and burial: i.e., festival games originate as funeral games for 'heroes.' Blood-offerings are likewise supposed

to honour 'heroes.' In both cases, a putative tomb is requisite to the festival site. Since the fighting with Sparta is attested chiefly by burials at the festival sites, it is evident that, as time passed, mythical heroes became legendary soldiers.

Our selection of festivals favours Apollo, Athena, and Zeus. At the Hecatombaea and the Gymnopaediae, Apollo presides over the reunion and enrolment of citizens and warriors; he was once a principal deity of war, as we see from the Boedromia and other widespread festivals. At the Panathenaea and the Oschophoria, Athena's interest in technology extends to weapons and ships. The Olympieia, Parparonia, and Ithomaea are addressed to Zeus as the weather god who was also potent in war; he and Athena are associated in the Synoecia as companion deities of the citadel and the adjacent city centre.

Such are the festivals considered here. Other deities and their ritual foster the staple livelihoods of the community; both sexes and all ages and conditions are recruited for various magic purposes. Greek festivals throw a flood of light on all aspects of society. Whether the present treatment will commend itself remains to be seen; there is, in any case, every incentive for others to do more, or do better.

PART ONE

Athens

1

The Hecatombaea,
the Enrolment of Citizens,
and Southeast Athens

Synopsis

Three Athenian festivals of the month Hecatombaeon, the first in the year, call for a reunion of the whole community: the Hecatombaea at the first quarter, the Synoecia at the full moon, the Panathenaea at month's end. These festivals did not flourish at the same period, nor do they reflect the same kind of society. Each in its turn was the chief new year's festival. The earliest is the Hecatombaea, a relic of the days when Athens was a fairly small community southeast of the Acropolis. The next is the Synoecia, which arose when Attica was first organized in phratries and a new area east of the Acropolis was marked out for their annual assembly. The latest to serve the purpose is the Panathenaea, though the festival itself is early.

The festival Hecatombaea is known only from its aetiology, the story of Theseus' arrival at Athens and his reception in the palace of Aegeus. Yet it belongs to a general type: a festival of Apollo at which youths just come of age are enrolled as citizens and warriors. At some cities such festivals were still important in the historical period. The Gymnopaediae of Sparta are examined later; a smaller instance, a rite on Myconos, is mentioned below. At Athens, however, society changed, and this observance was replaced by others.

The story of Theseus' 'enrolment' goes far back. There was no such ceremony in Classical Athens, nor indeed for much of the Archaic period. After Cleisthenes, young men were enrolled by the demes; before that, by the phratries. Enrolment at local phratry centres supersedes the enrolment ceremony in Athens. So the story arose at a time when Attica at large was not yet organized in phratries. That development can hardly be later than the early Archaic period, and may be earlier. The period during which our ceremony flourished was mainly or entirely the Dark Age. The festival business takes place in southeast Athens, and thus agrees with Thucydides' picture of Athens before Theseus enlarged it.

The southeast sector has a cluster of important shrines and festivals: Zeus *olympios* and the Olympieia, Apollo *pythios* and the Thargelia, Apollo *delphinios* and the Hecatombaea, Dionysus-at-Limnae and the Anthesteria. As Thucydides knew, they reflect the pattern of early settlement. It was remembered too that the spring Callirrhoe had once supplied the whole community. In Roman times, the surviving fountain-house was dismantled and removed to the Agora, like some other venerable monuments seen by Pausanias.

Thucydides' survey is not exhaustive: other shrines and festivals may be canvassed. The Acropolis festivals are the oldest of all, going back to Mycenaean times; one of them, however, was later amplified to take in the southeast. At the northwest, outside the settlement, potters and smiths were busy round Colonus-by-the-Agora. Their work was ceremonially linked with the Academy as a source of wood and fire, and this pattern continued when the Agora area was developed in the sixth century. At the northwest again, shrines of Demeter were planted along the main road so as to vie with Eleusis, until rivalry was superseded by the city Eleusinium.

The settlement at the southeast is also illustrated by the rural shrines at Agrae. Here are all the principal deities of agriculture, of pasturing, and, together with the Lyceium, of warfare. When they are added to Thucydides' instances, the calendar of early Athenian festivals is virtually complete.

Let us consider in turn the sources for Theseus' enrolment; the enrolment ceremony; southeast Athens; Thucydides on early Athens; the general distribution of Athenian shrines and festivals; and Agrae. (See maps 1 and 2.)

The Sources

Within the connected tale of Theseus' career, his arrival at Athens is a striking moment, and the story was told with little change (as compared with other episodes) long after the festival had lapsed. Bacchylides, Ovid, Plutarch, and Pausanias provide the main surviving accounts.[1] None of them draws on any nameable authority, though Plutarch's source is certainly one of the Attic chroniclers, and Pausanias' source is probably another. While Bacchylides comes long before the rest, he is not the most

---

1 Bacch. *Dithyr.* 17; Ov. *Met.* 7.404–52; Plut. *Thes.* 12.2–6; Paus. 1.19.1. Cf. Robert, *Heldensage* 724–9; H. Herter, *RE Suppl.* 13 (1973) 1080–3 *s.v.* Theseus 1; C. Sourvinou-Inwood, *Theseus as Son and Stepson* (*BICS Suppl.* 40, 1979) 18–58.

illuminating for the ritual. The details he gives of Theseus' appearance are only a realistic rendering of a young adventurer, as on vases.[2]

The story was treated in plays of Euripides and Sophocles, both called *Aegeus*, and afterwards by Attic chroniclers and Hellenistic poets. Like Bacchylides, they all depend in the first instance on epic poetry. The epics that survived were doubtless fairly late, but Theseus had been celebrated since at least the early Archaic period, when our evidence begins.[3]

To be sure, his exploits then were not the connected tale we know; the legend grew as Athens did, and some episodes were added at a late stage. The labours on the road from Troezen are as late as the last decades of the sixth century, and Medea's role is later still. Some infer that the story of Theseus' arrival and reception is equally late. Such a view ignores the ritual background, and not only the Hecatombaea. Our festival is the first of several rites, falling in successive months, that shaped the Theseus legend from the start. This larger background will be considered later, apropos of the Oschophoria (pp. 131–3). We must wait till then to see the full credentials of our story.

The Enrolment Ceremony

Plutarch mentions the date of Theseus' arrival in Athens, 8 Hecatombaeon, in two passages.[4] In the second he cites Diodorus the Periegete, but in the first he follows an Attic chronicler who went on to describe the reception in the palace. The palace proves to be the well-known shrine of Apollo *delphinios*. So the date is directly linked with an Apolline festival, obviously the ancient festival Hecatombaea from which the first month is named.[5] Apollo's holy day is the seventh, the first quarter serving as a signal for a community reunion. The eighth is specified instead either because this day was set apart for the enrolment of young men or because Theseus, and

---

2 Bacchylides' rendering of Theseus is thought to be significant in other ways by R. Merkelbach, *ZPE* 12 (1973) 56–62, and by J.P. Barron, *BICS* 27 (1980) 1–8. Merkelbach holds that Athens' *ephebeia* is mirrored in Theseus and his labours, and that the poem was composed for 'a festival of the ephebes,' a category which is said to include several festivals, e.g., the Theseia. But Theseus does not especially resemble a member of the ephebic corps as we know it later. Barron with remarkable ingenuity finds allusions in every line to Cimon and his family.

3 On epic poetry about Theseus, see L. Radermacher, *Mythos und Sage*[2] (Munich 1943) 252–3; Herter, *RE Suppl.* 13 (1973) 1046–7 s.v. Theseus 1.

4 Plut. *Thes.* 12.2, 36.5 (Diodorus *FGrHist* 372 F 38).

5 Cf. F. Graf, *MusHelv* 36 (1979) 14–18. C. Calame, *Thésée et l'imaginaire Athénien* (Lausanne 1990) 229, 319–24, ignores the Hecatombaea and associates Apollo *delphinios* with the Pyanopsia, for no visible reason.

also Poseidon, are otherwise associated with the eighth of a given month, especially 8 Pyanopsion.

Both in Plutarch and in Pausanias, Theseus on his arrival goes straight to this shrine of Apollo *delphinios*. In Pausanias we hear of a newly built temple, and in Plutarch of an open precinct, as it seems, with a gateway and a herm at the east; also of a fenced enclosure within the precinct, where the poison cup was spilt. The same setting comes into view again when Aegeus sacrifices the Marathonian bull to Apollo *delphinios*. Plutarch says that Aegeus lived here, and that the gateway was called by his name; in Ovid too the festival takes place at the king's palace.[6] There are other stories about a hero's reception, as we shall see below, in which a shrine of Apollo becomes a notional palace.

It is obvious at once that the occasion is the enrolment of young men as citizens, their transition from boyhood to manhood. In Pausanias, Theseus is jeered for wearing boyish finery, long braided hair and a robe down to his ankles, looking in fact like a marriageable maiden; then he proves himself a man.[7] Plutarch has an equivalent story about Theseus' coming of age at Troezen. He went to Delphi, as was the custom then for 'those graduating from boyhood,' οἱ μεταβαίνοντες ἐκ παίδων, and sheared his hair, but only in front, in the ancient warrior style (*Thes.* 5).

Theseus conducts himself like other youths just come of age, but with some exaggeration. They typically display their strength by hoisting up the oxen at the altar;[8] Pausanias tells how Theseus threw two cart oxen higher than the temple roof. In the more familiar version, Theseus wrestles the Marathonian bull, and breaks off a horn, and ties the animal with a rope, and drags it to the place of sacrifice.[9]

---

6 Plut. *Thes.* 12.4–6, 14.1; Paus. 1.19.1; Ov. *Met.* 7.427–9, 451–2; also Diod. 4.59.6.

7 Graf, *MusHelv* 36 (1979) 15, discerns a custom of dressing ephebes as maidens, said to be typical of 'initiatory rites.' In my opinion, both the custom and the category are misconceived. Cf. *Dining in a Classical Context*, ed. W.J. Slater (Ann Arbor 1991) 34, on exchange of dress; *HSCP* 87 (1983) 279–80 and *EMC*² 9 (1990) 426–9, 10 (1991) 62–5, on initiation rites.

8 Athenian ephebes are praised for αἴρεσθαι τοὺς βοῦς chiefly at the Mysteries, but also at the Proerosia and other rites unnamed: Pélékidis, *Éphébie* 223. Tanagra has an ephebic contest called βοάρσιον: L. Robert, *RevPhil* 65 (1939) 122–8 = *Op. Min. Sel.* 2.1275–81 line 21 (after AD 212). At Rhodes we find two groups of βοάρσαι called after 'Polycles' and 'Teisagoras' respectively: A. Maiuri, *Nuova silloge epigrafica di Rodi e Cos* (Florence 1925) 18 lines 27–9 (s. i a.); *IG* 12.1.102 line 8, cf. 1 (undated). They are not ephebes, but might be age-mates. Athena is called βοαρμία, among other warlike epithets, at Lycophr. *Alex.* 520; the scholiast explains it falsely as 'fitting,' ἁρμόσαι, oxen to the yoke.

9 Herter, *RE Suppl.* 13 (1973) 1083–90 s.v. Theseus 1.

It was also appropriate for the youths to help in cooking, as in the Apolline sacrifice of *Iliad* I: here they stand beside the old priest and hold the spits.[10] Athenian ephebes of the Hellenistic period are praised for 'distributing the meat' at the Mysteries.[11] Theseus too offers to cleave the meat, and draws his sword under the eyes of Aegeus, so that this is the means of recognition. Both the sword and the other token, the sandals, remind us that the young men are now invested with their arms, and that in very early days, before any hoplite armour was heard of, the main items were sword and sandals.

The young men are presented to the citizen assembly. In Plutarch, it is only after the sacrifice and recognition that Aegeus convenes the citizens and presents his son. In Ovid too, the festive crowd is mentioned at a later stage; both *patres* and ordinary people are now on hand – perhaps meaning the Council and the Assembly – to drink wine and sing and pray. Yet the preceding sacrifice is obviously part of the general celebration. In this respect Bacchylides' version is a little closer to the reality: the citizens muster in arms before Theseus' arrival.[12]

Such then is the festival that we see behind the story of Theseus' reception in Athens. The story must go back to that distant time when the festival was still of consequence. Later the occasion was neglected, though of course there may have been some token sacrifice by the authorities. The story could never be dropped, however, or even varied to any great extent; it forms an essential episode in Theseus' career. Furthermore, the Delphinium continued to exist and provided opportunity for a little more detail. For example, it may well have been an Attic chronicler who first said that the fenced area in the precinct was the spot where the poison was spilt. This exciting but obvious notion need not derive from any ritual.

In the fourth century, Apollo's shrine kept at least one association with the enrolment of citizens, as we see from the orators. An oath to be taken rather seriously was one which a mother swore in the Delphinium, attesting the paternity of her children.[13] In other cities, chiefly in Ionia and on Crete, Apollo *delphinios* long maintained a central role in civic life. His shrine might house the common hearth, or serve for the display of civic documents, particularly those awarding citizenship or *proxenia*.[14] As the pattern is strongest in Ionia, especially at Miletus and her colonies, it

10 *Il.* 1.465: νέοι δὲ παρ' αὐτὸν ἔχον πεμπώβολα χερσίν.
11 *Hesperia* 16 (1947) 170–2 no. 67 lines 15–16 (the first half of *IG* 2² 1009, 116–115 BC): καὶ καλλιερήσαντες διενείμαντο τὰ κρέα.
12 Plut. *Thes.* 12.5; Ov. *Met.* 7.430–4, 451–2; Bacch. *Dithyr.* 17.3–4.
13 Isaeus 12 *Euphil.* 9; [Dem.] 40 *Boeot.* (2) 11.
14 See Graf, *MusHelv* 36 (1979) 7–13.

is natural to suppose that Apollo *delphinios* had once spread from there to other places, including Athens.

There is also some corroborative evidence for the ritual.[15] The calendar of sacrifice published on Myconos in ca. 200, after two towns were united in one, includes an entry for 7 Hecatombaeon, the festival of Apollo *hekatombios*.[16] The animal victims are a bull and ten lambs, an economical form of 'hecatomb'; they answer to the oxen in our rite, or to the Marathonian bull. Two age groups are on hand, 'boys' and 'youths,' here called νυμφίοι.[17] Both the boys and the youths somehow assist in the sacrifice, for, like the priest, they are assigned certain portions of the victims. Perhaps the bull was manhandled by the youths. On the same day the river-god Achelous is separately honoured, and with a similar offering, a mature sheep and ten lambs. River-gods too watch over the rearing of boys and their coming of age.

One of Athens' homicide courts, that which dealt with pleas of lawful killing, is said to meet 'at the Delphinium.' The similar phrase used of another homicide court – 'at the Palladium,' i.e., at the statue so called – suggests that the court met in an adjoining area, and not within the very precinct. It is unlikely that these venues have any ritual or doctrinal significance. The courts presumably go back to the time when settlement was concentrated at the southeast; Delphinium and Palladium were obvious and contrasting landmarks.[18] We are told, but only by late sources, that Aegeus established the court at the Delphinium and that Theseus was tried here and acquitted.[19] The offence however may be either the killings on the road from Troezen or the killing of Pallas' sons; as to the former, Plutarch gives us instead, after some Attic chronicler, a purification at the

---

15 Nothing is known from the Attic demes that seems related to Athens' Hecatombaea. The calendar of Thoricus mentions 'the Delphinium' near the beginning (line 6), under Hecatombaeon, where the stone is mostly cut away: G. Daux, *AntClass* 52 (1983) 152–4. Yet this local shrine appears again a little farther on (line 11), probably under Metageitnion, in virtue of a sacrifice that took place 'beside' it, and for another deity than Apollo. The former sacrifice, which is a goat, probably took place 'beside' it too, and later in the month than the seventh.

16 *SIG*³ 1024.29–39 (*LSCG* 96). Cf. Nilsson, *Gr. Feste* 174, 425.

17 Elsewhere this word means always 'bridegrooms,' but the sense might easily pass into 'prospective bridegrooms,' youths of an age to marry.

18 It has been argued that the cases tried at the Delphinium and the Palladium are the residue of Athens' original homicide law, after other cases were transferred to the Areopagus: R. Sealey, *CP* 78 (1983) 275–96. R. Parker, *Miasma* (Oxford 1983) 142 n. 157, remarks that the Delphinium is 'suitable as a court' because the god is 'associated with civic life'; but it is not particularly suitable for homicide cases.

19 Paus. 1.28.10; schol. Patm. Dem. 23 *Aristocr.* 74; Poll. 8.119; Etym. Gen. *s.v.* ἐπὶ Δελφινίωι.

river Cephisus (*Thes.* 12.1). Theseus' connection with the homicide court is plainly secondary.

Southeast Athens

Pausanias locates the temple of Apollo *delphinios* in the farthest part of southeast Athens, somewhere between the Olympieium and the Ilissus (1.19.1). Excavation hereabouts has uncovered a Doric temple of the mid fifth century and not far away an Archaic building so substantial that it must have had some civic use. They have been claimed as Pausanias' temple and as the lawcourt 'at the Delphinium,'[20] but neither identification seems at all secure. In fact none of the shrines known to lie in this area can be precisely fixed.

The festival takes place at Apollo's shrine. There must have been some open ground to accommodate the citizen assembly; in early days, at the edge of the city, this is easy to imagine. In other cities the shrine of Apollo *delphinios* adjoins the agora.[21] We should note, however, that at Athens our shrine and festival are far removed from the city centre, as it later came to be: the area just below the east face of the Acropolis. Here was the agora, and the chief public buildings such as the Prytaneium, and some important shrines. This area too was venerable enough, and the agora was called 'Cecropian' or 'old' to distinguish it from the new Agora or 'Cerameicus' at the northwest. Yet when our festival first arose, the city centre did not exist. Its creation was ascribed to Theseus himself after he became king. He brought all the people of Attica into the city and gave them a government of magistrates, a legendary action described in various terms, as a 'synoecism' or a proclamation or the like. It too is deduced from a festival, one celebrated in the city centre: the Synoecia. The festival Synoecia and its aetiology are later than the festival Hecatombaea and its aetiology.

The Delphinium is in fact linked with the city centre in a rite of 6 Munichion, when girls parade from the Prytaneium to Apollo's shrine in order to make supplication for the launching of ships.[22] In this form the rite is later than the Hecatombaea, though it was likewise drawn into the tale of Theseus' youthful exploits.

Aegeus is said to reside as king in southeast Athens. To be sure, Aegeus has connections with other parts of the city; his role as Theseus' father and

---

20 J. Threpsiades and J. Travlos, *Deltion* 17 (1961) [1963] *Chron.* 9–14; R.E. Wycherley, *GRBS* 4 (1963) 166–8, and *Stones of Athens* 166–7; Travlos, *Pictorial Dict.* 83–90.

21 At Miletus, Olbia, Drerus, Aegina: cf. Graf, *MusHelv* 36 (1979) 5–6.

22 Plut. *Thes.* 18.1–2. Since Theseus and his companions start from the Prytaneium, the processioners will do likewise; the mythical action is projected from the rite.

hence as king is secondary to some independent role;[23] but only Aegeus the king is of interest here. Codrus is another king whose sole exploit takes place in extreme southeast Athens.[24] Disguised as a woodcutter, he was slain by the enemy somewhere near the Ilissus; the spot was always known, and in the Roman period was marked by a relief and an epigram. This adventure caused him to be associated in due course with Neleus, whose shrine was nearby. Again, Codrus' role as king is secondary – obviously so, since he belongs to the second line of kings, beginning with Melanthus and turning into virtual archons with Medon; this line is a late addition to Athenian myth and genealogy, but the several figures who make up the line existed independently before. Codrus the king is nearly the last of the second line, as Aegeus was of the first: Codrus and Medon are in this respect parallel to Aegeus and Theseus, different renderings of the same transition. In short, the last kings of Athens were sought and found at the southeast.

The time when kings ruled at the southeast was the Dark Age. In the Mycenaean period, Athens' wealth and power were based on the Acropolis. It is there that Athens' most ancient kings are firmly lodged: Cecrops, Erichthonius, Erechtheus, Pandion. Again, these figures do not originate as legendary kings. They are easily recognized as personifications of ritual in the Acropolis cults and festivals of Zeus and Athena. It is significant, however, that such figures were recruited as kings. In contrast to Aegeus and Codrus, earlier kings were invariably sought and found on the Acropolis.

The existing shrine of Apollo *delphinios* was equated with Aegeus' palace. In other cities too a notable shrine of Apollo is equated with the palace of a legendary king, and in a context somewhat resembling Theseus' reception: the king welcomes a hero from abroad.[25] Tydeus and Polyneices, coming from different quarters, happen to arrive together in Argos on a stormy night, and they fight each other for shelter or for animal hides as a covering. The setting is described now as Apollo's shrine, now as the porch of Adrastus' palace. Other details identify the shrine as that of Apollo *pythaeus* on the flank of the Aspis. Since Tydeus and Polyneices are at once betrothed to the king's daughters, we see that this is the spring festival of

23 For evidence and opinions about Aegeus, see Kron, *Phylenheroen* 120–40, and *LIMC* 1.1 (1981) 359–67 s.v. Aigeus; E. Kearns, *The Heroes of Attica* (*BICS Suppl.* 57, 1989) 142. For the shrine below the southwest bastion of the Acropolis, see L. Beschi, *ASAtene* 45–6 (1967–8) [1969] 520, 526–8. Aegeus founds Athens' cult of Aphrodite *ourania*, and is named for Aphrodite's animal, the goat, and always stands in need of women's magic: unmistakable clues to his nature.

24 For Codrus in cult and myth and quasi-history, see *GRBS* 29 (1988) 224–30, 259–60.

25 Cf. *Dining in a Classical Context* 29–33.

Apollo at which betrothals were commonly announced. Alcathous, another wandering hero, comes to Megara to win the king's daughter. The betrothal takes place in the palace, but forms an *aition* of the festival of Apollo *pythios*; his shrine was on the hill Alcathous.

These shrines and stories likewise take us back to the Dark Age. It is true that at Argos and Megara the shrines are built on hills that may once have served as Mycenaean citadels. The later settlements, however, occupied the same sites; and the stories point to later conditions.

Thucydides on Early Athens

Thucydides says that the earliest settlement at Athens was at the southeast (2.15.3–6). His first definition is 'the Acropolis ... and the part below it lying mainly to the south.' But when he proceeds to name five landmarks, they all point to the extreme southeast: the Olympieium, the Pythium, the shrine of Ge, the shrine of Dionysus-at-Limnae, the spring Callirrhoe. Of the last two, a word more in a moment.[26] Thucydides also contrasts this settlement, as we have just done, with the city centre east of the Acropolis. For the early settlement was first enlarged when Theseus 'synoecized everyone,' ξυνώικισε πάντας, and installed 'a single Council-house and Prytaneium' (15.2).

The point of Thucydides' digression has not always been grasped.[27] The Athenians love the countryside, he says; the disruption of 431, when they were forced to remove to the city, had no counterpart in history save only Theseus' synoecism (15.1–2). 'Before this,' τὸ δὲ πρὸ τοῦ, Athens itself was that small settlement at the southeast (15.3). After describing

26 The Olympieium, the Pythium, and the shrine of Ge should not require any subtle exegesis. To be sure, it is disputed whether Apollo's cave below the Acropolis was another 'Pythium' of note; against this, Wycherley, *AJA* 67 (1963) 75–9; Ernst Meyer, *RE* 24 (1963) 554–8 *s.v.* Pythion 2. It is also suggested, though with little warrant, that Zeus *olympios* was established near Apollo's cave; against this, Wycherley, *AJA* 63 (1959) 68–72. K. Clinton, *AJP* 94 (1973) 282–8, reaffirms both Acropolis locations. It is even conjectured that the shrines of southeast Athens were generally duplicated at the northwest; but any attraction that this view may once have had is now, one hopes, dispelled by evidence fixing the traditional city centre east of the Acropolis. These vexed questions are relevant only for one who believes that Thucydides, having pointed to the south, immediately talks about the north; or else that the Devil has substituted νότον for βορρᾶν in his text.

27 Gomme for once is far astray (on Thuc. 2.15.3). He refuses to see a contrast between Athens before and after Theseus ('What, in that case, was his picture of Athens between the age of Theseus and that of Kylon?'), and sees instead a description of Athens' growth, down to the tyrants.

the settlement, he continues: 'So the Athenians were attached for the most part to an independent abode in the countryside,' τῆι τε οὖν ἐπὶ πολὺ κατὰ τὴν χώραν αὐτονόμωι οἰκήσει μετεῖχον οἱ Ἀθηναῖοι – independent, that is, until Theseus abolished Council-houses and Prytaneia up and down Attica – 'and when they had in fact been synoecized,' καὶ ἐπειδὴ ξυνωικίσθησαν, many still went on in the old style, right until 431 (16.1). Thucydides' demonstration of Athenian rusticity consists partly in the smallness of the original settlement at Athens, partly in the numerous country towns or *poleis* which are a precondition for the legendary 'synoecism.'

The original settlement is attested by those 'ancient shrines'; Thucydides knew of others, which he does not name,[28] and the Delphinium was doubtless among them. With the shrines go festivals, including the Anthesteria, 'the older Dionysia,' as the festival of Dionysus-at-Limnae. In mentioning the Olympieium and the Pythium, Thucydides doubtless thought of the festivals Olympieia and Thargelia;[29] but the festival Hecatombaea was altogether too obscure. The Anthesteria were much the best example, being common to all Ionians, and so indubitably of ancient origin.

Dionysus-at-Limnae is mentioned last among the shrines. Topographers have long been baffled or deceived in their attempts to locate this shrine, but perhaps it is at last within our ken. Actual 'marshes' have been traced archaeologically southwest of the Olympieium.[30] Dionysus' shrine was probably close to that of Neleus, which we know to have been somewhere at the extreme southeast. In a decree of 418–417 on behalf of Neleus' shrine, a large catchment area is marked off on one side by 'the Dionysium.'[31]

---

28 'Still other ancient shrines are situated here' (2.15.4).

29 The Pythium and the Thargelia are associated in the decree published by W. Peek, *AthMitt* 66 (1941) 181–95 no. 2 (129–128 BC) lines 26–7, 33–4 (*LSCG Suppl.* 14), and in the Suda *s.v.* Πύθιον.

30 Travlos, *Pictorial Dict.* 332.

31 *IG* 1³ 84 line 35. The other three sides are indicated by two of the city gates and by 'the public building,' ἡ οἰκία ἡ δημοσία. Wycherley, *BSA* 55 (1960) 64–5, thought that the Dionysium was the shrine at the theatre, marking the northern boundary of a long narrow strip running south towards the Ilissus. Yet Dionysus-at-Limnae seems far more likely. Cf. Travlos, *Pictorial Dict.* 291, 332–3 (but the precise coordinates for the shrine of Neleus may be doubted); N.W. Slater, *ZPE* 66 (1986) 259 (but the spot where Codrus fell, which was outside the city wall, is not to be identified with the shrine of Neleus, still less with the catchment area). Slater 255–64 holds that the Lenaea were celebrated at the shrine of Dionysus-at-Limnae, but this festival requires a setting distinct from that of the Anthesteria.

In the festival Anthesteria, leading roles were reserved for the archon Basileus and his wife, the Basilinna.[32] These roles devolve from the early kingship and suggest that the king was called 'Basileus' instead of 'Anax' because his function was to manage community resources such as the new wine.[33] The shrine of Dionysus-at-Limnae was perhaps the starting-point for the procession of the Oschophoria, which brings the season's bounty from Athens to a nautical shrine at Phalerum. As we shall see, this too is an early element of the Theseus legend.

As to the spring Callirrhoe, embellished by the tyrants as the fountain-house Enneacrunus, there has been quite needless controversy or *parti pris*.[34] Thucydides turns to Callirrhoe after the four shrines; it must have been a little farther off, perhaps outside the settlement, on the Ilissus bank. Other good evidence squarely supports a location beside the Ilissus.[35] But since Pausanias saw a like-named work of Peisistratus in the Agora (1.14.1), it is easy to suppose that the main elements of that famous fountain-house were brought there and reassembled in the Roman period. This was done with several Classical items, including the entire temple of Ares and Athena – which Pausanias also records as if it had never moved.[36] His mention of

---

32 [Dem.] 59 *Neaera* 73–9; [Arist.] *Ath.* 3.5. G.H. Macurdy, *AJP* 49 (1928) 276–82, holds that the term 'Basilinna' or 'Basilissa' for the archon's wife is only an invidious comment of the orator; but ἡ τοῦ ἄρχοντος βασίλισσα appears as a title in the Athenian decree for Julia Domna: J.H. Oliver, *HSCP Suppl.* 1 (1940) 527–30 lines 30–1. For other details of the Anthesteria, *HSCP* 94 (1992).

33 Though the office of Basileus in Linear B is far from clear, it has much to do with the collection or distribution of commodities: Carlier, *Royauté* 108–16. Early 'kings' constantly appear in the myths of Dionysus: *GRBS* 29 (1988) 217.

34 Cf. Wycherley, *Testimonia* 137–42 nos. 434–55; E.J. Owens, *JHS* 102 (1982) 222–5. Owens reviews the controversy once more, and suggests that the name 'Enneacrunus' was transferred from the Ilissus area to the Agora in the first half of the fourth century BC. Yet Isocrates, and much later Alciphron, do not at all imply that Enneacrunus was in the Agora (a view adopted by Owens from the Agora excavators); in the Hellenistic period, [Plato] and 'Tarantinus' *apud* Hierocles still point to the Ilissus. Pausanias is wholly isolated.

35 Hdt. 6.137.3; schol. Ar. *Eq.* 526a (Cratin. fr. 198 Kassel and Austin); [Pl.] *Ax.* 364 A, D; Hierocl. *Hippiatr. praef.* (Wycherley, *Testimonia* 139 no. 443); Him. fr. 1.7; Etym. Magn. *s.v.* Ἐννεάκρουνος. A likely site has been found; I come to it below, apropos of the Metroüm in Agrae.

36 For material transplanted to the Agora between Augustus and Hadrian, see Thompson and Wycherley, *Agora of Athens* 160–8; T.L. Shear, Jr., *Hesperia* 50 (1981) 364; W.B. Dinsmoor, Jr., *Hesperia* 51 (1982) 410–52; Camp, *Ath. Agora* 184–7. Some of it comes from other parts of Attica, but not, it seems, the large altar in front of the Metroüm: the Agora excavators trace it to the Pnyx; I argue below that it is the altar of Eirene, and comes from the old agora.

Enneacrunus does not show exactly where it was in the Agora.[37] Several fountain-houses were constructed under the early Empire, and in all cases the superstructure is very little known.[38]

Thucydides says that the early community relied on Enneacrunus for most of its need of water, so that nuptial baths and other ritual always continued to use water from this source. Herodotus too, citing Athenian tradition, says that in early days Athenian girls typically fetched water from Enneacrunus, being thus exposed to lascivious Pelasgians who dwelt 'under Hymettus.' In the same context, though on the word of Hecataeus, which Herodotus impugns, the Acropolis is said to have been fortified just beforehand by Pelasgian workmen.[39] The two indications give us a settlement of the same extent as in Thucydides: the Acropolis and the southeast sector. Pausanias knows of a small settlement that includes the Acropolis, for he says that Athena's olive-wood statue was held in honour 'for many years before they came together from the demes,' i.e., long before the synoecism (1.26.6).

We see then that the general shape of Dark-Age Athens was well remembered in later days. This is hardly surprising; an inhabitant of London or Paris could tell us where the early settlement lay. The next stage of Athens' development, the old agora east of the Acropolis, does not depend on later memory; it was always preserved and recognized as the centre of the city after it spread beyond the southeast area.

The General Distribution of Athenian Shrines and Festivals

Thucydides names four ancient shrines at the southeast. A further question comes to mind. Taking all the old shrines and festivals of which we have some knowledge, how are they distributed throughout the city? Though perfectly feasible, the question seems not to have been asked before. Instead, the door is open to misleading assertions. We are told, for example, that Athenian worship is focused on the Acropolis as the ancient seat of royal power, in contrast to the 'bipolar' scheme of other Greek cities,

---

37 At this stage of his tour, Pausanias advances 'in a series of jumps': Thompson and Wycherley, *Agora of Athens* 205. Although the Southeast Fountain-house is now the favourite candidate for Enneacrunus, it was formerly the larger and handsomer fountain-house at the southwest. Owens, *JHS* 102 (1982) 224, raises some objections to the Southeast Fountain-house.

38 Two fountain-houses were constructed in the Agora in the first century BC, both at the southwest, and a century later the Nymphaeum at the southeast, this as part of larger changes in the water system: Thompson and Wycherley, *Agora of Athens* 201–3.

39 Hdt. 6.137 (Hecataeus *FGrHist* 1 F 127).

where the outlying territory is fully integrated by various shrines and processions.[40] But Greek worship is not a means of expressing spatial or social relationships. The cults of the Acropolis are concerned with Acropolis business, so to speak; those of the lower city, with all the other resources and activities on which the community depends. At the southeast, Zeus and Apollo and Dionysus account for several of the principal concerns. A little farther off, in the same direction, the cults of Agrae account for most of the others. This is the overall pattern; let us examine some details.

On the Acropolis, Zeus and Athena go back to Mycenaean times. The festivals of Zeus – the Pandia and the Dipolieia – mark the seasonal transitions for the two staple livelihoods, pasturing and agriculture, that are conspicuous in the respective aetiologies. The myth of the Pandia reflects a far-ranging transhumance, as between the king of Athens and a shepherd chief of central Greece, that can hardly have existed after the Mycenaean period.[41] Zeus is worshipped under the open sky, but Athena has a temple, at Athens as everywhere in Greece: the daughter of the weather god is the fire from heaven that once was kept within the palace as a wooden fetish and the flame beside it. The festivals of Athena – the Plynteria, the Arrhephoria, and the Panathenaea – celebrate the turning of the year and the recruitment of fresh resources for the palace economy. Her servitors in cult, weavers and millers, resemble the several corps of female craftsmen in the Linear B tablets;[42] indeed the goddess herself acquires the same features.

Whereas the rites of Zeus and Athena are proper to the Acropolis, it is remarkable that one of them, the Arrhephoria, includes an excursion to the lower city by two of Athena's servitors.[43] They leave the Acropolis

---

40 So F. de Polignac, *La Naissance de la cité grecque* (Paris 1984) 87–91. Note in passing that the bipolar scheme is quite illusory, resting on partial evidence and on the unwarranted assumption that the siting and the popularity of a given shrine are determined by abstract relationships rather than by elementary needs. As for the evidence, Polignac relies entirely on excavated shrines, both in the homeland and overseas. Although this evidence is now abundant, it cannot reveal the pattern of worship in any single city, much less a universal pattern; for excavation is always limited and sporadic, and favours the rural or isolated site; whence Polignac's emphasis on extra-urban shrines.

41 Cf. *Ancient Economy in Mythology: East and West*, ed. M. Silver (Savage, Md. 1991) 5–8.

42 Cf. J.-C. Billigmeier and J.A. Turner in *Reflections of Women in Antiquity*, ed. H. Foley (New York 1981) 2–6, 15–18; P. Carlier in *La Femme dans les sociétés antiques*, ed. E. Lévy (Strasbourg 1983) 14–22.

43 *HSCP* 87 (1983) 243–88. Earlier studies of the Arrhephoria were often far astray. P. Brulé, *La Fille d'Athènes* (Paris 1987) 79–98, reviews the question once again, and

at night, obviously by the path at the northeast that starts just at the temple of Athena, and go to a point in southeast Athens that Pausanias identifies as 'an enclosure not far from the so-called Aphrodite-in-the-Gardens' (1.27.3). Pausanias described this shrine of Aphrodite earlier in his tour of Athens, and in some detail (1.19.2); there too he insisted on the nomenclature – 'the place which they name the Gardens' – presumably because actual gardens were no longer to be seen. The shrine is mentioned after all the other shrines of southeast Athens, Olympieium, Pythium, and Delphinium, and just before Cynosarges and the Lyceium; so it must have lain on the periphery.[44] Now the destination of the two girls is not itself another shrine, but simply an 'enclosure,' in which there is 'a natural underground descent'; the girls go down it and leave their burden.

This observance, says Pausanias, 'is not generally known,' and he leaves it still a mystery, the carrying of some burden by two girls to a place underground. To judge from the several parallels that can be cited, to judge also from the tale of Cecrops' daughters, it is the feeding of a sacred snake. A sacred snake dwelt likewise on the Acropolis, and was likewise fed with anxious ceremony. Archaeological evidence makes it very probable that sacred snakes and their feeding had a part in Mycenaean religion; this will be the origin of the Acropolis snake. If then Athena's servitors duplicate the ceremony in southeast Athens, they mean to join this area to the Acropolis and to endow it with the same magical protection. The ceremony originates in the Dark Age, and shows once more that early Athens was chiefly the southeast sector.

So much for the Acropolis. As we cast our eyes round the lower city, the southeast sector is conspicuous; much less so the ground just east of the Acropolis, though antiquarians like Plutarch knew it as the city centre. The other area that is often claimed as a focus of early settlement, and also of festive games and processions, is the northwest. It happens that this is the only sector to be explored by sustained, large-scale excavation, in the Agora and the Cerameicus and over a large area north and west of the Areopagus; so it has naturally attracted most attention. From the earliest moment when there was any habitation at Athens, this was an area of roads and cemeteries. The most important road of all ran west-northwest to the middle Cephisus valley and thence to Eleusis, where it met the north-south

---

accepts my reconstruction, save that for the destination he posits a notional shrine called the 'Kourotropheion,' which might be either in southeast Athens or close by the east face of the Acropolis. Such a shrine cannot be reconciled with Pausanias.

44 The decree of 129–128 BC concerning the Pythium refers to 'the Gardens' as an area nearby: W. Peek, *AthMitt* 66 (1941) 181–95 no. 2 lines 27, 53 (*LSCG Suppl.* 14). According to Pliny, Aphrodite-in-the-Gardens was 'outside the walls': *Hist. Nat.* 36.16.

route through Greece; another, more nearly west to the lower Cephisus and thence to Peiraeus and Salamis; and yet another, more nearly north to the Academy and the upper Cephisus. Cemeteries lined the roads.

The Agora and adjoining ground are commonly described as a residential quarter, or even as a distinct village, in the Dark Age and the early Archaic period.[45] This gives a wrong emphasis. Houses there were, many of them by the eighth and seventh centuries, almost solely represented by wells and discarded pottery; but the same evidence shows that the houses were poor, and bunched together here and there, and joined with workshops, including the remnant of a kiln.[46] The occupants were potters and smiths, people who are generally placed apart, because they use fire and produce smoke and smells;[47] they also need abundant water, wood, and drainage. The sloping ground (finally levelled for the Agora), the northeast winds, the stream Eridanus are all suited to industry; so are the nearby woods of the Academy and Colonus.

Athens' craftsmen have an ancient festival, the Chalceia, falling on the last day of Pyanopsion; the festival Promethia must be theirs as well.[48] The ritual in question is doubtless the fetching of new fire before the winter season, when potters and smiths are busiest.[49] The fire is brought from a grove at the Academy, for it is an old belief that fire resides in the wood of living trees; as seen from the Cerameicus, the grove is the 'far land,' ἑκαδήμεια.[50] The destination, we may assume, is Colonus-by-the-Agora, the site of the later temple of Hephaestus and Athena. In Plato's account of Athens before the flood, this hilltop shrine is singled out as the abode of the warriors, with both craftsmen and farmers settled below. Although the picture is unreal – Plato makes Athens larger then than later – the antiquity of the shrine on Colonus is the authentic detail that lends colour to the rest.[51]

45 So, e.g., Travlos, *Poleodomikē exelixis* 30; R. Martin, *L'Urbanisme dans la Grèce antique*² (Paris 1974) 76–9, 292–4; E.J. Owens, *The City in the Greek and Roman World* (London 1991) 13–14.

46 See E.T.H. Brann, *The Athenian Agora VIII: Late Geometric and Protoattic Pottery* (Princeton 1962) 108–11.

47 Cf. *RDAC* 1978 204–5.

48 Cf. Deubner, *Att. Fest* 35–6, 211–12; C. Bérard, *AntK* 19 (1976) 101–14 (Chalceia).

49 Homer, arriving on Samos in the autumn, finds the potters stoking their kiln; just before, a fire is kindled in a phratry lodge for the festival Apaturia: *Vit. Hom. Herod.* 29–32. According to Ister, the hearth fire at the Apaturia commemorates the first use of fire: Harp. *s.v.* λαμπάs (*FGrHist* 334 F 2).

50 Trees contain fire: Hes. *Theog.* 563, with West's note. The spelling ἑκαδήμεια: Travlos, *Pictorial Dict.* 42, 47 figs. 56–8.

51 Pl. *Critias* 112 B. Cf. Thompson and Wycherley, *Agora of Athens* 143.

The ritual of the craftsmen is the starting-point for several picturesque ceremonies that were undoubtedly devised in the sixth century or even the fifth, during the development of the northwest sector. The cult of the fire-god Hephaestus was introduced from abroad, and with it the custom of racing with torches.[52] Several torch-races were now run over the Academy road. At least two processions, at the Olympieia and the Panathenaea, now started from the Cerameicus. Fallen soldiers were now buried on the Academy road, and this became the site of the funeral games conducted by the Polemarch. The physical arrangements for the races and processions will be examined when we come to the Panathenaea.

In dealing with the Panathenaea, we shall also find reason to reject the view that the Agora itself was a traditional setting for games and festivals (pp. 94–6). The installation of government offices in the sixth century shows rather that this large tract was not pre-empted by any earlier public use. The earliest shrines were planted on the west side of the Agora in the later sixth century or the early fifth: Zeus *sōtēr*, Apollo *patrōios*, Meter. These cults, all pertaining to the work of government, are filials of much older ones in the older parts of Athens: of Zeus in the old agora, of Apollo in southeast Athens, of Meter in Agrae.[53]

One other group of shrines on this side of Athens requires mention. They are shrines of Demeter assignable to one or other of her seasonal festivals. The excavated Eleusinium stands on a high terrace beside the Panathenaic Way as it approaches the west end of the Acropolis. Since the shrine was used for a celebration preliminary to the Mysteries at Eleusis, it can be no earlier than the moment, perhaps in the sixth century, when the Mysteries became a civic festival; the temple dates from the early fifth century.[54] Three other shrines on the same road are likely to be older, since they go with Athens' own festivals.

Demeter *chloē*, who belongs to the spring festival Chloaea, occupies a terrace below the southwest bastion of the Acropolis, beside the original west ascent.[55] The shrine where Aristophanes locates the city Thesmophoria lies a little to the west of the Eleusinium, on the north slope of the

---

52 *RhM* n.s. 128 (1985) 240–1, 258–61, 269–88.

53 In a similar vein, Thompson *apud* C.W. Hedrick, *AJA* 92 (1988) 209 n. 224, sees 'a shift in the centre of gravity' from the Ilissus to the Agora (at the Ilissus he evidently thinks of Zeus *olympios* as well as Apollo *pythios*, but that cult was unrelated to the one in the Agora). Hedrick, *ibid.* 185–210, insists that Apollo was not brought to the Agora until the later fourth century. This goes against the evidence, and creates an odd vacancy in the earlier years.

54 Thompson, *Hesperia* 29 (1960) 337; Thompson and Wycherley, *Agora of Athens* 152.

55 Beschi, *ASAtene* 45–6 (1967–8) [1969] 517–18, 526.

Areopagus, as we shall see in a moment. Much farther off, outside the
city at the Cephisus crossing, is a shrine of Demeter and certain partners,
those worshipped at the festival Scira; here too are the stream Scirus and
the place Scirum (Paus. 1.36.4, 37.2).

The Thesmophorium has proved elusive, but sufficient indications are
now in hand. It is obvious that a considerable area was needed to accommodate all the women who sojourned in the festival huts. At the southeast,
the Thesmophorium adjoined the shrine of the *Semnai*, mentioned by
Aristophanes in the *Thesmophoriazusae*. At the northwest, it adjoined the
prison, also intimated in the play by the judicial punishment of 'the plank.'
At the west again, the Demeter Cistern contained a deposit of figurines
similar to those found at excavated shrines of Demeter *thesmophoros*. The
officiating priestess who appears in an inscription belongs to Melite, the
district north of the Areopagus. No trace of the Thesmophorium was found
during the excavation of the north slope; the reason must be that this large
open precinct was afterwards given up to residential use. Statues of Pluto
and others that Pausanias saw in the shrine of the *Semnai* had probably
been taken from the Thesmophorium, for a shrine of Pluto is tended by
the priestess of the inscription.[56]

The shrines then are all beside the road that leads from the west, the
direction of Eleusis, up to the Acropolis. Each of the associated festivals,
not only the Chloaea, brings the worshippers to or from the Acropolis. At
the Thesmophoria, the herald calls for prayers first to Demeter and other
deities of the Thesmophorium, then to Ge *kourotrophos* and Hermes and
the Charites, deities of the Acropolis – Ge *kourotrophos* is beside Demeter
chloē below the bastion, Hermes and the Charites at the gate above.[57] To
honour these deities, the women must have gone from the Thesmophorium
to the Acropolis. Such a visit is included in Sophocles' account of the death
of Oedipus, which centres on our Thesmophorium and on the drastic rite
at the *megaron*. When Oedipus arrives at the pit in which he is soon to
disappear, his daughters go off to 'the opposite hill of Demeter *euchloos*' to
draw water. Within the sanctuary of the *Semnai*, Pausanias also saw statues
of Ge and Hermes and the tomb of Oedipus, further relics of the ritual
of the Thesmophoria.[58] As for the Scira, it is described as a procession

56 *Semnai*, 'plank': Ar. *Thesm.* 224, 931, 940. Figurines: D.B. Thompson, *Hesperia* 23
  (1954) 87–107. Priestess: *Hesperia* 11 (1942) 265–7 no. 51. Statues: Paus. 1.28.6.
57 Ar. *Thesm.* 295–302; Paus. 1.22.3, 8. For the shrine of Ge *kourotrophos*, Beschi,
  ASAtene 45–6 (1967–8) [1969] 517–18.
58 Soph. *Oed. Col.* 1590–1, 1600–1, 1660–1; Paus. 1.28.6–7. The *megaron* rite is also
  reflected in the traditional story of Swellfoot's mutilation and confinement: *GRBS* 29
  (1988) 217–22, and *EMC*² 9 (1990) 436–7, 10 (1991) 62, and *Anc. Econ. in Myth.* 20–1.

from the Acropolis to the Cephisus; the processioners are priests of the Acropolis cults of Athena and Poseidon.[59] These are the deities who are associated with Demeter in the shrine at the Cephisus.

It is surprising to find several shrines of Demeter sited along the road and linked with the Acropolis. As a rule, a community conducts each of the successive festivals of the grain at the same shrine, where the same furnishings, notably the *megaron*, are in use throughout the year. At Peiraeus it is the Thesmophorium, at Paeania the Eleusinium; at both shrines the series continues until the Scira, the last festival of the cycle, at the season of the threshing.[60] Now in the Athenian celebration of the Scira, Scirum and Scirus are both named for the festival, perhaps ostentatiously, but at this outlying site we hear nothing of Demeter's ritual, only of a sacrifice to Athena. Furthermore, early Athens had a shrine of Demeter at Agrae. Though later famous for a version of the spring festival, the Lesser Mysteries, it must once have served for the full series. On this topic a little more is said below, apropos of the shrine at Agrae.

The northwest shrines evoke the memory of an ancient rivalry between Athens and Eleusis. According to a late inscription, the Delphic oracle once exalted the shrine of Demeter *chloē* as the place where grain first came into ear; this flies against the usual tradition that grain was first sown and harvested at Eleusis.[61] And whereas Athens conducted a ceremonial ploughing at three fields round about – at Scirum and the Rharian field and the Buzygium – it was the one at Scirum, says Plutarch, that derived from the very first sowing.[62] Most striking of all, the ritual of the Scira inspires the tale of Erechtheus' war with Eleusis;

The place where Oedipus disappears in Sophocles is where Kore was carried down to the underworld (schol. *Oed. Col.* 1590), and this in turn is where Eubuleus' pigs were swallowed up as an explicit *aition* of the Thesmophoria (Clem. *Protr.* 1.17; schol. Luc. *Dial. Meretr.* 2.1, p. 275 Rabe; cf. Ov. *Fast.* 4.466).

59 Harp. *s.v.* Σκίρον (Lysimachides *FGrHist* 366 F 3); cf. schol. Ar. *Thesm.* 834, schol. Ar. *Eccl.* 18; Steph. Byz. *s.v.* Σκίρος. The oddity of this procession has prompted W. Burkert's interpretation of the Scira as a symbolic dissolution of society at the year's end: *Homo Necans* (Berlin 1972) 161–8; *Griechische Religion* (Stuttgart 1977) 349–50. This is to forget that the Scira originate as a seasonal festival of Demeter, celebrated in her shrines at many places (our dossier happens to consist of Attic demes and far-off Iasus, with its month Scirophorion). The procession and no doubt the place-name 'Scirum' are untypical and secondary.

60 *IG* 2² 1177 (Peiraeus); *IG* 1³ 250 (Paeania). Cf. n. 81 below.

61 *IG* 2² 5006 line 6, οὗ πρῶτον στάχυς εὐξη[ται, i.e., ηὔξηται. F. Jacoby, *Das Marmor Parium* (Berlin 1904) 61–75, documents the tradition of Eleusis' primacy.

62 Plut. *Conj. Praec.* 42, 144 A. Cf. Deubner, *Att. Feste* 47: 'a compromise between the claims' of Eleusis and Athens.

for his daughters (or daughter) are sacrificed near the Cephisus, and Erechtheus himself is thunderbolted at the shrine of Poseidon on the Acropolis.[63]

Our conclusion must be that in early times, whether the Dark Age or the beginning of the Archaic period, Athens was jealous of Eleusis and installed several shrines to advertise her own agriculture in the Cephisus valley. Later, when Athens took control of Eleusis' Mysteries, the rivalry was abolished by the Eleusinium and its processions. Accordingly, we shall not take these shrines and festivals of Demeter as evidence of early settlement at the northwest.

So far as the record shows, no other part of Athens has any venerable shrines. Or rather, none but Agrae, the extra-urban district at the southeast. Thucydides could have made his point just as well by citing Agrae.

Agrae

From the very outset, any community will place certain shrines beyond the settled area, because space is needed or because the gods foster the livelihoods of farm and pasture. The river Ilissus and later the city wall separate the southeast sector from the rural district Agra or Agrae, 'Field' or 'Fields.' Here we find another concentration of important shrines, equal to the southeast sector or even surpassing it: 1 / Zeus *meilichios*, 2 / Artemis *agrotera*, 3 / Demeter, 4 / Meter alias Rhea, 5 / Poseidon *helikōnios*. North of Agrae, east of the settlement, is 6 / Apollo *lykeios*, whose precinct the Lyceium is a large open ground for warlike exercises. We shall glance at each of these gods in turn, together with their respective festivals, in order to appreciate just how early and important they are.

1 / Zeus *meilichios* was honoured at the Diasia of 23 Anthesterion, on Thucydides' reckoning 'the greatest festival of Zeus at Athens' – ahead of the Olympieia and those on the Acropolis.[64] Outside Attica, the only record of the Diasia by name is on Thasos; but the shorter form 'Dia' is equivalent, and this, or the derivative month name 'Dios,' we find in all dialect branches. Indeed a corresponding festival can be inferred for every town with a cult of Zeus *meilichios*. Διάσια is formed from the locative *Διᾶσι and means 'Rites at the place Δῖα'; a place on Thasos is denoted by the redundant form Διάσιον.[65] The festival was attended by a huge

---

63 Eur. *Erechtheus* frs. 39–65 Austin; for later sources, Austin pp. 22–3. Cf. *CQ*² 34 (1984) 4 n. 0, and *RhM* n.s. 128 (1985) 233–8.

64 Thuc. 1.126.6. For other details, M.H. Jameson, *BCH* 89 (1965) 159–66.

65 Diasia, Diasion on Thasos: F. Salviat, *BCH* 82 (1958) 195, 234–6; Salviat and J. Servais, *BCH* 88 (1964) 268–70, 285. Diasia < Dia: Wilamowitz, *Glaube*² 1.222 n. 2. Pellene

gathering (πανδημεί, πολλοί, says Thucydides), so that a spacious setting was required.

It is this festival, celebrated in Boeotia as elsewhere, that gives rise to Hesiod's story of the first sacrifice. The epithet *meilichios* is conciliatory, and the festival Diasia is in fact described as somewhat gloomy; therefore the story feigns that Zeus is angry at the division of the meat. In Aristophanes a celebrant at the Diasia makes a black pudding from the sacrificial victim; so does Prometheus in Hesiod.[66] Hesiod's story is commonly taken as an *aition* of 'Olympian' sacrifice, i.e., of a large category of ritual, but Hesiod surely did not think in such terms. Almost every *aition* refers to a particular rite – this is true even of later stories about the origin of animal sacrifice. Hesiod lays the scene at Mycone 'Poppy field': a rural landscape in early spring, the setting and the season of the Diasia. Afterwards Mycone was equated with Sicyon, where Pausanias found a notable cult of Zeus *meilichios*.[67]

The Diasia belong in spirit to an early and undifferentiated society, in which kinsmen are reunited round a sacrificial victim (so Aristophanes). For Hesiod, this is the oldest festivity in the world.

2, 6 / Artemis *agrotera* and Apollo *lykeios* are some distance apart, but these two warlike deities can be recognized as joint recipients of the festival Boedromia of 6–7 Boedromion. The festival was conducted by the Polemarch, as we see from several aetiological myths, wherein the Polemarch is prefigured by either Ion or Theseus or Menestheus.[68] It is therefore one of 'the ancestral rites,' τὰ πάτρια, which led [Aristotle] to believe that the offices of Basileus and Polemarch were the most ancient elements of Athenian government (*Ath.* 3.3).

Among the Polemarch's duties, the festival appears as 'sacrifices to both Artemis *agrotera* and Enyalius' (*Ath.* 58.1). Enyalius, the personified war whoop, also personifies the Βοηδρόμια, 'rites of running with a shout.'[69]

---

has a festival Dia, and a bronze snake is dedicated to '*Mellichios* at Pelana': schol. Pind. *Nem.* 10.82a; *ArchAnz* 1922.76 no. 25; cf. H. Schwabl, *RE* 10 A (1972) 336, and *RE Suppl.* 15 (1978) 1054, 1098 s.v. Zeus.

66 Ar. *Nub.* 409–10; Hes. *Theog.* 538–9.

67 Hes. *Theog.* 536; Paus. 2.9.6.

68 Ion: Harp. s.v. Βοηδρόμια (Philochorus *FGrHist* 328 F 13); *Etym. Magn.* s.v. Βοηδρομιών; cf. Hdt. 8.44.2; [Arist.] *Ath.* 3.2; Str. 8.7.1, p. 383; Paus. 1.31.3, 7.1.5; schol. Ar. *Av.* 1527. Theseus: Plut. *Thes.* 27.2–7 (Cleidemus *FGrHist* 323 F 18); Macrob. *Sat.* 1.17.18; cf. schol. Callim. *H. Ap.* 69. Menestheus: Alcid. *Od.* 23; Philostr. *Her.* 23, p. 25 De Lannoy; cf. *Il.* 2.552–5; Hdt. 7.161.3, 9.27.4; Aeschin. 3 *Ctes.* 184, the third Eion herm; [Arist.] *Peplus* 34. Cf. *AJP* 105 (1984) 392–3; *Historia* 35 (1986) 162–3.

69 Enyalius and the war whoop: e.g., *Il.* 5.590–3; Aesch. fr. dub. 451c 30–1 Radt; Xen. *Anab.* 1.8.18, 5.2.4, whence Arr. *Anab.* 1.14.7; Plut. *Sol.* 9.5–7. The name is read in the Cnossus tablets, KN V 52, and is not less expressive in its Mycenaean form, *enuwarijo*.

So does *Phobos*, the personified battle rout. In Cleidemus' *aition*, Theseus as a virtual Polemarch sacrifices to *Phobos* before joining battle with the Amazons. The Athenian right wing, which decides the battle, is drawn up at the Lyceium, so that this is the place of sacrifice. 'A certain oracle,' said Cleidemus, enjoined the sacrifice; in Macrobius, Delphi bids Theseus to invoke Apollo with the paean.[70] Enyalius and *Phobos* stand for Apollo *lykeios* because this god of war and military exercises had faded away by the fourth century. He is still seen in a few passages of tragedy and in a decree '*ante a.* 434' which levies a tax on soldiers for the upkeep of his sanctuary, rather like a decree for Enyalius at Lindus.[71] Perhaps the reason for Apollo's decline was that Artemis alone received the honours of Marathon. And the reason for this must be that 6 Boedromion was the actual anniversary, if not of the battle, then of the day on which the army mustered at Athens; this was the time for prayers and vows.[72]

Admittedly, the festival Boedromia is nowhere assigned to Artemis, only to Apollo *boēdromios*. But since it must come at the seventh of the month, Apollo's holy day, it cannot be dissevered from the attested ritual of Artemis on the previous day; at other seasons Artemis and Apollo share many a festival on these successive days. We saw that [Aristotle] brackets two of the Polemarch's sacrifices, those for Artemis and Enyalius. Plutarch regards the commemoration of Marathon, which honours Artemis, as part of the Boedromia, for he puns upon the name while chafing Herodotus: ἀλλὰ τοῦτό γε βοηθεῖ τῶι Ἡροδότωι πρὸς ἐκείνην τὴν διαβολὴν κτλ. Demosthenes refers to a costly procession at the Boedromia, undoubtedly the procession to Agrae.[73] Furthermore, the mythical Amazons who figure

70 N. 68 above. The names *Phobos* and Enyalius are used interchangeably of a fearsome god at Sparta who is kept in close confinement: Plut. *Cleom.* 8.3–9.7, from Phylarchus (*Phobos*); Paus. 3.15.7 (Enyalius).

71 IG 1³ 138; S. Accame, *Clara Rhodos* 9 (1938) 211–39 (*LSCG Suppl.* 85). On Apollo *lykeios*, M.H. Jameson, *Archaiognosia* 1 (1980) 213–36. Ephebic decrees of later times, which always mention the procession to Agrae, have not a word of Apollo or the Lyceium.

72 As Philippides set out at about the same time and reached Sparta on the ninth day of a lunar month (Hdt. 6.106.3), this schedule implies that the festival calendars of both Athens and Sparta were then roughly in step with the moon. Others have come to about the same result: e.g., N.G.L. Hammond, *Studies in Greek History* (Oxford 1973) 207 n. 1, 256 (on the seventh the Persians land, on the eighth the Athenian army is at Marathon). It is not far-fetched to suggest that Herodotus' account of the battle charge is deduced from the festival name or the ritual: so Wilamowitz, *Aristoteles und Athen* (Berlin 1893) 1.250 n. 132; Mommsen, *Feste* 176; *contra*, Jacoby on Philochorus *FGrHist* 328 F 13 (*Text* pp. 281–2).

73 Plut. *De Herod. Mal.* 26, 862 A; Dem. 3 *Olynth.* 31. In Plutarch the commemorative rite 'rescues' Herodotus from the imputation of flattering the Athenians for money, since they would never have put up with his lies. Despite Simon, *Festivals* 82–3, the

in the *aition* of the Boedromia are elsewhere linked with Artemis, being but another avatar of the pubescent girls who conduct her ritual; the name Ἀμάζων denotes their newly swelling breasts (a- copulative, μαζός = μαστός 'breast'). At this season they perform warlike dances, as described by Callimachus.[74]

The festival produces a month name, Boedromion *vel sim.*, attested in every part of Greece; a festival so widespread is very old.[75] At Pyrrhichus south of Gythium, Pausanias found neighbouring shrines of Artemis and Apollo that were said to mark the limit of the Amazon invasion (3.25.3). The respective epithets are ἀστρατεία and ἀμαζόνιος: Artemis and her girls are joined with the 'army,' στρατός, as Apollo is joined with the girls. These are the two deities of the Boedromia.

At Athens a procession went from the city to Artemis' shrine at Agrae: what was the starting-point in the city? The answer is given by the co-ordinates of the festival *aition*, the battle against the Amazons. In Cleidemus' version, the two battle lines extend across the south side of Athens from west to east, with the Athenians outside the city, which the Amazons have occupied (more of this later, apropos of the festival Olympieia: pp. 137–8). The Athenian right is said to be stationed 'at the Palladium and Ardettus and the Lyceium': i.e., it faced the Amazons in southeast Athens, the area of the Palladium, but extended farther east to Ardettus, and then made a turn to the north, as far as the Lyceium. Thus the Athenian right outflanked the Amazons. The Amazon left rested on 'the Amazoneium as it is now called'; here some fallen Amazons were buried, and doubtless it was here that a 'sacrifice to the Amazons' was once conducted, though later it was only a memory. The Amazoneium is a point in southeast Athens near the Palladium – and we shall see that the Palladium goes with the Olympieium. Another source known to Plutarch said that the Amazon Hippolyte was buried 'beside the shrine of

---

term *charistēria*, 'thank-offering,' which Plutarch uses in this context is not distinctive enough (unlike *procharistēria*) to serve as a festival name. In Demosthenes the Athenians are cajoled by politicians who 'dispense festival-money and stage the procession at the Boedromia,' ἀγαπῶντες ἐὰν μεταδιδῶσι θεωρικῶν ὑμῖν ἢ Βοηδρόμια πέμψωσιν οὗτοι. Even if there was a procession for Apollo on 7 Boedromion, Demosthenes thinks mainly of that extravagant sacrifice of goats on the sixth.

74 Callim. *H. Dian.* 237–58, on Ephesus. The earlier name of Caesareon, the Ephesian month corresponding to Boedromion, was probably Badromion: R. Merkelbach, *ZPE* 36 (1979) 157–62. By one account, Ephesus' shrine of Artemis was founded when the Amazons marched against Athens: Paus. 7.2.7 (Pind. fr. 174).

75 Boedromion, Badromion, Boadromius, Badromius, Boathous (< *Βοάθοα). Our festival does not appear in W.K. Pritchett's chapter on 'War festivals and the calendar': *The Greek State at War*[3] (Berkeley 1979) 154–229.

Ge *olympia,'* where a certain stele stood: obviously the same site as Cleidemus' 'Amazoneium.' For [Plato], this is 'the Amazon stele' near 'the
Itonian Gate'; for Pausanias, it is the tomb of Antiope just within the gate
on the Phalerum road.[76] The site in question, with its stele, its sacrifice,
its putative burials, belongs to the ritual of the Boedromia. It will be the
starting-point of the procession to Agrae, and perhaps of another to the
Lyceium.

A war festival that takes its name from 'running with a shout' goes
back to a time when the general levy did not wear hoplite armour or fight
in close formation. They were lightly armed, and attacked on the run, as
do the mercenary troops in Xenophon.[77] That is, the festival goes back to
the Dark Age, or even before.

3 / Demeter's festival at Agrae is the Lesser, or Little, Mysteries, falling
sometime in Anthesterion.[78] Obviously, the festival was not so called until
the Mysteries of Eleusis were adopted as a civic observance; yet it must
have been renowned in its own right, in order to be placed on a footing with Eleusis. Now Demeter has a festival cycle that runs from the
ploughing and sowing in autumn to the threshing in summer.[79] Some
calendars, notably those of Attic demes, register a full series, or nearly so.
But one festival may be favoured over the rest. The Mysteries of Eleusis doubtless originate as a local version of the Thesmophoria, the most

76 Plut. *Thes.* 27.6; [Pl.] *Ax.* 365 A; Paus. 1.2.1. Travlos, *Pictorial Dict.* 160, associates 'the
   Itonian Gate' with some remains on the ground. 'The Amazoneium' is also mentioned
   by Diod. 4.28.2, Ammonius *FGrHist* 361 F 4, and Steph. Byz. *s.v.*, but they give no
   help with the location. Cleidemus forbids us to identify 'the Amazoneium' with the
   Amazon camp on the Areopagus, as known to Aeschylus and [Apollodorus].
77 N. 69 above. Cf. *A.P.* 7.231 = *HE* Damagetus 4, on a soldier of Ambracia killed while
   charging and described as βοαδρόμος. We should reject the view of W. Schulze, *SBBerl*
   1918.504–11 = *Kleine Schriften* (Göttingen 1933) 182–9, that the words βοηδρομεῖν
   and βοηθεῖν denote an ancient customary duty of 'running to a shout' (βοὴν θέειν, with
   accusative of the end of motion), i.e., of assisting one who cries out in distress – if only
   because this duty could not produce a public festival. Cries for help are often raised in
   tragedy, where Schulze finds most of his examples of the custom; it is not surprising
   that the words βοηδρόμος, βοηδρομεῖν should sometimes appear.
78 Both the festival and the shrine where it took place are expressly assigned to Demeter,
   not Meter: Him. *Or.* 3.4, 'Deo'; schol. Pl. *Gorg.* 497 C, 'Deo and Kore'; Bekker, *Anecd.*
   1.334, Phot., *s.v.* Ἄγραι, 'Demeter'; Eust. *Il.* 2 (Paus. Att. *a* 20 Erbse), 'Demeter'; cf.
   Ath. 7.63, 253 D (Hermocles *Coll. Alex.* p. 173 lines 3–6), 'Demeter,' 'Kore.' Cleidemus
   probably spoke of Demeter at Agrae in his first book, as he certainly spoke of Meter
   at Agrae in his fourth: Bekker, *Anecd.* 1.326–7 (Cleidemus *FGrHist* 323 F 1, 9). In
   general, see Nilsson, *Gesch. der gr. Rel.*[2] 1.667–9. It is sometimes held, as by Jameson,
   BCH 89 (1965) 159–62, that Zeus *meilichios* had a place in the Lesser Mysteries; the
   question does not matter here.
79 Cf. Jameson, *Athenaeum* 54 (1976) 443–4; R. Parker, *Boreas* 15 (1987) 141–2.

widespread festival of autumn; for both exhibit the same ritual pattern, and the same myths, of Kore's abduction and Iambe's teasing, are told of both. In early spring, the time of the Lesser Mysteries, the grain is coming into ear. It is as if the seed grain re-emerges on the stalk. In mythical terms, Kore has been confined beneath the earth for about a third of the year, but now returns to the upper world. So within the larger series, the two festivals of Eleusis and Agrae are complementary. Nor is it surprising that the ritual at Agrae was thought to evoke Dionysus as well, doubtless the infant Dionysus;[80] though proper to the cognate realm of viticulture, he much resembles the infant Plutus, another image of the new crop of grain.

It is at Agrae that the Athenians had always celebrated Demeter's festival of early spring. But here too they must once have celebrated the other festivals of Demeter, including the Thesmophoria. For all our evidence indicates that in each community the worshippers returned to the same shrine of Demeter the year round. The shrine was typically called 'Thesmophorium,' after the first festival in the series; yet the pit called *megaron* was in use both then and later; whereas pigs were thrown into the pit at the Thesmophoria, one might conjecture that the carrion was removed at the next festival, the Proerosia, to be mixed with the seed grain.[81] On this showing, Agrae was the focus of Demeter's worship for early Athens. The Thesmophorium and other shrines at the northwest were installed later.

80 Agrae is a place 'at which the Little Mysteries are performed so as to re-enact Dionysus' adventure,' ἐν ᾧ τὰ μικρὰ μυστήρια ἐπιτελεῖται, μίμημα τῶν περὶ Διόνυσον (Steph. Byz. s.v.). This is a normal way of saying that the ritual, whatever it might be, was explained by a certain myth of Dionysus. There is no reason to imagine a cult drama or pantomime as a late embellishment. The aetiology may well be early, and may stand behind the role of Dionysus both in Orphic poetry and in Eleusinian iconography. Graf, *Eleusis und die orphische Dichtung Athens* (Berlin 1974) 76, errs on this point.

81 At Eleusis, the Proerosia appear to be conducted within the great sanctuary, for the *megaron* is in use: S. Dow and R. Healey, *A Sacred Calendar of Eleusis* (LSCG 17) lines 15–27 (I take this passage to refer throughout to the Proerosia, not the Thesmophoria). At Peiraeus, the Thesmophorium and its *megaron* are in use at the festivals Thesmophoria, Proerosia, Calamaea, and Scira: IG 2² 1177. At Paeania, the festivals Proerosia, Chloaea, Antheia, and Scira all take place at the local Eleusinium: IG 1³ 250. At Thoricus, all the offerings assignable to festivals of Demeter (Proerosia in both summer and autumn, Chloaea, Antheia) are probably made at the same shrine, since there is no indication to the contrary: G. Daux, *AntClass* 52 (1983) 152–4. The same *megara* are in use at the festivals Thesmophoria, Scirophoria, and 'Arrhetophoria': schol. Luc. *Dial. Meretr.* 2.1, pp. 275–6 Rabe.

4 / Meter in Agrae is almost lost to view in modern accounts, being equated with the goddess of the Lesser Mysteries, who is clearly Demeter.[82] For this there is no warrant. Meter and Demeter are always distinct, except in speculative syncretism (Eur. *Hel.* 1301–68, etc.). Each has her own domain in nature and her own magic ritual, above all her own seasonal festivals. Those of Meter are the Galaxia and the Cronia, well attested both at Athens and elsewhere. As these festivals are very old, they presuppose a shrine of Meter other than the one in the Agora, which is thought to date from the early fifth century. We must consider first the shrine, then the festivals.

'Meter in Agra' is named in fifth-century inscriptions, and 'the Metroüm in Agrae' is known to the lexica, one of them citing Cleidemus.[83] According to Philodemus, Cleidemus had something to say of Μήτηρ θεῶν, her fuller title. Philochorus traced the altar back to Cecrops, a very ancient pedigree.[84] In Macrobius' report it is 'an altar for Saturn and Ops,' i.e., Cronus and Rhea, literary names that evoke the actual cult of Meter – Cronus, as we shall see in a moment, is nothing but a mythical projection of the Cronia, a festival of Meter. Philochorus said that Cecrops chose to honour Cronus and Rhea 'in place of Jupiter and Terra,' i.e., Zeus and Ge, and that he instituted the festival Cronia, a merry, rural, egalitarian custom (a festival in the 'Fields' is pre-eminently rural). Cecrops, more than any other founding hero, is mild and benign; therefore he prefers Cronus to Zeus, just as he insists upon a vegetarian form of sacrifice for Zeus on the Acropolis.[85] It was natural for Philochorus to draw out the contrast between Zeus and Cronus, since the shrine of Zeus *olympios* in southeast Athens was close to the shrine of Meter in Agrae. As we know from Thucydides, Ge too was conspicuous; Zeus and Ge were therefore set against Cronus and Rhea. Other sources say that the shrine of Zeus *olympios* was founded by Deucalion, a close contemporary of Cecrops.[86] In Philochorus, Cecrops was doubtless reacting to this foundation.

82 This opinion seems universal, though the emphasis may be put on one name or the other, Meter or Demeter. For example, Simon, *Festivals* 26–7, insists on Meter alias Rhea, and even denies the equation with Demeter, but still regards her festival as the Lesser Mysteries.

83 *IG* 1³ 234 line 5, 369 line 91, 383 line 50, cf. 138 lines 11–12; Bekker, *Anecd.* 1. 273, 327 (Cleidemus *FGrHist* 323 F 9).

84 Philod. *De Piet.* p. 23 Gomperz (Cleidemus F 25); Macrob. *Sat.* 1.10.22 (Philochorus *FGrHist* 328 F 97).

85 Paus. 8.2.3: Cecrops gave the title *hypatos* to Zeus, and sacrificed cakes on his altar instead of any living thing.

86 Marm. Par. *FGrHist* 239 A 4; Paus. 1.18.8.

Thus far all is clear. In the fifth and fourth centuries, as illustrated by inscriptions and Cleidemus, Meter and the Metroüm are in Agrae. We may assume that they are still there in the third century, when Philochorus points a contrast between the Olympieium and the Metroüm. A temple is not mentioned, only an altar. Now for Pausanias. He does not refer to Meter in his brief tour of Agrae; instead, 'in the enclosure' of the Olympieium, he remarks both the shrine of Ge and 'a temple of Cronus and Rhea' (1.18.7). As everyone allows, the phrase 'in the enclosure' causes difficulty, for in other sources both the shrine of Ge and something called the 'precinct of Cronus' are apart from the Olympieium, though near it, and in fact the only likely remains on the ground are outside the enclosure, on the south. The text of Pausanias may be at fault. The 'precinct of Cronus,' Κρόνιον τέμενος, is defined in a lexicon as 'the one beside the present Olympium, as far as the Metroüm in Agrae.'[87] Perhaps 'the Metroüm in Agrae' is only a traditional site. At all events, 'the present Olympium,' τὸ νῦν Ὀλύμπιον, seems to refer to Hadrian's construction; if so, the source is about as late as Pausanias. South of the Olympieium are the foundations of a temple which has often been claimed for Cronus and Rhea; in front of the temple are the foundations of a substantial altar. All the foundations are Roman, of the second century after Christ.[88]

The 'temple of Cronus and Rhea' in Pausanias, the 'precinct of Cronus' in the lexicon, are names for the shrine of Meter. Like several other monuments mentioned by Pausanias – the fountain-house Enneacrunus, the temple of Ares and Athena and its statues, the statues of Eirene and Callias – the Metroüm had been transplanted not long before Pausanias saw it. The original Metroüm was very likely on the left bank of the Ilissus at the point closest to the Roman temple. This suits the definition of the lexicon; moreover, it is just here that a relief of Pan is carved on a wall-face dressed in the native rock – Pan is Meter's favourite companion.[89] In the adjoining Ilissus bed are the cisterns and tunnels that have been plausibly associated with the original Enneacrunus. Since this area of the left bank saw extensive building in the time of Hadrian, perhaps for Pausanias' Gymnasium

---

87 Plut. *Thes.* 27.6 (the shrine of Ge serves to locate the Amazon stele); Bekker, *Anecd.* 1.273 (precinct of Cronus).

88 'Temple of Cronus and Rhea': Travlos, *Pictorial Dict.* 335–9.

89 Relief of Pan: Travlos, *Pictorial Dict.* 114 fig. 154, 289, 296 figs. 386–7; Wycherley, *Stones of Athens* 171–3. Pan and Meter: F. Brommer, *RE Suppl.* 8 (1956) 1003 *s.v.* Pan; E.D. Reeder, *AJA* 91 (1987) 429 n. 13. Travlos like others thinks of the Agrae Metroüm as a temple, and points to the foundations of a building uncovered in 1962: *Pictorial Dict.* 112, 114 fig. 154, 291 fig. 379. This is a little to the east of the site suggested here.

of Hadrian, it was doubtless necessary to remove both the fountain-house and Meter's altar.[90]

The festival Galaxia appears in decrees for the ephebes, in Theophrastus, and in the lexica; the Cronia in decrees for the Councillors, in literature, and in scholia and lexica.[91] At the Galaxia offerings are made to Meter under her full title, ἡ Μήτηρ τῶν θεῶν, and to her alone. The Cronia are described in the lexica as a festival for Cronus and Meter, again styled Μήτηρ τῶν θεῶν, or just for Cronus. The decisive item is an inscription, conjecturally dated to 267/6, in which the Councillors are busy at the Cronia: on the only reasonable supplement of a fragmentary passage, they honour ἡ Μήτηρ τῶν θεῶν, and her alone.[92] The god Cronus has long been recognized as a creature of myth rather than cult; the instances of cult are few and late.[93] The truth is that the very name Κρόνος was deduced from Κρόνια, the festival of Meter, and understood to be an imaginary figure of long ago. The real meaning of Κρόνια is different. Most festival names denote ritual actions; for example, Γαλάξια 'Milk rites' denotes such offerings as the milk porridge recorded at Athens. Hesychius has an entry κέρνεα, described as offerings to ἡ Μήτηρ τῶν θεῶν – obviously made on the dish called κέρνος, which was characteristic of her cult. The form κρόνια has been differentiated from the obvious, like many words of magic power (γαλάξια is differentiated from *γαλάκτια).

The festivals are early, as we see from the Ionian month names Galaxion and Cronion. The goddess Meter is native to Greece since at least the Mycenaean period, when she receives an offering at Pylus as *matere teïja*, the same title as Μήτηρ τῶν θεῶν (PY Fr 1202). Her cults have

90 Enneacrunus at the Ilissus: Travlos, *Pictorial Dict.* 204–5. Hadrianic buildings: Travlos 340 (excavation of 1896–97), 579 (excavation of 1968).

91 Galaxia: *Hesperia* 24 (1955) 228–32 lines 27–8, 125–6; IG 2² 1006 lines 23–4, 79–80; *Hesperia* 16 (1947) 170–2 no. 67 line 31 + IG 2² 1009 line 37; IG 2² 1011 lines 12–13; 1028 lines 40–1; 1029 lines 24–5; 1030 lines 35–6; Theophr. *Char.* 21.11 (τὰ Γαλάξια Wilamowitz: τὰ γὰρ ἄξια mss.); Bekker, *Anecd.* 1.229, Hsch. s.v. Γαλάξια. Cronia: B.D. Meritt and J.S. Traill, *The Athenian Agora* XV: *The Athenian Councillors* (Princeton 1974) no. 81 lines 5–6, no. 180 lines 9–10; Arist. *Nub.* 398; Dem. 24 *Timocr.* 26; etc. Cf. Dem. *Proem.* 54.

92 Meritt and Traill, *Ath. Councillors* no. 81 lines 5–6, is thus restored by Meritt: τοῖς [θεοῖς] οἷς π | [άτριον ἦν· τῶι δὲ Διὶ εὐσεβῶς συνετέλεσα]ν τὰ Κρ[όνια· ἔπεμψαν] δὲ | κτλ. 'Zeus' is not wanted, and 'piously performed' is not a customary phrase. On the analogy of no. 180 lines 9–10, lege τοῖς [θεοῖς] οἷς π | [άτριον ἦν· ἔθυσαν δὲ καὶ τεῖ Μητρὶ τῶν θεῶ]ν τὰ Κρ[όνια· ἔπεμψαν] δὲ | κτλ.

93 Wilamowitz, *SBBerl* 1929.35–53 = *Kleine Schriften* 5.2 (Berlin 1938) 157–83, and *Glaube*² 1.332–5. Cf. L. Robert, *REG* 79 (1966) 746: 'The cult of Cronus has left virtually no trace in Greece' apart from the Ionian month name and Ionian personal names.

a corresponding range, Boeotia and Arcadia and the Ionian domain. Her myths articulate Hesiod's account of the succession in heaven; for the nursing of Zeus is an *aition* of the Galaxia, as Cronus and his reign are an *aition* of the Cronia. The title 'Mother of the Gods' also contributes to the story; but in cult, where the title originates, it refers to the lesser male gods who stand beside Meter, Pan and Hermes and many local variations; Μαῖα as 'mother' of Hermes is an equivalent name.

The 'milk rites' of spring promote both the moistness of the earth and the lactation of animals as herds go out to pasture; the '*kernos* rites' of summer sustain the vegetation in the dry season.[94] Meter is goddess of pasturing as Demeter is of agriculture; the younger goddess is distinguished from the elder as 'Mother' of the settled community, Δημήτηρ < δημο-μήτηρ. Since the pastoral regime is much the same in both Greece and Anatolia (as agriculture is not), the presiding goddess is also much the same throughout this area. At Athens, however, there was reason, a little after 500 BC, to install a new cult of Meter in the Agora, and to invest her with the features of Ionian iconography that derive from native Anatolia.[95] The reason is that here the goddess had the special function of caring for the public records, which were kept on sheepskin or goatskin, her materials, and that this use of hides was especially developed in coastal Ionia (Hdt. 5.58.3). But Meter's age-old festivals continued as before. It was doubtless at the shrine in Agrae that the Councillors and the ephebes made their offerings in the Hellenistic period.

5 / Cleidemus is cited for a cult of Poseidon Ἑλικώνιος in Agrae – more precisely, for a hearth altar, *eschara*, that stood at the top of a hill called Ἑλικών.[96] The setting and the epithet are characteristic. In the homeland Poseidon is often found atop some inland hill or mountain: on the citadels of Athens, Corinth, Troezen, and Pheneus; on the hill Colonus in Attica and on a hill at Tricoloni near Megalopolis; on Mount Helicon, on Mount Boreus near Asea, and above Lycosura.[97] The epithet *helikōnios* goes back to Homer, and is widespread in Ionia. The Ionian cults are conventionally explained as deriving from Mount Helicon, or even worse, from the city Helice; but it is far more likely that *Helikōn* is a descriptive term that recurred at each cult site, as it does at Agrae.

What does the term describe? The meaning 'black' is attributed to the adjective ἑλικός *vel sim.* by Homeric exegesis and Hellenistic poets.[98]

94 Cf. *EMC*² 10 (1991) 67–8; *Anc. Econ. in Myth.* 8–10.
95 For the shrine in the Agora, Thompson and Wycherley, *Agora of Athens* 30–1, 35–8.
96 Bekker, *Anecd.* 1.326–7 (Cleidemus *FGrHist* 323 F 1).
97 Cf. F. Wüst, *RE* 22.1 (1953) 510–22 s.v. Poseidon (list of cults).
98 Callim. *Hec.* fr. 299 (= 116 Hollis); [Theocr.] *Id.* 25.127; schol., Eust. *Il.* 1.98; Hsch. *s.vv.* ἑλίβοτρυς, ἑλικόν, ἑλίκωπες; etc. Cf. D.L. Page, *History and the Homeric Iliad*

This can hardly be pure invention; moreover, an adjective with some such meaning is presupposed by a considerable series of personal names, e.g., Ἑλίκων, Ἑλικώ, Ἑλίκανδρος.[99] In Lycophron the name Μέλανθος 'Black' signifies Poseidon (*Alex. 767*); the scholiast explains that he was so called 'at Athens'; as this ordinary word is not a credible cult epithet, it must have been offered as a synonym by some antiquarian writer. The cult at Agrae will be in view. Callimachus says of a river that its water is the 'blackest,' ἑλικώτατον. Water, especially an abundant source of water, is often called 'black' or 'dark,' and this is Poseidon's element: all the gushing or flowing waters that fertilize the earth. A descriptive word has conjuring force; springs have names like 'Amymone' and 'Aganippe.' Hence the name Ἑλικών for Poseidon's cult sites.

Poseidon's commonest festival comes in winter, in the month Poseideon. At Sinope the priest of Poseidon *helikōnios* is active at the festival, which lasts three days in mid-month.[100] At Athens too the festival must have honoured Poseidon *helikōnios*; for Poseidon's cult on the Acropolis, the only other attested for the city, goes with the summer festival Scira.

Such then is Agrae. To sum up, our survey of shrines and festivals proves that for a long time the town of Athens was confined to the area southeast of the Acropolis. It did not spread to the north and west until Athenians were set in their ways of worshipping all the principal deities.

(Berkeley 1959) 244–5; Chantraine, *Dict. étym.* s.vv. ἑλίκωψ, ἕλιξ; Hollis on Callim. *loc. cit.*

99 Besides the three above, the *Lexicon of Greek Personal Names* 1 (Oxford 1987) gives Ἑλικάων, Ἑλίκιν, Ἕλιξ, Ἕλιξος.

100 *SIG*³ 1017 (*LSAM* 1). For the festival pattern, *CQ*² 34 (1984) 1–16.

2

The Synoecia,
the Old Agora,
and Attic Phratries

Synopsis

In the course of the Dark Age, society and government changed. In Attica a growing population came to be organized round the city of Athens in a system of phratries. The phratries now effectively enrolled young men as soldiers and citizens. This procedure, conducted at phratry lodges throughout the countryside, became so ingrained that it continued even after Cleisthenes transferred the main responsibility to the demes. With the advent of the phratries, the ceremony of the Hecatombaea in southeast Athens lost all significance. The phratries did not join together in the city, so far as one can see, in any corresponding ceremony.

If we look ahead to the tyrants, we find that another civic ceremony has been devised: an oath-taking in the sanctuary of Aglaurus, followed by the *pannychis* and procession of the Panathenaea. The ceremony continued when citizens were enrolled by the demes. Later still, young men underwent a period of training to qualify as soldiers and citizens, and the demesmen came to Athens just beforehand, in the month Metageitnion, in order to elect the supervisors. These developments took place in the old agora east of the Acropolis – an 'old' agora as it later seemed, but a new one in the days of the phratries.

Though citizens were enrolled locally, phratry members came to Athens at the beginning of the civic year for another purpose: to elect or acclaim the officers of government. The occasion, at the full moon of the first month, was called Συνοίκια, 'rites of the combined houses,' i.e., of the phratry lodges. The worship was addressed to Zeus and Athena, the deities of the Acropolis who had been adopted by every phratry.

The ground chosen for the gathering lay below the east face of the Acropolis, so that Zeus and Athena looked down upon their worshippers.

This was now the agora of Athens, and an altar of Zeus was set up which became the most famous altar in the city – 'the Altar of Pity,' where suppliants sought a hearing from the assembled people. A Prytaneium and other offices of government were built beside the open ground.

Attica was served by the phratry organization down to the sixth century, when conflict arose between different regions. The phratry members had always assembled under arms at the Synoecia, but the practice was now too dangerous. The tyrant Peisistratus suspended the gatherings, though not of course the ritual, and transplanted the archons' quarters to the northwest sector of the city. From then on, civic business was divided between the old agora and the new one, the Agora we know from excavation. The whole body of citizens no longer assembled in either place, but on the Pnyx or in the theatre of Dionysus.

Yet the old agora still accommodated certain traditional gatherings, and also emergency musters. In the fifth century some of the ground was turned into a spacious sanctuary of Theseus, and in the Hellenistic period some more of it was laid out as a gymnasium; both the Theseium and the gymnasium had civic uses deriving from the agora. The agora itself was never lost to view; indeed it became a literary fashion to reserve the term 'agora' for this area, and to speak of the new Agora as the 'Cerameicus.'

The festival Synoecia, like the Hecatombaea, is imprinted in the life of Theseus. But the episode is plainly secondary. After the cycle of adventures that culminates in the slaying of the Minotaur, when Theseus has succeeded to the kingship and the paradigm of a young Athenian is complete, the next step, before the rather disparate adventures of Theseus' maturity, is the institution of the Synoecia. Theseus summons all the people of Attica to the centre of Athens so that they may share in government on equal terms. More precisely, he gives them a common Prytaneium and Council-house, and makes offices elective.

It is true that nothing is said of phratries in this context. The reputed effect of Theseus' action is to level Athenian society, to introduce a virtual 'democracy,' and also to unify Attica, to bring about a virtual 'synoecism.' The first notion is anachronistic, and the second is unreal. The phratries installed Athens' magistrates and councillors, by what procedure we do not know; this has been assimilated to the elections or allotments of later Athenian democracy. The reunion of phratry lodges gives the festival name, Synoecia; this has been misinterpreted as a 'synoecism' of the familiar kind, and we are told, quite absurdly, that people from far and wide took up residence in Athens, and that throughout Attica innumerable Prytaneia and Council-houses were closed down.

The phratries of the Synoecia have left their mark elsewhere, in the antiquarian reconstructions of early Attica that are cited from the lost beginning of [Aristotle's] *Constitution of Athens* and from the Attic chronicler Philochorus. Their reconstructions are largely drawn from the festival business. For this we have independent testimony in Athens' calendar of sacrifice. The reconstructions of [Aristotle] and Philochorus are too schematic, but by comparing them with the calendar, we can see how they erred. The residue of truth constitutes our knowledge of early Attica.

The argument proceeds as follows. First the sources, and the range of evidence they provide, direct and indirect. Next the direct evidence for the ritual, at first sight contradictory; the sacrifice on the Acropolis; the festival deities, Zeus *phratrios* and Athena *phratria*. Then some questions of topography: the location of the old agora; Apollodorus' notion of Aphrodite *pandēmos*, which has always been misunderstood; 'the Altar of Pity'; the altar and statue of Eirene, a latecomer to the festival. Finally, the early organization of Attica: [Aristotle] on phratries and *trittyes*, and Philochorus on 'the twelve cities' and the *phylai*, and the reality that they both presuppose; [Aristotle] and others on the three occupational classes, a theory for which support was sought in the officiants of the festival; the ritual identity of the Eupatridae, the Geomori, and the Demiurgi. (See maps 3 and 4.)

The Sources

Thucydides and Plutarch hold up the Synoecia as commemorating Theseus' synoecism; the herald's proclamation quoted by Plutarch is clearly part of the ritual, and some other ritual details are deducible from the story. The festival appears on stone in the early regulations of the deme Scambonidae, and, as a biennial celebration, in the civic calendar of sacrifice set up in ca. 399.[1] This civic calendar carried great authority. A more eclectic and extensive body of ritual was compiled in the late fifth century, but the compiler, the clerk Nicomachus, was prosecuted for it, and his work was erased. The calendar that replaces it is restricted to authentic old observances, chiefly Solonian, and inscribed in very elegant lettering and format.[2] So the festival was carefully kept up long after the public gatherings of the Synoecia had ceased; indeed it continued in some form down to Plutarch's day.

1 Thuc. 2.15.1–2, 16.1; Plut. *Thes.* 24.1–4. *IG* 1³ 244.16–19; *Hesperia* 4 (1935) 19–21 no. 2 lines 31–59. Some current accounts of the festival: Mommsen, *Feste* 35–40; M.P. Nilsson, *RE* 4 A 2 (1932) 1435 s.v. Συνοίκια; Deubner, *Att. Feste* 36–8; Parke, *Festivals* 30–3; T.J. Figueira, *Hesperia* 53 (1984) 465–6. All save Mommsen ignore the evidence of aetiology.

2 *Phoenix* 43 (1989) 372–3; *JHS* 110 (1990) 65–75. P.J. Rhodes, *JHS* 111 (1991) 94–5, disagrees.

The goddess Eirene was associated later with the annual celebration of 16 Hecatombaeon. The Lycurgan record of hide-moneys gives a rough confirmation of the date, and shows that the sacrifice to Eirene was then on a very large scale.[3] Other sources have more to say of the altar, or altars, of Eirene, and of the statue by Cephisodotus, and of the date when the cult was reputedly established, 375–374. As we shall see below, the statue and altar of Eirene shared the fate of several Classical monuments in early Roman times, being removed from the old agora to the new.

Theseus' synoecism, as described by Thucydides and Plutarch, is not the only *aition* of our festival. An ancient and important rite will always give rise to sundry stories. The Synoecia can be discerned behind stories of Demophon, Theseus' son, and of Solon, and of Peisistratus. These stories dwell upon the muster under arms, which was a leading feature of the festival in early days; the phratries were above all a means of organizing society for war. The only trace of this that afterwards survived in the ritual was the herald's proclamation, addressed to men in arms. It is, moreover, the only trace we find in the story of Theseus' synoecism, which may therefore be later than any of the other stories. Thucydides tells it as if it were a novelty.

In Euripides' *Heracleidae*, as war with Argos threatens, Demophon the king of Athens musters the people in the city (lines 335–8). It is true that his action is only briefly reported. The setting of the play is not Athens but Marathon, where the Heracleidae have taken refuge, rather oddly, and where Demophon has left them, rather oddly. But the tradition outside Euripides brings the Heracleidae to Athens, not Marathon, and the altar of Zeus to which they cling belongs in the city, in the old agora. The supplication of the Heracleidae and the muster of Athenians make another *aition* of the Synoecia.

In early days soldiers wore a leather cap. Solon put on a leather cap when he rushed into the agora and mounted the herald's stone to urge war on Megara.[4] The story was inspired in the first instance by the opening lines of his poem on Salamis, but the details are taken from the ritual of the Synoecia. Sparta has a rather similar story about the Partheniae.

[Aristotle] and Polyaenus describe a ruse of Peisistratus by which he divested the Athenians of all their arms.[5] He first summoned them to muster under arms, then removed the arms while their attention was distracted. The two writers give different but parallel indications of the general

---

3 IG 2² 1496.94–5, 127–8.
4 Dem. 19 *De Fals. Leg.* 255; Plut. *Sol.* 8.1; Justin 2.7.10.
5 [Arist.] *Ath.* 15.4; Polyaenus 1.21.2.

setting, which is unmistakably the old agora. It was no doubt Peisistratus who ended the custom of mustering under arms at the Synoecia – but not in the manner alleged. We shall see later, while examining the Panathenaea, why the story says that the arms were sequestered at a place near the agora (pp. 117–18).

[Aristotle's] account of early Attica is known only from Plutarch and the lexica, but the context in Plutarch and the terminology of the lexica point directly to our festival. As for Philochorus, the remnants of his account are more substantial and coherent than has been generally recognized.[6]

The Direct Evidence for the Ritual

Let us examine the evidence for the festival setting and for the deities honoured. The first two items are the most distinct, but they are also contradictory.

Our festival appears in the cult regulations of the deme Scambonidae, inscribed on three sides of a stele in 'c. a. 460'; the lettering of the side in question is said to be a little earlier than that of the other two sides. The deme sacrifices a mature animal on the Acropolis, and the meat is sold raw.[7] It is sold, we may suppose, either for the sake of economy or because there was not space on the Acropolis for a general feast. The animal must be large, doubtless an ox. It is the Acropolis setting that conflicts with the next item.

The Solonian calendar inscribed in the year 399 or just after prescribes sacrifice on both days of the biennial celebration. On 15 Hecatombaeon, the *phylē* Geleontes and the *trittys* 'Bright-headbands' are on hand, and the victim is a young sheep. On 16 Hecatombaeon, the *phylē* Geleontes are again on hand, the sacrifice is addressed to Zeus *phratrios* and Athena *phratria*, and the victims are two young oxen, doubtless one for each deity.[8] On the first day we are not told to whom the young sheep is offered; it is extremely common in cult regulations (e.g., those of Scambonidae) to give only the festival name, then the victim.[9] Here too the sacrifice will

6 Plut. *Thes.* 25.1–3; [Arist.] *Ath.* fr. 2 Chambers (lexica and scholia). Philochorus *FGrHist* 328 F 94; Poll. 8.109; Steph. Byz. *s.v.* Ἀκτή (Apollodorus *FGrHist* 244 F 185).

7 *IG* 1³ 244 C 16–19: Χσυνοικίοις ἐμ πόλει τέλεον· τὰ δὲ κρέα ἀποδόσθαι ὀμά.

8 *Hesperia* 4 (1935) 19–21 no. 2 lines 35–8: Γλεόντων φυλῆι, Λευκοταινίων τριττύι, οἶν λειπογνώμονα. Lines 47–51: Γλεόντων φυλῆι. Διὶ φρατρίωι καὶ Ἀθηναίαι φρατρίαι. βόε δύο λειπογνώμονε.

9 H. Hansen, *GRBS* 14 (1973) 325, wrongly infers that the animal 'is offered to no deity in particular,' and that the *trittys* simply 'receives' it.

be addressed to Zeus *phratrios* and Athena *phratria*, or possibly to Zeus alone, the senior partner. The *trittys* 'Bright-headbands' do not represent any other sphere of interest; we shall see that they are in fact the whole group of phratries attached to the *phylē*.

On the second day the sacrifice is much larger, costing fifty drachmas instead of four, and 16 Hecatombaeon is recorded elsewhere as the single day of the annual celebration.[10] We may suppose that in early times secular business was transacted on 15 Hecatombaeon, the full moon and hence a good signal for a general reunion, and was followed next day by sacrifice and festivity. Later the secular business was dropped, and only the biennial celebration kept a small remembrance. The calendar entry is clear in itself, but phratry gods do not belong on the Acropolis.

A priesthood in Roman Athens evokes the Synoecia without naming it. In the time of Trajan, Titus Coponius Maximus the elder was 'priest of Ares Enyalius and Enyo and Zeus Geleon.'[11] The first two deities, Ares and Enyo, belong together. Statues of both, by Classical sculptors, stood in the fifth-century temple of Ares that was transplanted to the Agora in the time of Augustus, about a hundred years before the priesthood of Titus.[12] Near the temple Pausanias saw the statue of Eirene, again by a Classical sculptor, and near this was a transplanted altar. It is argued below that the altar is Eirene's, and that her altar and her statue came from the old agora. The temple of Ares is usually traced to Acharnae, but the reasons are not conclusive; perhaps Ares, like Eirene, came from the old agora. Zeus and Eirene also belong together as deities of the Synoecia. On this argument, the deities served by Titus have a common background in the old agora. But Ares and Enyo cannot be considered here; the trail would take us much too far. For the present purpose, Zeus Geleon must stand alone.

Zeus Geleon derives his epithet from the *phylē* Geleontes. In the Solonian calendar, this *phylē* worships Zeus *phratrios* at the Synoecia. It is true that, again on the evidence of the calendar, the Ionic *phylai* had at least one other ritual engagement, on the fifth of an unknown month; but that was a very small occasion (we shall come to it below, apropos of the Eupatridae).[13] The Ionic *phylai*, with the Geleontes to the fore, are

10 Plut. *Thes.* 24.4; schol. Ar. *Pax* 1019.
11 *IG* 2² 1072.5–6: ἱερεὺς Ἄρεως Ἐνυαλίου καὶ Ἐννοῦς καὶ Διὸς Γελέοντος. The archonship of Titus *fils*, which dates the inscription, is to be placed within the years 96–7 through 102–3, perhaps in 101–2: Follet, *Athènes* 170–3, 303, 365.
12 For this cult of Ares, Wycherley, *Testimonia* 54–5. For the temple, Thompson and Wycherley, *Agora of Athens* 162–5.
13 *IG* 2² 1357 a 6–8; *Hesperia* 4 (1935) 22–3 lines 6–8.

chiefly concerned with the Synoecia. About the time that Titus was priest, Plutarch wrote of our festival as a contemporary observance – he may have witnessed it.[14] Zeus Geleon is therefore another name for the presiding deity of the festival.

Thucydides says of the Synoecia that 'the Athenians down to this day conduct a popular festival for the goddess,' i.e., Athena. It is hardly surprising that Zeus is ignored in favour of his daughter, Athens' eponym and patron.[15]

Eirene was a latecomer to the festival, but she had long been celebrated in poetry, and here she is another daughter of Zeus. It was in this quality, as we shall see, that she was adopted at the Synoecia.

The Sacrifice on the Acropolis

Thus the evidence for the deities of the Synoecia is self-coherent, apart from that contradiction between the Solonian calendar and the regulations of Scambonidae. Whereas Zeus and Athena are worshipped as phratry gods in the calendar, the Acropolis has no phratry gods for Scambonidae to worship. None of the Acropolis cults of Zeus and Athena is at all related to phratries.

We should pause for a moment over Zeus *herkeios*, god of the yard or garth, whose altar stood near the Pandroseium.[16] As worshipped by families or by larger kinship groups, he too serves to establish one's lineage, and he is sometimes named beside Zeus *phratrios*, but as distinct from him.[17] He belongs to an older and simpler society, being joined with Apollo *patrōios* in the question put to prospective archons.[18] The term *patrōios*,

14 Plut. *Thes.* 24.4: ἔθυσε δὲ καὶ Μετοίκια ... ἦν ἔτι νῦν θύουσι. The festival name is distorted, but perhaps this is current usage rather than a slip by Plutarch; for Theseus' legendary action might equally be described as μετοικίζειν, which was then a more familiar word and phenomenon. The words ἔτι νῦν echo Thucydides; but despite Mommsen, *Feste* 39 n. 3, and Deubner, *Att. Feste* 36 n. 9, Plutarch would not sound the echo unless it were appropriate.

15 Thuc. 2.15.2: Ἀθηναῖοι ἔτι καὶ νῦν τῆι θεῶι ἑορτὴν δημοτελῆ ποιοῦσιν. Given the evidence of the Solonian calendar, one would not now label the Synoecia a festival of Athena, as Deubner did.

16 Dion. Hal. *De Dinarch.* 3 (Philochorus *FGrHist* 328 F 67). Cf. G.P. Stevens and J.M. Paton, *The Erechtheum* (Cambridge, Mass. 1927) 474–5; K. Jeppesen, *The Theory of the Alternative Erechtheion* (Aarhus 1987) 69 fig. 7.

17 Pl. *Euthyd.* 302 D; Ath. 11.3, 460 F (Cratin. Jun. fr. 9 Kassel and Austin). W.S. Ferguson, *Hesperia* 7 (1938) 32–3, rightly dismissed the notion that Zeus *herkeios* and *phratrios* are identical. Zeus *herkeios* has a very different range, as may be seen from H. Sjövall, *Zeus im altgriechischen Hauskult* (Lund 1931) 7–48.

18 [Arist.] *Ath.* 55.3; Harp. *s.v.* ἑρκεῖος Ζεύς (Deinarchus fr. 27 Sauppe).

'ancestral,' is applied to various deities by kinship groups of various kinds.[19] Apollo *patrōios*, like the Ionic *phylai*, goes with Ion's dispensation, which is more or less common to all Ionic peoples.[20] The phratries are a later development, and when they are drawn into legendary aetiology, as in [Aristotle], they are the work of Theseus.

Zeus *herkeios* then has no integral connection with phratries. His altar on the Acropolis possessed some notable civic function, for in the early Hellenistic period a portent at the altar was held to signify an impending change of government (so Philochorus). We can divine what this function was. Altars of Zeus *herkeios* were the place for swearing solemn oaths, and others not so solemn, as we see from the tale of Demaratus and his mother (Hdt. 6.67.3–68.1). So it was doubtless at the Acropolis altar that the board of archons swore the oath of office a second time ([Arist.] *Ath.* 55.5).

On this showing, it is only right to entertain the possibility that the deme Scambonidae sacrificed to Zeus *herkeios*. Zeus *polieus* should be canvassed too, and of course Athena *polias*. But these two have important festivals of their own. Since the Panathenaea like the Synoecia are a re-union of the whole community with a military flavour, Athena *polias* may seem a natural candidate;[21] but at the Synoecia, Zeus takes precedence of Athena. Wherever we turn on the Acropolis, we shall not find a setting entirely suited to our festival.

The regulations of Scambonidae are aberrant in another respect. We have much fuller regulations for other demes, all later, and mostly of the fourth century: two or three deal fully with the month Hecatombaeon, and yet there is no trace of the Synoecia.[22] In this period the festival was not of general concern to the demes; probably it was of no concern at all.

19 Cf. C. Rolley, *BCH* 89 (1965) 458–9, and Sjövall 34 on Zeus *herkeios patrōios*.
20 The mythical subordination of Ionia to Athens is now seen to go back to the Hesiodic *Catalogue* (fr. 10a lines 20–4 West). The story of Apollo's begetting Ion, hitherto regarded as late, may well have been told by [Hesiod] later; cf. M.L. West, *The Hesiodic Catalogue of Women* (Oxford 1985) 106. Early or late, the story like the archon's *dokimasia* implies that Apollo as well as Zeus was worshipped in each Athenian household, presumably as *agyieus*. The household god was adopted by the phratries, then by the city in the new Agora. Perhaps it was he for whom the festival Thargelia was first celebrated; cf. Mommsen, *Feste* 485–6. This view of Apollo *patrōios* is close to Nilsson's, *Gesch. der gr. Rel.*[2] 1.556–7. For other opinions, Jacoby, *CQ* 38 (1944) 73 = *Abhandlungen zur griechischen Geschichtsschreibung* (Leiden 1956) 255; J.K. Davies, *CJ* 73 (1977) 110; E. Kearns in *Crux: Essays Presented to G.E.M. de Ste. Croix* (Exeter 1985) 205.
21 Cf. Deubner, *Att. Feste* 36: 'It was naturally Athena, the goddess of the state.'
22 Cf. the calendars of the Tetrapolis, Erchia, and Thoricus: the last is fragmentary for the first month, but still does not encourage any thought of the Synoecia. J.D. Mikalson, *AJP* 98 (1977) 430, notes the omission and casts about for reasons. The lettering of the

The Solonian calendar specifies phratry gods. When we take up the aetiology of the festival, we shall find that it is indeed a gathering of phratries, the essential unit of social organization before Cleisthenes. Although it can be said of Theseus' synoecism that he brought Athenians together 'from the demes,' this expression is not to be relied on.[23] The deme Scambonidae has no business with phratry gods. Admittedly, these gods are worshipped not only by phratries, but sometimes by hieratic *genē* too. Hieratic *genē*, however, have a close relationship with phratries, as demes do not. In any case our festival is ancient; the participation of a deme can be no earlier than Cleisthenes.

It all goes to show that the sacrifice on the Acropolis is an exceptional measure. We should remember how early these regulations are. They come within fifty years of Cleisthenes' reforms. When Cleisthenes substituted demes for phratries as the essential unit, the change was duly signalized by including demes in the festival Synoecia. Since it was not appropriate for them to worship at the phratry shrine, they were directed instead to a prominent civic altar of Zeus or Athena, perhaps the altar of Zeus *herkeios*. The Acropolis was not far away from the phratry shrine, as we shall see; indeed they were directly linked by the northeast ascent. In short, the regulations give us a rather arbitrary innovation, which did not continue for very long.

Zeus *phratrios* and Athena *phratria*

We must look elsewhere for Zeus *phratrios* and Athena *phratria*. At Athens they are sufficiently attested as the deities common to every phratry, no matter what other cults a given phratry might possess. As others have remarked, this unitary worship strongly suggests that the phratries themselves were created at a single stroke.[24] Zeus and Athena are also, and as a very ancient heritage, worshipped on the citadel of nearly every Greek city; no other major deities are such constant partners in cult. It follows

---

Thoricus calendar points to the fifth century rather than the fourth: D.M. Lewis, *ZPE* 60 (1985) 108 n. 3; R. Parker, *Boreas* 15 (1987) 138 n. 11 (but the archaic form of the dative feminine plural should not be called in evidence, since it is retained even in the later addition on the left side).

23 Paus. 1.22.3, 26.6: ἀπὸ τῶν δήμων. Pausanias follows Apollodorus in deriving Aphrodite's epithet *pandēmos* from the synoecism: more of this below. But it is not clear that Apollodorus spoke of 'demes' rather than the *dēmos*; the expression 'from the demes' may originate with Pausanias. Even Apollodorus comes too late to signify.

24 K. Latte, *RE* 20.1 (1941) 757 *s.v.* Φράτριοι θεοί; cf. D. Roussel, *Tribu et cité* (Paris 1976) 135 n. 1.

that they were installed among the phratries as a means of attaching them to the centre of the community.

Whereas the festival Apaturia was celebrated at each phratry shrine of Zeus and Athena, the Synoecia brought the phratries together at a common shrine in Athens. We must try to locate this shrine. Two shrines of Zeus *phratrios* and Athena *phratria* have been excavated in the city, both elegant if not imposing, but much too late for the republication of the Solonian calendar, not to speak of any earlier time. In fact both come very late in the history of phratries. [25]

On the west side of the Agora, a very small temple was built in the mid fourth century right beside the south wing of the Stoa of Zeus; the altar in front was inscribed for our two deities, and a pedestal at the back of the temple probably supported statues of both. [26] Soon after this, a much larger temple of Apollo *patrōios* was built to the south, obviously as part of the same design, since it is nearly symmetrical with the wings of the Stoa of Zeus, and the temple of Zeus and Athena is nestled between. Now Apollo's temple occupies exactly the site of an Archaic apsidal building, so that this cult goes far back. [27] Zeus *sōtēr*, whose statue and altar stood in front of the great stoa, was also worshipped from of old; for remains of another Archaic shrine were found beneath the stoa. But in contrast to these, the temple of Zeus *phratrios* and Athena *phratria* is a new departure. Though it complements the other cults, it comes from a different background. As explained above, Apollo *patrōios* stands for another kind of kinship, earlier and more general than the phratries.

The other shrine came to light farther north, right beside the main thoroughfare that leads from the northeast corner of the Agora to the gates in the northeast sector of the city wall, and about halfway along it. [28] Here too an altar was inscribed for Zeus *phratrios* and Athena *phratria*; what else there may have been we do not know, since the excavation was quite restricted. This shrine is to be dated somewhat later than the other, in the late fourth century or even at the beginning of the third.

25 It must be conceded, however, that a shrine of Zeus *phratrios* and Athena *phratria* was constructed or refurbished at Paeania in the later fourth century. The document in question is dated on prosopographical grounds to the 320s: Davies, *Ath. Prop. Fam.* 68.
26 H.A. Thompson, *Hesperia* 6 (1937) 84–90, 104–7; Thompson and Wycherley, *Agora of Athens* 139–40; Thompson, *Agora Guide*[3] 76–8; S.I. Rotroff, *Hesperia* 52 (1983) 270.
27 Thompson *apud* C.W. Hedrick, Jr., *AJA* 92 (1988) 187 n. 8, 194 n. 54, 209 n. 224, gives a *mise-au-point*.
28 N. Kyparisses and Thompson, *Hesperia* 7 (1938) 612–25; Travlos, *Pictorial Dict.* 573–5.

Both shrines presuppose some kind of phratry worship that was still of moment at a rather late stage, but what was it? As the shrine at the northeast is near the periphery of the ancient city, it can hardly be regarded as the centre of a particular phratry, unless we believe that phratries were rather numerous; and even then it is odd that the phratry did not trouble to put its name upon the altar, and that the construction is so late. The Agora shrine must have been somehow meant for general use. But it is hardly satisfactory to suppose that it was newly built for the festival Synoecia, now transferred from some other site. The altar is too small for a sacrifice of oxen, even young ones; moreover, Eirene needs a substantial altar of her own.

The festival Apaturia suggests an explanation.[29] This festival called for all the members of each phratry to gather for three days at the phratry centre, wherever that might be in the Attic countryside. Yet even in Cleisthenes' day the membership of a given phratry was often widely scattered, as we see from the deme affiliation of phratry members. In 396–395 the phratry Demotionidae, whose centre was at Deceleia, resolved to post notices in Athens of business to be transacted at the Apaturia. In 406 a good many phratry members, evidently from different phratries, were in Athens even during the festival, for they wore mourning garb to the Assembly; they must have forgone the celebration at the phratry centres.[30]

Since the festival was the time for welcoming or rejecting new members, it was conducted perforce as long as phratries lasted. But to gather at some distant lodge became ever more difficult and irksome. So some reunions, we may suppose, were held in the city instead;[31] the chief need then was for a decent altar to accommodate the offering of small animals, and this was provided in the Agora. The reason for building the other shrine on the northeast thoroughfare was perhaps that the city reunions had become still more common and required another facility.

We have yet to identify the setting of the Synoecia; the argument so far has been entirely a process of exclusion. The direct evidence for the

29 Isaeus 7 *Apollod.* 15 does not permit the inference that phratry business was normally conducted at the Thargelia, a city festival; see Wyss *ad loc.*
30 Posting notices in Athens: *IG* 2² 1237 lines 61–4, 121–3. The Apaturia of 406: Xen. *Hell.* 1.7.8.
31 The calendar of the Salaminian *genos* inscribed in 363–362 includes an offering, worth forty drachmas, to Zeus *phratrios* at the Apaturia: Ferguson, *Hesperia* 7 (1938) 1–9 no. 1 lines 92–3 (*LSCG Suppl.* 19). Ferguson 28–9 infers that the festival was celebrated jointly by several phratries, and doubtless in the city. It is just as likely, however, that the *genos* was associated with a particular phratry: A. Andrewes, *JHS* 81 (1961) 9. Whether members of the *genos* belonged to more than one phratry remains unclear: Ferguson 28 n. 7; Andrewes 10; S.C. Humphreys, *ZPE* 83 (1990) 247–8.

ritual, as cited above, does not suffice. But we can see from the various aetiologies that our festival was held in the centre of Athens. What and where that centre was will soon emerge. Briefly, Thucydides and Plutarch point to the Prytaneium and a hypothetical Council-house;[32] [Aristotle] and Polyaenus, to the Theseium and the Anaceium; Apollodorus, to 'the old agora.' We shall also find that the old agora had a notable altar of Zeus, variously called the altar of Zeus *agoraios*, or the Altar of Pity; but these are only descriptive terms. The altar of Eirene was nearby. So it is the shrine of the Synoecia, and the further argument turns upon topography.

The Old Agora

It is but recently that the location of the old agora has become apparent. The only mention of it that was allowed was an enigmatic text of Apollodorus: admittedly, an important witness, a native Athenian and the leading scholar of his age. There can be no doubt, however, that the old agora was very close to certain shrines and public buildings that are better known. Chief among them is the Prytaneium, mentioned by [Aristotle] as one of four buildings that once served as quarters for the archons (*Ath.* 3.5). In the new Agora the three stoas at the northwest corner, which dominate the square, were all used by the archons. The earliest of them, the Stoa of the Basileus, was probably once used by the whole board; for the laws which they administered were displayed there on the *kyrbeis*, and the stone on which they swore their oath of office lay in front. In other cities too the archons' quarters, or the quarters of chief magistrates however styled, adjoin the agora.[33]

Now the Prytaneium, as Pausanias shows us (1.17.2–18.3), was near the Theseium, the Anaceium, and the sanctuary of Aglaurus, which included an Acropolis cave. It is reassuring that both the Theseium and the Anaceium are known for accommodating large assemblies. In the story of Peisistratus' ruse the Athenians muster at either the Theseium or the Anaceium. Historical musters are attested for both. Demesmen assemble at the Theseium for elections. We are clearly in the orbit of the old agora.

Yet a series of misunderstandings caused all these landmarks to be misplaced. It was supposed that Peisistratus, having mustered the Athenians, addressed them from the Propylaea on the west side of the Acropolis; that

---

32 Mommsen, *Feste* 38–9, inferred too strictly that the festival was celebrated *in* the Prytaneium, and so that Hestia was honoured too. We shall see below that the Council-house is a hypothetical building, equated by Thucydides with the actual Prytaneium.

33 Cf. *AJA* 88 (1984) 257; *Historia* 35 (1986) 168–73.

Herodotus locates the sanctuary of Aglaurus close to the Propylaea on the north side of the Acropolis; that Pausanias came to the Theseium and the other places just after leaving the new Agora, presumably at the southeast corner. Apollodorus only made confusion worse confounded; for he was thought to associate the old agora with a well-known shrine of Aphrodite *pandēmos* below the southwest bastion of the Acropolis.

In consequence, the area round the west end of the Acropolis became a Procrustes' bed for Athenian topographers. The cave of Aglaurus was identified as the next cave to the east of the caves of Apollo and Pan. The Prytaneium, Theseium, and Anaceium were lodged precariously on the slope above the Eleusinium – though some put the Theseium close beside the new Agora, or even within the Agora. The old agora, which, like the new one, ought to be a broad level area, was installed on the saddle between the Acropolis and the Areopagus, or farther south and west, or even on the south slope of the Acropolis.[34]

Ex oriente lux. In 1980 a stele was found *in situ* beneath the east face of the Acropolis, a stele that had been posted, according to the instructions it bore, in the sanctuary of Aglaurus.[35] Directly above is a large cave, the cave of Aglaurus. The other landmarks find their place close by, and we begin to grasp the full meaning of ancient writers who refer to these landmarks. We also see that this area east of the Acropolis was always known, right down to Pausanias' time, as the old agora and the true centre of Athens.

In 480, says Herodotus (8.52–3), the Persians occupied the Areopagus as a vantage point 'opposite the Acropolis,' and their main assault was 'at the gates,' where the defenders rolled down rocks; these gates are plainly at the west, like the later Propylaea. But the defenders were surprised by a few men who climbed up elsewhere, 'in front of the Acropolis, behind the gates and the ascent,' ἔμπροσθε ὢν τῆς ἀκροπόλιος, ὄπισθε δὲ τῶν πυλέων καὶ τῆς ἀνόδου, just at the sanctuary of Aglaurus, 'even though the place was very steep.' The east side is the front because the Acropolis shrines face this way and the city centre lies below. It is indeed very steep; before the south side was built up with a temple platform and a massive wall, it was the steepest part. No wonder then that it was left unguarded in 480.[36]

---

34 E.g., Travlos, *Poleodomikē exelixis* 28–9 and pl. I, and *Pictorial Dict.* 1–2, 8 fig. 5, 576–9; A.N. Oikonomides, *The Two Agoras in Ancient Athens* (Chicago 1964) 1–50; Wycherley, *Phoenix* 20 (1966) 285–93, and *Stones of Athens* 5, 178. But according to Kolb, *Agora* 20–3, Athens' agora always lay at the northwest, on the excavated site.

35 G.S. Dontas, *Hesperia* 52 (1983) 48–63. Cf. *AJP* 105 (1984) 386, 392–3; *Historia* 35 (1986) 157–68; also N.W. Slater, *ZPE* 66 (1986) 263–4.

36 D.M. Lewis in A.R. Burn, *Persia and the Greeks*[2] (London 1984) 607–8, refuses to believe that Herodotus moves from the west side of the Acropolis to the east side.

Lucian describes the same feat of climbing by a different party. In *Piscator* the tribe of philosophers, attracted by a promise of money, storm the Acropolis from every side, by every route. The last route to be mentioned, the most difficult of all, is taken by those who 'even set up ladders against the Anaceium,' καὶ πρὸς τὸ Ἀνακεῖον προσθέμενοι κλίμακας, and swarm up like hiving bees. The Anaceium, as we see from Pausanias, is the broader area below the sanctuary of Aglaurus. The daunting precipice also inspires Philochorus' story that the Athenians resolved to honour Aglaurus after she gave her life by leaping from the Acropolis wall.[37]

Herodotus' phrase 'in front of the Acropolis' is rather like the phrase 'in the middle of the city,' ἐν μέσηι τῆι πόλει, urbe ... media, which is used by Plutarch and Statius to locate the Theseium and the Altar of Pity.[38] In recounting Theseus' synoecism, Plutarch says that the common Prytaneium and Council-house were built 'where the lower city is now centred,' ὅπου νῦν ἵδρυται τὸ ἄστυ (*Thes.* 24.3) – a periphrasis for the agora.

After Peisistratus had mustered the Athenians in the Theseium ([Aristotle]) or the Anaceium (Polyaenus), he withdrew to higher ground so as to make himself heard – to the Acropolis entrance, πρὸς τὸ πρόπυλον τῆς ἀκροπόλεως ([Aristotle]) or εἰς τὸ προπύλαιον (Polyaenus). The shrine of Aglaurus, where the arms are secured in [Aristotle's] version, was situated 'round' the Acropolis entrance, περὶ τὰ προπύλαια τῆς πόλεως (Philochorus, as rendered by a scholiast). The entrance in question is clearly not at the west. The ramp on that side was constructed in the time of Peisistratus;[39] until then there was only a path beside the southwest bastion. A very ancient route, direct and rather steep, ascends the northeast slope of the Acropolis and emerges at the main place of worship: right in front of 'the old temple,' right beside the presumed site of Athena's altar.[40] Here then is the Acropolis entrance envisaged in the stories of Peisistratus' ruse and Aglaurus' suicide.

These conclusions are dictated by the stele uncovered in 1980. Another clue had been provided a few years earlier, when it was observed

---

According to Lewis, Herodotus' description cannot in fact be reconciled with the new reality, so that he stands convicted of fundamental error, and of pretending to more knowledge than he possesses.

37 Luc. 28 *Piscator* 42. Paus. 1.18.2: 'Above the shrine of the Dioscuri is a precinct of Aglaurus.' Schol. Dem. 19 *De Fals. Leg.* 303 (Philochorus *FGrHist* 328 F 105).

38 Plut. *Thes.* 36.4; Stat. *Theb.* 12.481.

39 E. Vanderpool in *PHOROS. Tribute to B.D. Meritt* (Locust Valley, N.Y. 1974) 157–9.

40 S.E. Iakovides, *Hē mykēnaikē akropolis tōn Athēnōn* (Athens 1962) 97–9, 136–43; J.A. Bundgaard, *Parthenon and the Mycenaean City on the Heights* (Copenhagen 1976) 26–31 and pl. D.

that Pausanias does not in fact locate the Theseium near the new Agora, which, like other late writers, he calls 'the Cerameicus,' but near a different square, which he calls precisely 'the agora.'[41] Yet the full significance of this has not been seen, for 'the agora' is thought to be a commercial agora, perhaps even the Roman Market. The notion does not do justice either to Pausanias' customary language or to his customary method.[42] In every city he visits, Pausanias uses the term 'agora' for the ancient ceremonial centre. He would not do otherwise at Athens, especially when he begins so formally (1.17.1). 'The Athenians have in their agora some monuments that are not familiar to everyone, notably an altar of Pity,' Ἀθηναίοις δὲ ἐν τῆι ἀγορᾶι καὶ ἄλλα ἐστὶν οὐκ ἐς ἅπαντας ἐπίσημα καὶ Ἐλέου βωμός. Nor would he draw attention to a workaday milieu, a commercial agora, or to a very recent construction, the Roman Market. Nor do we expect to find the ancient Altar of Pity in such a setting. Pausanias' 'agora' is the old agora.

It has generally been supposed that the old agora disappeared in later times.[43] Pausanias, and also Plutarch, show us that it did not disappear; it was always known and preserved as an agora. Other late writers testify to its celebrity, even if they have no firsthand knowledge. The rhetorician Sopater, living at Athens in the fourth century, says orotundly that the Athenians 'worship Pity' and 'fashion an altar of Kind-heartedness,' φιλ-ανθρωπία – two names for the same thing; the 'altar of Kind-heartedness' he situates, like Pausanias, 'on the agora,' ἐπὶ τῆς ἀγορᾶς. Alciphron, listing the main scenes of public activity at Athens, speaks of 'the Cerameicus, the agora' in succession.[44]

Pausanias and Alciphron distinguish the old agora and the new as 'the agora' and 'the Cerameicus.' In surviving sources, the new Agora is first called 'the Cerameicus' by Poseidonius in his satirical account of the philosopher-tyrant Athenion.[45] Athenion mounts the speaker's platform at the Stoa of Attalus as people clutch at his hem. Just before this, Poseidonius said that 'the Cerameicus was full of citizens and foreigners,' all rushing together to hear Athenion. There was no reason for anyone to gather on the road leading from the Dipylon to the Agora;[46] Athenion had entered

41 Vanderpool, Hesperia 43 (1974) 308–10. The distinction did not go unremarked in the nineteenth century: Vanderpool 309 n. 2.

42 Wycherley, Stones of Athens 65 n. 83, rightly objected, but wrongly preferred to equate 'Cerameicus' and 'agora.'

43 E.g., Wycherley, Phoenix 20 (1966) 293; Thompson and Wycherley, Agora of Athens 19 ('We can surmise that most Athenians had never heard of it').

44 Sopat. Rhet., Walz, Rhet. Gr. 8.210; Alciphr. Epist. 4.18.11.

45 Ath. 5.49–50, 212 E–F (Poseidonius FGrHist 87 F 36 = fr. 253 Sandbach).

46 'I.e., the route into the Agora': Sandbach ad loc. But Thompson and Wycherley, Agora of Athens 51, correctly say, 'i.e., the Agora.'

the city the day before (by whatever gate) and had been lodged overnight in a rich man's house. 'The Cerameicus' is therefore the new Agora, and the usage implies that only the old agora deserves that name, 'the agora.'

In the middle Hellenistic period, when we may assume that the old agora was no longer needed for some of the earlier business, the area was embellished by the construction of the Gymnasium of Ptolemy, named for its founder. This was almost certainly Ptolemy III Euergetes, who was Athens' leading 'benefactor' in the years after 229.[47] Pausanias comes to the Gymnasium between 'the agora' and the Theseium, and says that it was close to both.[48] No doubt the Gymnasium made use of some open ground which had once served the purposes of the agora. And since a gymnasium was typically shaded by trees, it will be the trees of Ptolemy's Gymnasium that Statius describes as growing near the Altar of Pity.[49]

In the fifth century, there is a very probable reference to the old agora by the poet Melanthius, under the expressive name 'Cecropian agora.' According to Plutarch, Melanthius spoke thus of the painter Polygnotus: 'At his own cost he adorned the temples of the gods and the Cecropian agora with the exploits of demigods,' αὐτοῦ γὰρ δαπάναισι θεῶν ναοὺς ἀγοράν τε | Κεκροπίαν κόσμησ' ἡμιθέων ἀρεταῖς.[50] Plutarch, to be sure, has his eye on the Painted Stoa in the new Agora. He has just told how Polygnotus 'painted the stoa,' ἔγραφε τὴν στοάν, not for hire but for free, and also how he included among the Trojan women a portrait of Elpinice, Cimon's sister, because he had enjoyed her favours. Part of this clearly goes back to Melanthius. A little farther on, Plutarch cites poems in which Melanthius, by way of 'sporting with Cimon,' πρὸς τὸν Κίμωνα παίζων, named the ladies whom Cimon had conquered. Melanthius sported with Elpinice too, and named Polygnotus.[51] As we see from the lines quoted, Melanthius did not refer expressly to the Painted Stoa. The story of the portrait is not from Melanthius, but was no doubt suggested by his poem.

47 So C. Habicht, *Studien zur Geschichte Athens in hellenistischer Zeit* (Göttingen 1982) 112–17. In remarking that the Ptolemaeum is not attested before 122–121 (apart from a conjectural suppletion of an earlier document), Habicht overlooks Apollodorus *FGrHist* 244 F 59, a chronographic notice of a philosopher who, having studied with Carneades, subsequently opened a school at the Ptolemaeum. The man's career begins in the archonship of Aristophantus, sometime round the mid second century: 154–3, according to B.D. Meritt, *Historia* 26 (1977) 183.

48 Paus. 1.17.2: the Gymnasium is 'not far from the agora'; the Theseium is 'beside the Gymnasium.' Cf. Plut. *Thes.* 36.4: the Theseium is 'in the middle of the city next to the present gymnasium.'

49 Stat. *Theb.* 12.491–2.

50 Plut. *Cim.* 4.7 (Melanthius fr. 2 Bergk / West).

51 *Elpinicae amores a Melanthio diffamatos esse puto, sicut Cimonis; ideo de Polygnoto dicit*: West *ad loc.*

All the evidence linking Polygnotus with the Painted Stoa is very dubious. In Melanthius' lines, something else is meant by 'the temples of the gods'; and the phrase 'the exploits of demigods,' i.e., of heroes, does not well describe the range of paintings in the stoa, of which at least half were historical rather than heroic.[52] Although some writers say, quite predictably, that one or other of the paintings in the stoa was by Polygnotus, it is Panaenus, a much lesser figure, to whom both Pausanias and Pliny attribute the battle of Marathon, the most famous of all the paintings.[53] Harpocration s.v. Πολύγνωτος (cf. Suda s.v.) indicates that Polygnotus was dissociated from the stoa by the best authorities. 'He received Athenian citizenship,' we are told, 'either because he painted the Painted Stoa for free, or as others have it, ἢ ὡς ἕτεροι, the paintings in the Theseium and the Anaceium.'[54] For all details of Polygnotus, Harpocration cites at the end 'Artemon in his book On Painters and Juba in his books On Painting' (FGrHist 275 F 21). Artemon and Juba are obviously those 'others.'

The paintings in the Anaceium and the Theseium are heard of elsewhere; they depict heroic subjects.[55] For the Anaceium a literal 'temple,' ναός, is not attested, and but doubtfully for the Theseium;[56] a poet, however, might use the word for any shrine. Since the Theseium and the Anaceium are both close to the old agora, it seems likely that Melanthius' allusion is chiefly to these two shrines, and that 'Cecropian agora' means precisely the old agora. It is a fitting epithet, since the name of Cecrops evokes the Acropolis that towers above.

Thus far the evidence locating the old agora. We now turn to Apollodorus, who speaks of 'the old agora' by this very name. He does not, however, help to locate it; for his purpose is only to explain an epithet used elsewhere, pandēmos, by referring to a custom of the agora. Since he has always been misunderstood, and since the misunderstanding has bedevilled Athenian topography, we must pause to set the record straight.

---

52 See Wycherley, Phoenix 7 (1953) 20–35; Testimonia 31–45 nos. 47–98, and the summing-up on p. 31. Of the paintings alleged for the stoa, Marathon, Oenoe, Phlius, Salamis, and Sophocles are historical subjects; only Amazons, Troy, and Heracleidae are heroic.

53 Paus. 5.11.6; Plin. Hist. Nat. 35.57. Cf. Wycherley, Testimonia 45, additional note 3.

54 ἐν τῶι θησαυρῶι καὶ τῶι 'Ανακείωι mss: Θησείωι Valckenauer: Θησέως ἱερῶι Reinesius.

55 Anaceium: Paus. 1.18.1 (Leucippids by Polygnotus, Argonauts by Micon); 'Polygnotus' hare' was a byword. Theseium: Paus. 1.17.2–3 (Amazons, Centaurs, young Theseus by Micon). J.P. Barron, JHS 92 (1972) 20–45, finds the Theseium paintings reflected on contemporary vases.

56 Hsch., Etym. Magn. s.v. Θησεῖον.

Aphrodite *pandemos*

Apollodorus is cited by Harpocration *s.v.* πάνδημος 'Αφροδίτη (*FGrHist* 244 F 113). 'Apollodorus in his work *On the Gods* says that the title *pandēmos* had been given at Athens to the goddess who was established round the old agora, inasmuch as all the people would gather here of old for public assemblies, which they called *agorai*,' πάνδημόν φησιν 'Αθήνησι κληθῆναι τὴν ἀφιδρυθεῖσαν περὶ τὴν ἀρχαίαν ἀγορὰν διὰ τὸ ἐνταῦθα πάντα τὸν δῆμον συνάγεσθαι τὸ παλαιὸν ἐν ταῖς ἐκκλησίαις, ἃς ἐκάλουν ἀγοράς. Apollodorus attributes this use of the epithet *pandēmos* to the past, not to contemporary Athens. 'The title had been given,' or 'She had been called,' κληθῆναι. Harpocration does not say, 'The title was given,' or 'She was called,' καλεῖσθαι.

As to Apollodorus' own time, there is no question that Aphrodite *pandēmos* was worshipped southwest of the Acropolis, and that the old agora was to be seen east of the Acropolis. Apollodorus could not possibly hold a wrong opinion about the location of either Aphrodite *pandēmos* or the old agora. Instead, he ventures an explanation of why Aphrodite was called *pandēmos* in the first place. Another explanation was current before Apollodorus, and it was somewhat closer to the truth. For the nature of this cult is not in doubt.

The cult furnishings are better known in the light of recent work.[57] The setting is a narrow terrace below the south face of the Nike bastion; a small temple or aedicula with marble front and wooden roof was erected here in the second half of the fourth century. Though the furnishings were modest, the worship was renowned. A procession took place at the beginning of the civic year, doubtless on 4 Hecatombaeon, Aphrodite's holy day.[58] The occasion thus resembles other festivals of Aphrodite that are associated with magistrates and the annual transition of office.[59] Such cults and festivals are of fairly recent origin, like the magistracies themselves. They arose when offices were opened to a wider field of candidates. The rich and noble who held power in early days never lacked for entertainment; now it was provided for persons of ordinary means.[60] Hence the

---

57 Dontas, *Praktika* 1960 [1961] 4–9; Wycherley, *Phoenix* 20 (1966) 289–90, and *Stones of Athens* 178–80; L. Beschi, *ASAtene* 45 / 6 (1967–8) 517–28; E. Simon, *Schweizerische Numismatische Rundschau* 49 (1970) 5–19, and *Festivals* 48–9. The reconstruction of the aedicula is due to Beschi.

58 *IG* 2² 659 (*SIG*³ 375; *LSCG* 39).

59 Cf. F. Sokolowski, *HThR* 57 (1964) 1–8; F. Croissant and F. Salviat, *BCH* 90 (1966) 464–71.

60 A similar development took place at Miletus in 525–524, when the Molpi admitted some lesser persons to their festivity: *Phoenix* 41 (1987) 359–78.

epithet *pandēmos*. Elsewhere Aphrodite is called *agoraia* or *timouchos* or *synarchis*, or takes her title from a particular magistracy.

The Athenians mostly said that the cult of Aphrodite *pandēmos* was instituted by Solon.[61] It was doubtless prescribed in the Solonian laws or calendar, and in terms that marked it as an innovation. Pausanias gives a dissenting view. When he comes to our terrace shrine, he ascribes the cult to Theseus, to the time 'when Theseus brought the Athenians from the demes into one city' (1.22.3, cf. 26.6). Although Pausanias does not mention the old agora, and Harpocration does not mention Theseus, Pausanias' notion of the cult undoubtedly goes back to Apollodorus. Consider the following points.

This notion is a rather late one. In his *Life* of Theseus, Plutarch draws on the Attic chroniclers, and very fully, as they drew on tragedy and epic and any other Athenian tradition. Yet there is nothing here about Aphrodite *pandēmos*; instead, Theseus honours Aphrodite at the time he sails for Crete, obviously a nautical rite of 4 Munichion.[62] But when Apollodorus spoke of all the people assembling in the old agora, he must have spoken too of Theseus; for this is the custom of the Synoecia, which was traced to Theseus. The shrine of Aphrodite *pandēmos* was near other monuments, of Aegeus and Hippolytus, which evoked the Theseus story; so it was easy to bring her into it. Perhaps the usual tale of Solon was thought unseemly by Apollodorus; for Solon was said to have endowed the cult with the avails of prostitution.[63]

Apollodorus was therefore both tendentious and hypothetical.[64] He said in effect that Aphrodite *pandēmos* was first established not by Solon, nor on the site where we see her now, but by Theseus, and 'round the

---

61 Ath. 13.25, 569 D (Philem. *Adelph.* fr. 3 Kassel and Austin; Nicander *FGrHist* 271–2 F 9a); Harpocr. *s.v.* πάνδημος Ἀφροδίτη (Nicander F 9b).

62 Plut. *Thes.* 18.3. The aetiologies that situate Theseus' departure in Munichion are not among the earliest; Theseus' career was first projected from the Hecatombaea and ensuing festivals. In the story of Aphrodite *epitragia*, the oracle and the prodigy are suggestive of tragedy.

63 It is true that Apollodorus discoursed of Aphrodite as patron of prostitutes (F 112, cf. F 114); but a civic cult at Athens might require a different approach.

64 He is probably responsible for another element in Pausanias' description of the sanctuary on the terrace. Theseus, says Pausanias, set up a cult of both Aphrodite and Peitho. 'The ancient statues did not exist in my time, but those that did were the work of no inconsiderable artists.' The decree of 287–286 provides for the bathing of 'the images,' plural. It does not seem very likely that after this date the sanctuary was newly furnished with statues by 'no inconsiderable artists.' The statues that were bathed in 287 are doubtless the statues seen by Pausanias. 'The ancient statues' are then a figment subserving the hypothesis of an earlier sanctuary.

old agora.' If these words represent Apollodorus fairly, he was also vague. He was bound to be, for the old agora and all its cults were right before the eye. We may wonder whether Apollodorus looked to some actual cult of Aphrodite, just close enough to be described as 'round the old agora.' If he did, it was very likely the cult of Aphrodite and Eros on the north slope of the Acropolis, which is just to the west of the lower stretch of the northeast ascent.[65] The question is not important, however: Apollodorus may well have left it open.

In sum, Apollodorus' mention of 'the old agora' has value only as another indication that this was indeed a familiar area in Hellenistic Athens. It is the reality that lends colour to his notion of a vanished form of Aphrodite *pandēmos*.

'The Altar of Pity'

Pausanias admires the Altar of Pity which he found in the old agora. So do many other writers.[66] It was a commonplace to extol the Altar as attesting the wise humanity of the Athenians. And it is often said of both the Heracleidae and the Argive mourners of the Seven that they sat here in supplication.[67] To be sure, none of these writers is earlier than the Roman period; their immediate sources are perhaps only of the Hellenistic period.[68] Yet this is plainly a venerable monument.[69] It was fifth-century tragedy that invented and spun out the mythical themes of supplication; if later writers always associate the Heracleidae and the Argive mourners with the Altar of Pity, this must be true to the tragic presentation.

A personification like 'Pity,' Ἔλεος, would not be worshipped in the fifth century. 'The Altar of Pity' is therefore a descriptive term for an altar that served some other deity. When the term originated we cannot tell; but

65 Cf. Travlos, *Pictorial Dict.* 229 fig. 293.
66 Wycherley, *Testimonia* 67–74 nos. 163–190.
67 Heracleidae: [Apld.] *Bibl.* 2.8.1.2 (2.167); Stat. *Theb.* 12.497–9 (the Heracleidae found the Altar); schol. Ar. *Eq.* 1151; Zenob. 2.61; etc. Cf. Robert, *Heldensage* 656 n. 1. Argive mourners: [Apld.] *Bibl.* 3.7.1.2 (3.79); Stat. *Theb.* 12.512–13; Zenob. 1.30; etc. Cf. Robert, *Heldensage* 944 n. 3.
68 The Altar of Pity appears in Diodorus during the debate at Syracuse on the fate of the Athenian prisoners (13.22.7). Old Nicolaus, the exponent of clemency, is not heard of elsewhere, and it is impossible to be sure where this long debate comes from (13.19.4–33.1). E. Schwartz, *RE* 5.1 (1903) 681 s.v. Diodoros 38, thought it might be Diodorus' own fabrication, otherwise Ephorus embellished; Jacoby, on Philistus *FGrHist* 556 F 51–6 and Timaeus *FGrHist* 566 F 99–102, argues for Timaeus, as does L. Pearson, *The Greek Historians of the West* (Atlanta 1987) 146.
69 Cf. G. Zuntz, *ClMed* 14 (1953) 74.

once it was abroad, writers were sure to say, as Pausanias does and many others, that the Athenians worshipped Pity. To whom did the altar truly belong? Until lately it was common, as a consequence of confusing 'the agora' and 'the Cerameicus,' to equate the Altar of Pity with the altar of the Twelve Gods;[70] but now we must think again. The answer is given by the inscription on a votive relief that was set up at a certain altar, depicted in the relief. The stone was found in the Odeium of Herodes, but like much else was brought here from another quarter.[71] A Thracian family living in exile have received the opportunity of returning home, perhaps in AD 44 or 46, when Thrace was annexed by Rome, or a little earlier. The relief is a thank-offering. The family speak of themselves as suppliants at the Altar of Pity; and they invoke the presiding deity. 'O highest ruling on high, father of rich-fruited Eirene, we supplicate your Altar of Pity,' ὑψιμέδων ὕπατε, πάτερ εἰρήνης βαθυκάρπου, σὸν Ἐλαίου βωμὸν ἱκετεύομεν ἡμεῖς. The deity is Zeus.[72]

We should not be surprised to learn that the principal altar in the old agora was an altar of Zeus. Zeus was worshipped in every agora of which we are sufficiently informed; the cult of Zeus *sōtēr* on the west side of the new Agora appears to be the oldest in the area, and was in the hands of the archons. Hesychius s.v. ἀγοραῖος Ζεύς records an 'altar of Zeus *agoraios* at Athens,' and the same title is used a few times in literature and even in a couple of epigraphic oaths.[73] Though most of these references are not illuminating, an important point emerges. Zeus *agoraios* is not another title for the cult of Zeus *sōtēr* or *eleutherios* in the new Agora; that cult has its own nomenclature and a separate tradition in the lexica. The title can only denote the cult of Zeus in the old agora.

One reference to Zeus *agoraios* stands out from the rest. In Euripides' *Heracleidae* Iolaus and the Heracleidae sit as suppliants at an altar of Zeus which is repeatedly mentioned and was no doubt a prominent fixture in the theatre. Only once does Zeus receive a title, and it is *agoraios* (line 70).[74] The setting is professedly Marathon (lines 32, 37–8, 80–1), but there is no local colour, nothing but the altar, and a nameless temple to shelter

---

70 Thompson, the leading exponent of this view, renounced it at *Agora Guide*[3] 98.

71 *IG* 2[2] 4786. For the date and circumstances of the inscription, see L. Robert, *Studii Clasice* 9 (1967) 107–10 = *Op. Min. Sel.* 6.251–4.

72 The Altar of Pity was rightly equated with the altar of Zeus *agoraios* by Oikonomides, *Athenaika* 16 (1960) 1–13, and *Two Agoras* 32–9; but he blunted the argument by bringing in Zeus *meilichios* and *philios* as well.

73 Wycherley, *Testimonia* 122–4 nos. 379–86.

74 V.J. Rosivach, *ParPass* 178 (1978) 32–47, argues mistakenly that this epithet points to the new Agora and the cult of Zeus *eleutherios*.

Alcmena and the girls. Another part of Attica is prominent in the reports of Eurystheus' invasion and its outcome. It is at Pallene that the invaders encamp, and the battle is fought, and Eurystheus' head is buried as a talisman (lines 393–7, 849–50, 1030–1).[75] Euripides then has brought the Heracleidae to Marathon so as to justify a battle at Pallene: such a battle cannot take place unless the enemy's target is Marathon, not Athens. In other tragedies that are lost to us, the altar of Zeus *agoraios* was at Athens, and must have figured very largely in the action; for Euripides simply reuses it as a stock item.[76]

We should ask why Euripides situates the battle at Pallene; the answer throws further light on the supplication of the Heracleidae. Pallene saw other battles too, mythical or legendary: Athena against the Giants; Theseus against the eponym Pallas; Peisistratus against his opponents.[77] The last is always taken as a historical event, but we shall see below, apropos of the Olympieia, that several incidents of Peisistratus' career, including the sequel to Pallene, look very much like aetiology. At all events, certain curious details recur in the several battles of Pallene (and in still other legendary combats): troops of young men, and chariot riders, and gorgonian talismans. These details, as also the proverbial phrase Παλληνικὸν βλέπειν, are likely to reflect a ritual combat at the festival of Athena Pallenis.[78] The festival took place at the same time as the Panathenaea; for the latter is evoked by the chorus of the *Heracleidae* as they await news of the battle (lines 781–3, cf. 788–9).[79]

---

75 The battle takes place near a 'hill,' the site of Athena's shrine (line 849); this is obviously the 'rocky brow' which Eurystheus occupied in order to study the terrain (lines 394–5). He has slipped past Athens, but Euripides prepares us with talk of scouts and rapid marches (lines 337–9). Zuntz, *The Political Plays of Euripides* (Manchester 1955) 99–104, holds that Eurystheus encamps on the western border of Attica, west of Eleusis. As he admits, a battle at Pallene is then completely unexpected and unexplained.

76 Another Athenian custom, children begging with the *eiresiōnē*, was sometimes traced to the Heracleidae, as if they were 'thus nourished by the Athenians' (Plut. *Thes.* 22.7).

77 Athena against the Giants: F. Vian, *La Guerre des géants* (Paris 1952) 198–202, 265–74. Theseus against Pallas: Vian 274–6; H. Herter, *RE Suppl.* 13 (1973) 1091–3 s.v. Theseus 1. Peisistratus: Rhodes, *Comm.* 208–9.

78 One explanation of the phrase speaks of 'casting stones,' βάλλειν λίθοις (Suda s.v. Παλληνικὸν βλέπειν; schol. Ar. *Ach.* 234); though the explanation is supported by a fictitious etymology, Βαλλήνη instead of Παλλήνη, it probably originates in a ritual λιθοβολία. The similarity of detail extends to the number of youthful combatants: fifty Giants, fifty Pallantidae, five sons of Eurystheus. The number is widely paralleled. Its ritual origin is clearly seen in Justin's version of a portentous combat beside the Palladium of Siris – fifty lads are slain as they embrace the statue (20.2.3–8).

79 The calendar date agrees with the Theseus story; for Theseus overthrows the Pallantidae soon after his arrival at Athens, on 8 Hecatombaeon.

The festival Synoecia comes shortly before this, in mid Hecatombaeon. According to Euripides, the Athenians mustered in the city before the battle at Pallene (lines 335–8). No doubt it was the ritual of the Synoecia that first prompted the story of how Athens took up arms in defence of the Heracleidae. The familiar *aition* is now spliced together with an *aition* of the festival of Athena Pallenis, which is perhaps Euripides' own invention. Hence the peculiar topography of the play.

The upshot is that 'the Altar of Pity' where the Heracleidae are found in later literature corresponds to the altar of Zeus *agoraios* in tragedy. The inference is confirmed by a vase painting of ca. 400 BC, an early Lucanian column crater, which depicts a scene from tragedy; for Iolaus wears the embroidered costume of the stage.[80] He and two little Heracleidae are beside an altar; Copreus, the herald of Eurystheus, lays hands upon them; but two young horsemen, perhaps Demophon and Acamas, gallop towards the group. Whose altar is it? Alcmena, also standing near, holds a small statue of Zeus.

The same tragedy probably accounts for a tradition mentioned by Philostratus. It was said of the Athenian ephebes that they wore their dark cloaks as a sign of penance for killing Copreus when he attempted to drag the Heracleidae from the altar.[81] In Euripides' play, Copreus departs without injury after an exchange of words (line 287). Some other tragedy made an end of him, doubtless at the hands of the two young horsemen. In later days the ephebic cloaks were traced back to this occasion.

In [Apollodorus], Adrastus too comes to the Altar of Pity, and in Statius it is the womenfolk of the Seven;[82] so the altar of Zeus *agoraios* appeared in still other tragedies.

We shall come back to the role of Zeus at the Synoecia in considering the phratries. Let us take Eirene next.

Eirene

The goddess Eirene, 'Peace,' came to be worshipped at the Synoecia on 16 Hecatombaeon (schol. Ar. *Pax* 1019). In 375–374, when a Common Peace was composed at Athens after years of fighting, the Athenians celebrated this military and diplomatic triumph by honouring Eirene. The honours are variously described as the building of an altar or altars, the institution

80 Berlin (West) 1969.6 (*LIMC* 1.1 [1981] 439 no. 20 *s.v.* Akamas et Demophon).
81 Philostr. *Vit. Soph.* 2.1.8. Elsewhere the dark cloaks commemorate the dark sail of the tribute ship. Cf. Münscher, *RE* 8.1 (1912) 942 *s.v.* Herodes 13; P. Roussel, *REA* 18 (1941) 163–5.
82 [Apld.] *Bibl.* 3.7.1.2 (3.79); Stat. *Theb.* 12.512–13.

of sacrifice, the spreading of a couch.[83] Perhaps it was now that the elder Cephisodotus created his famous statue of the mother Eirene holding the child Plutus with a horn of plenty.[84] In the Lycurgan period too, Eirene received sacrifice on a very large scale, as we see from the hide-moneys of 333 and 332.[85] Much later, in the second half of the second century, some magistrate is honoured for sacrificing to Eirene, as the second of a pair of deities; the missing name before hers was probably Zeus.[86] The Thracian family who made a dedication at the Altar of Pity, i.e., the altar of Zeus, addressed the god in Hesiodic style as father of Eirene.

On this evidence one supposes that Eirene was worshipped beside Zeus in the old agora, but at a separate altar. Pausanias saw a statue of Eirene as well as one of Hestia in the Prytaneium (1.18.3), which was beside the old agora, or very near it. Yet Cephisodotus' statue was seen by Pausanias on the west side of the new Agora, and near it was a statue of Callias, a reputed peacemaker, as Pausanias recalls, of the mid fifth century (1.8.2). Plutarch, moreover, implies that at one time the altar of Eirene and the statue of Callias were to be seen together; for in a discussion of 'the Peace of Callias,' he records the view that the altar dates from this occasion, when Callias too was highly honoured, scil., with a statue (*Cim.* 13.6).

The results of excavation allow us to follow Pausanias' steps in the Agora as he speaks of Cephisodotus' statue and the statue of Callias.[87] These and three other statues (of Amphiaraus, Lycurgus, Demosthenes) he locates between the monument of the Eponymi and the temple of Ares and Athena, both securely identified on the ground. There are statue bases hereabouts, though of course they cannot now be individually assigned. There is also, near the northeast corner of the base of the Eponymi, a monument which Pausanias does not mention: a large marble altar of the fourth century, 'the handsomest altar found in the Agora.' It was, however,

---

83 Isocr. 15 *Antid.* 109–10: annual sacrifice since 375–374. Didym. *in Dem.* 10 *Phil.* 34, col. 7.62–71 (Philochorus *FGrHist* 328 F 151): altar set up in 375–374. Nep. *Timoth.* 2.2: altars set up, couch spread in 375–374.

84 Paus. 1.8.2, 9.16.2. Pliny puts Cephisodotus' *floruit* in 372–368, but Eirene is not one of the two masterpieces that he mentions (*Hist. Nat.* 34.50, 87). H. Jung, *JdI* 91 (1976) 97–134, argues for a date just before 360–359, when the statue is prominently depicted on six or seven Panathenaic amphoras. Simon, *LIMC* 3.1 (1986) 703 *s.v.* Eirene, prefers the earlier date.

85 *IG* 2² 1496.94–5 (333 BC, 874 dr.), 127–8 (332 BC, 713 dr.). The sacrifice is made by the Strategi, and is the first of the year.

86 *IG* 2² 1000.5–6. 'Non ΣΤΟΙΧ. 30–34.' Lines 7–13 of this fragmentary decree have been plausibly restored to this length. Line 6 might run, ὑπὲρ τῶν θυσιῶν ὧν ἔ[θυσε τῶι τε Διὶ καὶ] | τεῖ Εἰρήνηι; or just τῶι Διί. Most divine names are too long.

87 Cf. Thompson, *Agora Guide*³ 304–5, 'Walk I,' and the fold-out plan.

brought here in the Roman period, after being dismantled and removed from some other site.[88] Round the same time, the temple of Ares and Athena was also brought here in pieces and reassembled, a large undertaking. At least three statues came with it, of Ares and Athena and Enyo. Perhaps then Cephisodotus' statue and the statue of Callias are migrants too.

The full dimensions of the altar, at the bottom step, are 8.76 m by 5.43 m. At the Pnyx, on the high ground behind the speaker's platform, a bedding just a little larger, 8.90 m by 6.00 m, is cut in bedrock; it is suggested that the Agora altar formerly stood here.[89] Yet this does not seem a proper place for an altar. The bedding, like the speaker's platform, is on the axis of the assembly area, so that the presumed altar faces north, or slightly east of north. In the Agora our altar faces due east, as one expects of any altar. Surely the bedding on the Pnyx was for a statue base, like the row of somewhat smaller beddings farther south. It is also suggested that an altar transferred from the Pnyx to the Agora is likely to be one of Zeus *agoraios*.[90] But aside from the arguments, I hope conclusive, for placing Zeus *agoraios* in the old agora, there is no reason to think that Zeus would be worshipped with this title at the Pnyx, which is not an agora.[91] On the other hand, the altar of Zeus *agoraios* in the old agora, alias the Altar of Pity, was still *in situ* in the time of Pausanias.

The Agora altar stood very close to Cephisodotus' statue of Eirene and the statue of Callias.[92] Plutarch associates the statue of Callias with the altar of Eirene; Cephisodotus' statue belongs with the altar of Eirene; the Agora altar is as large and elegant as the altar of Eirene should be.

---

88 R. Stillwell, *Hesperia* 2 (1933) 140–8; Thompson, *Hesperia* 21 (1952) 91–3, and *Agora Guide*[3] 68–70; Thompson and Wycherley, *Agora of Athens* 160–2 (whence the words quoted); T.L. Shear, Jr., *Hesperia* 50 (1981) 365.

89 So Thompson.

90 Thompson cites schol. Ar. *Eq.* 410, 'Zeus *agoraios* is set up in the agora and in the *ekklēsia*.' This scholium has every appearance of being improvised to explain the mention of Zeus *agoraios* in the play; it certainly does not hint at a transfer of the cult from the Pnyx to the Agora.

91 There is a further complication. D.G. Romano, *AJP* 89 (1985) 441–54, has argued that the facilities of Lycurgan date on the Pnyx are 'the Panathenaic stadium and theatre' of Lycurgan documents. This is a strained hypothesis; objections are raised by R.A. Moysey, *AJA* 90 (1986) 212, cf. A.J. Heisserer and Moysey, *Hesperia* 55 (1986) 182 n. 25, and by G.R. Stanton and P.J. Bicknell, *GRBS* 28 (1987) 88–9. At p. 454 n. 61, Romano promises to reinterpret the presumed altar in the light of the hypothesis.

92 The Agora excavators looked for the altar of Eirene just at this point, but could not find it. 'No doubt the altar stood close by. Thus the site is known to within a few yards and the area has been thoroughly excavated, but no identifiable traces have been found': Thompson and Wycherley, *Agora of Athens* 168.

Surely this is indeed the altar of Eirene, so that both altar and statues were brought here from the old agora.[93] It might be argued too, though this is not the place, that the temple of Ares and Athena also came from the old agora. In Pausanias' day the old agora seems to have been largely denuded (Paus. 1.17.1).

The cult of Eirene poses one or two questions of chronology. The Agora altar has been dated on stylistic grounds to the late fourth century. If this is right, it was a replacement for an earlier altar, for one used since at least 375–374. Given those very large sacrifices of the Lycurgan period, we may well believe that a replacement was in order. More important is the question of when the cult began. The prevailing view is that it was created *ab ovo* in 375–374 to signalize the peace treaty.[94] This seems indicated by the sources who describe the celebrations of that year. Yet we should beware of taking them at face value. Isocrates, the earliest source, was concerned in 354–353 to magnify the achievements of Timotheus, above all the peace treaty. Later sources perhaps depend in the first instance on the official record of offerings and construction work, which might suggest a new departure when it was not. Furthermore, Eirene was a popular figure who had always been praised in song. She meant much more than a peace treaty; and despite Isocrates, the treaty of 375–374 lasted no more than a year and a half.[95] In any case, there is no reason to suppose that 16 Hecatombaeon was the day on which the treaty was made.[96]

The cult evokes that popular figure. Cephisodotus' rendering adopts an image of earlier poetry, Eirene as a bountiful mother bearing or nursing

93 Some infer that Amphiaraus too is associated with Eirene, since Pausanias mentions both statues in the same breath. But he mentions Callias farther on, between Lycurgus and Demosthenes, so that the closer grouping need not be significant. Mommsen, *Feste* 40, thinks that Amphiaraus is a man of peace because he opposed the expedition against Thebes; I. Krauskopf, *LIMC* 1.1 (1981) 701 no. 57 *s.v.* Amphiaraos, that he is the healing deity of Oropus, and was represented like Asclepius.

94 So Deubner, *Att. Feste* 37–8; Jacoby on Philochorus *FGrHist* 328 F 151; Parke, *Festivals* 32–3; Simon, *LIMC* 3.1 (1986) 701 *s.v.* Eirene. An earlier origin is argued by S. Accame, *La lega ateniese* (Rome 1941) 248–51, but on insufficient grounds; it is unconversantly assumed by F.W. Hamdorf, *Griechische Kultpersonifikationen* (Mainz 1964) 53–5.

95 Cf. T.T.B. Ryder, *Koine Eirene* (Oxford 1965) 61.

96 As usual, Xenophon and Diodorus make for controversy in the reconstruction of events; but the normal range for dating the treaty is from autumn 375 through spring 374. The battle of Alyzeia, which preceded any negotiation, fell on the day of the Scira, 12 Scirophorion (Polyaenus 3.10.4) – much too close to the following 16 Hecatombaeon, even if there was intercalation. For some opinions, see Jacoby, ns. 2, 28 to Philochorus *FGrHist* 328 F 151; G.L. Cawkwell, *Historia* 12 (1963) 90 n. 56; V.J. Gray, *CQ*[2] 30 (1980) 314.

Plutus, and so a counterpart of Demeter.[97] In the late fifth century, Euripides and comedy have much to say of Eirene.[98] Aristophanes brought both Eirene and Plutus onto the stage, and though he is far from attesting any cult observance, he exemplifies a climate in which the cult was bound to flourish. The festival Synoecia provided an obvious setting. It was a time, at least in legend, for all Athenians to gather in concord and worship Zeus. Zeus (we do not need a Thracian to remind us) is parent of Eirene, as she of Plutus. It is these associations, rather than the peace treaty of 375–374, that provide the background for the cult of Eirene.

[Aristotle] on Phratries and Trittyes

We may now consider the early organization of Attica that gives rise to the festival Synoecia and is reflected in the ritual. Thucydides and Plutarch have very similar accounts of Theseus' 'synoecism,' of people removing from the country to the city, as a professed *aition* of the Synoecia.[99] After the 'synoecism,' Plutarch quotes two relevant oracles, then describes another step that Theseus took to strengthen Athens, a proclamation summoning everyone together on equal terms but in orderly fashion, in three occupational classes. Finally, he cites 'Aristotle,' i.e., the lost beginning of the *Constitution of Athens*, for the view that Theseus was the first to favour the mob – a view repeated, though in more moderate language, in the surviving portion of the work.[100] It is sometimes held that in Plutarch 'Aristotle' contributes nothing but this judgment, that the proclamation comes from a different source.[101] This is unlikely in itself, and doubly so when we find that the proclamation recurs in Heracleides' epitome of the *Constitution of Athens* (§1).

[Aristotle] represented Theseus as organizing Attica quite thoroughly, after an earlier start by Ion. Just before Theseus, in the time of Pandion and his sons, Attica was in complete disarray: διετέλουν οὗτοι στασιάζοντες, as Heracleides says (*ibid.*). Ion had instituted the Ionic *phylai* – in this

---

97 Bacch. *Paean* 4.61–2; *Vit. Hom. Herod.* 33 (Carm. Pop. 1 Diehl).

98 We should note the context of her appearance in the *Heracleidae*. Demophon has just departed to muster the Athenians; Iolaus still clings to the altar of Zeus. The chorus in their song cry defiance to Argos. 'Though Eirene pleases me,' they say (lines 371–2), Athens has the armed strength to meet Eurystheus. This would suit the Synoecia exactly.

99 Thuc. 2.15.2; Plut. *Thes.* 24.1–4. Both use the verb συνοικίζειν; but a true commemorative ritual would be called *συνοικιστήρια (cf., e.g., οἰνιστήρια, προχαριστήρια).

100 Plut. *Thes.* 25.1–3; [Arist.] *Ath.* 41.2.

101 E.g., Jacoby, *Atthis* (Oxford 1949) 247 n. 49; cf. n. 12 to Philochorus *FGrHist* 328 F 19, n. 11 to F 110, n. 17 to F 200.

[Aristotle] is at one with Herodotus and Euripides – but not their subdivisions.[102] Theseus' 'constitution,' the second in a long series, coming after Ion and before Solon, was the first that had any proper 'order,' δευτέρα δὲ καὶ πρώτη μετὰ ταύτην ἔχουσα πολιτείας τάξιν (*Ath.* 41.2).

Plutarch gives us both a 'synoecism' and a proclamation. Although he represents them as two steps taken in succession, there can be no doubt that they are rival and equivalent accounts of the same dispensation. Finding the two accounts in different authorities, Plutarch made use of both to fill out the biography of Theseus. The proclamation is [Aristotle's] account; it is easily recognized as another *aition* of the Synoecia, a somewhat more realistic *aition* than a 'synoecism.'

The entry for the biennial Synoecia in the Solonian calendar of sacrifice gives us the following items: the Phylobasileis, the heads of the four Ionic *phylai*, and the *phylē* Geleontes that is always named first among them; a *trittys*, 'the Bright-headbands'; phratries, in the epithet *phratrios* accorded to both Zeus and Athena; *oikoi*, the term for phratry lodges, in the festival name; a herald, mentioned twice.[103] [Aristotle], as we find him in Plutarch and Heracleides and also in the lexical tradition to be noticed in a moment, gives us the Ionic *phylai*; the *trittyes*; the phratries; a herald, implicit in Theseus' proclamation (κήρυγμα Plutarch, ἐκήρυξε Heracleides). Moreover, Plutarch quotes the proclamation as a familiar phrase, one still in use, obviously in the ritual of the Synoecia.[104] 'Come hither, all ye (armed) hosts,' δεῦρ' ἴτε πάντες λεώι. 'Armed hosts' is a suitable term for men ranged in phratries, which once had a military character.

There is a third account, neither a 'synoecism' of Athens nor a proclamation summoning the people, which forms yet another *aition* of the Synoecia. Whereas [Aristotle], as we shall see, dwelt on the twelvefold division of Attica that was produced by subdividing the Ionic *phylai*, Philochorus told how Attica had once been 'synoecized' into twelve cities distributed throughout the whole area.[105] Moreover, this multiple

---

102 Hdt. 5.66.2; Eur. *Ion* 1575–6; [Arist.] *Ath.* 41.2. According to H.T. Wade-Gery, *Essays in Greek History* (Oxford 1958) 88–99, Theseus in the *Constitution of Athens* did no more than add the class Eupatridae, after Ion had created two occupational classes together with *phylai*, phratries, and *genē*. Neither Plutarch nor the lexical tradition can be thus interpreted. *Phylai* and phratries, moreover, have no integral connection with either the occupational classes or the alleged system of *genē*. A thorough refutation will emerge as we proceed.

103 J.H. Oliver, *Hesperia* 4 (1935) 5–6, 19–21, 25–9 no. 2 lines 31–59 (*LSCG Suppl.* 10A).

104 Plut. *Thes.* 25.1; Heracleid. *Epit. Ath.* 1; [Arist.] *Ath.* fr. 3 vulg. / 2 Chambers (Harpocration *s.v.* τριττύς, Pollux 8.111, etc.).

105 Str. 9.1.20, p 397 (Philochorus *FGrHist* 328 F 94); Etym. Gen., Etym. Magn., Suda *s.v.* ἐπακρία χῶρα; Steph. Byz. *s.v.* ἐπακρία, *s.v.* Ἀθῆναι (Charax *FGrHist* 103 F 43).

'synoecism' had a military purpose, to repel invading Carians and Boeotians. To be sure, Philochorus traced the arrangement right back to Cecrops; the first of the twelve cities, Athens itself, was called 'Cecropia.' The twelve names recorded by Philochorus were very likely used at the festival Synoecia; they undoubtedly survived in related customs, as we shall see. Cecrops then might well come into it. But Philochorus also said that Theseus was responsible for 'synoecizing' the twelve cities into one; so he did not disavow entirely the usual view of the Synoecia. Philochorus, we should remember, was well versed in Athenian ritual.

An important feature of [Aristotle's] account, a twelvefold division of Attica and the terms used for it, does not appear in Plutarch or Heracleides, but is quite insistently described in a good many lexica and scholia that cite 'Aristotle.' These sources are listed, and partly quoted, as either fr. 3 or fr. 2 in editions of the *Constitution of Athens*; the effect is somewhat misleading, for [Aristotle] cannot possibly be responsible for all the details in all the sources. The tradition will be examined more closely below, when we turn to two other matters, the occupational classes and the system of 360 *genē*. Let us focus here on the evidence for the twelvefold division.

Harpocration *s.v.* τριττύς has a note briefer and clearer than the rest, and more to the point. 'Trittys' and 'ethnos' and 'phratry' are said to be equivalent names for a threefold division of a *phylē*, i.e., an Ionic *phylē*, and hence for a twelvefold division overall, 'as Aristotle says in the *Constitution of Athens*.' Pollux has the same note without Aristotle's name; it comes just after an authentic description of the Phylobasileis, and just before mention of the 360 *genē*. All the other lexica and scholia are concerned to explain the 360 *genē*, for which they cite 'Aristotle,' and part of the explanation is that a *phylē* is divided into three parts, called either 'trittys' or 'phratry.'

It is generally and rightly agreed that the threefold division of the *phylē*, making twelve parts in all, derives from [Aristotle], as do 'trittys' and 'phratry' as equivalent names for the units. 'Ethnos' as yet another equivalent name is sometimes discounted, but for no compelling reason.[106] The notes in Harpocration and Pollux do not seem inferior to the others; they seem rather better. *Ethnos* might easily drop out, but there was no reason for adding it. It cannot be an attempt to fuse the accounts of

---

106 E.g., Rhodes, *Comm.* 71 n. 1 ('certainly wrong'). It is accepted as [Aristotle's] term by Jacoby, ns. 15, 28 to Philochorus F 94, and by F.R. Wüst, *Historia* 6 (1957) 182. H. Hommel, *RE* 7 A 1 (1939) 333–4 *s.v.* Trittyes, holds that the *ethnē* are properly the occupational classes.

[Aristotle] and Philochorus; there is no other trace of this, and *ethnos* is not an obvious rendering of Philochorus' *polis*. [Aristotle] and Philochorus, moreover, draw on the same evidence, customs existing in their own day; whatever evidence led Philochorus to speak of twelve local communities was already available to [Aristotle], and might lead him in turn to speak of twelve *ethnē*.

Another consideration points the same way. [Aristotle] undoubtedly conceived the twelve parts as territorial divisions, which for the purpose of description seem to require a name other than *trittys* or phratry. The twelve *trittyes* are mentioned twice again, apropos of Solonian naucraries and of Cleisthenes' reforms (*Ath.* 8.3, 21.3). These are passing references, and [Aristotle] had no reason to repeat any other term, phratry or *ethnos*. Each Ionic *phylē*, says [Aristotle], was divided into three *trittyes* and twelve naucraries. One cannot be sure, at least from these words, that [Aristotle] thought of the naucraries as a subdivision of the *trittyes*, four to each; but to be thus bracketed together, they must be divisions of the same kind. Though [Aristotle] happens not to say so here, the naucraries were generally known to be territorial divisions – they are precursors of Cleisthenic demes (*Ath.* 21.5). Farther on, [Aristotle] says of Cleisthenes' reforms that the twelve *trittyes* of the old days would only be perpetuated if Cleisthenes made a like number of territorial *phylai*. We must infer that in [Aristotle's] view the twelve *trittyes* corresponded to natural divisions of the Attic terrain; Cleisthenes' *phylai* did not, at least globally; but [Aristotle] forgets this. Since then [Aristotle] conceived the twelve parts as territorial divisions, the likelihood is that he also described them as such, as *ethnē*.

Thus far [Aristotle's] reconstruction of early Attica, which depends upon the ritual of the Synoecia. The ritual misled him, at least in part; for his reconstruction is too schematic. Yet the actual organization of early days was indeed reflected in the ritual, and the ritual was conducted with punctilio for long ages after the organization disappeared. Moreover, one element of the organization, and that the main one, did not disappear at all. The phratries survived though their larger purpose was superseded; even in the later fourth century many Athenians belonged to phratries. It follows that [Aristotle's] reconstruction contains much truth. By comparing the reconstruction with the ritual, we should be able to determine where the truth lies. Surprisingly, this has never been attempted since our main source for the ritual, the fragment of the Solonian calendar, came to light sixty years ago.[107]

---

107 Wade-Gery, *Essays* 96–8, writing before this, thought that the ritual would show 'how to correlate those accounts of the Synoikisis which have survived'; but he did

Almost everyone agrees that [Aristotle's] reconstruction is implausible. *Trittyes*, phratries, and *ethnē* cannot be three names for the same thing, for a twelvefold division of Attica. Most go on to say that the twelvefold division, if it existed, was not important. They may accept twelve *trittyes*, but then suppose that the phratries were not closely correlated, and were indeed very numerous, perhaps as many as the later demes.[108] The *ethnē* are mostly left aside. Philochorus has not often been matched with [Aristotle], and he is sometimes claimed by the fundamentalists who believe in miracles, and who say that 'the twelve cities' preserve a memory of the Bronze Age.

The phratries are the key. They were still on hand in [Aristotle's] day; he observes that Cleisthenes did not abolish them, no more than he abolished old family connections, *genē*, or hereditary priesthoods (*Ath.* 21.6). In private lawsuits, as we see from the orators, the phratries could help establish both citizenship and family affiliation. Decrees for new citizens extend the right to choose a phratry. Inscriptions refer to phratry shrines and property, and show the phratries conducting business like other property-holding associations. As one living in Athens, [Aristotle] encountered phratries every day, the same phratries as existed before Cleisthenes.

How could he say that they were twelve, if he saw, and everyone knew, that they were about as many as the demes, some hundred and forty? How could he say this if the number was at all greater? For if it was a small number, it must have been exactly known, and indeed perfectly familiar.[109] Other evidence, to be considered below, supports the number twelve as well as we could expect from our fragmentary record.

If, however, there were twelve phratries, there will not have been twelve *trittyes*. Yet we can see how the mistake arose. In [Aristotle's] day the pre-Cleisthenic *trittyes* surely did not survive in any form, except perhaps as represented by some officiant at the festival Synoecia. Even here it might be no more than a token representation, the *trittys*

---

not pursue the matter, beyond pointing to the words quoted as Theseus' proclamation. J. Sarkady, *Acta Ant. Hung.* 17 (1969) 6, after remarking that [Aristotle] fathered a certain constitution on Theseus because he was linked with the Synoecia, adds parenthetically, 'It is immaterial what the concrete substance of the tradition about the Synoikia may have been.' Scholars are furtively aware of aetiology as an enormous shadow that falls across all their efforts; but they dare not confront the giant.

108 Rhodes, *Comm.* 68–71, gives a *mise-au-point*.

109 Roussel, *Tribu et cité* 142–3, reverses the argument: since there were in fact 'a great number of phratries of very diverse size,' [Aristotle] cannot have made them twelve. But we know that he did, and do not know that the reality was otherwise.

'Bright-headbands' of the *phylē* Geleontes. [Aristotle] would then assume that these *trittyes*, like the Cleisthenic, were each 'a third part' of a larger body, the *phylē*, and hence twelve in number, like the phratries. Yet the word τριττύς properly means not 'a third part,' but 'a body formed of three parts,' 'threesome'; and this linguistic fact must not be thrust aside.[110] The three parts of a pre-Cleisthenic *trittys* can only be phratries. A group of three phratries was incorporated in each *phylē*.

The Solonian calendar rather intimates that within a *phylē* the *trittys* is coextensive with the phratries. On 15 Hecatombaeon sacrifice is offered 'for the *phylē* Geleontes, for the *trittys* Bright-headbands.' It has been supposed that as Geleontes come first among the four *phylai*, 'Bright-headbands' come first among three *trittyes*. One then asks why the *trittys* 'Bright-headbands' should come first, and be singled out. There is an obvious reason why the *phylē* Geleontes should come first, and be singled out; they are, as we shall see below, the *phylē* particularly associated with the city, as distinct from other parts of Attica. But it is hard to think of a reason for favouring one *trittys* over two others. Moreover, on the following day we find an entry which seems parallel. Sacrifice is offered 'for the *phylē* Geleontes, to Zeus *phratrios* and Athena *phratria*.' If the sacrifice is made on behalf of all the phratries in the *phylē*, the *trittys* 'Bright-headbands' will comprise all those phratries.

It can hardly be fortuitous that the name of the *trittys* echoes the name of the *phylē*. Whereas the *phylē* is called the 'Shining-ones,' Γελέοντες, a participle of Ionic form (Hsch. γελεῖν· λάμπειν, ἀνθεῖν), the *trittys* is called the 'Bright-headbands,' Λευκοταίνιοι. The *phylē* names come first, and are very archaic; so far as we can understand them, they are purely ornamental. Afterwards four matching names were invented for the *trittyes*. When the *phylai* of Perinthus were renamed in later times, 'Geleontes' was replaced by Εὐανθίς, yet another word meaning 'Bright.'[111]

This interpretation has the further advantage of explaining the use of the term *trittys* over the long term. The Ionic *phylai* undoubtedly came before the phratries. Ion (at the latest) instituted the *phylai*, as all our sources agree; as a rule nothing is said of phratries, and on the argument above [Aristotle] ascribes them to Theseus. The *phylai* are common to Ionia, and must have originated there; but the phratry organization is not

---

110 The meaning 'threesome' is as evident at Athens as elsewhere, in the term for a sacrificial offering: *IG* 1³ 5.5 (τρίττοα), 1³ 78.37 (τρίττοια), 1² 845.6 (τρίττοια), 2² 1126.34 (τρικτεύα). It is inconceivable that τριττύς as a parallel form was used from the outset with the meaning 'a third part.'

111 N.F. Jones, *Public Organization in Ancient Greece* (Philadelphia 1987) 286–7.

so general.[112] The phratries then were created later, for a new purpose. We expect them to be made commensurate with the pre-existing *phylai*, and to be distributed among them. The number of phratries was determined approximately by the population and the territory of Attica; it was determined exactly by the correlation with the four *phylai*. A *trittys* was so called as a new body of three phratries, the body assigned to each *phylē*. When Cleisthenes reorganized Attica once again, the population was much larger, and the basic units assigned to each *phylē* were much smaller and more numerous, the demes. A certain number of demes likewise made a body called a *trittys*. But this *trittys* was again a subdivision of the *phylē*; and just as an Ionic *phylē* had three phratries, a Cleisthenic *phylē* had three *trittyes*.

The Phratries of the Classical Period

[Aristotle] can be tested against the evidence for phratries in the Classical period, though this evidence is not extensive.[113] We have, I think, just six phratry names, all known from inscriptions: Αἰχνιάδαι, *Γλεωντίδαι, Δημοτιωνίδαι, Θερρικλεῖδαι, Θυμαιτάδαι, Μεδοντίδαι.[114] Two of the names are found only in adjectival forms, Γλεωντίς and Θυμαιτίς, which are appropriate for large and eminent bodies of citizens, like Cleisthenic *phylai*. The original names, however, are all patronymics and disclose a unitary system. One name commonly included, Δυαλεῖς, must be stricken: it is not a patronymic, and the body is described as a 'league,' κοινόν, and a pair of phratriarchs officiate. The decree of 300–299 emanating from this body is one of our latest documents. Two phratries, one of them in the area of Myrrhinus, had by this time pooled their resources and chosen a name acceptable to both.[115] Other bodies with patronymic names mentioned in

---

112 Roussel, *Tribu et cité* 153 ('Very few are the Ionian cities where the existence of phratries is attested'); Jones, *Public Organization* Index I A 30, φρατρία (Andros, Chios?, Delos, Miletus, Tenos).

113 Cf. Ferguson, *CP* 5 (1910) 257–84, and in *Classical Studies Presented to E. Capps* (Princeton 1936) 152–4, 157; M. Guarducci, *L' istituzione della fratria* 1 (*MemLinc*[6] 6, 1937) 11–57, 83–94; Roussel, *Tribu et cité* 139–51. In 1910, Ferguson thought that the phratries were truly twelve; in 1936, that 'the chances are against their having been as few as twelve.'

114 Αἰχνιάδαι: *IG* 2² 2621, 4974 (Guarducci, *Fratria* 1.91 nos. xi, x). Γλεωντίς: *Hesperia* 17 (1948) 35 no. 18. Δημοτιωνίδαι: *IG* 2² 1237 (*SIG*³ 921; Guarducci, *Fratria* 1.83–6 no. i). Θερρικλεῖδαι: *IG* 2² 4973 (Guarducci, *Fratria* 1.91 no. ix). Θυμαιτίς: *IG* 1² 886 (Guarducci, *Fratria* 1.90–1 no. viii); *Hesperia* 57 (1988) 81–2. Μεδοντίδαι: *IG* 1² 871–2; *Hesperia* 10 (1941) 15–30 no. 1 lines 17–18, cf. 30–1; *IG* 2² 1233; cf. Paus. 4.13.7.

115 *IG* 2² 1241 (Guarducci, *Fratria* 1.89–90 no. vi). Cf. Guarducci, *Fratria* 1.51–2. Admittedly, a phratry or part of it may also be called a κοινόν: *Hesperia* 10 (1941) 15–30

the epigraphic record, mostly as possessing shrines, are far more likely to be *genē* than phratries.[116]

If the phratries were as many as the demes, they make a remarkably poor showing. By contrast, the surviving names of Attic *genē* number several score, and appear alike in literature, in the lexica, and in inscriptions.[117]

The phratry best known to us, in virtue of regulations inscribed in 396–395, is the Demotionidae.[118] The membership is numerous and dispersed. Whereas the phratry has its centre at Deceleia, with a 'lodge' and an altar and priest of Zeus *phratrios*, important notices are posted in the city of Athens, 'wherever the Deceleians congregate.'[119] As in other phratries that we hear of, the members are subdivided into smaller groups called *thiasoi*, who alone have personal knowledge of each other. 'The Deceleia lodge,' ὁ Δεκελειῶν οἶκος, is evidently formed of members still living at Deceleia, or perhaps rather of the more active members; for they assume special duties in the scrutiny of candidates.[120] 'The shrine of Leto' where

---

no. 1 lines 17–18, 30–1, the phratry Medontidae and a group of *orgeōnes*. In the very fragmentary inscription republished by C.W. Hedrick, Jr., *Hesperia* 52 (1983) 299–302, it is quite unnecessary to take the plural *phratriarchoi* (line 7) as indicating dual phratriarchs; they could as well be successive phratriarchs, or phratriarchs in general. The restoration of the phratry name *Therrhik]leidai* (lines 9–10) is also very dubious.

116 Guarducci, *Fratria* 1.55–6, canvasses two names in the lexica and six on stone, and is inclined to discount them all. Two of these, together with Dyaleis, are included by Ferguson, *Studies Pres. to Capps* 154, in a list of seven known phratries.

117 Toepffer, *Att. Gen.*, discusses fifty-eight *genē*, and lists twenty-nine demes with patronymic names that may derive from *genē*. It is true that even among the main entries a few are either wrong, e.g., Alcmaeonidae, or late, e.g., Eupatridae, and that only an optimist will rely on all the names in the lexica. On the other hand, some likely names have turned up on stone since 1889. Andrewes, *JHS* 81 (1961) 14, offers reasons, but not nearly enough, why *genē* should in any case be recorded or remembered in greater numbers.

118 *IG* 2² 1237 (*SIG*³ 921; Guarducci, *Fratria* 1.83–6 no. i; *LSCG* 19, an excerpt); C.W. Hedrick, Jr., *The Decrees of the Demotionidai* (Atlanta 1990) 7–11. Cf. U. von Wilamowitz-Moellendorff, *Aristoteles und Athen* (Berlin 1893) 2.259–79; Wade-Gery, *Essays* 116–34; A. Diller, *TAPA* 63 (1932) 193–205; Andrewes, *JHS* 81 (1961) 3–5; W.E. Thompson, *SymbOslo* 42 (1967) 51–68; Hedrick, *Decrees of the Demotionidai*.

119 *IG* 2² 1237 lines 63–4, 122–3. Ever since Wilamowitz, a sharp distinction has been drawn between 'Demotionidae' and 'Deceleans' in the terms of the decree; it is supposed that one of them is a select group within the phratry, perhaps a *genos*. No such distinction is warranted. 'The Deceleians' who congregate at a place in Athens are not precisely 'the Deceleia lodge,' however that be understood; they are Deceleians in a broader sense, including demesmen of Deceleia, and no doubt other residents or proprietors – all who are associated with the district. Wade-Gery, *Essays* 123 n. 1, 124 n. 1, 133–4, gives the evidence but forces the conclusion.

120 *IG* 2² 1237 lines 32–3, 42. 'Five men above thirty years of age' will be chosen to carry out these duties. A very fragmentary decree found in the same area, near the royal estate,

notices are also posted (lines 124–5) is another place more frequented than the phratry lodge: perhaps in the agora of the deme Deceleia.

The location of other phratry centres is not recorded. A boundary stone for the 'lodge' of an unnamed phratry has survived, but without provenance.[121] There was, however, a phratry centre at or near Paeania: a phratry decree found at Liopesi honours two members for a contribution towards the construction or embellishment of a shrine of Zeus *phratrios* and Athena *phratria*. From the same area comes a list of twenty phratry members headed by the names of the two phratry gods; these members likewise have some closer connection with the shrine.[122] Finally, two boundary stones of Aechniadae can be feasibly attributed to the centre of this phratry; both were found at Keratea (Cephale) in southeast Attica.[123] One of them is inscribed simply, 'Boundary of the phratry Aechniadae,' ὅρος φρατρίας Αἰχνιαδῶν. It might perhaps mark just a piece of property, but the phratry centre seems more likely. The other is inscribed, 'Shrine of Apollo *hebdomeios* of the phratry Aechniadae.' As the god of civic reunions and hence of the enrolment of citizens, Apollo was often worshipped by the phratries too, presumably at the phratry centre. The phratry Therrhicleidae have also left behind a boundary stone for their shrine of Apollo *patrōios*, but it has no provenance.[124]

The provenance of other phratry inscriptions does not as a rule point to the phratry centre. Phratries had possession of various shrines and properties, and it was there that the pertinent documents were posted.[125]

---

seems to speak of five men 'dwelling at Deceleia' as chosen for some purpose (*IG* 2² 1242 lines 4–5). But this decree is half a century later, and may not even be the phratry's.

121 *IG* 2² 2622 (Guarducci, *Fratria* 1.92 no. xiii): ὅρος οἰκίας φρατέρων.

122 The decree: W. Peek, *AthMitt* 66 (1941) 219–21 no. 2; *SEG* 3.121 (Guarducci, *Fratria* 1.87 no. iii). The list: *IG* 2² 2344 (Guarducci, *Fratria* 1.92 no. xiv). The list is usually regarded as a *thiasos*; it cannot be a whole phratry, as maintained by M.A. Flower, *CQ*² 35 (1985) 232–5.

123 *IG* 2² 2621, 4974.

124 *IG* 2² 4973. There is no great temptation to associate this phratry with a stele, perhaps bearing cult regulations, which Meritt reconstructed from many fragments: *IG* 1³ 243, 'a. 480–450.' Meritt's restorations give us the deme Melite and even a decree of Melite (lines 32, 72), and also 'the Thericleium' (line 30). Meritt, *Hesperia* 36 (1967) 72–3, 83–4, thinks of 'the shrine of the eponym of the phratry of the Therrhikleidai,' and of observances resumed after the Persian Wars. But in truth it seems impossible to extract any sense at any point from these battered remnants. '*De poculo* Θηρικλείῳ *interdum cogitavimus*,' Lewis on *IG* 1³ 243. See also n. 115 above.

125 The Medontidae are placed at Keratea by S. Solders, *Die Ausserstädtischen Kulte und die Einigung Attikas* (Lund 1931) 92, 119, 123; just south or just north of the city of Athens by M. Crosby, *Hesperia* 10 (1941) 22–3. The evidence for these locations is evanescent.

To get a little farther, we must summon our other witness, Philochorus on 'the twelve cities' of Attica. As rendered by Strabo, Philochorus said that Cecrops 'synoecized the population into twelve cities,' εἰς δώδεκα πόλεις συνοικίσαι τὸ πλῆθος. This is not a normal use of the verb συνοικίζειν, 'synoecize' or 'settle together.' A given group of people in a given area are 'settled together' in one settlement, not distributed into twelve settlements. Philochorus has his eye on the Συνοίκια and hence on the phratry organization of Attica.

Strabo gives the following names: Cecropia, Tetrapolis, Epacria, Deceleia, Eleusis, Aphidna, Thoricus, Brauron, Cytherus, Sphettus, Cephisia. One name has dropped out, at least in most of Strabo's manuscripts (we shall come back to it); the eleven that remain are nearly all familiar place-names, but in the Cleisthenic system the areas so denoted are not of comparable extent. Seven are Cleisthenic demes (Deceleia, Eleusis, Aphidna, Thoricus, Cytherus, Sphettus, Cephisia), ranging however from very large demes (Eleusis, Aphidna) to a small one (Cytherus). At least four, including three deme-names, are Cleisthenic *trittyes* (Tetrapolis, Eleusis, Thoricus, Sphettus). Although another Cleisthenic *trittys* was called Epacreis, this transparent name, 'On-the-hills,' was likely used of more than one district, and Philochorus, as we shall see in a moment, seems to mean a district other than the *trittys*. Brauron, often remarked as an odd omission from Cleisthenic nomenclature, was always a place-name in common use. Cecropia evokes the Acropolis.

The distribution of these places will be considered below, when we take up Philochorus' account in earnest. Here we need only observe that most of the places are on the periphery, and yet are true to the boundaries of Attica as they were before the mid sixth century; for the northwest sector, the area of Phyle and Oenoe, is not represented (though one name is missing). As others have said, 'the twelve cities' have the air of an authentic tradition of some kind. No one has yet explained how later conditions might have led Philochorus to this result.

How then do 'the twelve cities' consort with twelve phratry centres? Four phratries in the epigraphic record can be readily aligned with the names in Philochorus' list.[126]

The Demotionidae have their lodge at Deceleia. The Aechniadae appear to have their centre at or near Cephale; this is close enough to Thoricus.

126 It is a pity that the 'phratry' Titacidae of the lexica cannot be taken seriously, since their eponym is very much at home at Aphidna. The two 'phratries' Titacidae and Thyrgonidae give the lie to each other, as may be seen from J.S. Traill, *The Political Organization of Attica* (Princeton 1975) 121–2 nos. 41–2.

Another phratry have their centre at or near Paeania; this is close enough to Sphettus. The most striking case is the phratry Gleontidae.

A boundary stone found in the Agora names 'the shrine of Cephisus of the Gleontis phratry,' [ἱερὸν] Κηφισῶ Γλεωντίδος φρατρίας.[127] The name Γλεωντίς, *Γλεωντίδαι is a variant of the name of the first Ionic *phylē*, spelt Γλέοντες in the Solonian calendar. Only the quantity -o- serves to differentiate the two names. Both the *phylē* and the phratry belong to the city of Athens, and more precisely to the Acropolis. According to a doctrine which we shall examine in a moment, the Ionic *phylai* had other names before the time of Ion. From Cecrops onward, the *phylē* Geleontes was called successively Κεκροπίς, Κραναίς, Διάς. The names come from Cecrops, the hero of the Acropolis; from the physical aspect of the Acropolis, κραναός, 'craggy'; from Zeus, the deity of the Acropolis. The phratry Gleontidae possessed a shrine of the river Cephisus, the western boundary of Athens, where Theseus was purified before entering the city. We must conclude that the phratry centre was Cecropia, the first of Philochorus' 'cities.'

[Aristotle's] account of early Attica is not so far off the mark. In reality, a fourth part of Attic territory, a *trittys* of three phratries, was assigned to each Ionic *phylē*. The *phylai* themselves did not correspond to a fourfold division of Attica, for they went back to a time when Athens itself was a small community southeast of the Acropolis, and the king of Athens did not rule in Marathon as well, and there was no one with authority to carve up Attica into four parts or twelve.

The *trittyes* gave new life to the old Ionic *phylai*, and served Attica so well that even Cleisthenes retained a version of the *trittyes*. [Aristotle] was right to link the *trittyes* with the Solonian naucraries, and right again to see 'the pre-existing *trittyes*' as a pattern to be avoided by Cleisthenes; but he went astray in making the *trittyes* twelve instead of four. As Attica grew in population and resources, each *trittys* was divided once more into twelve naucraries, as in Solon's laws. And when Cleisthenes made his *phylai* ten instead of twelve, a more normal number, he had his eye upon the twelve phratries grouped in *trittyes* according to the natural division of the land.

This reconstruction is confirmed by Philochorus, to whom we now turn.

Philochorus on 'the Twelve Cities'

'The twelve cities' of Philochorus answer to the twelve phratries or *ethnē* of [Aristotle]. Philochorus ascribed this organization to Cecrops instead of

127 *Hesperia* 17 (1948) 35 no. 18: 'boundary stone of Hymettian marble,' 'c. 400 BC.'

Theseus, though he kept a certain role for Theseus.[128] 'Once again, later on, πάλιν δ' ὕστερον, Theseus is said to have brought the twelve cities together into one, the existing city.'[129] This act of Theseus, another 'syn-oecism,' was expressly indicated as an *aition* of the Synoecia.[130] 'Once again,' because Athens alone had existed in the time of Cecrops, until the inhabitants were dispersed throughout Attica to deal with those Carians and Boeotians. We may assume, however, that the twelvefold division was not wholly undone by Theseus. While restoring Athens to its primacy, he did not leave Attica a blank, as it had been in the time of Cecrops. Philochorus will have said that the twelve cities now became something else, such as phratries.

Our next step is to determine as far as possible the distribution of 'the twelve cities.'[131] There is indeed quite other evidence for the territorial organization of Attica that was envisaged by Philochorus; we shall come to it below. But 'the twelve cities' should first be taken by themselves.

These settlements were allegedly planted in the face of enemy attack, by Carians at sea and Boeotians on land. Perhaps they were equally di-vided for defence against the two enemies. Strabo's list does not, however, observe any consistent geographic order: Cecropia, Tetrapolis, Epacria, De-celeia, Eleusis, Aphidna, Thoricus, Brauron, Cytherus, Sphettus, Cephisia. We can try to place the names in better order. But if the distribution is to be credible for the purpose stated, we shall find it necessary to make one or two assumptions.

The east coast is well defended against the Carians by Tetrapolis, Brau-ron, and Thoricus, situated at due intervals. The south coast from Sunium to the bay of Phalerum is about as long and vulnerable; it needs about as many settlements. Can we identify them?

Epacria, one of the twelve cities, is also the name of a district where Philochorus situates the deme Semachidae. Philochorus' city or district is sometimes equated with the Cleisthenic *trittys* Epacreis. The deme Semachidae, however, does not belong to the same *phylē* as the *trittys* Epacreis, and the evidence for its location distinctly favours the area of

128 Jacoby, n. 5 on Philochorus FGrHist 328 F 94, makes it a question whether Hecataeus, in calling Thoricus a *polis* (Steph. Byz. s.v. [FGrHist 1 F 126]), 'already knew the tradition about Kekrops.' But to judge from Stephanus, *polis* was Hecataeus' word for every sort of community.

129 Str. 9.1.20, p. 397 (Philochorus F 94).

130 Steph. Byz. s.v. 'Αθῆναι (Charax FGrHist 103 F 43): 'Theseus, in synoecizing the twelve cities of Attica into Athens, instituted a festival Synoecia.'

131 Hommel, RE 7 A 1 (1939) 335–9 s.v. Trittyes, and Klio 33 (1940) 181–200, identified 'the twelve cities' with twelve pre-Cleisthenic *trittyes*, but only because the names are mostly repeated in the Cleisthenic system.

Laureium, which might well be called Epacria, 'On-the-heights.'[132] More-over, the other location that has been canvassed for both the deme Semachi-dae and the *trittys* Epacreis, namely the north side of Pentelicus, has little room for the 'city' Epacria, since three other of 'the twelve cities' are nearby (Tetrapolis, Aphidna, Deceleia).[133] So a case can be made for situ-ating Epacria near the east end of the south coast.

Sphettus, though later counted an inland deme, can also be recruited for the south coast. It lies at the south edge of the central plain and has easy access to the coast; indeed Pausanias records a tradition that Sphettus, like the harbour town Anaphlystus, was founded from Troezen (2.30.9).

Finally, there is a little hope that the missing name has not been lost irretrievably, and that it completed the south-coast roster. Late manuscripts of Strabo have Φαληρός at the end of the list, and the name also appears in a partial list which Psellus took from Strabo: an authentic remnant, or a Byzantine conjecture? Another piece in the puzzle is a lexical entry suggesting that Philochorus named a second Tetrapolis, the Tetracomi that included Phalerum. One might ask whether 'Phalerus' was not a gloss for Tetracomi.[134] Perhaps then the south coast like the east was defended by three settlements: Epacria, Sphettus, and Tetracomi or Phalerum.

On the landward side Attica was threatened by Boeotia. To counter the threat, we have six inland cities. Cephisia, Deceleia, and Aphidna lie towards the north, and Eleusis towards the west. Athens itself need not be tied to the lines of defence. Cytherus as a deme has not yet been located; it could fit almost anywhere.[135]

---

132 Steph. Byz. *s.v.* Σημαχίδαι (Philochorus *FGrHist* 328 F 206). Hsch. *s.v.* Σημαχίδαι, a deme of Antiochis. IG 2² 1582 lines 53–4, a shrine Σημάχειον at Laureium. The coastal *trittys* of Antiochis is near Laureium. Cf. Lewis, *Historia* 12 (1963) 27 n. 56.

133 This location is preferred by Traill, *Political Organization* 54, and *Demos and Trittys* (Toronto 1986) 139, but (as with many other demes) it has shifted somewhat between the two publications.

134 Φαληρός recc.; τά Φάληρα Psellus, *De Op. Daem.* 44–5 Boissonade. Etym. Gen., Etym. Magn., Suda *s.v.* ἐπακρία χῶρα· δύο δὲ τετραπόλεις ἐκάλεσεν ἐκ τεσσαρῶν πόλεων ἑκατέραν μοῖραν καταστήσας. Jacoby firmly rejected Phalerum and firmly embraced Tetracomi; but the evidence and opinion which he cites at length (ns. 5–6) make any decision very painful. At all events, if the name is not preserved here, it is gone forever. Gemistus Pletho thought of Athens; Wilamowitz of Munychia; Ferguson, *CP* 5 (1910) 274, of Agrae; Solders, *Ausserst. Kulte* 111, of Pallene.

135 The deme Cytherus belongs to the *phylē* Pandionis. The only known city deme of Pandionis, Cydathenaeum, lies north of the Acropolis; its inland demes lie on the west side of the central plain, north of Sphettus; its coastal demes lie on the east coast, south of Brauron. On this showing, any location of Cytherus next to other demes of Pandionis will be uncomfortably close to another 'city' of the twelve, and will make the general distribution quite uneven. But as everyone knows, a few demes

Philochorus on the Four *Phylai*

Philochorus' picture of 'the twelve cities' of early Attica is more or less in focus. But for the period from Cecrops to Theseus, it was not enough to say that Attica was organized as twelve cities. 'The twelve cities' have been deduced from the twelve phratries of the Synoecia, but the phratries are bound up with the four Ionic *phylai*. The normal view was that the *phylai* were created and named by Ion, and that the phratries were created later. This view will not do for Philochorus; if the twelve cities go back to Cecrops, so must the *phylai*. Ion could not be dismissed altogether, when Herodotus and Euripides tell us that the *phylai* were named for his sons. We require an earlier system of four *phylai* under other names. Such a system is described by Pollux; it was already known to Apollodorus, who provides a valuable detail.[136]

In this system, the four *phylai* are named and renamed four times, under Cecrops, Cranaus, Erichthonius, and Erechtheus, i.e., in the time of Ion. It is only under Erechtheus that the *phylai* get their familiar names from Ion's sons. At the beginning of history, Cecrops gives his name to the first *phylē*, the later Geleontes, and all four names signify different parts of Attica. Cranaus in his turn gives his name to the first *phylē*, and all four names signify the same parts of Attica. Under Erichthonius the *phylai* are named after four deities: Zeus, Athena, Poseidon, and Hephaestus. This should not persuade us that the four *phylai* actually worshipped four tutelary gods.[137] The *phylē* Geleontes did indeed worship Zeus; the priesthood of 'Zeus Geleon' survives in Roman Athens as a vestige of the Synoecia. But the Geleontes also worshipped Athena as Zeus' partner, as we see from the Solonian calendar of sacrifice. One might guess that the

---

are strays, lying far away from other demes of the same *trittys*. One of these is Probalinthus, another deme of Pandionis; and Probalinthus is also detached from the other parts of the Tetrapolis, one of the twelve cities. The twelve cities might well call for special treatment in the new system. The only other evidence for locating Cytherus is [Demosthenes'] description of the estate of Phaenippus, which lay in the deme. The estate was very large, but in 'a far quarter,' *eschatia* (42 *Phaenipp.* 5–7, 20–4); the whole deme was not populous, contributing only one or two Councillors. Was it northwest of Athens, at the edge of the plain, as another city deme of Pandionis? Two recent suggestions about Cytherus illustrate the range of uncertainty. P.J. Bicknell, *REG* 89 (1976) 599–603, thinks of Cytherus as a cult association comprising an inland deme and other elements, and points to three sites near Spata (Erchia). Traill, *Demos and Trittys* 33–4, 39 n. 2, 45, 47–51, makes Cytherus a coastal deme and proposes a site very close to Brauron.

136 Poll. 8.109; Steph. Byz. *s.v.* Ἀκτή (Apollodorus *FGrHist* 244 F 185).
137 So Rhodes, *Comm.* 68.

other three *phylai* worshipped Zeus and Athena in other settings, as did the phratries in due course. Instead, the four deities evoke once more the four parts of Attica. The undoubted worship of Zeus by the Geleontes, as perpetuated in the Synoecia, was only the starting-point.

The successive names for the Geleontes are Κεκροπίς, Κραναίς, Διάς. For the Hopletes, Αὐτόχθων, Ἀτθίς, Ἀθηναίς. For the Aegicoreis, Ἀκταία, Μεσογαία, Ποσειδωνιάς. For the Argadeis, Παραλία, Διακρίς, Ἡφαιστιάς. The names for the Geleontes signify the Acropolis, as we saw above. The names for the other *phylai*, though of transparent meaning, would still leave much room for dispute – were it not for Apollodorus, who fixes the Aegicoreis and the Argadeis on the south and east coasts respectively. Whereas some said that Attica was called Ἀκτή 'Shore' after a man Actaeus, Apollodorus said, 'It was so called because a large part of it comes down to the sea; inasmuch as it forms a triangle, the two sides converging on Sunium from either hand are on the sea, because of which, when the *phylai* were four under Cecrops, they called two of them Ἀκταία and Παραλία.'

Pollux's nomenclature seems very arbitrary; it could not fail to be. In part, it makes use of old descriptive terms for various districts, as if to show why these terms are so inveterate: they go right back to the primaeval world of Cecrops and other kings. Yet the terms here applied to a fourfold division of Attica cannot agree very well with the terms actually applied to a threefold division – scil., the terms for the three contending regions of the sixth century, which include παραλία and διακρία, or the terms for the three groups of Cleisthenic *trittyes*, which include παραλία and μεσόγειος.[138] We must approach the nomenclature in a spirit of goodwill.

For the south coast, the domain of the Aegicoreis, *Aktaia* and *Poseidonias* are acceptable. Ἀκτή, when it is not the whole of Attica, is the peninsula at Peiraeus. At the fourth-yearly festival of Poseidon, boats bound for a *theōria* and a regatta sailed along the south coast from the Peiraeus to the harbour town of Sunium.[139] It is a trifle disconcerting to find a coastal region also called *Mesogaia*, 'Interior'; but if this term must be used in a partition of Attica that does not include a precisely suitable area, the south coast is at least more open to the interior and the central plain than is the east coast.

The east coast, the domain of the Argadeis, may well be called Paralia, 'By-the-sea,' as in other contexts the whole coast is so called, or the south

---

138 D. Kienast, *Historische Zeitung* 200 (1965) 274–7, does his best to assimilate Pollux to the regional divisions of the sixth century. But Apollodorus, though mentioned (274 n. 3), is not called to testify; without him, everything is mere conjecture.

139 Deubner, *Att. Feste* 215; Parke, *Festivals* 97.

coast. *Diakris* (not the only form), which could be understood as either 'Among-the-hills' or 'Beyond-the-hills,' was a familiar term for northeast Attica, but was also known to have once extended to Peisistratus' base at Brauron. *Hēphaistias* is surprising at first sight, since Hephaestus hardly appears in cult anywhere in Attica save at Athens, and as a partner of Athena. Indeed this alien god of fire and metallurgy was first brought to Athens to adorn the Panathenaic festival, when the year's new fire was fetched, by means of a torch-race, from the Academy to the altar of Athena.[140] Now the same rite of fetching new fire was conducted at Marathon in the famous cult of Athena *hellōtis*; the very epithet *hellōtis* appears to denote the new fire, as does also *Hēphaistia* as an epithet of Athena. For our purpose the proof is supplied by Nonnus, with his insistent allusions to Hellenistic poetry, especially Callimachus. We find that Marathon was then celebrated (like the Academy) as the scene of Athena's sexual encounter with Hephaestus, an image of the new fire that is widely paralleled.[141] Hellenistic poets draw on Attic chroniclers; Philochorus will have known this aetiology – he may even be the source of it. As a name for the east-coast *phylē*, *Hēphaistias* evokes Marathon.

Apollodorus gives no help with the domain of the Hopletes, for which names are used that might seem most appropriate either to the city of Athens (*Autochthōn, Athēnais*) or to Attica at large (*Atthis*); but of course neither can be meant. It is a fourth part of Attica, matched against the city and the south and east coasts: either the northern border, one supposes, or the middle. If the middle, it should not lie chiefly in the central plain, since the term *Mesogaia* was reserved for the south coast. A reasonable choice is a north-central domain attached to Pallene, on the saddle between Hymettus and Pentelicus. The earth-born giants are denizens of Pallene; hence *Autochthōn*. Athena Pallenis is worshipped by a League of some extent; hence *Athēnais*. Of *Atthis* we can only say that the name is better given to middle Attica than to any other part. It should perhaps be added that the Hopletes were sometimes linked with *hopla*, 'arms,' as if this were a *phylē* of men in arms;[142] Pallene is the site of ancient battles and of ritual combat.

Such is the system of four *phylai* reaching back to Cecrops and corresponding to a fourfold division of Attic territory. The system can be safely attributed to Philochorus, for it complements 'the twelve cities' of Cecrops. When the twelvefold division was carried back to the beginning, so perforce was the fourfold division. Philochorus was put to the necessity of inventing earlier names for the Ionic *phylai*.

---

140 *RhM* n.s. 128 (1985) 231–95. For Athena *hellōtis* at Marathon, 241–5.
141 Nonn. *Dion.* 27.313–23.
142 Plut. *Sol.* 23.5.

The four *phylai* like the twelve cities are deduced from the festival Synoecia, and the festival truly reflects the organization of early Attica. The twelve local phratries were distributed among four larger areas. But just as the twelve phratries were wrongly labelled as 'cities,' so the four areas are wrongly labelled as *phylai*. It was not the four Ionic *phylai* but the four *trittyes* that served to group the phratries in larger areas, three in each. The four areas of Attica that we have just examined constitute the pre-Cleisthenic *trittyes*.

Philochorus' 'twelve cities' reproduce the twelve phratries, or phratry centres; his four *phylai* reproduce the four *trittyes*. We can now match up phratries and *trittyes*. That they do somehow match is obvious at once; for in Strabo 'the twelve cities' guard Attica both by sea and by land, and in Apollodorus two of four *phylai* lie along the coast.

The *trittys* of the *phylē* Argadeis lies along the east coast; the phratry centres are at Thoricus, Brauron, and Tetrapolis. For this *phylē* Philochorus chose successive names – *Paralia, Diakris, Hēphaistias* – that correspond to the phratry centres in geographic order; for *Diakris* evokes Brauron, and *Hēphaistias* evokes Marathon. The *trittys* of the *phylē* Aegicoreis lies along the south coast; the phratry centres are at Tetracomi or Phalerum, Sphettus, and Epacria. The successive *phylē* names – *Aktaia, Mesogaia, Poseidōnias* – again correspond to the phratry centres; for *Aktaia* evokes the peninsula beside the bay of Phalerum, and *Mesogaia* evokes Sphettus, and *Poseidōnias* evokes Sunium and the area of Epacria. In this coastal domain, the correspondence between *Mesogaia* and Sphettus is so odd as to be distinctly reassuring.

The *trittys* of the *phylē* Geleontes, called 'Bright-headbands,' lies round the city; the phratry centres are at Cecropia and Eleusis and somewhere else, perhaps Cytherus. The *phylē* names, however – *Kekropis, Kranais, Dias* – all evoke the Acropolis. The *trittys* of the *phylē* Hopletes lies round Pallene, or rather beyond it to the north, the avenue of attack; the phratry centres are at Cephisia, Deceleia, and Aphidna. The *phylē* names, however – *Authochthōn, Atthis, Athēnais* – all evoke Pallene.

The location of 'the twelve cities' and the location of the four *phylai* have been argued independently. Yet the results coincide. With such evidence as we have, the argument cannot always be secure. But even if every doubtful case is set aside, there will still be a large measure of agreement.

[Aristotle] and Others on the Occupational Classes

Ancient theorists liked to say that early or ideal societies were divided into large occupational classes, usually three. This is of course a deduction of a very general kind (we have such theories still), not an aetiology of any particular custom or institution. One class was always farmers; another nearly always craftsmen; but a third class, superior to the others, was somewhat variable. It might be priests, or warriors, or guardians; or both priests and warriors, or both priests and guardians, making four classes in all. Though Plato at different times imagines both three classes and four, Aristotle in the *Politics* regards three classes as standard.[143]

The scheme of classes was naturally adopted in antiquarian accounts of early Attica. Four versions survive; doubtless there were others. We shall first distinguish them, then ask what warrant they may have in Athenian custom.

One is [Aristotle's] version, expounded in the lost beginning of the *Constitution of Athens*, as part of his *aition* of the Synoecia – i.e., the second *aition* in Plutarch's *Theseus* (25.1–2). The proclamation 'Come hither, all ye hosts' brought a swarm of people into the city to somehow live on equal terms. Theseus 'did not, however, allow the democracy to become disordered or tangled up by the influx of an indiscriminate mass of people. Instead, he was the first to separate Eupatridae and Geomori and Demiurgi,' ἀλλὰ πρῶτος ἀποκρίνας χωρὶς εὐπατρίδας καὶ γεωμόρους καὶ δημιουργούς, 'and to reserve it for the Eupatridae to know religion, and to provide magistrates, and to be teachers of the laws and interpreters of the sacred and the profane, so that he put them on a footing with the other citizens: the Eupatridae seemed to excel in reputation, the Geomori in usefulness, the Demiurgi in numbers.'

Pollux has the same three classes (8.111). After describing the Ionic *phylai* and the twelvefold subdivision, and also a further subdivision into *genē*, he comes at the end to the classes. 'There were three *ethnē* in old times, Eupatridae, Geomori, Demiurgi,' τρία δ' ἦν τὰ ἔθνη πάλαι, εὐπατρίδαι γεωμόροι δημιουργοί. It is through simple inadvertence that the term *ethnē*

143 Pl. *Resp.* 2, 369 C–375 E: society should be divided into farmers, craftsmen, and warriors or guardians. Pl. *Tim.* 24 A–B: ancient Egypt and ancient Attica have priests, craftsmen, farmers (also shepherds and hunters), and warriors. Pl. *Critias* 110 C, 112 B: ancient Attica has craftsmen, farmers, and warriors. Arist. *Pol.* 2.8, 1267 B–1268 A, citing Hippodamus: society should be divided into craftsmen, farmers, and warriors. Arist. *Pol.* 4.4, 1291 B: as against any theory of classes, like Plato's, it is observed that the same persons may serve as warriors, farmers, and craftsmen. Arist. *Pol.* 7.8, 1328 B: if we distinguish six groups of people who provide necessary services in any state, the first three are farmers, craftsmen, and warriors, but only the fifth are priests, coming between men of property and policy makers. Diod. 1.28.4–5: ancient Egypt like ancient Attica has Eupatridae as priests, Geomori as both farmers and warriors, and craftsmen.

is used here instead of, for example, βίοι: in the preceding passage the twelvefold unit has been referred to repeatedly as *ethnos* (as in Harpocration *s.v.* τριττύς). There can be no doubt that [Aristotle] is the source for the three classes, as for the twelvefold subdivision of the *phylai*. The farmers are again called γεωμόροι, a somewhat unusual term; elsewhere they are γεωργοί.

In Plutarch, the function of the Eupatridae is described in some detail. There are two reasons for dwelling on this class. Whereas the function of the other two classes is perfectly transparent, theirs is not. And the very name Eupatridae makes us wonder if this is indeed a democratic regime, or one less monarchical – 'the democracy' is doubtless Plutarch's term, for [Aristotle] will say hereafter, in listing the successive 'constitutions,' that the constitution of Theseus 'deviates a little from the monarchical' (*Ath.* 41.2). It has been suggested that two of the classes, the Geomori and the Demiurgi, had existed before, as the creation of Ion, not of Theseus, and that Theseus now added the Eupatridae.[144] There are decisive objections. First, if Theseus' role was only to add a class excelling in reputation to others excelling in usefulness and numbers, it was a plain step backward from democracy. Second, in [Aristotle's] view Attica before Theseus was in *stasis*, and Theseus' constitution was the first to impart any order to society.[145] Third, the normal scheme is of three classes: we meet with four as a refinement, we even meet with two, but we expect to meet with three in a work of Aristotle's school that deals with the leading city of Greece.

The other three versions of Attica's class society are subsequent refinements; they give us either four or two classes. None can be attributed, though one thinks first of the several Attic chroniclers, who could not well keep silent on this topic. These other versions, while refining an earlier version with three classes, may or may not be later than [Aristotle]; he would not prefer them in any case.

Strabo in his account of Achaea as an earlier Ionia mentions Ion's activity at Athens (8.7.1, p. 383). 'At first he divided the population into four *phylai*, and next into four occupations. Some he designated as farmers, others as craftsmen, others as ritual officiants (*hieropoioi*), and a fourth group as the guardians.' This looks like a purely arbitrary variation, and need not be considered further.

Dionysius of Halicarnassus thinks that Romulus may have copied Athens when he created the Patricians and Plebeians (*Ant. Rom.* 2.8.1–2). The Athenian system, which 'still existed' in the time of Romulus, is described

144 So Wade-Gery, *Essays* 88–92; followed by Rhodes, *Comm.* 67.
145 Heracleid. *Epit.* 1; [Arist.] *Ath.* 41.2.

as follows. 'For they, having divided the population into two parts, gave the name Eupatridae to those from distinguished families and with sufficient wealth, to whom the leadership of the city was entrusted, and the name Agroeci, ἄγροικοι, to the rest of the citizens, who were not competent to take any part in public affairs. But in time these too were admitted to the magistracies.' The outlook here requires a less flattering term for the farmers, 'Agroeci.' Given Dionysius' purpose, to find another perfect correspondence between Rome and Greece, it would not be safe to conclude that in his Greek source the 'Agroeci' were indeed firmly excluded from government, as if they were Plebeians. The term Eupatridae for the superior class, as in [Aristotle], is an authentic Athenian name, which we shall examine below. For the rest, this too is an arbitrary variation without any real interest.

The last version, again with only two classes, but now Georgi and Demiurgi, appears in a number of lexica and scholia that explain the system of Attic *genē*. They cite 'Aristotle,' and partly overlap both with Pollux and with Harpocration *s.v.* τριττύς, where 'Aristotle in the *Constitution of Athens*' is precisely the authority for *trittyes* and *ethnē* and phratries as twelve subdivisions of the four *phylai*. *Trittyes* and phratries (but not *ethnē*) are again so described in those other lexica and scholia; to this extent they undoubtedly draw on [Aristotle]. But they also speak of a division of the people into those two classes, Georgi and Demiurgi, and of an elaborate system of *genē*: thirty *genē* in each *trittys* or phratry, and thirty men in each *genos*. The system is thus analogous to the natural world, as we are told in the fuller lexica and scholia: the *phylai* are like the year's four seasons, and the *trittyes* or phratries like twelve months, and the *genē* like 360 days. 'Aristotle' is cited at the beginning or in the middle of this rigmarole. Pollux is much briefer on the *genē*, though he alone preserves the term *triakades*, 'thirtieths,' as a synonym (8.111).

These lexica and scholia have a long history as a 'fragment' of [Aristotle]. Before the discovery of the papyrus copies of our work, they formed about the longest of the many scattered fragments culled from the lexica (fr. 385 Rose[3]). In editions of the papyrus work, they were at first printed as fr. 3, after the passage of Plutarch's *Theseus* as fr. 2: it was supposed that they give further details of Theseus' dispensation.[146] Lately, they have been printed as fr. 2, before Plutarch: it is supposed that they describe Ion's dispensation, with two occupational classes, which it fell to Theseus to complete by adding a third class.[147] Even so, few are willing

146 So, e.g., Sandys, Kenyon[3], Oppermann.
147 So Chambers (Teubner 1986), after Wade-Gery.

to believe that [Aristotle] is responsible for everything in the 'fragment,' for 360 genē and 10,800 genos members and that beautiful analogy with the year.[148] But once we pass beyond the details that are authenticated by Harpocration s.v. τριττύς, there is no discernible place to draw the line.

Everything beyond those details is falsely ascribed. Two occupational classes instead of three is not a colourable view for an Aristotelian.[149] Nor was Ion credited by [Aristotle] with any order more intricate than the four phylai; phratries and the rest were due to Theseus as an aition of the Synoecia. Furthermore, it is very unlikely that genē had any part to play in the organization of early Attica as conceived by [Aristotle]. He does not refer to them later, as he does to the phylai and the trittyes. The word γένος is regularly used by [Aristotle] in its ordinary, untechnical sense of 'family,' 'lineage,' especially a distinguished one.[150] We are told that Cleisthenes 'allowed all to keep their genē and their phratries and their priesthoods' (Ath. 21.6), and it is sometimes thought that these are hieratic genē, and so a tautology for hereditary 'priesthoods';[151] but the ordinary meaning is better suited to the context.

It has not been noticed that in the system described by the lexica, the genē are in effect a substitute for the Eupatridae; the system is therefore wholly incompatible with [Aristotle]. 'And each genos had thirty men, those enrolled in the genē, who were called gennētai, among whom the priesthoods appertaining to each genos were allotted,' καὶ γένος ἕκαστον ἄνδρας εἶχον τριάκοντα τοὺς εἰς τὰ γένη τεταγμένους, οἵτινες γεννῆται ἐκαλοῦντο, <ἐξ> ὧν αἱ ἱερωσύναι <αἱ> ἑκάστοις προσήκουσαι ἐκληροῦντο.[152] Consider what this system implies.

In Classical Athens a great many cults, from the most obscure to the most renowned, were partly or entirely in the hands of hereditary groups who all came to be called genē, though they were not real 'families.' In general, cults are an ancient and constant feature of the landscape; some arrangements for tending cults existed before, or outside, any proper organization of society, and were never the subject of any reform, as by Cleisthenes or the ensuing democracy. But now it is asserted that such

---

148 Cf. Rhodes, Comm. 68.
149 In the past, some editors inserted the third class, Eupatridae, into the text of all the lexica and scholia. This is an act of violence, when the tradition is so uniform; there is no likelihood that a common source has been universally misrepresented. In any case the Eupatridae are not wanted, as we shall discover in a moment: the genē have taken over their function.
150 Ath. 1, 13.5, 16.10 (a document), 20.1, 21.2, 28.2, 35.4, 42.5.
151 If it is also thought that each phratry was virtually managed by a hieratic genos, then the three terms are one, and [Aristotle] writes with unaccustomed amplitude.
152 Lex. Demosth. Patm. p. 152 Sakkelion, s.v. γεννῆται.

cults and such *genē* are part of the original system. Or rather, they are the system, for *trittyes* (phratries) and *phylai* are only groupings of *genē*. No doubt the notion is that all cults, in effect all religion, were thus provided for. The system dispenses with the Eupatridae or any other class of priests. So there are only two classes, Georgi and Demiurgi.

It would probably be misguided to suppose that the system expresses any strong social or political conviction, that the author was pious or democratic. The system is extremely artificial, and the author's main concern was symmetry.

According to the lexica and scholia, the twelvefold unit intermediate between the 4 *phylai* and the 360 *genē* is called interchangeably *trittys* or phratry; according to Pollux, it is also called *ethnos*. If this detail is truly reported, then the system presupposes [Aristotle's], and is very late and bookish. But the twelvefold unit was generally known (Philochorus has it too); some other term, or either 'trittys' or 'phratry' or 'ethnos' alone, may well have been assimilated to [Aristotle's] usage in the lexical tradition. For within this tradition [Aristotle] was first compared, and then confused, with our author. After the words quoted above about the *genē* and the priesthoods, the entry continues, 'such as Eumolpidae and Ceryces and Eteobutadae, as Aristotle reports in the *Constitution of Athens*, speaking thus'; there follows the extended analogy between social units and parts of the year.[153] Now [Aristotle] mentions Eumolpidae and Ceryces rather prominently (*Ath.* 39.2, 57.1), not however the Eteobutadae, unless it was in the lost beginning. Such mention is very different from all the lore of *phylai* and seasons and the rest. It was just at this point that some confusion caused the whole system to be falsely ascribed to 'Aristotle.'

The Eupatridae

Returning to [Aristotle's] version, we ask what further warrant these three classes may have in Athenian institutions. [Aristotle] would say anyway that early Attica had three classes; he would trace them back anyway to Theseus' fundamental ordering of society as an *aition* of the Synoecia. Yet these predispositions do not account for the names of the three classes, especially the name 'Eupatridae.'

It is for the Eupatridae 'to know religion, and to provide magistrates, and to be teachers of the laws and interpreters of the sacred and the profane,' γινώσκειν τὰ θεῖα καὶ παρέχειν ἄρχοντας ... καὶ νόμων διδασκάλους

---

153 καὶ γένος ἕκαστον ... ἐκληροῦντο, οἷον Εὐμολπίδαι καὶ Κήρυκες καὶ Ἐτεοβουτάδαι, ὡς ἱστορεῖ ἐν τῆι ᾿Αθηναίων πολιτείαι ᾿Αριστοτέλης λέγων οὕτως· φυλὰς δὲ αὐτῶν συννενεμῆσθαι δ' ἀπομιμησαμένων τὰς ἐν τοῖς ἐνιαυτοῖς ὥρας κτλ.

εἶναι καὶ ὁσίων καὶ ἱερῶν ἐξηγητάς (Plut. *Thes.* 25.2). Two main functions are described as four, in chiastic order. 'To know religion' and 'to be interpreters of the sacred and the profane' is to be the priests. 'To provide magistrates' and 'to be teachers of the laws' is to be the secular rulers or the government. The terminology, whether it is chiefly Plutarch's or [Aristotle's], has no great significance; it is meant to sound wise and solemn. The terms for the priestly function are suitable to any prominent ritual officiants. The terms for the ruling function happen to be more closely suitable to Athens' chief magistrates, the board of nine 'archons' who administer the laws, and also to the Council of the Areopagus as the *ex officio* body of all archons past and present.[154]

The Eupatridae are seen in a slightly different light in Pollux, just before the passage which combines some details from [Aristotle] with others from the system of thirty *genē* (8.111). That passage resembles the tradition of the lexica and scholia examined above; it is a different branch of the tradition, fuller on [Aristotle] and less full on the *genē*. 'The Phylobasileis, being four, and from the Eupatridae, had charge especially of ritual, sitting as a body in the Basileium beside the Bucoleium,' οἱ δὲ φυλοβασιλεῖς ἐξ εὐπατριδῶν δ' ὄντες μάλιστα τῶν ἱερῶν ἐπεμελοῦντο, συνεδρεύοντες ἐν τῶι βασιλείωι τῶι παρὰ τὸ βουκολεῖον. Then comes the passage on *phylai* and *trittyes* and *genē*. At the very end we hear of the three classes, miscalled *ethnē*, Eupatridae and Geomori and Demiurgi. Hesychius *s.v.* φυλοβασιλεῖς has a fragment of the information in Pollux, saying that these officers 'are chosen from the *phylai* as those who perform the sacrifices,' ἐκ τῶν φυλῶν αἱρετοί. οἱ τὰς θυσίας ἐπιτελοῦντες.

In the surviving portion of the *Constitution of Athens*, the four Phylobasileis are mentioned together with the Ionic *phylai* as constituting Ion's dispensation (41.2); also in the resumptive note about *phylai* and *trittyes*, i.e., about Theseus' dispensation, that gives the background to Solonian naucraries (8.3); and finally in the survey of homicide courts (57.4). Athens' Basileium is nowhere else referred to; [Aristotle] is, however, the only authority to take an interest in Athens' most ancient civic buildings, as illustrating how the board of archons grew.[155] It is nearly certain then

---

154 W.G. Forrest and D. Stockton, *Historia* 36 (1987) 235–40, have argued that the pool of men from whom archons and Areopagites were drawn was at all times much smaller than commonly supposed.

155 Bucoleium, Prytaneium, Epilyceium or Polemarcheium, Thesmotheteium: *Ath.* 3.5; whence Suda *s.v.* ἄρχων; Bekker, *Anecd. Gr.* 1.449. 'The Basileus had the Bucoleium, as it is now called,' τὸ νῦν καλούμενον βουκολεῖον. Rhodes *ad loc.* infers that in [Aristotle's] view the Bucoleium was formerly called 'Basileium,' just as the Epilyceium was

that the Phylobasileis appeared in the lost beginning as part of Theseus' dispensation as well as Ion's; it is very probable that [Aristotle] is the source for Pollux's account of the Phylobasileis as recruited from the Eupatridae, and taking charge of ritual, and sitting in the Basileium. If it is not [Aristotle], it is some other factual authority who had his eye on the same kind of evidence.

The Phylobasileis are rather prominent in the entry of the Solonian calendar for the biennial Synoecia. On both days, 15 and 16 Hecatombaeon, they are the first recipients of priestly perquisites, *hierōsyna*, and receive the best part, the chine or the leg. Phylobasileis, plural, are on hand on 15 Hecatombaeon, doubtless all four; but Phylobasileus, singular, on 16 Hecatombaeon, doubtless he of the *phylē* Geleontes.

It is true that the Phylobasileis are active at other festivals besides the Synoecia. The Solonian calendar was compiled, at least in part, from earlier collections of ritual observances; those named in the surviving fragments are 'the rites occurring month by month,' 'the rites occurring on no fixed day,' and 'the rites pertaining to the Phylobasileis,' τὰ φυλοβασιλικά. These last are the source for the festival Synoecia, being named as such on both days. In another fragment of the calendar the same source is cited for some observance on the fifth of an unknown month; the Phylobasileis themselves appear in the following line, the last that is legible.[156] There is an important difference, however. At the Synoecia the Phylobasileis are solely responsible, and for a considerable expenditure, fifty-four drachmas. On the fifth of that unknown month another source is cited first, 'the rites occurring month by month,' and the expenditure appears to be significant.[157] 'The rites pertaining to the Phylobasileis' come only in second place – and the expenditure is only an obol and a half!

Both 'the rites pertaining to the Phylobasileis' and the Phylobasileis themselves have been restored in another small fragment of the calendar.

---

formerly called 'Polemarcheium.' Yet the latter change of name is explained at length – falsely, as it seems – and the words about the Bucoleium merely acknowledge that it does not take its name from the Basileus; 'Basileium' can just as well be a building beside it. Carlier, *Royauté* 359 n. 211, suggests that 'Basileium' is another name for the Prytaneium, but this building would not be obscurely indicated as 'the Basileium beside the Bucoleium.' For the complex of buildings, see *Historia* 35 (1986) 160–3.

156 *IG* 2² 1357a (*LSCG* 17B); Oliver, *Hesperia* 4 (1935) 22–3, 29–30.

157 The sums and the arrangement are a little clearer in Oliver's text, which supersedes Kirchner's: cf. *Hesperia* 4 (1935) 23 n. 1. Part of 'the rites occurring month by month' is an offering for Erechtheus worth six drachmas, but the total in the line above had another figure before 'six,' probably sixteen drachmas. The observances prescribed for the fifth continue for fourteen lines until we reach the sixth of the month; some or all of these observances were again 'the rites occurring month by month.'

One cannot tell whether the restoration is secure; in any case nothing more is to be learned.[158] Another proposal to restore the Phylobasileis, but in the Archaic calendar of the Eleusinium, also seems rather doubtful.[159]

In sum, the Phylobasileis had much more to do at the biennial Synoecia than on any other occasion that is known to us.[160] We may conclude that [Aristotle's] scheme of three classes looks first to the Phylobasileis as they preside at the Synoecia. While describing Theseus' dispensation as an *aition* of the festival, he says that the Eupatridae were put in charge of religion. Pollux says that the Phylobasileis were Eupatridae and had charge of ritual.

The Eupatridae are also said to provide the archons who administer Athens' laws.[161] Now it is evident that the original purpose of the Synoecia was to bring the phratries together at the new year for the purpose of installing a new government. In the first *aition* of the Synoecia, the one known to both Thucydides and Plutarch, Theseus establishes a single Council-house and Prytaneium at Athens (while closing down many others throughout Attica). In the second *aition*, besides the role of the Eupatridae, there is the notion that Theseus gave everyone a share in government; Plutarch begins by saying, 'He summoned everyone on equal terms,' ἐκάλει πάντας ἐπὶ τοῖς ἴσοις (*Thes.* 25.1). In Philochorus' bifurcated *aition*, Cecrops founds twelve self-governing 'cities' and Theseus brings them together into one.

As another vestige of their former power, the Phylobasileis of the historical period adjudicate certain homicide cases at the Prytaneium.[162]

158 S. Dow, *Hesperia* 10 (1941) 34 fr. E; cf. *Hesperia* 30 (1961) 65 fr. D. In the latter place Dow explains, 'The squeeze had been marked with soft black pencil ... In printing, the image was reversed ... The readings are indubitable throughout – fortunately, because the fragment disappeared even before it could be catalogued ...' Dow has restored two other headings, novel ones, in another battered fragment: *Hesperia* 10 (1941) 35 fr. F; *ProcMassHistSoc* 71 (1953–7) [1959] 16, 20. They should be rejected: *JHS* 110 (1990) 70.

159 *IG* 1³ 232 line 43. The proposal, which is Jeffery's, is noted by Lewis and favoured by Carlier, *Royauté* 355 n. 190.

160 Carlier, *Royauté* 355–8, after examining the evidence as I do, observes that whereas the fragments of the civic calendar refer to nineteen festivals, the Phylobasileis appear in three, a proportion of 'about one to six.' If Dow's restoration is discounted, the proportion is 1:9.5.

161 [Dem.] 59 *Neaera* 75 says that although Theseus' 'synoecism' made Athens a democracy, 'the people still elected the Basileus from chosen candidates, voting for the best man,' τὸν μὲν βασιλέα οὐδὲν ἧττον ὁ δῆμος ἡιρεῖτο ἐκ προκρίτων κατ' ἀνδραγαθίαν χειροτονῶν. 'Chosen candidates' and the criterion of excellence are perhaps allusions to 'Eupatridae.'

162 Poll. 8.120; cf. [Arist.] *Ath.* 57.4, where the building is not mentioned. For other details, D.M. MacDowell, *Athenian Homicide Law* (Manchester 1963) 85–9.

This is the place to ask why Thucydides and Plutarch mention Prytaneium and Council-house in the same breath. It has always been assumed that these are separate buildings,[163] but the assumption is unjustified. According to Thucydides, Theseus 'abolished both the Council-houses and the magistracies of the other cities in favour of the present city, creating one Council-house and Prytaneium,' τῶν ἄλλων πόλεων τά τε βουλευτήρια καὶ τὰς ἀρχὰς ἐς τὴν νῦν πόλιν οὖσαν, ἓν βουλευτήριον ἀποδείξας καὶ πρυτανεῖον (2.15.2). The earlier Council-houses of other Attic cities are of course deduced from the Council-house at Athens, whatever that was; earlier magistracies are added for good measure. The logical replacement is one Council-house at the centre, not one Council-house and one Prytaneium. It should be obvious that the phrase καὶ πρυτανεῖον is epexegetic – the Council-house is in fact the Prytaneium. Plutarch's language is more ambiguous, but need not be examined here; in such a matter, Plutarch is not an independent authority.

Other considerations point the same way. The story of the 'synoecism' has regard to Athens' Prytaneium, an old building in the old agora; it cannot also have regard to a new building in the new Agora, the only Council-house we ever hear of at Athens.[164] But if the Prytaneium alone is to warrant the story, then it must have served as a Council-house as well, replacing all the Council-houses of Attica; for any independent city will have not only magistrates, but a council. Moreover, the Prytaneium resembled a Council-house in some respects. The Council-house in the Agora contained a public hearth; so did the Prytaneium. Documents were displayed on stone outside the Council-house, and were also deposited nearby; the *axones* as the first publication of Solon's laws were kept in the Prytaneium. The very name 'Prytaneium' recalls the *prytaneis* as the presiding committee of the Council of Five Hundred.

Since the Phylobasileis were active at the Prytaneium, [Aristotle] inferred that these 'Eupatridae' had a leading role in government. But his language is vague; and with the same evidence we cannot do better now.[165]

What then does it mean to say that the Phylobasileis are εὐπατρίδαι? A *genos* of this name appears in later Hellenistic and Roman times, but

---

163 E.g., Gomme, HCT 2.49, 59; Wycherley, Testimonia 132 no. 404; Thompson and Wycherley, Agora of Athens 148.

164 For the sources, see Wycherley, Testimonia 128–37 nos. 387–433.

165 F. Gschnitzer, RE Suppl. 13 (1973) 803 s.v. Prytanis 7, thinks that the Phylobasileis, when sitting at the Prytaneium, formed 'the oldest and closest council' of the Basileus; but this is only a conjecture.

earlier usage is different: it is a fairly broad term of commendation that is somehow sanctified by tradition.[166] How the term arose, and why it was associated with the festival Synoecia, is not hard to guess. The phratries are self-professed kinship groups; their names all take patronymic forms. Any given phratry is the offspring of some noble sire; together, they might all be styled 'the offspring of noble sires,' εὐπατρίδαι. This name for phratry members matches the name for the phratry festival at which children were first admitted: ἀπατούρια, glossed as ὁμοπατόρια.[167]

No other group but the phratries deserve this collective name. The bodies later known as *genē* whose business is to tend certain cults are not invariably called by patronymic names (cf. Buzygae, Ceryces, Heudanemi, Salaminians); their names are in fact taken from the ritual actions they performed, less commonly from the ritual setting, and a patronymic suffix, where it occurs, does little to disguise this origin (cf. Praxiergidae especially, but also Eumolpidae, Phytalidae, and many others). Like any specialists, doctors for example, such a body would rely on family transmission, though not of course in a single line; but this form of recruitment was not ostentatious, as with the phratries. Finally, the bodies tending cults were of every size and quality, like the cults themselves, and, as explained above, did not form any recognizable subdivision of society. For such *genē*, no collective name was possible.[168]

In early days the name 'Eupatridae' was doubtless given to all phratry members: it suits them all. Later, when phratries no longer joined together, as at the Synoecia, to conduct the most important public business, this imposing collective name had no use. To be sure, Athenians continued to be proud of phratry membership, but it was only the individual phratry that counted. A name like 'Demotionidae' carried weight; 'Eupatridae' did not. In the fourth century the name was plainly a fossil. In the context of the Synoecia, [Aristotle] equates it, not with the general attendance, but with the presiding officers, the Phylobasileis.

---

166 Isocrates says of Alcibiades that he belonged through the male line to the Eupatridae, through the female to the Alcmaeonidae; much is said thereafter of the family Alcmaeonidae, but of the Eupatridae only that 'it is easy to perceive their fine lineage from the very name' (16 *De Big.* 25). For the later *genos*, see Davies, *Ath. Prop. Fam.* 11; for general usage, Bourriot, *Genos* 1.407–22.

167 Schol. Ar. *Ach.* 146; Suda *s.v.* ἀπατούρια. Frisk, *Gr. etym. Wörterb. s.v.* 'Απατούρια, thinks of 'an original form *ἀπατορϝος = ὁμοπάτωρ "from the same father." '

168 Kearns, *The Heroes of Attica* (BICS Suppl. 57, 1989) 64–77, shows that the cults and ceremonies of the *genē* are not much concerned with descent and kinship – unlike those of the phratries.

The Geomori and the Demiurgi

If the Phylobasileis are 'Eupatridae,' the rest of the attendance will be 'farmers' and 'craftsmen.' The terms for these classes, γεωμόροι and δημιουργοί, are not taken from Athenian institutions, but both are strongly eulogistic. They support the proposition that Theseus created a fairly even society, that he put the Eupatridae 'on a footing with the other citizens,' τοῖς ἄλλοις πολίταις ὥσπερ εἰς ἴσον κατέστησε (Plut. Thes. 25.2).

Γεωμόροι is not a usual synonym at all for γεωργοί (except perhaps in later poetry), but denotes instead wealthy 'landowners.'[169] Yet the term was never in current use in Attica, as it was in some places, for a particular group. The only reason one can see for ascribing it to Theseus' dispensation is to suggest that he exalted the farming class. This tendency appears again in the legendary coinage of Theseus. Plutarch, having cited 'Aristotle' as saying that Theseus 'inclined towards the masses,' goes on: 'He struck coins and stamped them with an ox, whether it was for the Marathonian bull or for Minos' commander or to win over the citizens to farming,' ἢ πρὸς γεωργίαν τοὺς πολίτας παρακαλῶν (Thes. 25.3). Athens' early didrachms include a type with ox's head that in later estimation stood for the whole series, perhaps not undeservedly.[170] [Aristotle] in a subsequent chapter appears to credit Solon with the first tetradrachms, and there refers to the didrachm as 'the ancient type' (Ath. 10.2). To judge from Plutarch, he said that the type went back to Theseus and subserved his ordering of society.[171]

Δημιοεργοί is Homer's term for no ordinary craftsmen, but for specialists like seers, doctors, master carpenters, and minstrels, who all rove from land to land (Od. 17.383–6, cf. 19.135). It is doubtless the connotation of 'specialists' or 'experts' that caused the term to be used for boards of magistrates in many cities. Granted, the class of craftsmen was already so

---

169 At Diod. 2.28.5 'Geomori' is used for the second of three classes common to Attica and Egypt; it is easy to suppose that the ultimate source is [Aristotle].

170 C.M. Kraay, Archaic and Classical Greek Coins (London 1976) 57–8, and pl. 9 no. 170, cf. no. 174. Schol. Ar. Av. 1106 (Philochorus FGrHist 328 F 200); Poll. 9.60–1. The type was popular in its day, for it was used again on the reverse of the first tetradrachms. In fact it seems the handsomest of all the Wappenmünzen. The Gorgoneium has more detail, but the ox's head, with bulging nose and shell ear and tufted brow, looks just like the animal we know.

171 There is a possibility that [Aristotle] interpreted the word γεωμόροι as 'land-dividers,' i.e., those who plough, as with the ox on the coins. The adjective is an epithet of a plough ox at Apoll. Rhod. Argon. 1.1214, and the derivative verb and noun may take the meaning 'till,' 'tillage,' i.e., the crops (LSJ s.vv. γεωμορέω, γεωμορία).

called by Plato, but he too flatters them: craftsmen have a leading role in Plato's imagery, and in his latest works the term is used for the craftsman who is creator of all, the Demiurge. For Aristotle in the *Politics*, even in passages concerned with Plato, craftsmen in general are τεχνῖται, a more ordinary term.

Such 'Geomori' and such 'Demiurgi' must have been discernible in the attendance of the Synoecia. The first, as farmers, are squarely in the picture, for Theseus summons people from the Attic countryside. According to Thucydides, Theseus' 'synoecism' was counter to the Athenian fondness for country living, and even after it the majority of people preferred to dwell 'in the fields' (2.14.2, 16.1). In Dionysius of Halicarnassus, the Athenians are divided into two classes only, Eupatridae and 'farmers' or 'rustics,' ἄγροικοι; but we cannot be sure that he drew on a source directly acquainted with the Synoecia.

The 'Demiurgi' are represented by another officiant, but a lesser figure than the Phylobasileis. Penelope speaks of heralds as δημιοεργοί (*Od.* 19.135). This is an extension of normal usage, for heralds go abroad not to exercise a needed skill, but to convey important messages. Penelope's words are memorable: it is her first encounter with Odysseus. At the Synoecia a herald stood upon a stone in the old agora and cried, 'Come hither, all ye hosts!' In the Solonian calendar he is mentioned after the Phylobasileis, receiving a lesser perquisite on both days of the biennial celebration. In [Aristotle] the herald's cry becomes Theseus' proclamation. It also gives rise to another story current in the fourth century, of Solon's masquerading as a herald.

It is true that in [Aristotle's] day a herald was not a craftsman in any proper sense. Yet the herald of the Synoecia looked like a craftsman, since he wore a leather cap. The cap goes back to very early days, when the festival was a muster under arms, and it was worn by every soldier. In military use it soon gave way to the metal helmet,[172] but for the herald it was retained as ritual attire. Solon, in order to summon the Athenians to war, goes to the agora, puts on a leather cap, and mounts the herald's stone. He then recites his poem on Salamis; in another version, a herald recites it for him.[173] In the actual poem, Solon describes himself as a herald, the starting-point for the story. To don the cap and mount the stone is to

---

172 See Lamer, *RE* 11.2 (1922) 2493 s.v. Κυνέη.
173 Dem. 19 *De Fals. Leg.* 251–6; Plut. *Sol.* 8.1–2. Demosthenes says πιλίδιον λαβὼν περὶ τὴν κεφαλήν, Plutarch πιλίδιον περιθέμενος. Cf. Cic. *De Off.* 1.30, 108; Justin 2.7.9–11; Paus. 1.40.5; Polyaenus 1.20.1; Diog. Laert. 1.46. In Diogenes Laertius, Solon reads his poem 'through a herald.'

become the herald of the Synoecia, who summons the people to muster under arms.[174]

The story keeps its full meaning only when the cap is understood as a military emblem. It is so understood in the earliest allusion to the story, by Demosthenes in the year 343. Solon and his stirring poems are contrasted with Aeschines, a self-styled patriot who puts a leather cap upon his head and goes round denouncing others – making war on them, as it were.[175] It is a perversion of the story, probably a rather late one, to say that in pretending to be a herald, Solon was also feigning madness, and that the cap was intended as a plaster for a sore head.[176]

The leather cap was also shown or named in Spartan ritual to signify a muster under arms, as we see from the story of the Partheniae. These sturdy youths, having just come of age, are bent on revolution. In the version of Antiochus of Syracuse, their leader is to give the signal by putting on a leather cap at the festival Hyacinthia; but the plot is completely foiled when the herald forbids him to put on a leather cap. In the version of Ephorus, the signal is for the Partheniae to 'raise a Laconian cap in the agora,' but the herald forestalls them by crying, 'Ye who are about to raise the

174 For the phratries as military units, cf. Andrewes, *Hermes* 89 (1961) 129–40. In Homer they are a novel form of organization, mentioned only twice (*Il.* 2.362, 9.63), but we should observe that on both occasions the narrative has already shown us a general muster of the army. In Book 2 and again in Book 9 all the men are summoned 'to an agora' to be addressed by the chiefs. 'They filed into an agora in companies,' ἐστιχόωντο ἰλαδὸν εἰς ἀγορήν (2.93–4), an expression as unique as 'phratry.' 'Nine' heralds to form them up are also unique (2.96–7), and recall the nine tents in which Spartan phratries are brigaded at the Carneia. Thersites as an ordinary soldier says in effect that wars are won by soldiers and not by generals (2.237–8). Furthermore, in the usual story of Thersites that the *Iliad* presupposes, satisfaction for his death is sought by Diomedes as a virtual phratry brother, and a settlement is reached on Lesbos, which has a month Phratrius, and Achilles sacrifices to Apollo and Artemis and Leto as virtual phratry gods; cf. *Phoenix* 43 (1989) 263–4. It is not only in vocabulary that the epic gives evidence of social change.

175 It is sometimes held, e.g., by Piccirilli on Plut. *Thes.* 8.1, that even in Demosthenes the cap may signify madness. On this view, Demosthenes accuses Aeschines of feigning madness while advocating policy.

176 So Plutarch. Cicero, Justin, Polyaenus, and Diogenes Laertius speak of his feigning madness, and Justin (or rather Trogus) also thinks of the cap: *deformis habitu more vaecordium*. Demosthenes may have contributed unwittingly when he transferred his scorn from Aeschines to the cap, calling it πιλίδιον, 'a wee leather cap.' This is just the term for medicinal plasters to the head (Pl. *Resp.* 3, 406 D). In later times the story would be best known through Demosthenes' allusion; R.A. Pack, *The Greek and Latin Literary Texts from Greco-Roman Egypt*² nos. 291–8, lists eight papyrus copies of *De Falsa Legatione*.

cap, leave the agora.'[177] Antiochus and Ephorus presuppose the same piece of ritual, but one cannot be sure what it was exactly. Perhaps the young men were told by the herald to form up for parade at a separate location. We should also glance at the Roman *pilleus*. The 'cap of liberty' derives from the soldier's leather cap, and has a large place in public ceremony. Under the Republic, even under the early Empire, it often stands for political rather than civil freedom, for freedom from foreign domination or freedom from tyranny – as when citizens returning from captivity march with the cap in the triumphal procession, or when it is carried or worn after the death of Caesar and Nero.[178] This use explains why it is worn by emancipated slaves and by revellers at the Saturnalia; the reverse development is not credible. Two aetiologies in Livy show that the cap was worn in assembly, as at Athens and Sparta; they also suggest that the custom was borrowed from Greece.

As Lucumo arrives at Rome by way of the hill Janiculum, an eagle lifts the *pilleus* from his head, then restores it (1.34.8–9).[179] The omen points to the social organization introduced by the Etruscan dynasty: the centuriate assembly for enrolling and mustering soldiers. The cap was either worn in this assembly, or removed at a given moment, as at Sparta; it was undoubtedly worn by the watch posted on Janiculum while the assembly met.[180] Lucumo is half Greek, and the Etruscans transmitted Greek culture to Rome.

Again, Livy tells how the battle of Beneventum in 214 BC was won by a levy of Roman slaves; all the details, such as valiant slaves taking heads as trophies, are fantastic (24.14–16). It is easy to see that the slaves and their conduct and their reward have been entirely deduced from a

177 Str. 6.3.2, pp. 278–9 (Antiochus *FGrHist* 555 F 13). Str. 6.3.3, pp. 279–80 (Ephorus *FGrHist* 70 F 216); Polyaenus 2.14.2. In Antiochus it is περιθέσθαι κυνῆν; in Ephorus, ἆραι πῖλον Λακωνικόν. The herald's cry is given verbally by Polyaenus, after Ephorus.

178 For a collection of instances, see S. Weinstock, *Divus Julius* (Oxford 1971) 136–7, 142, 144, 147–8. It is in effect the soldier's cap that was worn at auction by slaves sold without guarantee (Gel. 6.4). As Gellius says, following a learned source, the custom arose when prisoners of war were offered for sale: i.e., the *pilleus* of a captured soldier served to indicate his origin.

179 Tanaquil tells her husband to expect a high calling, since the omen comes from the sky and fixes on his head, a man's highest part. This proves that structuralism was not invented yesterday, but fails to explain why the head-gear is precisely a *pilleus*. Ogilvie *ad loc.* thinks of the *apex* as a priestly hat, and hence of the *rex sacrorum* as a virtual king. But the *apex*, being worn by many Etruscan and Roman priests, could not by itself identify the *rex sacrorum*; nor was there any reason to link this office with the advent of the Etruscan kings.

180 For the watch, T. Mommsen, *Römisches Staatsrecht*[3] (Leipzig 1887) 3.1.387.

commemorative painting in the shrine of Jupiter *libertas* on the Aventine. As described by Livy, it showed men wearing caps and feasting; some of the celebrants reclined, others stood and ministered. That is, they are all citizen soldiers; those who minister, according to the custom we observed at Athens, are newly enrolled youths. Jupiter *libertas* is Zeus *eleutherios*, and the ritual like the god was presumably adopted from Syracuse or Tarentum.

In sum, the herald of the Synoecia wore a leather cap, and it was subject to misunderstanding. In [Aristotle's] scheme, it served to show that the herald was a craftsman, and hence that the class of craftsmen were entitled to the flattering name 'Demiurgi.'

Such then are the occupational classes which [Aristotle], in the light of Aristotelian and other theory, deduced from the ritual of the Synoecia. Unlike the twelvefold division of Attica, they are quite unreal.

3

The Panathenaea, Northwest Athens, and the Enrolment of Citizens

Synopsis

In the early sixth century regional conflict broke out in Attica. The phratries as local associations must have played a large part in this conflict. Peisistratus was able to unite Attica once more; to do so, he placed the phratries under some constraint. Many citizens were enrolled through procedures that were called in question after the end of the tyranny, in the brief interval before demes superseded phratries. Philochorus quotes a law of Archaic aspect that compels each phratry to admit two new classes of persons.[1]

The changes were sanctified by ceremony. Peisistratus suspended the general reunion of phratry members at the Synoecia, in so far as it entailed a muster under arms. He introduced instead, at the Great Panathenaea, a procession of armed citizens which displayed the unitary strength of Athens. At the annual Panathenaea, young men were enrolled as citizens at the city centre: on the night before, they swore an oath of loyalty in the sanctuary of Aglaurus, then raised the paean on the Acropolis. When the Great Panathenaea came round, they bore arms with other citizens.

While Attica was at peace, the city of Athens grew and prospered. A large tract was reserved for the new Agora, and new offices of government were installed on the west side. The whole northwest sector was developed, and enclosed by a city wall. This change is likewise reflected in the Panathenaea; the northwest sector now becomes the setting for both the procession and the torch-race. The processioners formed up beside the northwest gate at a new muster-ground, the Leocoreium. They

---

1 [Arist.] *Ath.* 13.5; Phot., Suda *s.v.* ὀργεῶνες (Philochorus *FGrHist* 328 F 35a).

paraded across the Agora and ascended the Acropolis by a new ramp at the west. The torch-race was run from the Academy through the northwest gate to the west side of the Acropolis. Most of the route had long been used for the ritual fire-bringing of potters and smiths. But the Academy precinct and the termini of the racetrack were newly embellished by the tyrants.

We shall take the following points in order: the enlargement of the festival program; northwest Athens; the processional route; the Leocoreium; the facilities for the torch-race; the *pannychis* and the enrolment of young men; the armed processioners. (See map 5.)

The Enlargement of the Festival Program

The fourth-yearly celebration of Athens' Panathenaic festival, with athletic and equestrian games and a great procession, was already renowned in the second half of the sixth century. Peisistratus and his sons are generally given credit, and reasonably so. It may be doubted, however, whether their contribution to the festival has been correctly identified. The date 566–565 is handed down for the establishment of the games,[2] and the earliest prize amphorae cannot be much later.[3] A large temple of Athena was built on the Acropolis in the early sixth century, perhaps in the years round 570.[4] Behind these innovations, scholars often see the hand of Peisistratus. Yet the tyrant comes just a moment too late.

Peisistratus' first coup is reliably dated to 561–560, the archonship of Comeas.[5] Before this Athens was beset by faction, the usual prelude to tyranny. Such large projects as the Panathenaic games and the temple on the Acropolis required general support; we must infer that they did not advance the aims of any faction leader, such as Peisistratus. Had they done so, either they would have been opposed until Peisistratus as tyrant was able to carry them through or other faction leaders would have come forward as equal sponsors. But clearly there is no warrant for supposing

---

2 Euseb. *Can. a.* 566–565; Marcellin. *Vit. Thuc.* 2–4 (Pherecydes *FGrHist* 3 F 2). Cf. T.J. Cadoux, *JHS* 68 (1948) 104.

3 Cf. J.A. Davison, *JHS* 78 (1958) 26–9 = *From Archilochus to Pindar* (London 1968) 35–8; P.E. Corbett, *JHS* 80 (1960) 57–8; J. Boardman, *Athenian Black Figure Vases* (London 1974) 167–8; Kyle, *Athletics* 34–5.

4 W.H. Plommer, *JHS* 80 (1960) 127–59; I. Beyer, *ArchAnz* 1974.639–51, 1977.44–84; T.L. Shear, Jr., in *Athens Comes of Age: From Solon to Salamis* (Princeton 1978) 2–3, 12.

5 [Arist.] *Ath.* 14.1; Marm. Par. *FGrHist* 239 A 40; Plut. *Sol.* 32.3. Cf. Cadoux, *JHS* 68 (1948) 104–8.

that the Panathenaic games were conjured up by a prospective tyrant.[6] The Pythian, Isthmian, and Nemean games had been founded not many years before;[7] now the fashion came to Athens.

It is true that a scholiast on Aristeides says precisely, 'Peisistratus created the Great (Panathenaea).'[8] The fourth-yearly celebration is here distinguished from the annual one, founded by Erichthonius. Another scholiast gives a full account, after the Aristotelian *Peplus*, of the mythical origins of the Panathenaea and other ancient agonistic festivals,[9] so that the distinction between the annual and the fourth-yearly celebrations has been added as a corollary to this account. It was doubtless prompted by the story that Peisistratus caused the Homeric poems to be recited in a proper form at the fourth-yearly Panathenaea (and perhaps also at the fourth-yearly Brauronia); for this story, as elaborated in the doctrine of Peisistratus' 'recension,' was widely current in later times.[10] The scholium must not be conflated with the tradition that the games were established in 566–565.

Peisistratus is more likely to be responsible for the general dimensions of public festivity, notably the great procession. The procession and the games took place in different quarters. Then as later, the Stadium for athletic events was probably beside the hill Ardettus, southeast of Athens; the Hippodrome was at Phalerum.[11] But the procession went through the northwest sector of the city, starting from a gate in the wall, which was later the Dipylon, and crossing the Agora, and finally ascending the Acropolis by the ramp on the west side. After sacrifice on the Acropolis, the

6 Jacoby, n. 2 to Ister *FGrHist* 334 F 4, objects as I do to the usual notion, but spoils the effect by suggesting that the games were established by aristocrats in order to counter 'the agitation of Peisistratos.'

7 Admittedly, the Pythian games of Sicyon were instituted or enlarged by the tyrant Cleisthenes (schol. Pind. *Nem.* 9 inscr., 20, 25b). His action was quite notorious, as may be seen from Hdt. 5.67. Adrastus as a 'hero' goes with Apollo's spring festival at Sicyon (as also with the corresponding rite at Argos), and was diminished when the musical contests of the festival gave way to athletic games; see *Dining in a Classical Context*, ed. W.J. Slater (Ann Arbor 1991) 26–8.

8 Schol. Arist. *Panath.* 362, 3.323 Dindorf: τὰ δὲ μεγάλα Πεισίστρατος ἐποίησεν.

9 Schol. Arist. *ibid.* ([Arist.] fr. 637 Rose³).

10 So Jacoby, n. 1 to Ister *FGrHist* 334 F 4. For the development of the story, see R. Janko, *The Iliad: A Commentary* vol. 4 (Cambridge 1992) 29–32. Hesychius *s.v.* Βραυρωνίοις tells of 'rhapsodes' reciting the *Iliad* at Brauron; this may be part of the improvement ascribed to Peisistratus by Photius *s.v..* Βραυρωνία (ed. Theodoridis, 1982).

11 For the Stadium, see Kyle, *Athletics* 94–5; as to the proposed location on the Pnyx, n. 91 on the Synoecia; for the Hippodrome, n. 24 on the Olympieia. Steph. Byz. *s.v.* Ἐχελίδαι says that the athletic contests of the Panathenaea were conducted here, i.e., at or near the Hippodrome; but this is doubtless a mistake. For games in the Agora, see below.

meat was distributed, at least in the fourth century, in the Cerameicus, presumably the area just outside the Dipylon.[12] On the previous day the torch-race, a popular spectacle, was run from the Academy to the Acropolis: it too traversed the northwest sector. Such are the Great Panathenaea; the annual celebration has a smaller procession and sacrifice, and perhaps a torch-race.[13]

Northwest Athens

We have already seen that the northwest part of the city is not a usual setting for festivals (pp. 16–21). The Agora is bordered by government offices, and its shrines and ceremonies are modest. At the Dionysia, the statue of Dionysus was conveyed in procession from a temporary lodging at the Academy to Athens' theatre on the south side of the Acropolis; but since this festival is no earlier than the second half of the sixth century, the route may well have been suggested by the business of the Panathenaea.[14] At the Olympieia, a cavalry parade started from the Dipylon, as did the Panathenaic procession; but since the rest of the festival (an ancient one) took place at the Olympieium in southeast Athens, and even farther off, at the Hippodrome, we may suppose that the route of the parade has been extended to the northwest. At the Epitaphia, sacrifice was offered, and games were probably conducted, in the public cemetery on the Academy road; but again the cemetery is no earlier than the late sixth century. Finally, half a dozen festivals included torch-races, which were perhaps always run over the same track, from the Academy to the Acropolis or thereabouts; but the Panathenaic torch-race will be the model for most of the others.

---

12 *Hesperia* 28 (1959) 239–47 and *IG* 2² 334 (337/6–330/29 BC) B 24–5 (*LSCG* 33; C.J. Schwenk, *Athens in the Age of Alexander* [Chicago 1985] no. 17): at the Lesser Panathenaea, the meat will be distributed in [Κεραμεικῶ]ι – a nearly certain restoration – 'as at the other distributions of meat.' It is understandable that the deme Scambonidae preferred to conduct its own distribution in the deme agora: *IG* 1³ 244 A 19–21. The road outside the Dipylon has post-holes along the edge, whether for structures at the Panathenaea or at the public funeral: R. Stupperich, *Staatsbegräbnis und Privatgrabmal im klassischen Athen* (Münster 1977) 1.32, 2.26 n. 2; C. Clairmont, *Patrios Nomos* (Oxford 1983) 1.36, 2.263–4 n. 44. Plommer, *Gnomon* 50 (1978) 663, suggests that post-holes on the site of the Pompeium served for the Panathenaic distribution, but the archaeological dating is too early.

13 The matter of the torch-race is unclear: for opinions, Deubner, *Att. Feste* 24, 212; L. Ziehen, *RE* 18.3 (1949) 459, 487–8 *s.v.* Panathenaia; J.K. Davies, *JHS* 87 (1967) 37; Simon, *Festivals* 64.

14 It is usually thought that the city Dionysia were instituted by the tyrants, but W.R. Connor, *ClMed* 40 (1989) 7–32, has argued for the first years of the democracy.

We have also seen that two festivals are likely to be early and proper to the northwest sector: the Promethia and the Chalceia. Though details of both are wholly obscure, they plainly belong to potters and smiths respectively, the denizens of the Cerameicus, 'Potters' Quarter.' Prometheus is honoured at the Academy; Athena and Hephaestus, the deities of the Chalceia, both there and on the hill overlooking the Agora. They are all associated with a ceremonial fire-bringing, and it must have been the custom from of old to fetch new fire each year from the Academy to the craftsmen's quarter, probably to the hill-top shrine. The original fire-bringing need not have been a torch-race; indeed there is reason to think that torch-races came to Athens from abroad, together with the fire-god Hephaestus. The Promethia and the Chalceia have helped to inspire the arrangements of the Panathenaea.

It is urged by some, notably the Agora excavators, that the area of the Agora was traditionally used for festival games.[15] The argument, as it emerges from several expositions, may be summarized as follows.

Burials were made in the area for a very long time, until the practice finally stopped about 600 BC. In early days, burials were often accompanied by funeral games; chariot races were especially favoured, to judge from Geometric vases; the vases are found as offerings in Agora burials. Some of the Agora burials, moreover, may have given rise to hero cult: certain caches of offerings, certain small shrines in the Agora are interpreted as hero cult inspired by the discovery or the memory of ancient burials. Games would then be regularly celebrated as an element of hero cult; a racetrack in Corinth, on the presumed site of the agora, was associated with hero cult by the excavator there. Such games prepared the way for the Great Panathenaea as an agonistic festival uniting the whole community. Perhaps the Agora continued to be the setting of the Panathenaic games right down to the construction of a proper stadium in the Lycurgan period. In any case, in the late fifth century foot races were apparently run over a track in the Agora, and in the middle Hellenistic period the *apobatēs* event is thought to have terminated at the Eleusinium nearby. Victories in equestrian events, not necessarily at the Panathenaea, were sometimes commemorated by dedications placed at the northwest corner of the Agora.

The hypothesis of early games in the Agora cannot be tested by direct evidence; any installation will have been too slight to be traced

15 Travlos, *Poleodomikē exelixis* 36–40, and *Pictorial Dict.* 2; H.A. Thompson, *ArchAnz* 1961.224–31, and EpistEpetAth 14 (1963–4) 276–84, and *Agora Guide³* 104–6; Thompson and Wycherley, *Agora of Athens* 121, 193–4; Wycherley, *Stones of Athens* 36; Kolb, *Agora* 24–5, 52; Camp, *Ath. Agora* 46; Kyle, *Athletics* 57–64, 93–4.

archaeologically. So the hypothesis depends entirely on the chain of inference presented above. Every link is frail.

If funeral games were celebrated at the burial site, then they took place on every side of the city, along all the roads where burials were made. But a regular setting was doubtless adopted; when the body was cremated beforehand, games and burial were easily separated, and easily deferred until a convenient or statutory time. The festival Epitaphia as an ancient duty of the Polemarch also calls for a regular setting;[16] yet this was not the Academy road, which must have been largely free of important burials in the late sixth century, in order to be chosen for the public cemetery. We should look rather to the southeast sector, where settlement was concentrated in the Dark Age; the only undoubted Stadium and Hippodrome lay in this direction. The most likely setting for early funeral games and for the early Epitaphia is the road to Phalerum.

'Hero cult' as an intermediate factor between funeral games and festival games is only another hypothesis, and one that seems ill considered. The ancient view of agonistic festivals as originating in the death and funeral of heroes (or of giants, or monsters, or fallen gods) is plainly a matter of aetiology; 'heroes' as a class are a matter of aetiology, men of old who are said to be commemorated by games, blood-offerings, or other peculiar rites.[17] In other words, the ritual is prior to the belief, at least in early days. To say that games must have been conducted in the Agora so as to honour 'heroes' is to argue in a circle. As for Corinth's racetrack, the principal evidence for 'hero cult' is a deposit of Hellenistic figurines in a water basin – a momentary episode in the long history of this racetrack. The case is not even relevant until it is shown that this part of Corinth was the agora: both the terrain and the remains are unpromising.[18]

Finally, although it seems established that athletic and equestrian events were sometimes held in the Agora, this is not the place for the whole program of Panathenaic games. Furthermore, it is obvious that the use of the Agora for certain events need not be due to ancient custom. The Agora came to be a favourite vantage point for watching the Panathenaic

---

16 *Ath.* 3.3, 58.1: Boedromia and Epitaphia as the Polemarch's 'ancestral' duties.

17 Something more will be said of 'hero cult' apropos of the Parparonia and of a festival at Phigaleia.

18 For the 'hero cult' at Corinth, see O. Broneer, *Hesperia* 11 (1942) 128–61; for further investigation of the racetrack, C.K. Williams, II, *Hesperia* 50 (1981) 1–33. Williams does not dispute the hero cult (pp. 16, 21). That Corinth's agora lay beneath the Roman Forum was once a natural assumption, but is now virtually disproved. So Williams, *Hesperia* 39 (1970) 32–9, and 50 (1981) 21; *contra*, Thompson *apud* Kolb, *Agora* 81 n. 16.

procession, whether from the stoas or from grandstands erected by the road.[19] When the facilities and perhaps the spectators were already on hand, it would be natural to conduct such events as were suited to the time and place. Perhaps they were events of the same day as the procession and the banquet, 28 Hecatombaeon. The *apobatēs* event presumably took place on this day, since the Parthenon frieze shows the participants joining the procession.

There is then no reason to suppose that funeral or festival games were somehow native to the Agora. Apart from games, it is agreed by almost everyone that the Agora had no public use until the early sixth century.[20] At this time private use ends: burials are discontinued and wells are filled up. The early buildings on the west side, though very indistinct, can still be recognized as predecessors of the public buildings of the Classical period: dining and working quarters for councillors or other officials; shrines of Meter, Apollo, and Zeus; other dining quarters; the small and simple stoa that was later reserved for the Basileus. Within the sixth century, the dating and sequence of the various elements are often in doubt. But it is clear that the work of government greatly increased in the second half of the sixth century, the time of Peisistratus and his sons. Peisistratus is very likely responsible for the stoa and hence for the *kyrbeis*, the second publication of Solon's laws. As the *kyrbeis* in the stoa supersede the *axones* in the Prytaneium, this is the moment when government is effectively transferred from the old agora to the new.[21]

The Agora area was open ground when it was first set aside for public use; so the northwest sector was not then much developed. We may assume that, as government devolved upon the Agora, other activities quickly

---

19 POxy 2889 lines 1–16 (Aeschin. *Milt. init.*); Ath. 4.64, 167 F (Hegesander *FHG* 4.415 fr. 8). Aeschines evokes 'the Great Panathenaea' of either 414 or 410 – not of 411, as H. Patzer has it, *ZPE* 15 (1974) 274–5 – when Socrates, Euripides, and Hagnon father of Theramenes 'were sitting in the stoa of Zeus *eleutherios*' to watch the procession. Hegesander speaks of an occasion in the third century (under 'Antigonus') when a wooden platform was erected 'at the Herms,' i.e., near the Stoa of the Basileus at the northwest corner; it must be the Great Panathenaea (Athenaeus says only 'at the Panathenaea'), inasmuch as the man who thus provides for his mistress is a Hipparch, concerned with equestrian games; possibly these games were also conducted in the Agora.

20 For the Agora in the sixth century, see Shear in *Athens Comes of Age* 4–8; Camp, *Ath. Agora* 37–57. No one but Kolb, *Agora* 23–6, has argued that the Agora site was used as such before the sixth century.

21 Cf. *Historia* 35 (1986) 168–76.

started up nearby. The bustling commerce which we hear of later probably began in the sixth century.[22]

It thus appears that the Panathenaic festival was expanded by Peisistratus so as to give a share, a very large one, to the newest part of Athens.

The Processional Route

The Panathenaic procession went through the northwest sector up to the ramp at the west side of the Acropolis. The broad earthen ramp is chiefly meant for the procession; until it was built, the approach from the west was by a path beside the southwest bastion. The archaeological dating points to Peisistratus. A house that was demolished to make way for the ramp yielded pottery of the second quarter of the sixth century.[23]

Where, in the tyrants' day, did the procession start? A normal starting-point would be the edge of the city, a gate in the city wall, if there was a wall – and Athens must have had a wall by this time; many lesser cities did.[24] If we can locate the starting-point of the procession, we shall know the line of the city wall at the northwest.

In later days, the procession started at the Pompeium, right inside the later wall and right between the Dipylon Gate and the Sacred Gate. This facility, an enclosed peristyle court with some adjacent dining-rooms, was not built until the end of the fifth century;[25] but the arrangement of the two gates implies that the ground had been used for the purpose since the Themistoclean wall was built.

For the wall before Themistocles, Thucydides is our principal authority. In describing the assassination of Hipparchus, he says that Hippias was outside the city gate in the Cerameicus, and that Hipparchus was inside (6.57.1, 3). The gate is referred to offhandedly, as if it were the same then as later. The building of the Themistoclean wall, on which Thucydides digresses, calls for mention of its predecessor. In 489, he says, very little was left of the earlier circuit (1.89.3; cf. Hdt. 9.13.2): to build another wall required a huge effort. We are further told that with the new wall, 'the

---

22 For trades and crafts in the area, see Wycherley, *Testimonia* 185–206 nos. 610–89; Thompson and Wycherley, *Agora of Athens* 170–3, 185–91.

23 E. Vanderpool in *PHOROS. Tribute to B.D. Meritt* (Locust Valley, N.Y. 1974) 157–9.

24 Cf. *ibid*. 156–60; Wycherley, *Stones of Athens* 9–11; F.E. Winter in *Studies Presented to E. Vanderpool* (Princeton 1982) 199–204.

25 The construction can be dated between 404, the razing of the Themistoclean wall, and ca. 393, the building of the Cononian wall: W. Hoepfner, *Das Pompeion* (Athens 1971) 34, 112, and A. Hönle, *ibid*. 240–5.

circuit was everywhere extended' (1.93.2). There may be some exaggeration in these words, for Thucydides is most insistent on the magnitude of the task and on the confidence and determination of the Athenians when they set about it. Or rather, there must be some exaggeration: at the southeast, the later wall ran about as close to the Olympieium as any earlier wall could have done.[26] In any case, the earlier wall had a considerable circuit.

Such are the *prima facie* indications that in 514 the procession was marshalled at about the same point as later, beside the Dipylon Gate. In spite of them, modern opinion holds that the procession started much closer to the Acropolis – in the Agora. If there was a wall, it ran close to the Agora. Hippias may have been just outside, or farther off, at the site of the Pompeium. On this view, the early Panathenaic procession was a short one. Moreover, the only level ground traversed by the procession was in the Agora itself; the slope to the Acropolis begins at the southeast corner. This is not an attractive reconstruction.

The Leocoreium

The question turns on the 'Leocoreium': on what it was, and where it was. We should consider the location first; for on this point there is broad agreement, but it is mistaken. The Leocoreium is thought to be somewhere in the Agora, probably on the north side; on the strength of this conviction the most diverse remains have been canvassed.[27]

Both Thucydides and [Aristotle] name the Leocoreium as the place where Hipparchus was engaged in marshalling the procession, or part of it. Herodotus too, without naming the Leocoreium, says that Hipparchus was so engaged.[28] Before they killed Hipparchus, the tyrannicides were stalking Hippias; but whereas Thucydides puts Hippias 'outside in the Cerameicus, as it is called' (6.57.1), [Aristotle] puts him on the Acropolis (*Ath.* 18.3). Thucydides is generally preferred,[29] and this is reasonable; in any case, we need only inquire how he envisaged the action, not whether he was

26 For the line of wall here, see Travlos, *Pictorial Dict.* 160, 172, 402.

27 Judeich, *Topogr.*[2] 338–9; Travlos, *Poleodomikē exelixis* 41, and *Pictorial Dict.* 3, 578; O. Broneer, *ArchEph* 1960 [1965] 62–7; S. Brunnsåker, *OpAth* 8 (1975) 77–86; J.S. Boersma, *Athenian Building Policy from 561–560 to 405–404 BC* (Groningen 1970) 205; Thompson and Wycherley, *Agora of Athens* 121–3; Thompson, *Agora Guide*[3] 87–90, and in *Athens Comes of Age* 101–2; Kron, *Phylenheroen* 199–200; S.N. Koumanoudes, *ArchEph* 1976 pp. 195–7; Wycherley, *Stones of Athens* 63–4; Kolb, *Agora* 47–52.

28 Thuc. 6.57.3; [Arist.] *Ath.* 18.3; Hdt. 5.56.2.

29 So, e.g., C.W. Fornara, *Historia* 17 (1968) 408–9; K.J. Dover, *HCT* 4.334; Rhodes, *Comm.* 231.

right about the actual event. According to Thucydides, Hippias was like-wise marshalling the procession, placing the different elements in order (6.57.1).[30] Thinking that they were betrayed to Hippias, the tyrannicides, 'just as they were, rushed inside the gates and fell upon Hipparchus at the Leocoreium, as it is called' (6.57.3). When the news was brought to Hippias, he did not come at once to the scene, but took the precaution of disarming the armed processioners (6.58).

Thucydides makes us see that Hippias and Hipparchus were stationed close together, at the starting-point of the procession; but the city wall was between them. With all the crush and hubbub of the holiday, the assassination inside the wall was not remarked by those outside. It is not remotely plausible that, while providing this full description, Thucydides had in mind a different line of wall, and a different starting-point for the Panathenaic procession, from those familiar in his own day.

Phanodemus, as rendered by the lexica, situates the Leocoreium 'in the middle of the Cerameicus,' ἐν μέσωι τῶι Κεραμεικῶι.[31] To be sure, the Agora is sometimes called 'the Cerameicus' – but only by late and learned writers, from Poseidonius onwards, who reserve the term 'agora' for the old agora. Neither Phanodemus nor the lexica would use 'Cerameicus' to denote the new Agora. Here 'the Cerameicus' is plainly the old Potters' Quarter, the district northwest of the Agora, bisected by the city wall. Phanodemus doubtless spoke of the Leocoreium while recounting the as-sassination.[32] In respect of the location he agrees exactly with Thucydides.

The Cerameicus district had a bad reputation, as the haunt of prosti-tutes.[33] The Leocoreium, as a landmark in the Cerameicus, shared this repu-tation. Alciphron, who tells us so (3.2.1), depends on fourth-century comedy and the orators,[34] and in fact a speech of Demosthenes shows the Leocoreium in this light. The speaker, a young man, was injured in a drunken brawl at

---

30 Dover, HCT 4.334, speaks as if a distinction were to be made, in the several accounts of the assassination, between 'dispatching' (πέμπειν, ἀποστέλλειν) and 'marshalling' (κοσμεῖν, διακοσμεῖν) the procession. The former is only a more general term; the latter is used by Thucydides of both Hippias (6.57.1) and Hipparchus (1.20.2).

31 Harpocr. s.v. Λεωκόριον (Phanodemus FGrHist 325 F 8); cf. Phot., Suda s.v., schol. Dem. 54 Conon 7.

32 The citation is from Book 9, too far on for Leos and his daughters, even if this tale were known to Phanodemus; cf. Jacoby ad loc.

33 Ath. 6.72, 258 C (Alexis fr. 206 Kassel and Austin); Alciphron 2.22.2, 3.12.3, 28.3; schol. Pl. Parm. 127 C; schol. Ar. Eq. 772; etc.

34 Menander's dyskolos mentions τὸ τοῦ λεώ, together with any 'stoa,' as a place for idlers (line 174). The Leocoreium has been generally thought of (cf. Sandbach ad loc.), but perhaps this is only a periphrasis for (ἡ) λεωφόρος. 'Never tread the highways,' said Pythagoras (Vorsokr 58 C 4, 6).

the Leocoreium. He presents himself, however, as a very decent, sober, quiet young man; lest we jump to conclusions about the brawl, he explains at great length how he happened to be waylaid just at the Leocoreium. Scholars have failed to grasp the purport of his explanation. It is largely through this misunderstanding that the Leocoreium has been sought in the Agora.

Young Ariston (in the company of one friend) was assaulted by Conon and his son and several others, all of them insolent ruffians.[35] Earlier in the evening, Conon's son, already drunk, passed by Ariston in the street, 'at the Leocoreium, near Pythodorus' place,' κατὰ τὸ Λεωκόριον, ἐγγὺς τῶν Πυθοδώρου, and bawled an insult, and went off mumbling to himself as a drunken man will do.[36] His destination was a drinking party at a house in Melite; here he gave the scent to Conon and others who followed him back to Ariston; it was 'just about at the Leocoreium,' κατ' αὐτό πως τὸ Λεωκόριον, that they pounced upon their victim. Ariston calls witnesses to the assault; they will have testified as well to the first encounter, that drunken shout and mumbling. Thus the Leocoreium is the scene of all the action. But according to Ariston, this was pure chance.

It was his custom, he says, 'to stroll at evening in the Agora,' περιπατοῦντος, ὡς εἰώθειν, ἑσπέρας ἐν ἀγορᾶι μου. He was so occupied when Conon's son passed him by at the Leocoreium. Afterwards Conon's son was leading the other assailants to the Agora, ἐπορεύετ' εἰς τὴν ἀγοράν, and Ariston and his friend were heading back from the Pherrhephattium, ἀναστρέφουσιν ἀπὸ τοῦ Φερρεφαττίου, when the assault took place at the Leocoreium. Admittedly, one might infer from the first stage of this narrative that the Leocoreium was right in the Agora. But the second stage shows that 'strolling in the Agora' must include getting there and going away again. Moreover, Conon's son needs some time to reach the house in Melite, to persuade the drinkers that there is sport to be had, and to return with them.[37]

---

35 Dem. 54 *Conon* 7–10. The tombstone of Conon's son, set up by the father, was reported by Pittakys (*IG* 2² 7103); no doubt he drank himself to death. Elsewhere Pittakys cited, from the vicinity of the Agora, a most enigmatic fragment mentioning the Leocoreium: Wycherley, *Testimonia* p. 113. This is sometimes held up as further evidence for the Agora location.

36 'Pythodorus' place,' τὰ Πυθοδώρου, might be the establishment of Pythodorus ὁ σκηνίτης, an associate of Pasion in the 390s, especially if this associate had a grandson with the same name and the same connections: for the proposed affiliation, Davies, *Ath. Prop. Fam.* 430, 481. Harpocration says of Pythodorus 'Who-keeps-a-stall' that he was *not* so called 'as a man of the agora,' ὡς ἀγοραῖος, inasmuch as goods were sold in stalls everywhere (*s.v.* σκηνίτης). 'Pythodorus' place' clearly does not belong in the Agora we know.

37 'He went on towards Melite further up,' παρῆλθε πρὸς Μελίτην ἄνω (Dem. 54 *Conon* 7). The deme Melite was a large area west of the Agora; 'further up' will mean further south, to higher ground.

The Pherrhephattium, where Ariston turns about, must lie within the Agora; Hesychius has an entry Φερεφάττιον· τόπος ἐν ἀγορᾶι, perhaps deriving from a note on our passage. It is almost certainly the shrine at the northwest corner that was first uncovered in 1971.[38] This shrine has indeed been identified by some as the Leocoreium,[39] but its nature as well as its location imposes a different interpretation. A small square precinct wall encloses a rocky outcrop in the ground; right beside it is a well, with a well-head as carefully constructed as the precinct. The well and the precinct were installed at the same time, in the late fifth century, and were used together: offerings of the same kind were thrown into the well and left in the precinct.[40] The pottery and other articles show that a female deity is honoured. It is a deity of the underworld, for the pottery includes white-ground lecythi, otherwise used as grave offerings. The well also yielded curse-tablets and a lead tablet with a repeated ritual cry, BAXXIOE.[41] Even without Ariston, one would think of Persephone.

The precinct and the well are right beside the Panathenaic Way at the corner of the Agora, suitably placed to mark the limit of one's stroll. It thus appears that Ariston went no farther than the northwest corner: he strolled along the Panathenaic Way from a point near the Dipylon Gate, the Leocoreium, and then back again. If this seems a little short of 'strolling in the Agora,' remember that Ariston was at the Leocoreium both earlier and later in the evening, to be shouted at and to be assaulted. These matters of record dictate the length of the stroll.

It is interesting to see what happened to Ariston. His assailants tripped him up and threw him 'into the mire,' εἰς τὸν βόρβορον. He was so beslimed that he had to be carried to a bathhouse to be sluiced off before a doctor could inspect his injuries. Such mire was hardly to be found in the Agora. But the Eridanus river ran out between the Dipylon Gate and the Sacred Gate; close beside it on the south ran the city's main sewer.[42]

The latest contemporary source to mention the Leocoreium is Hegesias of Magnesia, in the early third century.[43] He trumpets the great sights of Athens: the Acropolis and the trident mark; Eleusis and the Mysteries; 'there the Leocoreium, here the Theseium.' Hegesias was a silly writer, but if these words are to make even a minimum of sense, the Leocoreium cannot

38 T.L. Shear, Jr., *Hesperia* 42 (1971) 126–34, 360–9.
39 So Thompson, Wycherley, Koumanoudes, and Kolb (n. 27 above). Kron is sceptical; so is Camp, *Ath. Agora* 78–9.
40 It seems more likely that offerings were thrown directly into the well than that they were periodically removed from the precinct and discarded here.
41 D.R. Jordan, *AJA* 90 (1986) 212.
42 Cf. *AR* 1983–84 pp. 9–10.
43 Str. 9.1.16, p. 396 (Hegesias *FGrHist* 142 F 24).

be some minor fixture in the Agora. The area of the Dipylon Gate, however, where processions are marshalled, might well be evoked in this context.

Of the sources who know the Leocoreium at first hand – Thucydides, [Aristotle], Demosthenes – none can be pressed to show what sort of place it was: an open area, or a building, or a complex of ground and buildings. It was not precisely the Pompeium or its site, for the names 'Leocoreium' and 'Pompeium' are used concurrently in the second half of the fourth century.[44] But it might be an area nearby, or an area which included the Pompeium.

Thus far the location. If we ask what the Leocoreium was, there is a most beguiling answer. It was a hero shrine of the three maiden daughters of Leos, who were sacrificed by their father, as an oracle required, to deliver Athens from a plague or famine. The earliest reference to the story, in the Demosthenic *Epitaphios*, does not mention the Leocoreium; but it is clearly implied in the phrase τὰς Λεὼ κόρας (Dem. 60 *Epit.* 29). All other sources for the story are very late: Pausanias and Aristeides and Aelian and several lexica and scholia.[45] Besides accounting for the name 'Leocoreium,' the story also makes a heroic paradigm for the *phylē* Leontis, first in the *Epitaphios* and again in Pausanias (1.5.2).

Everyone sees that the story is an aetiology: the name Λεωκόρειον is said to commemorate an event that is deduced from it, the fate of Λεὼ κόραι. And everyone is aware that the story very much resembles that of Erechtheus and his daughters, and that of Hyacinthus and his daughters; these two stories are both attached to a cult-site west of Athens, the shrine of the Ὑακινθίδες (a title which Euripides equates with the celestial Ὑάδες).[46] The similarity extends to the name 'Praxithea' for Erechtheus' wife and one of Leos' daughters. We may accordingly suspect that the story of Leos' daughters makes use of a narrative motif in order to explain a name, Leocoreium, of which the true meaning was forgotten.

It is sometimes maintained that the story of Leos' daughters comes first, and inspires the others; or that, whatever the relationship, the story is still significant for the true nature of the Leocoreium.[47] We shall then infer that heroines or chthonian deities were worshipped here or, at the least, that the Leocoreium was a shrine. The story, however, has every appearance of being a mere doublet. In the *Epitaphios* it comes soon after the story of Erechtheus' daughters, the paradigm for the *phylē* Erechtheis;[48]

44 'Pompeium': [Dem.] 34 *Phorm.* 39; *IG* 2² 1673 line 20 (327–326 BC).
45 For these, see Wycherley, *Testimonia* 108–13 nos. 317–38.
46 For the relationship between the two stories, see Wilamowitz, *Glaube* ² 1.104 n. 1.
47 So, e.g., Robert, *Heldensage* 141–2; Kron, *Phylenheroen* 196–8; Kolb, *Agora* 49–51.
48 Dem. 60 *Epit.* 27, 29, whence Diod. 17.15.2; cf. Cic. *De Nat. Deor.* 3.50.

for most of the *phylai*, the paradigms are very far-fetched, and can hardly be regarded as a traditional element of the funeral speech. There is nothing in any source to indicate where Leos belongs in Athenian history; we only hear of plague or famine, seemingly a variant for enemy attack, as in the story of Erechtheus' daughters. Furthermore, although the story leads up to the Leocoreium as a shrine or memorial, no detail is offered about the aspect or the location of the shrine, or about the manner of worship. Later sources knew the story only from such passing mention as we find in the *Epitaphios*; it had no place in tragedy or in Attic chronicles.

To explain 'Leocoreium' as commemorating Λεὼ κόραι was almost inevitable, since a hero Λεώς, or rather two such heroes, existed independently. A sacrifice for Leos of Agnus was recorded in the *axones*;[49] but Leos the eponym of Leontis was a different person, a reputed son of Orpheus, and father of a certain Cylanthus as well as of three daughters.[50] Any son of Orpheus belongs in the neighbourhood of Eleusis. In 357–356 the *epimeletai* of Leontis made a dedication to the eponym, which was reused in a building at Daphni.[51] The regulations of Scambonidae, a deme of Leontis, call for sacrifice to Leos by 'the demarch and the *hieropoioi*.' At this early date, ca. 460, a board of *hieropoioi*, otherwise unspecified, are likely to be those of Eleusis.[52] Thus the hero Leos who became the eponym of Leontis has nothing to do with the Leocoreium.[53]

We conclude that the story of Leos' daughters is worthless. The name 'Leocoreium' was altogether mysterious, and open to any plausible explanation.

Perhaps we can now do better with the name; a compound form like Λεωκόρειον should not be impenetrable.[54] The first element is likely to

---

49 Steph. Byz. *s.v.* 'Αγνοῦς (Solon fr. 83 Ruschenbusch). Cf. Plut. *Thes.* 13.2–3; schol. Eur. *Hipp.* 35 (Philochorus *FGrHist* 328 F 108).

50 Phot., Et. Magn. *s.v.* Λεωκόριον.

51 *IG* 2² 2818; cf. W.E. McLeod, *Hesperia* 18 (1959) 126. Kron, *Phylenheroen* 200–1, adduces other dedications of Leontis, but they are not informative.

52 *IG* 1³ 244 C 4–5; cf. *IG* 1³ 6 line 2, and K. Clinton, *AJP* 100 (1979) 3–4, 8–9. E. Kearns, in *Crux: Essays Presented to G.E.M. de Ste. Croix* (Exeter 1985) 195, and again *The Heroes of Attica* (BICS *Suppl.* 57, 1989) 86, 181, makes it a question whether the deme sacrifice was conducted at the Leocoreium.

53 Strictly, a *phylē* named for Λεώς should be Λεωΐς; cf. Μινωΐς from Μίνως, which in Attic is declined like Λεώς. No doubt the form Λεωντίς sounded better, as suggesting λέων. In the late fourth century, a victory dedication by the cavalry of Leontis displays a 'lion' in relief: *Hesperia* 40 (1971) 271–2, and pl. 57 c. Lead tokens of Leontis also have a lion's head or striding lion: Kron, *Phylenheroen* 194 n. 941.

54 Kron, *Phylenheroen* 197–8, gives a critique of several theories; she herself sides with the legend. One view derives the name from λεώς and κορεῖν 'sweep': to sweep the host

be λεώς 'host'; for a host is often marshalled by a leader, and Hipparchus was marshalling the Panathenaic procession. The word was recognized by ancient readers, though they personified it as a hero. The second element has hitherto defied interpretation. One expects it to match up with the marshalling of the host.

The regular word for 'marshall' is κοσμεῖν; it is used of Hipparchus and Hippias marshalling the Panathenaic procession. 'Marshaller(s) of the hosts' is a Homeric formula, κοσμήτορι/ε λαῶν. Similar phrases were traditional at Athens. The epigrams commemorating Eion and other Athenian victories speak of both κοσμητῆρα μάχης and κοσμητὰς πολέμου τ' ἀμφὶ καὶ ἠνορέης.[55] The chief ephebic supervisor is κοσμητής. Now in the word κόσμος the suffix -μος has been added to a root about which linguists are still doubtful.[56] The root also appears as κορ-. Hesychius has an entry κορμηταί· κοσμηταί. At Gortyn, κόρμος and πρόκορμος are the older forms of κόσμος and πρόκοσμος, civic magistrates.[57] The Cretan dialect is not otherwise given to rhotacism.

The old word νεωκόρος is also relevant, being used of one who 'adorns' a temple, another meaning of κοσμεῖν. To be sure, the title is generally taken as 'temple-sweeper'; there is a touching scene in Euripides' Ion to subserve this etymology (112–45, cf. 795). Sweeping, however, is a task much too trivial to produce a common title. The Suda insists on the correct meaning: ὁ τὸν ναὸν κοσμῶν καὶ εὐτρεπίζων· ἀλλ' οὐχ ὁ σαρῶν. The form κόρ-μος should convince us that this is an authentic definition, and not a lame attempt to enhance the dignity of a neōkoros.

The magistrates κόρμος and πρόκορμος are anticipated by a pair of officials in the Linear B tablets. The korete and porokorete (pl. koretere and porokoretere), i.e., κορητήρ and προκορητήρ, appear at different places and supply bronze and other commodities.[58] The agent suffix -τήρ is the same as in κοσμητήρ. Though the terms have puzzled experts, it seems reasonable to interpret them as 'marshaller' and 'deputy marshaller.'

The upshot then is that the root κορ- had about the same meaning as the derivative verb κοσμεῖν, and that Λεωκόρειον is the place for

---

is to purify them, and 'Leocoreium' is the place for doing it. This is only half right. Neither κορεῖν nor any of its compounds is ever used in a sense approaching 'purify.' To purify a host (typically an army) was an uncanny business that would not be done at the same time, or even in the same place, as the marshalling of the Panathenaic procession.

55 Aeschin. 3 Ctes. 185.
56 Frisk, Gr. etym. Wörterb. s.v. κόσμος; Chantraine, Dict. étym. s.v.
57 Guarducci, ICret 4 p. 31.
58 See J.T. Hooker, Linear B. An Introduction (Bristol 1980) 107 (bibliography), 110–11.

'marshalling the host.' The term is apt for the starting-point of the Panathenaic procession, which was meant to represent the whole citizen body; it would not be not apt for the starting-point of any lesser procession. But why is this ancient term attached to a site at the northwest? The earliest community was at the southeast; then a new centre was laid out east of the Acropolis. It was only in the time of Peisistratus that the northwest area was developed. Peisistratus must have transferred the name from some other quarter.

The Facilities for the Torch-race

Literary sources associate the tyrant family with the Academy and hence with the torch-race. 'Hipparchus' wall,' τὸ Ἱππάρχου τειχίον, was a byword for an expensive public project; the Suda and the paroemiographers explain that it was a wall 'round the Academy.'[59] A boundary stone of the Academy found *in situ* may be coeval with the wall-building or slightly later.[60] 'In front of the entrance to the Academy,' πρὸ δὲ τῆς εἰσόδου τῆς ἐς Ἀκαδημίαν, Pausanias saw an altar of Ἔρως, 'Desire,' bearing a dedication by Charmus the Polemarch, reputed to be both lover and father-in-law of Hippias.[61] As Pausanias came to the Academy by the road from the Dipylon, 'the entrance' must be the gate which gave on the road.

The altar of Eros is elsewhere said to be the starting-point of the Panathenaic torch-race, where the torches were lit.[62] Cleidemus quotes the epigram upon the altar: 'O Eros, god of various resource, to you Charmus

59 Suda s.v. τὸ Ἱππάρχου τειχίον; Zen. Ath. 2.13 = vulg. 6.29: Hipparchus built a wall περὶ τὴν Ἀκαδημίαν. Cf. W. Bühler, *Zenobii Athoi Proverbia* 4 (Göttingen 1982) 123–7. As Bühler says, the proverb arose at a time when tyrants were notorious for their monuments and their exactions; but the starting point is an actual wall built by Hipparchus. In place of the words quoted, a nonsense phrase, παρὰ τὴν Πυθίαν, appears in three late collections. As they all belong to one forlorn offshoot of the mediaeval vulgate, there is no possibility that they alone preserve an original reading, even if it were not nonsense. J.P. Lynch in *Studies Presented to S. Dow* (GRBS Monogr. 10, 1984) 173–9 attempts to defend παρὰ τὴν Πυθίαν as a *lectio difficilior* – which it is not, since Πυθία, Πύθια, Πύθιος, Πυθώ appear up and down the corpus of proverbs. Lynch bids us think of the 'Pythium,' τὸ Πύθιον, associated elsewhere with Hipparchus' father. The argument finally collapses on itself. For Lynch also postulates an 'oracle' which authorized the building of a wall: i.e., it is the literal Πυθία after all. How then do we deduce the 'Pythium'? Or any location?

60 *Deltion* 22 (1967) [1968] *Chron.* 46–9; *AAA* 1 (1968) 101–2: hόρος τές hεκαδεμείας. Cf. Travlos, *Pictorial Dict.* 42, 47; Wycherley, *Stones of Athens* 222–4.

61 Paus. 1.30.1. Cf. Plut. *Sol.* 1.7; Apul. *Plat.* 1.1; Ath. 13.12, 561 E; *id.* 13.89, 609 C-D (Cleidemus FGrHist 323 F 15 = Anticleides 140 F 6).

62 Schol. Pl. *Phaedr.* 231 E; cf. Plut. *Sol.* 1.7.

set up this altar at the shaded limits of the gymnasium.' It was predictably interpreted as the testimony of a gratified *erastēs*; Plutarch offers a confused variant in which Peisistratus is the *erastēs* and dedicates a statue instead of an altar. But Eros more truly evokes the torch-race, as we shall see in a moment.[63]

The altar of Eros at the Academy leads Pausanias to mention 'the altar in the city, of Opposite Desire, as it is called,' τὸν ἐν τῆι πόλει βωμὸν καλούμενον 'Αντέρωτος. This altar gave rise to an idle tale, told in slightly different versions by Pausanias and Aelian, about mismatched lovers who leapt to their death from the Acropolis.[64] In Aelian the affair is commemorated not by the altar but by a statue on the Acropolis which showed a boy holding a brace of cocks. We may infer that whereas the votive statue stood above, the altar stood below, so that both could be held to mark the lovers' leap.[65] The altars of Eros at the Academy and of Opposite Eros at the Acropolis may thus be the two termini of the Panathenaic torch-race.

Pausanias, however, says that the torch-race started from the altar of Prometheus within the Academy; he goes on to describe the race. Apollodorus, another firsthand authority, speaks of an altar of Hephaestus, an old one, within the Academy – 'in the precinct of the goddess,' i.e., Athena – and also of 'an ancient base at the entrance,' βάσις ἀρχαία κατὰ τὴν εἴσοδον, which showed in relief the two deities of fire, Prometheus and Hephaestus. 'Prometheus is placed first, and is the elder, with a sceptre in his right hand; Hephaestus is young, and placed second. And an altar common to both is rendered in relief on the base.'[66] Thus we see that the altar within the Academy could be assigned either to Prometheus, the older deity, or to Hephaestus, the newcomer.

There is still the contradiction about the starting-point of the race: either the altar of Prometheus or Hephaestus within the Academy (so Pausanias), or the altar of Eros at the entrance (so Plutarch and the scholiast to Plato).[67] The former is plainly appropriate. But the witnesses for the

---

63 Eros' epithet ποικιλομήχανος resembles other epithets applied to deities of consequence in early poetry: ποικιλομήτης (Zeus, Hermes), πολυμήχανος (Apollo), πολύμητις (Hephaestus).

64 Paus. 1.30.1; Suda *s.v.* Μέλητος (Ael. fr. 69 Hercher).

65 Judeich, *Topogr.*² 284, places the altar too on the Acropolis, beside the statue.

66 Paus. 1.30.2; schol. Soph. *Oed. Col.* 56 (Apollodorus *FGrHist* 244 F 147).

67 Deubner, *Att. Feste* 211–12, holds that the starting-point was changed, as from the altar of Prometheus to the altar of Eros, for the Panathenaic torch-race, but not for other torch-races. This is a possible interpretation, but not a likely one. It is true that only the scholiast to Plato expressly mentions the Panathenaic torch-race; Plutarch and Pausanias appear to speak of the torch-race in general. It is also true that Pausanias

latter cannot be set aside; in Plutarch the starting-point is referred to as a matter of common knowledge. Furthermore, Apollodorus situates the relief with Prometheus and Hephaestus 'at the entrance,' somewhere near the altar of Eros. We must ask what 'Eros' means in this context.

It is notorious that Hephaestus was once enamoured of Athena; the same is said of Prometheus too, though without further detail.[68] Since Athena as a perpetual virgin could not be overcome, her affair with Hephaestus had a strange consummation: Hephaestus' seed was spilt on the ground, and from it sprang the child Ἐριχθόνιος, 'He-of-the-very-earth.' The child was taken to the Acropolis and cherished in Athena's sanctuary. This myth is often treated as a queer distasteful aberration, but it reflects a deep-rooted belief which is not peculiar to Greece. The producing and fostering of new fire are a prodigy of nature; they are in fact the begetting and fostering of a marvellous child.

The altar of Eros is therefore equivalent to the altar of Prometheus or Hephaestus as a source of new fire. In early days, the fire was doubtless brought directly, with whatever ceremony, from the altar of Prometheus to the altar of Athena on the Acropolis. But the torch-race required a broad level track with a conspicuous start and finish. The altars of Eros and Anteros were installed as the termini. We may suppose that fire was carried from the altar of Prometheus to the altar of Eros in preparation for the race, so that the former could always be reckoned the true starting-point, as it is by Pausanias.

The altar of Eros and the Academy wall are ascribed to Charmus and Hipparchus respectively. The tyrants may have instituted the torch-race; if not, they at least improved the facilities.

---

in his tour of the Academy gives no special prominence to Athena; and true again that in describing the torch-race, he mentions only competing runners, not competing teams, though the Panathenaic torch-race is generally thought to be a relay. But the description may be elliptic, whether it is meant to apply to both single and relay races, or to relay races alone, as the only kind. It would be surprising if Pausanias did not have his eye on the Panathenaic torch-race as the leading instance of this Athenian event.

68 Hephaestus: Eratosth. *Catast.* 13 (Eur. fr. 925 Nauck² = 1246 Mette); etc. Prometheus: schol. Apoll. *Argon.* 2.1249 (Duris *FGrHist* 76 F 47). Cf. *RhM* n.s. 128 (1985) 258–69. On a calyx krater lately published, the birth of Erichthonius is watched by either Prometheus or Epimetheus (for the name is poorly preserved): J.H. Oakley, *AntK* 30 (1987) 123–30. Apollo is also on hand, with a tripod beside him. Oakley suggests, not very plausibly, that the vase is meant to commemorate a dithyrambic victory at the Thargelia, Apollo's festival. We should remember that Apollo is neighbour to Hephaestus and Athena in the Agora. In a learned genealogy, it is Apollo *patrōios*, not Erichthonius, who is their offspring: Cic. *De Nat. Deor.* 3.55, 57; Clem. *Protr.* 1.20.

The torch-race is perhaps referred to in three early dedications on the Acropolis. The dedications are made by boards of *hieropoioi* who have conducted a festival of Athena, evidently the Great Panathenaea. Their duties are described in two brief phrases: 'they made the race,' τὸν δρόμον ἐποίεσαν, and 'they did the games,' τὸν ἀγῶνα θέσαν. On the most natural interpretation, 'the games' comprise all the athletic and equestrian events. 'The race' which is distinguished from 'the games' is then the torch-race.[69]

Since the Academy was chiefly renowned for the ceremonial fire-bringing, it was doubtless in consequence of the new arrangement for the Panathenaic torch-race that a small grove of olive trees was planted here to supply the oil for Panathenaic prizes. The trees numbered twelve and were called μορίαι.[70] This is the adjective from μόρος 'part,' 'share,' though ancient explanations prefer the meaning 'fate' or 'doom.' The twelve 'parts' represented by twelve trees are the twelve phratries that make up the whole of Athens' territory. Later, when more oil was needed, it was natural to requisition it from trees throughout Attica.

The *Pannychis* and the Enrolment of Young Men

The *pannychis* was celebrated on the Acropolis on the night of 28 Hecatombaeon, to be followed at sunrise by the great procession.[71] Torches lit up the shrines where the festivity took place: those of Athena and her associates, Pandrosus and Curotrophus. Youths and maidens danced and

69 A.E. Raubitschek, *Dedications from the Athenian Akropolis* (Cambridge, Mass. 1949) nos. 326–8; Hansen, *CEG* s. *viii-v* nos. 434–5. According to Raubitschek, *dromos* means the games, *agōn* the ceremonial element. J.A. Davison, *JHS* 78 (1958) 30–1 = *From Arch. to Pindar* 41–3, is agnostic. Travlos, *Pictorial Dict.* 2, understands the first phrase to signify 'the construction and repair of the Dromos,' i.e., the festival racetrack, which he situates in the Agora. One does not see why three boards at different times should be engaged in the task. *CEG* s. *viii-v* no. 301 is the dedication of an official who 'made this handsome racetrack,' *dromos*, for the Eleusinia; but here the adjective and demonstrative pronoun determine the meaning.

70 Schol. Soph. *Oed. Col.* 701 (Ister *FGrHist* 334 F 30); Phot., Suda s.v. μορίαι; Etym. Magn. s.v. μορία.

71 According to W.K. Pritchett, in *Philia epē eis G.E. Mylōnan* (Athens 1986–7) 2.179–88, the day of the procession and sacrifice came before the night of the *pannychis*. Pritchett thinks that the meat from the sacrifice was consumed during the night by the whole body of citizens. Not, perhaps, the usual notion of a *pannychis*, nor yet of a banquet. But Pritchett has a brisk way with the evidence. Though Euripides speaks of youths and maidens dancing all night on the Acropolis, this is not the *pannychis*. And though the Lycurgan law on the Panathenaea turns from the *pannychis* to the procession at sunrise, the latter has been inserted 'parenthetically' (p. 188).

sang hymns of joy, respectively paeans and *ololygai*.[72] As we learn from a decree recently published, the priestess of Aglaurus kept order and set out a table of offerings.[73] The *pannychis* and the table of offerings can now be recognized in certain late sources who speak of food offerings and of 'mysteries' for Aglaurus and Pandrosus.[74]

If youths dance and sing paeans, we are bound to ask what part was played by the corps of ephebes in the later Hellenistic period. Now, although the ephebes are commended year by year for joining in a great many festivals, parading and sacrificing and competing, the Panathenaic festival is almost never mentioned. The usual round of festivals runs from early Boedromion (the procession to Agrae) to late Scirophorion (the Diisoteria).[75] As exceptions to the pattern, we encounter the Panathenaea

---

72 Eur. *Heracleid.* 777–83; *Hesperia* 28 (1959) 239–47 and *IG* 2² 334 (337/6–330/29 BC) B 32–3 (*LSCG* 33; Schwenk, *Athens in the Age of Alexander* no. 17); *HSCP Suppl.* 1 (1940) 520–30 (decree for Julia Domna, after AD 195) lines 32–4, cf. R.S. Stroud, *Hesperia* 40 (1971) 200–204 no. 53 (new fragments); Heliod. *Aeth.* 1.10.1–2. Julia Domna is honoured in various ways at the Panathenaic festival; it is at the *pannychis* that officiants will 'set up a torch' and 'dance.' For other comment on the *pannychis*, see Deubner, *Gr. Feste* 24, and *AbhBerl* 1941 no. 1.23 = *Kleine Schriften* (Königstein 1982) 629; Ziehen, *RE* 18.3 (1949) 459 *s.v.* Panathenaia, and 631 *s.v.* Παννυχίς 1.

73 *Hesperia* 52 (1983) 50–2 (247–246 or 246–245 BC). On 11 Metageitnion the Assembly, acting on a motion of the Council, honours a priestess of Aglaurus recently installed in office; besides offering her inaugural sacrifices (lines 11–14, 26–8), she has just conducted the *pannychis* (lines 28–30). *IG* 2² 948 (166–165 BC), which honours another priestess of Aglaurus, was passed about the same time of month, arguably the thirteenth, though the month is lost (lines 4–5): perhaps it was customary for a new priestess to take office just before the Panathenaea. The Salaminian *genos*, who supply the priestess, sacrifice a pig to Athena at the Panathenaea, and it is the only sacrifice that matches the priesthood: *Hesperia* 7 (1938) 1–9 no. 1 (363–362 BC) lines 87–8 (*LSCG Suppl.* 19). As the priestess of Aglaurus also serves Pandrosus and Curotrophus (lines 12, 45), and as the *genos* also supplies a *kanēphoros* of Curotrophus (lines 45–6), these deities too were honoured at the *pannychis*. The connection between the priesthood and the Panathenaic festival has been overlooked, as by W.S. Ferguson, *Hesperia* 7 (1938) 20–1, and G.S. Dontas, *Hesperia* 52 (1983) 56–7. They cast about for a separate festival of Aglaurus, but there is none.

74 Bekker, *Anecd.* 1.239 *s.v.* δειπνοφόρος; Athenagoras, *Leg. de Christ.* 1.1. Agraulus and Pandrosus are here the mythical daughters of Cecrops; the lexicon adds 'Herse' as well. The mythical Cecropids answer to the *arrhephoroi* of Acropolis ritual, and these appear to be associated with the *pannychis* in the decree for Julia Domna: τὰς [ἀρρηφόρ]ους τὰς ἀπολυ[ομένα]ς. J.H. Oliver's restoration can hardly be avoided: who but the *arrhephoroi* might be 'discharged' after a term of service? See the photograph, fig.1, and the epigraphical comment at p. 523. P. Brulé, *La Fille d'Athènes* (Paris 1987) 92–3, favours the restoration on similar grounds.

75 See Pélékidis, *Éphébie* 211–56. Admittedly, several festivals cannot be fixed in the calendar.

just once, and the Eleusinia, a festival of the following month, twice. In one year, the ephebes dedicated prizes and offered sacrifice at both festivals; in another, they offered sacrifice at the Eleusinia.[76] As a body, their participation was slight. Under the Empire, when the festival calendar was greatly changed, the ephebes took part in a different range of agonistic festivals. Though the Panathenaic festival is never mentioned by name (nor the Eleusinia), it is clear that the Great Panathenaea included a regatta of ephebes.[77] A curious item is the festival 'Athenaea' which came towards the end of the ephebic year: it was first 'revived' in the year 189–190, and thereafter the ephebes competed each year in various contests. The occasion is surely the annual Panathenaic festival.[78] In sum, the evidence suggests that the round of festivals at first stopped short of the Panathenaea, but was afterwards extended.

It is obvious and agreed that the ephebes were enrolled for service shortly before the procession to Agrae on 6 Boedromion; the enrolment and the procession are often conjoined in ephebic decrees. The time at which they were discharged from service is less obvious. Under the Empire, they served for a full year; gymnasiarchs were appointed month by month from Boedromion through Metageitnion. The concluding ceremony was then a sacrifice and banquet in the Diogeneium, the gymnasium chiefly used by the ephebes.[79] It is commonly assumed that ephebic service had always continued through Metageitnion; but as we have just seen, the round of festivals does not bear this out. Moreover, in Hellenistic times the concluding ceremony is different: the ephebes go up to the Acropolis with the *kosmētēs* and sacrifice 'to Athena *polias* and Curotrophus and Pandrosus.'[80] These are the deities of the Panathenaic *pannychis*; surely the sacrifice was made early on the evening of the *pannychis*.

76 *Hesperia* 16 (1947) 170–2 no. 67, completing *IG* 2² 1009 (117–116 BC), lines 27–8; *IG* 2² 1028 (102–101) lines 15–16. Cf. Pélékidis, *Éphébie* 224, 254–5.

77 See Follet, *Athènes* 339–43.

78 *IG* 2² 2116 (AD 189–90?) lines 18–21; etc. Cf. P. Graindor, *MusB* 26 (1922) 207–10; Follet, *Athènes* 320. The 'Athenaea' must be distinct from the Panathenaea, says Graindor 209, because the name first appears at a late date, and because it appears in a document which also bears the date 'Panathenais 35' (*IG* 2² 2245 lines 1–2, 181: AD 256, according to Follet). Neither objection is valid. The Panathenaea proper will go on as before beside these ephebic contests as purportedly revived; so will the Panathenaic era.

79 *IG* 2² 2221 (AD 216/7–219/20; now joined with other fragments [Follet, *Athènes* 236]) lines 20–1. Cf. Graindor, *MusB* 26 (1922) 223; Pélékidis, *Éphébie* 256.

80 *IG* 2² 1039 (79–78 BC) lines 4–6, 57–8. Cf. Graindor, *MusB* 26 (1922) 210; Pélékidis, *Éphébie* 256.

If the ephebes graduated at the *pannychis*, they were able to parade the next day as full citizens. This gives point to a remark of the orator Deinarchus; the target is a foreigner who had shamefully purchased his inscription on a deme register. The man's sons, Deinarchus tells the court, 'will go up to the Acropolis as ephebes instead of *skaphēphoroi*' – the role assigned to metic processioners of like age – 'owing their citizenship not to you but to this fellow's money.'[81]

No one doubts that the Hellenistic *ephēbeia* inherited the dates of enrolment and discharge from the Lycurgan period, although the term of service was then two years instead of one. In this period, there is clearly an advantage in separating the graduation of one group of ephebes from the enrolment of another by an interval of a month or so. Prospective ephebes were scrutinized by the demes and again by the Council, and those rejected by the demes could appeal to the lawcourts. Moreover, supervisors for the new group were elected in two stages: first the fathers gathered by *phylē* and chose a slate of candidates, and then the Assembly made the final choice. Ephebes from the group of two years before might be needed to testify at the scrutiny; supervisors of the group of two years before (supposing that they served for both years) might want to stand again.[82]

Since the ephebes were enrolled in early Boedromion, the scrutiny and the elections must fall in Metageitnion. Other evidence points to this month, and further shows that all the activity took place in Athens. The demes met to scrutinize the ephebes, and the fathers met to choose the supervisors, at the Theseium, in the old city centre east of the Acropolis. It would be easy to assume that the ephebes were scrutinized in each deme centre, and that the supervisors were chosen at the assembly place for each *phylē*. But an orator says that when a law of 346–345 required each deme to conduct a special scrutiny, the deme Halimus met somewhere in the city, so that the demesmen left again in time to get home.[83] Though this special scrutiny may not have come at the usual season, it was surely done at the usual meeting place; otherwise the orator would say not only that the meeting place was inconvenient, but also that the inconvenience was unwonted.

Elsewhere we learn that the demes conducted their regular scrutiny in Metageitnion or thereabouts, and that the scrutiny was associated with elections, *archairesiai*. Leostratus as an adopted son attempted to insert his

---

81 Harpocr. *s.v.* σκαφηφόροι (Deinarchus fr. 16 Sauppe). Cf. D. Whitehead, *The Ideology of the Athenian Metic* (Cambr. Philol. Soc. Suppl. 4, 1977) 50.

82 [Arist.] *Ath.* 42.1–2. It seems likely that the same supervisors served with the ephebes throughout their two-year term; otherwise the fathers' choice was only half effective.

83 Dem. 57 *Eubul.* 10. Cf. Whitehead, *The Demes of Attica* (Princeton 1986) 87–9.

name in the deme register on three successive occasions – 'at the *agora* of the magistrates,' i.e., at the election of deme officers, and so presumably in Scirophorion, before the beginning of the civic year; during the distribution of the *theōrikon* at the Panathenaea, and so at the end of Hecatombaeon; and 'at the past elections,' arguably in Metageitnion.[84] It was also 'at the elections' that Thrasyllus, another adopted son, was able to get his name inscribed on the deme register; he himself was away with a ceremonial delegation to Delphi, the so-called Pythais, which probably took place in summer.[85] Both the date and the setting of 'the elections' are made explicit by a decree of the deme Eleusis of the year 332–331: certain rent is due 'in the month Metageitnion at the elections, whenever the demesmen gather in the Theseium.'[86] Finally, under 12 Metageitnion the calendar of the deme Erchia prescribes sacrifice to some leading Athenian deities – Apollo *lykeios*, Demeter at the Eleusinium, Zeus *polieus*, Athena *polias* – as if the demesmen were flocking to Athens on that day.[87]

This evidence warrants the conclusion that the demes gathered in the Theseium towards the middle of Metageitnion in order to scrutinize ephebes. Erchia gathered on the twelfth, but it may have taken several days for all the demes to do their work. On the seventh, presumably at the Apolline festival Metageitnia, the Salaminian *genos* sacrifice to several deities concerned with kinship;[88] so perhaps the business started then and lasted through the second quarter. 'The elections' also take place at this time: it is by this name that the orators refer to the scrutiny, and the decree of Eleusis to the gathering in the Theseium. The elections must be those of the ephebic supervisors, first by fathers, then by the Assembly.

The calendar of Erchia is dated by the lettering to the first half of the fourth century; the speech of Isaeus cannot well be later than the mid century. They indicate, and so do other clues, that ephebic service of some kind antedates the Lycurgan period. On the other hand, it should be clear

84 [Dem.] 44 *Leochar.* 36–40.
85 Isaeus 7 *Apollod.* 27–8. A. Boethius, *Die Pythais* (Uppsala 1918) 15–19, errs in supposing that the 'elections,' *archairesiai*, are of deme officers and so must fall at the beginning of the civic year: [Demosthenes] places the 'elections' after the Panathenaea; the decree of Eleusis places them in Metageitnion. This chronology favours a connection between the fourth-century Pythais and the Pythian festival.
86 *REG* 91 (1978) 289–306 lines 27–8 (Schwenk, *Athens in the Age of Alexander* no. 43). For other views of these 'elections,' see D.M. Lewis, *CR* [2] 34 (1984) 345; Whitehead, *Demes of Attica* 89–90, 269–70, 289–90.
87 *BCH* 87 (1963) 603–34 A 1–5, **B** 1–5, Γ 13–18, Δ 13–17 (*LSCG* 18).
88 *Hesperia* 7 (1938) 1–9 no. 1 lines 89–90 (*LSCG Suppl.* 19): Apollo *patrōios*, Leto, Artemis, Athena *agelaa*.

that ephebic service is a relatively late development. As described by [Aristotle], it has two aspects, as military training and as light military duty: the ephebes are armed and trained as soldiers, and they serve in garrison and on patrol (*Ath.* 42.3–5). In either aspect the program is unlikely to be earlier than the fourth century.[89]

Whenever it was first devised, the program did not run with the civic calendar, from Hecatombaeon to Scirophorion. The calendar dates were determined instead by an older custom. The date for completing the program is the traditional date for enrolling youths as citizens: 28 Hecatombaeon, the Panathenaic festival. Given this date, the ephebes must start the program somewhat later in the year, after an interval that allows for scrutiny and elections: i.e., at the beginning of the month Boedromion. This date is a consequence of the other.

'The ephebic oath' is seen from its language to be a relic of an older time.[90] The several vows – not to shame one's arms and to fight bravely and to defend one's homeland, to obey the magistrates and the laws – are appropriate to one who is now enrolled as an adult citizen. Moreover, the oath was sworn in the precinct of Aglaurus, and so presumably on 28 Hecatombaeon: it was then that youths and maidens danced and sang under the eyes of the priestess of Aglaurus. Admittedly, our sources disagree on whether the oath was taken at the beginning or the end of ephebic service.[91] It might indeed be thought that in the two-year program the proper time for the oath is the beginning of the second year, when the ephebes (after thorough training in the use of several weapons) receive a token shield and spear in a public ceremony, and go forth to patrol the boundaries of Attica,

89 On ephebic service before 335, see P. Gauthier, *Un Commentaire historique des* Poroi *de Xénophon* (Paris 1976) 190–5; Rhodes, *Comm.* 494–5; N.V. Sekunda, *ZPE* 83 (1990) 149–58. But the myth of Melanthus, far from being the aetiology of an early form of service, has nothing to do with this age group: *AJP* 109 (1988) 284–5; *GRBS* 29 (1988) 204–24.

90 G. Daux, *REG* 84 (1971) 373, gives an accurate conspectus of the literary and epigraphic versions. P. Siewert, *JHS* 97 (1977) 109–11, insists on the archaic language and outlook. There is, however, no suggestion in the oath that political power is reserved for others than the oath-takers. It is obvious that an oath of this tenor would have been changed.

91 Lyc. *Leocr.* 76; Ulp. *ad* Dem. 19 *De Fals. Leg.* 303; Poll. 8.105. Ulpian puts it at the beginning, Pollux at the end; but Pollux is fuller – he gives a complete text of the oath, a better one than Stobaeus, nearly as good as the Acharnian stele. To be sure, he also says that inscription on the deme register came at the end of service, whereas [Aristotle] says that it came before; but he is not discredited thereby. For most purposes the inscription did not matter until the end of service, so that these are only different points of view. Lycurgus appears to say that Athenians swore the oath just when they became ephebes; but he might be speaking loosely. Pélékidis, *Éphébie* 111–12, with some hesitation puts the oath at the beginning of service.

which are prominently named in the oath. These uncertainties cannot be resolved; they go to show that ephebic service incorporates some earlier elements in an artificial manner.

In any case, the enrolment ceremony of 28 Hecatombaeon was itself an innovation. In the Dark Age, youths like Theseus were enrolled at the festival Hecatombaea, on the seventh or eighth of the month. Later, youths were enrolled locally at phratry centres throughout Attica, and there was no general ceremony at Athens. It was no doubt Peisistratus who fixed on the Panathenaea.

The Armed Processioners

The Panathenaic procession followed without interval upon the *pannychis*. The Lycurgan regulations provide that 'the *hieropoioi* ... shall conduct the *pannychis* in the finest way for the goddess and dispatch the procession at sunrise,' ἅμα ἡλίωι ἀνιόντι.[92] The priestess of Aglaurus, on taking office, sacrificed to several deities besides Aglaurus, obviously those who could help her to manage the *pannychis* and the youths and maidens: Ares, Helius, Horae, Apollo.[93] Ares and Apollo helped with the youths,[94] 'Sun' and 'Hours' with the schedule. The youths and maidens danced in the night and paraded at sunrise. It was for the priestess of Aglaurus to ensure that they reached the Cerameicus, where the procession formed up at first light, in good condition and in good time.

92 *Hesperia* 28 (1959) 239–47 and *IG* 2² 334 (337/6–330/29 BC) B 32–4.
93 *Hesperia* 52 (1983) 50–2 lines 12–13; *IG* 2² 948 lines 12–13.
94 Ares set a stern example by killing a youth who molested a maiden: Eur. *El.* 1260–2; Bekker, *Anecd.* 1.444, Etym. Gen., Etym. Magn., Suda *s.v.* ʼΑρειος πάγος (Hellanicus *FGrHist* 323a F 1); Steph. Byz. *s.v.* ʼΑρειος πάγος (Philochorus 328 F 3); Paus. 1.21.4; [Apld.] *Bibl.* 3.14.2.2 (3.180); schol. Pind. *Ol.* 11.83. The maiden was his daughter by Aglaurus, evoking the *pannychis*. The youth was Poseidon's son Halirrhothius 'Sea-plashing,' evoking the Acropolis cleft and 'sea,' i.e., the *pannychis* setting. According to Pausanias, the incident took place beside the fountain-house on the south slope of the Acropolis. This spring has no name that we know of, being referred to only as the spring in Asclepius' sanctuary (Xen. *Mem.* 2.13.3; Plin. *Hist. Nat.* 2.225; Paus. *loc. cit.*); a boundary stone of the late fifth century, the time when Asclepius was installed, says simply *hópos κρένες* (*IG* 1² 874). Not surprisingly, the Nymphs and perhaps other, kindred deities were worshipped nearby: Travlos, *Pictorial Dict.* 138, 142 figs. 192–3. In the light of these circumstances, it is hardly feasible to conjecture that the spring belonged especially to a certain hero or a certain nymph, one of the principals in the story. Since the water is warm and brackish – and Xenophon and Pliny indicate that these qualities were notorious – it may well have been associated with the 'sea' on the north side. Jacoby on Ister *FGrHist* 334 F 6 envisages confusion or contamination as between the 'sea,' the spring of Asclepius, and also Clepsydra.

One group of processioners is of interest here: those who bore arms. Harmodius and Aristogeiton chose to assail the tyrants at the Great Panathenaea of 514 BC, hoping that others would use their arms to help. Spears, rather than swords or daggers, were needed to engage with the tyrants' bodyguard of 'spear-bearers,' *doryphoroi*. Thucydides explains that some processioners carried a shield and spear, and that there was no other day for citizens to carry arms (6.56.2, 58.2). Custom had changed, for as we saw, the herald's summons at the Synoecia was to muster under arms. It changed again after this date, for Thucydides is speaking only of the past: 'it was not suspicious' to be under arms, οὐχ ὕποπτον ἐγίγνετο, and 'they were accustomed' to carrying spear and shield, εἰώθεσαν. In the late fifth century, the Great Panathenaea were an occasion widely known in the Greek world; had there been a procession under arms, Thucydides would appeal to common observation. Spears are altogether absent from the procession of the Parthenon frieze. There are helmets and shields for the *apobatai*, helmets for a few horsemen, a couple of corselets, even a sword or two. But no spears – though other reliefs and also vases are not at all averse to showing processions of horsemen with spears.[95]

Thucydides is directly contradicted by [Aristotle].[96] 'But the usual account, that Hippias separated the processioners from their arms and apprehended those with daggers, is not true. For they did not then parade with arms, but the democracy instituted this later.' It has been conjectured that [Aristotle] or his source knew of a decree which called for a procession under arms, whether this was indeed an innovation, as [Aristotle] thought, or a long-standing practice that was only reaffirmed. The conjecture is very strained. In Thucydides' day the procession with spears was not even a recent memory, and it is not shown in the Parthenon frieze; it was therefore discontinued before the mid fifth century. The hypothetical decree must be considerably earlier, and it must have been reversed by another hypothetical decree, seemingly unknown to [Aristotle]. We can hardly believe

95 For details, see F. Brommer, *Der Parthenonfries* (Mainz 1977) Text 228–9. Brommer finds it 'striking' that no spears are shown, and cites reliefs and vases where they are in fact carried by processions of horsemen. G.R. Bugh, *The Horsemen of Athens* (Princeton 1988) 15–19, thinks that a festival procession may be intended on two early red-figure cups which show youthful horsemen, each armed with two spears, presenting themselves for some kind of registration; but (as he also intimates) the number of spears is against this.

96 *Ath.* 18.4. The contradiction has been discussed many times. See, e.g., Mommsen, *Feste* 101 n. 5, 144–4; Brunnsåker, *The Tyrant-Slayers of Kritios and Nesiotes* (Lund 1955) 31–2; J. Day and M. Chambers, *Aristotle's History of Athenian Democracy* (Berkeley 1962) 20–1; Dover, *HCT* 4.335–6; Rhodes, *Comm.* 210. Dover and Rhodes as the latest in the field refuse to decide between Thucydides and [Aristotle].

that the first hypothetical decree would survive, or that it would be sought out by [Aristotle] or his source.

[Aristotle's] contradiction is undoubtedly polemical. There had always been controversy about the end of the tyranny, and one issue was whether Harmodius and Aristogeiton were chiefly responsible. A strong current of belief, and at least one authority, probably Hellanicus, said that they were. Everyone acknowledged, however, that Hippias clung to power for a certain time after the assassination of Hipparchus. One asks why the Athenians did not rise in arms at the very moment that Hipparchus was assassinated. The only feasible answer is that they had no arms, as [Aristotle] asserts, not only here but also in the tale of Peisistratus' ruse (Ath. 15.3–5). It is true that [Aristotle] does not regard Harmodius and Aristogeiton as responsible for ending the tyranny: in this he agrees with Thucydides. But his account is composite, and includes assorted novelties. In the matter of the arms we can follow Thucydides without any hesitation.

Who then were the processioners who carried shield and spear? Thucydides' phrases (and [Aristotle's] contradiction) only show that they were a certain group of citizens.[97] No doubt they represented the principal components of the army, however it was organized under the tyrants. But prominent among them, we may be sure, were Athens' youngest soldiers, those just enrolled as citizens. Consider the Parthenon frieze.

The horsemen of the frieze are all, apart from two bearded figures, very young. As some are even younger than others, two age groups must be represented: youths approaching manhood, and youths recently enrolled as men. It should be obvious that these youths take part in the procession in virtue of their age, not because they are typical or ideal members of the cavalry.[98] They are the wealthiest of Athenian youths, those who own and ride horses. Even in a democracy, the wealthy may supersede everyone else for ceremonial purposes; that, indeed, is the point of liturgies which recruit basket bearers and the like from wealthy families. So the procession of the Great Panathenaea gave a very prominent place to Athenian youths.

97 56.2: 'It was not suspicious for those of the citizens who were joining the parade to come together under arms.' 58.1: Hippias' first reaction was to disarm 'the processioners under arms.' 58.2: 'For it was with shield and spear that they were accustomed to parade.'

98 The youthful horsemen have often been associated with the cavalry, as by Ziehen, RE 18.3 (1949) 468 s.v. Panathenaia; Parke, Festivals 43; Bugh, Horsemen 77–8. Simon, Festivals 59–62, thinks of them as 'ephebes,' 'young riders in military training' who 'escort' the procession. Here as elsewhere in the book (e.g., pp. 25, 48) she makes two improbable assumptions: that a corps of ephebes were always on duty at Athenian festivals, as they are in the later Hellenistic period; and that these ephebes were mounted.

Perhaps the older age group, those just enrolled as men, were drawn from the graduating classes of the past four years.[99]

To be a man is to bear arms; youths at their enrolment take up arms and go on parade. 'The ephebic oath,' sworn on the night before the procession, begins with a vow not to shame one's arms. We may infer that the armed processioners of 514 included youths recently enrolled as men.

The bearing of arms is also in question in the tale of Peisistratus' ruse, of which [Aristotle] and Polyaenus give different but similar versions.[100] Polyaenus' ultimate source is doubtless of the same period as [Aristotle's]; both versions, full of local colour, probably derive from Attic chroniclers. In this tale Peisistratus divests all the Athenians of their arms, and so lives up to the usual expectation of tyrants in the fourth century; Aristotle reckons 'the seizure of arms,' ὅπλων παραίρεσις, as a standard tactic.[101] The tactic is of course illusory. An Archaic tyrant relied on popular support; he could not do worse than to take away everyone's arms, not only making enemies but forfeiting any effective support. And it is a poor sort of cunning to muster a large body of men under arms with the hope of filching their arms during some distraction.[102]

The tale also runs counter to the circumstances of Hipparchus' assassination: the tyrannicides were encouraged by the armed procession of the Great Panathenaea. The armed procession could be denied, as by [Aristotle]. But it is obvious that the true circumstances were long and well remembered before someone hit on this denial.

On the other hand, there is good reason to believe that the tale, though not literally true, is yet faithful to conditions of Peisistratus' day – in other words, that it is an aetiology. It takes place in the old city centre east of the Acropolis; the topography was examined above, apropos of the festival Synoecia, and we need only recall the main points. The different

---

99 The four cows and four sheep of the north frieze may well correspond to the festival cycle. Some think of the four Ionic *phylai*, but it seems unlikely that these would be perpetuated at the Panathenaea (they are indispensable to the Synoecia).

100 [Arist.] *Ath.* 15.3–4; Polyaenus 1.21.2.

101 Arist. *Pol.* 5.10–11, 1311 A 12–13, 1315 A 38.

102 Aristodemus of Cumae, it is said, called upon the citizens to give up their arms by bringing them to a sanctuary, or sanctuaries, as dedications (Dion. Hal. *Ant. Rom.* 7.8.2–3): a more feasible procedure, but surely not more authentic. There is a strong hint of intimidation in the procedure ascribed to the Thirty (Xen. *Hell.* 2.3.20). The Three Thousand and those excluded from their number were mustered under arms in separate places, and the latter were told to leave their arms, which were then collected and placed 'in the temple' on the Acropolis. Dionysius I, like Peisistratus, reportedly employed a ruse (Diod. 14.10.4). 'Having sent out the Syracusans to the harvest, he went round to the houses and seized everyone's arms.'

landmarks mentioned by [Aristotle] and Polyaenus – the Theseium and rooms nearby, the Anaceium and the shrine of Aglaurus – all converge on the old agora. This was once the regular muster-ground of Athens; musters were held in later days at the Theseium and the Anaceium, but they were exceptional. The most significant landmark is the Acropolis entrance and approach to which Peisistratus and his audience are said to withdraw. It is the northeast ascent, leading directly from the old agora to the old temple and altar of Athena. This ascent went out of use after the ramp and gates were built at the west, round the mid sixth century. The story then is faithful to conditions at the beginning of the tyranny, its ostensible date.

The tale was originally meant to explain a change of custom at this date. Athenians formerly mustered under arms in the old agora; the normal occasion was the festival Synoecia, a reunion of all the phratries of Attica. Peisistratus suspended this muster in the interest of public order. Henceforth arms were carried only by a few in the procession of the Great Panathenaea, and the few included Athens' youth. The tale feigns that the arms are sequestered either in the buildings near the Theseium (so [Aristotle]) or in the shrine of Aglaurus (so Polyaenus). It was in the shrine of Aglaurus that youths swore 'the ephebic oath' – not to shame their arms, and so on – on the night before the procession. The version with the Theseium will be a later variant, if, as seems likely, this civic shrine was first installed by Cimon.[103] But the Theseium is none the less appropriate.

In the fourth century, as we saw above, some of the preliminaries to ephebic service were conducted at the Theseium. Here the youths were first scrutinized, and a slate of supervisors was drawn up. In the Hellenistic and Roman periods the Theseium was a centre of ephebic activity. The festival Theseia consisted largely of athletic contests for Athenian youth, both ephebes and younger lads.[104] Some contests required the use of weapons, and the sanctuary had a facility called *hoplothēkē*. Ephebic catalogues of the Roman period were set up at the Theseium or somewhere near it, for many of them have the same provenance – the church of Haghios

103 The ritual here on 8 Pyanopsion was said, predictably, to mark Theseus' return from the port to the city (as was also the festival Pyanopsia of the day before). Apart from this, there is nothing in the legends of Theseus that points by way of aetiology to the civic shrine or festival. Our study of the Oschophoria will show that the Cretan adventure was inspired by other rites of early Pyanopsion. Rhodes, *Comm.* 211, assembles other indications that the Theseium is not very ancient.

104 Cf. n. 19 to the Oschophoria.

Demetrios Katephores – as records of the Theseia which undoubtedly come from the sanctuary.[105] Given the legend of Theseus, we may assume that the Theseium was associated right from its foundation with the warlike exercises of Athenian youth. Hence the variant.

105 *Hoplothēkē*: IG 2² 957 line 9, 958 lines 28–9, 963 line 6. IG 2² 956, 957, and 958, records of the Theseia posted at the Theseium, were found at the church, as were many of the catalogues, IG 2² 1960–2291. Cf. Vanderpool, *Hesperia* 43 (1974) 309; Bugh, *ZPE* 83 (1990) 21–2.

4

The Oschophoria and Seafaring

Synopsis

The port of Phalerum is linked to the city in certain rites which show Athens' concern with seafaring long before she became a naval power. In the Oschophoria, a festival of early autumn, a procession goes from Athens to the shrine of Athena Sciras at Phalerum to honour two nautical heroes, a pilot and a bow-officer; the two youths who lead the procession are dressed in old-fashioned finery. In another observance of the same season, a foot race is run over the same route, and the winning youth receives a cup of punch, an old-fashioned prize. Both observances are managed by an ancient hieratic *genos*, the 'Salaminians.' Still at the same season, a chorus of youths and maidens sail to Delos to honour Apollo with the crane dance. The same ship was always used to convey them: a very old-fashioned ship.

These rites, together with the festival Hecatombaea, have largely inspired the tale of Theseus' Cretan adventure. Plutarch, drawing on the Attic chroniclers, tells us how the rites commemorate the tale. In the *Life* of Theseus, as in hardly any other work, myth and ritual constantly illuminate each other. Moreover, the literary record can be compared with the epigraphic regulations of the 'Salaminians,' first published in 1938. The regulations help us to distinguish the Oschophoria and the race, and to date them, respectively, to late Boedromion and early Pyanopsion. The dancers who sailed to Delos were of the age group recently enrolled at the Hecatombaea. Thus we have the main elements of the Cretan adventure: Theseus, the ideal young champion, and 'the twice seven' youths and maidens, and a dangerous voyage across the sea. It is likely that the whole Theseus legend starts from this point.

Let us first examine the rites: the Oschophoria; the race for the cup of punch; the 'Salaminians'; the mission to Delos. Then we shall consider the origin of the Theseus legend.

The Oschophoria

A festive group parades from Athens to Phalerum, to the shrine of Athena Sciras. They are led by a herald and by two youths whose costume and adornment are so dainty that some observers imagined an expedient of Theseus when he sailed with the tribute of youths and maidens: he had smuggled in two extra youths among the maidens. The youths carry bunches of grapes as emblems or decorations, and behind them a chorus sings and dances 'grape-bearing songs,' ὠσχοφορικὰ μέλη, and women bring provisions for a feast. When this group reaches the sanctuary, they enjoy themselves to the full. Such in outline is the picture of the ritual given by our sources and generally accepted.[1]

Details are controversial, but some of them may be left aside as unimportant for our purpose. Others require examination. A foot race over the same route, as described by other sources, has been thought by some to be a part of the Oschophoria; this is mistaken, as we shall see. Our attention should be directed first to the deities of the sanctuary and to the calendar date.

The festival setting is the shrine of Athena Sciras; a little more will be said below about Athena as patron of seafaring, or rather of nautical skills. It is true that the starting-point in Athens (for both the procession and the race) is said to be a shrine of Dionysus, probably Dionysus-at-Limnae. But this need not have any great significance; the festival business takes place elsewhere.[2] At Athena's shrine we might expect Athena to be chiefly

---

1 Cf. Deubner, *Att. Feste* 142–7, and *AbhBerl* 1943 no. 12 = *Kleine Schriften* (Königstein 1982) 711–25; W.S. Ferguson, *Hesperia* 7 (1938) 18–21, 24–8, 33–41; H. Jeanmaire, *Couroi et Courètes* (Lille 1939) 338–63; L. Ziehen, *RE* 18.2 (1942) 1537–43 *s.v.* Oschophoria; Jacoby on Philochorus *FGrHist* 328 F 14–16; Pélékidis, *Éphébie* 226–8; Parke, *Festivals* 77–81; E. Kadletz, *GRBS* 21 (1980) 363–71; Simon, *Festivals* 89–92; C. Calame, *Thésée et l'imaginaire Athénien* (Lausanne 1990) 143–8, 324–7.

2 Deubner and Simon are persuaded that any festival with bunches of grapes must belong to Dionysus. But there seem to be only two bunches of grapes, in the hands of the two *ōschophoroi*; and nothing was done with them that would interest Dionysus. The calendar frieze of Haghios Eleutherios shows, in the month Pyanopsion, a naked figure holding a bunch of grapes and treading on a pile of them (but Kadletz admits only the former). If this evokes a festival, as maintained in different ways by Kadletz and Simon, it is not the Oschophoria, which fall in the previous month, as we are about to see. M.P. Nilsson, *JdI* 31 (1916) 321–2 = *Opuscula Selecta* 1 (Lund 1951)

honoured; yet the 'Salaminians,' who have both the shrine and the festival in their charge, do not in fact offer any sacrifice to Athena at this season. Now Athena shared her sanctuary with two heroes, Nauseirus and Phaeax, respectively pilot and bow-officer.[3] Most versions of the Cretan adventure give a prominent role to Theseus' pilot;[4] when Theseus returned safely, he established 'pilot rites,' *kybernēsia*. We are told elsewhere that Theseus on his return established the Oschophoria; indeed two accounts are offered of how he did so. The mention of the 'pilot rites' belongs to a third account: this is a descriptive term for the Oschophoria.[5]

Our festival was managed by the 'Salaminians,' as we learn from the regulations which this body set up in 363–362.[6] There are in fact two groups of Salaminians now joined as one; the group who officiate at Phalerum and Athens are those 'from the seven kindreds,' ἐκ τῶν ἐπτὰ φυλῶν. Their regulations include a calendar of sacrifice, and the entry for the two nautical heroes comes in the month Boedromion.[7]

185–6, rightly describes the grape-bunch of the Oschophoria as a 'harvest bough,' corresponding to the *eiresiōnē* as a 'may bough.'

3 *Hesperia* 7 (1938) 1–9 no. 1 (*LSCG Suppl.* 19) lines 91–2, 'Nauseirus' and Phaeax; Plut. *Thes.* 17. 7 (Philochorus *FGrHist* 328 F 111), 'Nausithous' and Phaeax. Plutarch, after Philochorus, speaks of the pair as occupants of 'hero shrines,' *hērōa*, 'at Phalerum at the sanctuary of Scirus.' Scirus is only a junior partner in the cult of Athena Sciras, but he too has a role in the story, and therefore serves to identify the sanctuary. Pausanias in his brief notice of Phalerum (1.1.4) mentions, among other items, 'altars' of 'heroes,' unspecified, but doubtless including Nauseirus and Phaeax. At the last he comes to the altar of a nameless hero, identified by some with Androgeos son of Minos: not the same as the pilot Nauseirus, we may be sure. This other altar will soon find its place.

4 Plut. *Thes.* 17.4–7 (Simonides fr. 550 Page, Philochorus *FGrHist* 328 F 111), 22.1; Diod. 4.61.4. Cf. Plut. *Thes.* 17.3 (Hellanicus 323a F 14): despite Jacoby *ad loc.*, it is likely enough that Hellanicus too mentioned the pilot.

5 Plut. *Thes.* 17.7 (Philochorus *FGrHist* 328 F 111), on the *kybernēsia*; 22.2–4, on the Oschophoria; 23.2–5 (Demo 327 F 6), on the Oschophoria again.

6 *Hesperia* 7 (1938) 1–9 no. 1 (*LSCG Suppl.* 19) lines 10 (priestess of Athena Sciras), 21–2 (*ōschophoroi* and *deipnophoroi*), 41 (loaves at Athena's shrine), 43–4 (herald and priestess), 49–50 (*ōschophoroi*, *deipnophoroi*, priestess, herald), 52 (stele posted at Athena's shrine), 63–4 (herald), 91–2 (sacrifices to Phaeax and Nauseirus). Cf. *IG* 2² 1232 lines 15–16, 23, 'fin. s. iv,' a decree of the Salaminians also posted at Athena's shrine.

7 Sacrifice is offered on the same day in Boedromion to Poseidon *hippodromios*, 'the hero Phaeax,' 'the hero Teucer,' 'the hero Nauseirus.' Teucer has been added here, as Eurysaces elsewhere in the calendar, to provide a link with the island of Salamis; more of this below. As for Poseidon *hippodromios*, who receives a larger offering than the others, we must suppose that the Hippodrome lay very close at hand, and was requisitioned for the festivities when room did not suffice in Athena's shrine. The

The Oschophoria are thus dated to Boedromion, not Pyanopsion, as usually said.[8] It was perhaps the twenty-seventh or the twenty-eighth, days favoured by Athena.[9] The calendar also prescribes sacrifice for Athena Sciras herself and her eponymous partner Scirus, but two months later, in Maemacterion.[10] The rites in Boedromion and Maemacterion span the closing period of navigation in the autumn, when a pilot's skill and Athena's favour are most required.[11]

Theseus' return to the city of Athens was dated either to 7 Pyanopsion, the Pyanopsia, or to the following day, the principal day of the civic

---

Hippodrome was a broad open area: even at cavalry reviews, people milled about until they were driven off the track (Xen. *Hipparch.* 3.10). It may or may not be Poseidon *hippodromios* who was served by the *genos* Phoenices, named in the title of a speech of Deinarchus as disputing 'the priesthood of Poseidon' with the deme Phalerum (Dion. Hal. *Din.* 10) – the ancient port of Athens probably had more than one cult of Poseidon. Despite Ferguson, *Hesperia* 7 (1938) 25, 27, and E. Kearns, *The Heroes of Attica* (*BICS Suppl.* 57, 1989) 38–41, 120, there is little warrant for supposing that the festival *kybernēsia* belongs to Poseidon. In Plutarch it goes with the nautical heroes, and they with Athena Sciras.

8 The date is always given as either 6 or 7 Pyanopsion. 6 Pyanopsion: Ferguson, *Hesperia* 7 (1938) 28; Ziehen, *RE* 18.2 (1942) 1543 *s.v.* Oschophoria; Deubner, *Kl. Schr.* 718; Jacoby, n. 137 to Philochorus F 14–16; Pélékidis, *Éphébie* 226. 7 Pyanopsion: Deubner, *Att. Feste* 146 (the seventh or a little later); Jeanmaire, *Couroi et Courètes* 338–46; Parke, *Festivals* 80; Simon, *Festivals* 89 (Parke and Simon are doubtless inadvertent, since they profess to follow Ferguson *et al.*). The seventh was formerly preferred because Plutarch says that Theseus' return to the city is commemorated on this day, scil. by the festival Pyanopsia. But in the same breath, Plutarch distinguishes the return to the city from the sojourn at Phalerum, to which the Oschophoria belong; moreover, the Oschophoria cannot coincide with a major Apolline festival. The sixth is now preferred because under this date the Salaminians sacrifice to Theseus (Ziehen wrongly says that they sacrifice to Athena Sciras). But a sacrifice to Theseus himself is not mentioned anywhere in the tradition about the Oschophoria, even though this tradition is fully cognizant of Theseus' return; moreover, we shall see in a moment that Plutarch mentions a sacrifice to Theseus that is distinct from both the Oschophoria and the civic Theseia.

9 The principal day of the Panathenaea, including the *pannychis*, is 28 Hecatombaeon, and either the third of the month or the third last day, i.e., the twenty-eighth, is Athena's holy day: W. Schmidt, *Geburtstag im Altertum* (Giessen 1908) 98–101. The Salaminians sacrifice at the Panathenaea, when one of their number, the priestess of Aglaurus, conducts the *pannychis*: cf. *Hesperia* 52 (1983) 50–7 lines 28–9. The deme Teithras prescribes sacrifice for Athena and Zeus on 27 Boedromion: *Hesperia* 30 (1961) 293–7 no. 1 lines 7–12. Thoricus too has a sacrifice for Athena near the end of Boedromion, 'at the salt flat': *AntClass* 52 (1983) 150–74 line 23. There is nothing to indicate whether these observances of Teithras and Thoricus are somehow related to ours.

10 *Hesperia* 7 (1938) 1–9 no. 1 lines 93–4.

11 Veg. *Mil.* 4.39: *incerta navigatio* from 14 September to 10 November.

Theseia.[12] But he made port some time before, and spent the interval at Phalerum, where he established other rites, and also buried his father. The Oschophoria belong to this interval.

The Race for the Cup of Punch

Another event, a foot race over the same route, is attested elsewhere (but the procession and the race are mentioned successively by Proclus).[13] The runners are said to be either 'ephebes' or 'children with both parents living,' παῖδες ἀμφιθαλεῖς; in either case, they represent different φυλαί. The winner receives a cup filled with a traditional punch. Not only is it the same route, from the shrine of Dionysus to the shrine of Athena Sciras; the runners like the processioners also carry the same seasonal emblem, bunches of grapes. The procession and the race are plainly related. Yet it cannot be that they were both conducted on the same day to make up the festival Oschophoria; for they have left quite separate trails of antiquarian comment.

Now between the Oschophoria and Theseus' return to the city, there is yet another commemorative rite at Phalerum. In the calendar of the Salaminians, Theseus himself receives sacrifice on 6 Pyanopsion, two days before the civic Theseia.[14] In Plutarch, after the festival Oschophoria is instituted, a sacrifice to Theseus is instituted next (*Thes.* 23.5). A precinct was marked out, we are told, and the cost of sacrifice was to be defrayed by the families who gave up sons and daughters as tribute. This is not the civic Theseia, which Plutarch knew to be a much later foundation, by Cimon.[15] Since the families in question number seven or 'twice seven,' they can be equated with the Salaminians 'from the seven kindreds.'[16] Here then is

---

12 Seventh: Plut. *Thes.* 22.3. Eighth: *ibid.* 36.4.

13 Ath. 11.92, 495 F (Aristodemus *FGrHist* 383 F 9); Procl. *Chrest.*, Phot. *Bibl.* 239, 332a; schol. Nic. *Alex.* 109. The phrase τοῖς Σκίροις in Aristodemus, i.e., in the epitome of Athenaeus, is a palpable confusion, more likely due to the epitomator than to Aristodemus. Though this has long been recognized, it is fiercely resisted by Jacoby on Philochorus *FGrHist* 328 F 14–16 (*Text* pp. 300–2). Yet he does not explain how the race might be appropriate to the festival Scira, nor why the text of Athenaeus is above suspicion. Elsewhere Jacoby is less respectful of the epitomator: cf. Sosibius *FGrHist* 595 F 5.

14 *Hesperia* 7 (1938) 1–9 lines 92–3.

15 Plut. *Thes.* 36.1–4, *Cim.* 8.5–7.

16 *Hesperia* 7 (1938) 1–9 no. 1 lines 3–4, 56–7, 75 (ἐκ τῶν ἑπτὰ φυλῶν); 9–12 no. 2 lines 5, 23–4, 42–3 (ἐξ ἑπτὰ φυλῶν). 'The seven kindreds' are generally taken, *faute de mieux*, as seven Cleisthenic *phylai*, but everyone sees how lame this notion is. Cf. Ferguson, *Hesperia* 7 (1938) 12–15; Nilsson, *AJP* 59 (1938) 387 = *Opuscula Selecta* 2 (Lund 1952)

a sacrifice to Theseus at Phalerum, doubtless beside the shrine of Athena Sciras, where the Salaminians belong.

The ritual is perhaps evoked by monuments which Pausanias saw at Phalerum. He remarks, very briefly, the temple of Athena Sciras and also altars for 'heroes' and for 'the children of Theseus': the last phrase, which seems a little dubious, might easily be emended as 'the children <with> Theseus.'[17] The 'heroes' will include the nautical heroes and possibly Theseus himself. If the emendation is accepted, the altar or altars for 'the children with Theseus' will represent a later form of the sacrifice that was once defrayed by their reputed families; the Salaminians may well have vanished long before Pausanias.[18]

In later days, the chief renown of the civic Theseia was as an agonistic festival for the young; 'boys' and 'ephebes' competed in a variety of athletic contests.[19] It must have grown from small beginnings. The Salaminians arrange a 'contest,' ἄμιλλα, not otherwise described; it goes unmentioned in the calendar, but the most natural place is with the sacrifice to Theseus.[20] This contest of 6 Pyanopsion can then be equated with the foot race of ephebes or children.[21] The φυλαί which they represent are those of the Salaminians, the legendary seven 'kindreds.'

734, and *Cults, Myths, Oracles and Politics* (Lund 1951) 32; Jacoby, n. 2 to Philochorus F 14–16; A. Andrewes, *JHS* 81 (1961) 9 n. 31; Kadletz, *GRBS* 21 (1980) 370.

17 Paus. 1.1.4: βωμοὶ δέ ... καὶ ἡρώων καὶ παίδων τῶν Θησέως: <μετὰ> Θησέως Robert. One does not expect 'the children of Theseus,' scil. Demophon and Acamas, to be sharply distinguished from the general category of 'heroes.' Pausanias' text is often at fault, and the correction is easy. It must be admitted, however, that Demophon and Acamas are not out of place at Phalerum; for it is here that one or other acquires the Palladium of Troy in a struggle with the Argives, and both may have been named together in some version that does not survive. In this sense καὶ <ἄλλων> ἡρώων would be an improvement. For other opinions, Robert, *Hermes* 20 (1885) 354, and *Heldensage* 691 n. 6; Jacoby, n. 137 to Philochorus F 14–16 and n. 4 to F 111; H. Herter, *RE Suppl.* 13 (1973) 1103 s.v. Theseus 1; Kron, *Phylenheroen* 145 n. 666; Kearns, *Heroes of Attica* 40.

18 Ferguson, *Hesperia* 7 (1938) 47, thinks that the Salaminians were still active at the turn of the era, but the evidence is very slight.

19 Cf. Mommsen, *Feste* 291–8, 306–7; A. Wilhelm, *AthMitt* 30 (1905) 213–19; E.N. Gardiner, *Greek Athletic Sports and Festivals* (London 1910) 245–8; Pélékidis, *Éphébie* 229–35; Herter, *RE Suppl.* 13 (1973) 1226–9 s.v. Theseus 1; G.R. Bugh, *ZPE* 83 (1990) 20–37. Bugh 35 n. 60 thinks that the games 'took place several days before the eighth.' The purported join between *IG* 2² 959 and 1014, which would give the date 6 Pyanopsion for a decree arising from the games, must be left for experts to judge.

20 *Hesperia* 7 (1938) 1–9 no. 1 line 61. The association of contest and sacrifice is fully argued on the evidence of the inscription by Ferguson, *Hesperia* 7 (1938) 34–5.

21 Ferguson, *Hesperia* 7 (1938) 36–8, identifies the contest with the foot race as an event of the Oschophoria; he has been generally followed.

The 'Salaminians'

Finally, the 'Salaminians' themselves. The name belongs to two groups uneasily reconciled, those 'from the seven kindreds' and those 'from Sunium.' The former are active at Athens and Phalerum, the latter at Sunium. In a later document the two groups are referred to as two *genē*.[22] In Attica the term *genos* is used of the many ancient bodies who have responsibility for conducting local rites. It is not inappropriate, since any sort of arcane knowledge is handed down in families or purported families (cf. Homeridae, Asclepiadae, and the like). The natural assumption is that the two groups of Salaminians are two hieratic *genē* of independent origin who now find themselves in confrontation, perhaps only because of the coincidence of name.

Modern scholars have a strong historicizing bent: with them the nature of Attic *genē* counts for less than the memory of great events. The Salaminians, we are told, are named for the island of Salamis; it is usually said that they were created as a body at the moment when Athens wrested the island from Megara, whether they were at first native islanders or Athenians entrusted with island cults.[23] On another view, they were an ancient group of islanders who somehow became assimilated to the type of the hieratic *genos*.[24] It is awkward for the theory that most of the rites or cults served by the Salaminians have nothing to do with the island. In outline, their mandate is as follows. At Athens, the Salaminians supply the priestess of Aglaurus and conduct the *pannychis* of the Panathenaea.[25] At Phalerum, they supply the priestess of Athena Sciras and conduct the Oschophoria. At Sunium, they supply the priest of Heracles 'at the ferry place,' obviously the harbour, and conduct a festival of Heracles in Munichion. But there is, after all, a connection with Salamis. The many lesser figures in the regulations include Eurysaces and Teucer, respectively son and half-brother of Ajax, the principal island hero. At Athens, the Salaminians supply the priest of Eurysaces, and sacrifice at his

---

22 *Hesperia* 7 (1938) 9–12 no. 2 line 3.

23 Ferguson, *Hesperia* 7 (1938) 12–47, especially 42–6; Nilsson, *AJP* 59 (1938) 385–93 = *Op. Sel.* 2.731–41, and *Cults ... and Politics* 30–6; M. Guarducci, *RivFil* 76 (1948) 223–53.

24 Bourriot, *Genos* 1.570–94, 685–91, 693, 698–702; S.C. Humphreys, *ZPE* 83 (1990) 246–8. According to Bourriot, the Salaminians are a local community of the kind called *homogalaktes*, 'the most ancient human cell in Attica which we can recognize' (p. 698).

25 For the priestess of Aglaurus, cf. *IG* 2² 3459, ca. 280 BC; *Hesperia* 52 (1983) 50–7, 247–246 or 246–245; *IG* 2² 948, 166–165.

shrine near the Agora. At Phalerum, Teucer is named beside the nautical heroes in the celebration of the Oschophoria.[26]

Eurysaces and Teucer do not dictate the interpretation of all the rest. It is obvious that they are latecomers. No doubt they were installed at Athens and Phalerum at some stage in Athens' occupation of Salamis, i.e., during the sixth century BC. Someone was needed to take charge, and our hieratic *genos* at Athens and Phalerum, ostensible 'Salaminians,' were the inevitable choice. Athena Sciras has also been regarded as an import from Salamis, but this is most unlikely. To be sure, she is worshipped there as well, on another headland; and the hero Scirus who is her partner at Phalerum is matched by like-named heroes on Salamis and on the cliffs of the Megarid. Not surprisingly, Megarian and Attic chroniclers gave priority to one or other of these homonyms; they did not, however, suggest that the cult of Athena was in contention. Athena is from of old the patron of nautical as of other technology (she built the *Argo*, and an even earlier ship that brought the Danaids from Egypt).[27] Her various shrines on the coast are therefore ancient and autonomous: they were not the fashion later.

It is far more significant that the regulations do not extend to any cult on the island of Salamis, as of Athena Sciras or Ajax. The omission would be incomprehensible, if the body of Salaminians had been created for the very purpose of emblazoning Athenian control over Salamis.

The theory rests upon a false premise: that the Salaminians as a *genos* or *genē* are named for the island. A hieratic *genos*, however, is always named for the ritual it conducts; sometimes a patronymic ending is added, sometimes not.[28] The Praxiergidae 'do the job' of cleansing Athena's temple and its furnishings. The Buzygae 'yoke oxen' for the first ploughing. The Eumolpidae 'chant sweetly' at the sowing of the seed. The Heudanemi 'still the winds.' And so on. Of the many names which are truly *genē* of the hieratic kind, some are quite obscure, as very ancient names will be; but wherever the name can be interpreted at all, this explanation fits.

---

26 *Hesperia* 7 (1938) 1–9 no. 1 lines 11, 34, 36, 53, 84–5 (priest and shrine of Eurysaces), 88 (sacrifice to Eurysaces), 91 (sacrifice to Teucer). Cf. *IG* 2² 1232 line 22 (shrine of Eurysaces).

27 Cf. L. Preller, *Griechische Mythologie* 1⁴ (Berlin 1887–94) 217–18 (but nautical technology is here separated from other kinds, on pp. 221–4). For a more intuitive approach, M. Detienne, *RevHistRel* 178 (1970) 133–77 = *Cunning Intelligence in Greek Culture and Society* (Eng. tr., 1978) 177–9, 183–4, 215–58.

28 Cf. Kearns, *Heroes of Attica* 69. But she thinks of the phenomenon as somewhat restricted.

The word σαλαμίς was once a descriptive term, since it was applied to two places which have no historical connection but the same physical appearance: Salamis town on the island, and Salamis town on Cyprus. A broad level beach, then; but more specifically, a 'salt flat,' as we see from the many cognate words like ἅλς, ἁλή, ἅλμη, which have lost initial σ-. The Salaminians are employed at two broad level beaches, Phalerum bay and the bay at Sunium (which has salt flats still). They serve such deities of the coast as Athena Sciras, the nautical heroes, Heracles 'at the ferry place,' even 'the hero at the salt flat,' ὁ ἥρως ὁ ἐπὶ τῆι ἁλῆι, who is honoured at Sunium shortly after the festival of Heracles. They also serve Pandrosus, the goddess of the sacred olive tree on the Acropolis; for salt is used in steeping olives.[29]

The Salaminians are accordingly two groups of 'Salt-flat men,' based at Phalerum and at Sunium. Their earliest function was to promote with suitable observance the harvesting and use of salt, a staple commodity like grain or wine. Those of Phalerum also began to conduct a procession from the city to the port, the Oschophoria. They must have joined hands with the king who reigned in early Athens, i.e., in the community by the Ilissus; for the Oschophoria were soon drawn into the Theseus legend. As a further consequence, the Salaminians sacrificed to Theseus, and called for young men to run a race in his honour, the remote beginning of the festival Theseia. With an eye upon the legend, they took a more imposing title, 'Salaminians from the seven kindreds.'

The Mission to Delos

As everyone knows, Athens conducted an observance on Delos each year that was thought to commemorate Theseus' return.[30] An ancient thirty-oared ship was fitted out, always the same one but kept in repair, and a chorus of youths and maidens embarked on it, together with chorus masters and a ritual ambassador, architheōros. They were understandably cautious in setting forth and in returning; and for the whole time the

29 Hesperia 7 (1938) 1–9 no. 1 lines 10–11, 16–17, 44, 84, 86 (Heracles 'at the ferry place'), 17, 53–4, 86 ('the hero at the salt flat'), 12, 45 (Pandrosus).
30 Pl. Phaedo 58 A–B; Xen. Mem. 4.8.2; [Arist.] Ath. 56.3; Callim. H. Del. 307–15; Plut. Thes. 21.1–2 (Dicaearchus fr. 85 Wehrli), 23.1 (Demetrius Phal. fr. 155 Wehrli), Quaest. Conv. 8.4.3, 724 A; Paus. 8.48.3, 9.40.3–4; Poll. 4.101; Hsch. s.v. Δηλιακὸς βωμός. The François vase shows the youths and maidens dancing, and Theseus playing the lyre: Florence 4209 (ABV 76.1). To be sure, the vase painter follows a version of the myth in which the dance was first performed on Crete, at the very moment of Theseus' triumph. But the ritual prototype is still the dance on Delos.

Athenians at home observed a regimen of purity, which in the year 400–
399 had the effect of delaying Socrates' execution. On Delos the chorus
danced the 'crane dance' round the ancient altar of Apollo that was formed
of goats' horns.

In modern books this observance is invariably associated with the chief
festival of Apollo on Delos: a gathering of Ionians in ancient days, in
Classical times mainly an Athenian spectacle, but always an occasion for
sending choruses and ritual embassies.[31] The month was Thargelion – not
Anthesterion, as often said, for that was not a time for anyone to sail to
Delos. The whole notion is misconceived. The old ship, the one chorus, the
crane dance – all were peculiar customs which Athens kept in memory of
Theseus. Later sources tell how Theseus also, on the same occasion, set up
a statue of Aphrodite, a wooden post with square bottom, and established
games in which the victor was wreathed with palm leaves; they too belong
to the Athenian observance. The general celebration in Thargelion is not
the time for any of this. Nor for the regimen of purity that allowed Socrates
to live on; else Plato had been spared a long explanation.[32]

Furthermore, it is agreed on all sides – by Plato, Callimachus, Plutarch,
Pausanias – that the customs originate with Theseus' return. In Plutarch
they are recounted just before the rites at Phalerum. If the customs belonged to the month Thargelion (not to speak of Anthesterion), we could
not have this result. For the Cretan adventure, the Attic chroniclers gave a
timetable extending from Munichion, when Theseus departed, to Pyanopsion, when he returned. A different timetable would be required by customs of Thargelion that everyone spoke of as marking the return. Or more
likely, the customs of Thargelion would be tied to the outward voyage. As
it is, the customs must belong to the proper season, round the beginning
of Pyanopsion. The name of the dance, γέρανος 'crane,' is doubtless taken
from the season; for cranes fly south in October.[33]

Xenophon says of Socrates that 'after the verdict he lived on for thirty
days because of Delian rites falling in that month': he thinks of a calendar

---

31 E.g, Rhodes on [Arist.] *Ath.* 56.3, cf. 54.7.
32 It is also relevant that legend placed Socrates' birthday on '6 Thargelion, when the
Athenians purify the city and the Delians say that Artemis was born': Diog. Laert. 2.44
(Apollodorus *FGrHist* 244 F 34, Demetrius Phal. 228 F 10 = fr. 153 Wehrli). Had
Socrates died at the same season, Diogenes would say so while noticing the dates of
birth and death.
33 The name is not explained by ancient sources, who say only that the dance imitated the
windings of the labyrinth (Callimachus, Plutarch, Pollux); cf. P. Bruneau, *Recherches
sur les cultes de Délos* (Paris 1970) 20–1, 29–32. For cranes as a seasonal indication,
A. Mommsen, *Mittelzeiten* (Schleswig 1870) 19 n.

month, Pyanopsion. The ship left early in the month, or was ready to leave, as soon as the winds fell. It was doubtless on the first of the month that the stern was wreathed in preparation by the priest of Apollo.[34] The altar of 'the Hero at the Stern,' so called by Callimachus and others, marks the place for the wreathing ceremony and the launching.[35] Pausanias mentions the altar last in his survey of Phalerum, and notes that the hero was identified by experts as Androgeos son of Minos. They had good reason to do so, since the youths and maidens first took ship in order to expiate the death of Androgeos. Callimachus, who adopted this identification from an Attic chronicler, began his story with the invocation 'O Hero at the Stern,' and then added, 'since this the *kyrbis* sings.' We may infer that the wreathing ceremony was prescribed in the Solonian calendar, and was accompanied by the singing of paeans.[36]

Scholars will have it that 'the Hero at the Stern,' alias the son of Minos, is none other than 'Nauseirus,' alias the pilot of Theseus' ship, who with his mate Phaeax is firmly situated at the sanctuary of Athena Sciras.[37] This makes little sense. Moreover, although memorials of Androgeos were sought in other quarters too, this identification of 'the Hero at the Stern' was undoubtedly current among Attic chroniclers who knew the pilot as a familiar figure.[38]

On Delos the observance included games as well as sacrifice and dance. Since these games took place round the same time as the race of ephebes from Athens to Phalerum, they are another antecedent of the civic Theseia. Games, or at least torch-races, were conducted on Delos under the name

34 Which priest of Apollo, we do not know: perhaps the one who officiated at the Pyanopsia a few days later. Apollo Delius had a shrine at Phalerum (*IG* 1³ 383.153–4, a. 429–428; cf. *IG* 1³ 130, as restored by Lewis), but like the Delium at Marathon, it was presumably used during the Delian festival of Thargelion. At Phlya, Apollo Delius was honoured during the Thargelia: Ath. 10.24, 424 E–F (Theophrastus fr. 119 Wimmer, Hieronymus fr. 28 Wehrli).

35 ἥρως ὦ κατὰ πρύμναν, ἐπεὶ τόδε κύρβις ἀείδει: Callim. *Aet.* Bk. 4, fr. 103; cf. Clem. Alex. *Protr.* 2.40.2; Paus. 1.1.4.

36 Paeans often go with wreathing, on shipboard as elsewhere. D. Wachsmuth, ΠΟΜΠΙΜΟΣ Ο ΔΑΙΜΩΝ (Berlin 1967) 90–3, assembles a wide range of evidence for the wreathing of the stern.

37 Deubner, *Att. Feste* 225; Ferguson, *Hesperia* 7 (1938) 25; Jacoby on Philochorus F 111 (*Text* pp. 440–1); Herter, *RE Suppl.* 13 (1973) 1104 s.v. Theseus 1 (doubtful); Kearns, *Heroes of Attica* 40 (doubtful).

38 According to Amelesagoras (*FGrHist* 330 F 2), Androgeos was buried in the Cerameicus and there called 'Eurygyes' – i.e., he is identified with the eponymous hero of the Academy road, a *locus* of funeral games. But Amelesagoras was a maverick. Callimachus' source may very well be Philochorus, as for the Hecale story.

'Theseia' during the last period of Athenian control, after 166: a relic of the old observance.[39]

The Origin of the Theseus Legend

We saw before that in early days Athenian youths were enrolled as citizens at the festival Hecatombaea: hence the story of Theseus' arrival in Athens and recognition by his father, a virtual 'enrolment.' This story is closely bound up with the further exploits of the youthful Theseus, and especially with the Cretan adventure.

From a narrative point of view, the 'enrolment' has two aspects. Theseus is an ideal youth: having come of age, he leaves his mother and proves himself a man, and now embarks on larger tasks. He is also the royal heir: having arrived in Athens, he is recognized by his father and accepted by the people, and now defends the kingdom against dangerous enemies. As to his coming of age, the labours on the road from Troezen are an amazing proof. As to the recognition, it depends on foiling Medea. Both the labours and Medea are late additions to the legend; it may seem that the 'enrolment' is only a consequence of these additions.[40] But in principle it is just as likely that the 'enrolment' was there from the start, and has only been embellished, first with the labours and then with Medea; long afterwards, with Hecale's cottage. The capture of the Marathonian bull is earlier than the labours on the road, but how much earlier does not appear; in any case one might think it separable from the 'enrolment.' Origin and development cannot be traced through the narrative structure alone: a general rule with Greek myth.

The whole Theseus legend has been analysed repeatedly with widely differing results.[41] Yet the analysis seldom focuses sharply or for long on the most important element, the ritual background. The Theseus legend is attached at every point to Athenian cults and festivals. Sometimes the connection is secondary: when the story was already abroad, some ritual or other was pointed out as a re-enactment of the story, and the ritual in turn caused the story to be told in a new light. The Attic chroniclers

---

39 IDél 1951–2, 1955. Cf. Bruneau, Cultes de Délos 35.
40 So U. von Wilamowitz-Moellendorff, SBBerl 1925.234 = Kleine Schriften 5.2 (Berlin 1937) 113–14; C. Sourvinou-Inwood, Theseus as Son and Stepson (BICS Suppl. 40, 1979) 26–8.
41 E.g., Robert, Heldensage 676–8, 689–90, 706; Wilamowitz, SBBerl 1925.234–9 = Kl. Schr. 5.2.113–20; L. Radermacher, Mythos und Sage² (Munich 1943) 290–303; E. Will, Korinthiaka (Paris 1955) 191–204; Herter, RE Suppl. 13 (1973) 1231–4 s.v. Theseus 1; Kearns, Heroes of Attica 117–24; Calame, Thésée 397–450.

used great ingenuity in working out such associations. But their practice only testifies once more to the original nature of the Theseus legend, as of all Greek and ancient myth. It is the aetiological and social reference that makes Greek myth what it is, rather than a corpus of *Märchen* or *novelle*.

The rites associated with the Theseus legend come in clusters. The Cretan adventure was always the most famous, and it is treated as a voyage out and back: Theseus departs in early Munichion as the sailing season opens, and returns late in the season, round the beginning of Pyanopsion.[42] Both junctures have their commemorative rites, but those of the return are much more notable. It is easy to see that this realistic chronology is contrived, and that the Cretan adventure was originally thought of as taking place round the beginning of Pyanopsion.

Other commemorative rites fall in Hecatombaeon and Boedromion. The Hecatombaea honouring Apollo are almost the first. Just before this, doubtless on the second of the month, are the rites of Zeus *meilichios* at the river Cephisus, recalling how Theseus was purified as he entered Athens.[43] Philochorus, and after him Callimachus, amplified the story of Theseus' reception with an *aition* hitherto unknown, taken from a cult of Zeus on Mount Pentelicus.[44] As the rites in question were rather sombre – the story tells of an offering to the dead – they were perhaps cognate with the rites for Zeus *meilichios*, and to be dated likewise to the second. Late in this month, the festival of Athena Pallenis at Pallene can be discerned behind the encounter with Pallas and his fifty sons.[45] The festival includes a ritual combat which gives rise to still other mythical combats; Euripides recounts one of them, about Theseus' son Demophon, and shows us that the festival came at the same time as the Panathenaea, on 28 Hecatombaeon (*Heracleidae* 777–83).

The festival Boedromia of 6–7 Boedromion commemorates the battle with the Amazons.[46] On the first day the festival honoured Artemis at her shrine in Agrae, and on the second Apollo at the Lyceium; both shrines

---

42 Departure in Munichion: Plut. *Thes.* 18. Return round the beginning of Pyanopsion: *ibid.* 22–3 (Demetr. Phal. fr. 155 Wehrli, Demo *FGrHist* 327 F 6), 36.4; Harpocr. *s.v.* ὀσχοφόροι (Philochorus *FGrHist* 328 F 16, Ister 334 F 8); Bekker, *Anecd.* 1.239 *s.v.* δειπνοφόρος (Philochorus F 183). Cf. Robert, *Heldensage* 695–7.

43 Plut. *Thes.* 12.1. We know from historical anecdotes that the Argive festival of Zeus *meilichios* was close in time to the Spartan Gymnopaediae, which fell in the month corresponding to Hecatombaeon.

44 Plut. *Thes.* 14.2–3 (Philochorus *FGrHist* 328 F 109); Callim. *Hecale* frs. 230–77; *Suppl. Hell.* frs. 280–91. Cf. A.S. Hollis, *Callimachus* Hecale (Oxford 1990) 7.

45 Schol. Eur. *Hipp.* 35 (Philochorus *FGrHist* 328 F 108); Plut. *Thes.* 13; etc.

46 Plut. *Thes.* 27.1–7 (Hellanicus *FGrHist* 323a F 17, Cleidemus 323 F 18), 28.1 (*Theseis* fr. 1 Davies); etc.

have helped to form the battle dispositions. Then we come to the rites marking the Cretan adventure. They extend from late Boedromion through early Pyanopsion.

So the festival Hecatombaea is in effect the first in the series of commemorative rites. The 'enrolment,' moreover, prepares Theseus to go forth from Athens as a young warrior and a young bachelor – to fight the sons of Pallas and to woo or abduct Ariadne. As to the battle with the Amazons, it is hard to decide whether Theseus was at first a young warrior, or a young bachelor, or both.

The Cretan adventure was always closely linked with Theseus' coming of age, or with his arrival and recognition, i.e., with the enrolment ceremony. Young Theseus was eager to go, and the Athenians demanded this of Aegeus' son. The tribute, returning at intervals of nine years, or eight as we would say, was now due for the third time.[47] A third time is always likely to be critical; and two such intervals must pass before the ideal youth is ready. Supposing that the tribute was a condition of life since Theseus' birth, supposing too that he grew up in Athens, he still could not come forward until this moment. The enrolment ceremony of Hecatombaeon is therefore fundamental to the Cretan adventure. The story is very old, and so is the ritual behind it.

---

47 On these details, says Plutarch, 'most of the historians agree': *Thes.* 15.1; cf. Marm. Par. *FGrHist* 239 A 19–20; Diod. 4.61.3–4; [Apld.] *Epit.* 1.7. For other sources, Herter, *RE Suppl.* 13 (1973) 1099–1100 s.v. Theseus 1. Diodorus with his usual inadvertence makes it only the second tribute. Something has gone wrong with the computation of the Parian Marble, which gives an interval of thirty-five years between the imposition of tribute in 1294–293 and Theseus' accession in 1259–1294 (the interval must in any case be a multiple of eight). The imposition of tribute should probably have been assigned to 1275–1274, year thirty-three of Aegeus' reign instead of year thirteen: so Jacoby, *Das Marmor Parium* (Berlin 1904) 144–5, and again in *FGrHist*.

5

The Olympieia and
the Calvary

Synopsis

Though Zeus *olympios* is chiefly known for the huge temple begun by
Peisistratus and completed by Hadrian, his cult and festival are very old.
In late spring, the weather god is asked to bring clear skies for the ripening of the grain; the requisite magic is a noisy, tumultuous display that
becomes the *anthippasia*, an equestrian contest. To witness the spectacle, the Palladium is conveyed to the Hippodrome, just as the statue of
Dionysus is conveyed to the theatre. The explanatory myth describes a
battle at Phalerum in which Athens takes possession of the Palladium of
Troy.

Peisistratus enlarged the festival as he did the shrine; it was still flour-
ishing in the fourth and third centuries, when inscriptions throw a little
light. After Peisistratus, it began with a great procession, like the Panathenaea. This procession too started at the northwest, and the cavalry
were prominent. The festival aetiology was now drawn from the tyrant's
exploits. The cavalry parade was said to re-enact the announcement of his
victory at Pallene; the conveyance of the Palladium was said to re-enact
the manner of his entering Athens.

We shall consider in turn the nature of the cult; the origin of the
festival; the cavalry parade; the *anthippasia*.

The Nature of the Cult

The sanctuary was one of the oldest in Athens: in Thucydides' opinion,
older than the legendary 'synoecism' that created the first agora east of the

Acropolis. The founding myth takes it back to Deucalion, when he came to Athens after the flood.[1]

Like every deity, Zeus *olympios* fostered the subsistence of his worshippers. We should ask how he did so.

Among Athenian cults of Zeus, only Zeus *meilichios* at Agrae and Zeus *polieus* on the Acropolis can be compared for general importance. Zeus *meilichios* is entreated at the end of winter, at the festival Diasia of 22 Anthesterion, when stores are running low; from this point until the harvest is the most difficult time of all. Zeus *polieus* is honoured by the city after the threshing, at the festival Dipolieia of 14 Scirophorion; bright hot weather has been needed hitherto, but now it is rather to be feared; so a plough ox is sacrificed as a signal for fresh weather and as an instrument for producing it.[2] The festival of Zeus *olympios* comes round on 19 Munichion.[3] Zeus must help once more: at this date the grain is in the last stage of ripening, and it will suffer unless the skies are clear and still throughout.

All the evidence we have for Athens' cult of Zeus *olympios* shows that crops and weather were the main concern. Pausanias records the foundation myth and a commemorative rite. After the flood, he says, the water ran off through a cleft nearby, and Deucalion himself built the first shrine. Each year wheat meal mixed with honey is thrown into the cleft. The flood myth, wherever it occurs in Greece, is bound up with ritual that signals the end of winter rains and the hope for abundant crops or pasture.[4] The rites mostly come in the month Anthesterion; that was probably the time for casting the wheat meal. Zeus *olympios* has a partner, the goddess Earth; like a wedded wife, she takes his name – Ge *olympia*. There is a similar pair at Sparta, Zeus *olympios* and Aphrodite *olympia*.[5] Whichever goddess it is, the shared epithet makes a magic union, of potent rain and fertile field.

Zeus *olympios* is thus a deity of agriculture, or at least of weather as it affects agriculture. At Sparta the cult of Zeus *olympios* was traced

---

1 Thuc. 2.15.4; Marm. Par. *FGrHist* 239 A 4; Paus. 1.18.7–8; cf. Str. 9.4.2, p. 425.

2 Cf. *Ancient Economy in Mythology*, ed. M. Silver (Savage, Md. 1991) 15.

3 Plut. *Phoc.* 37.1.

4 At Delphi, the favourite setting for the flood myth, the flood ends on 7 Bysius = Anthesterion, and is commemorated by a magic sprinkling and other rites: EMC² 9 (1990) 441, 10 (1991) 72. Athens' *hydrophoria* was perhaps an equivalent rite, but the date is not recorded. Other rites of the season come to be associated with the flood, e.g. the *chytroi* of 13 Anthesterion.

5 Paus. 3.12.11. Elsewhere at Sparta, Zeus *olympios* is worshipped alone: Paus. 3.14.5.

back to Epimenides, a legendary magician, and therefore a likely person to have invented agriculture. Indeed Epimenides always carried with him a talisman of agriculture, an ox's hoof that contained unfailing food.[6] Now at Athens too Epimenides was sometimes spoken of as the first to yoke an ox, i.e., as the inventor of agriculture. But this role he disputed with a literal 'Ox-yoker,' Buzyges the eponym of the Buzygae, a hieratic *genos*.[7] The *genos* supplied the priest for an old cult of Zeus: yet another old cult, beside those of Zeus *olympios*, Zeus *meilichios*, Zeus *polieus*. Or so it seems at first sight.

The official title of the *genos* priest is 'priest of Zeus at the Palladium.'[8] The Palladium, a small wooden statue of Athena, belongs to this cult of Zeus and forms an ancient landmark; the court for involuntary homicide was known as the court 'at the Palladium.' The priest also conducted a ritual ploughing in a field called the Buzygium, described as lying 'under the Acropolis,' but only to distinguish it from two other fields much farther off, one at the river Cephisus west of Athens, and another at Eleusis. The Buzygium cannot lie right beside the Acropolis.[9] Fertile land was wanted for a ritual ploughing, and is provided at the other two sites. In Athens, the most fertile land that lies 'under the Acropolis' is at the southeast, near the Ilissus. We also expect the Buzygium to be near the shrine of Zeus 'at the Palladium.'

6 Diog. Laert. 1.114 (Epimenides *Vorsokr* 3 A 1, *FGrHist* 457 T 1, Timaeus *FGrHist* 566 F 4).

7 Schol. Aeschin. 2 *De Fals. Leg.* 82; Serv. *Georg.* 1.19 ([Arist.] fr. 386 Rose³); *Etym. Magn. s.v.* Βουζυγία.

8 *IG* 2² 1096, and *Hesperia* 9 (1940) 86–8 no. 17, another fragment: τοῦ Βουζύγου καὶ ἱερέως Διὸς τοῦ ἐμ Παλλαδίωι. *IG* 2² 3177: ἱερεὺς τοῦ Διὸς τοῦ ἐπὶ Παλλαδίου καὶ Βουζύγης. *IG* 2² 5055: Βουζύγου ἱερέως Διὸς ἐν Παλλαδίωι. *IG* 2² 5075: ἱερέως Διὸς τελείου Βουζύγου. The last two are theatre seats which have been erased and reinscribed; indeed 5055 has been erased twice, and the existing inscription may be the latest of any seat in the theatre, '3rd/4th cent. after Chr.': M. Maass, *Die Prohedrie des Dionysostheaters in Athen* (Munich 1972) 125, 136–7. Perhaps the *genos* had previously held some other seat or seats; under Hadrian, seats were newly assigned to various dignitaries. For the Buzygae in general, see Toepffer, *Att. Gen.* 136–49; Bourriot, *Genos* 2.1270–91.

9 Plut. *Conj. Praec.* 42, 144 A: 'The Athenians conduct three ritual ploughings, the first at Scirum, a memorial of the most ancient sowing of all, the second in the Rharian plain, the third under the Acropolis, the Buzygium as it is called,' τρίτον ὑπὸ πόλιν τὸν καλούμενον βουζύγιον. Some think of the shrine of Demeter *chloē* below the southwest bastion of the Acropolis, but the rock ledge here would not lend itself to ploughing (Demeter's shrines at the northwest were discussed above: pp. 18–21). According to schol. Aeschin. 2 *De Fals. Leg.* 82, Buzyges' plough 'was dedicated on the Acropolis,' ἀνέκειτο ἐν τῇ ἀκροπόλει. Wherever the ploughing, this is the place for a dedication, and the Acropolis 'slopes' are not – *pace* E. Kearns, *The Heroes of Attica* (*BICS Suppl.* 57, 1989) 152.

The site of the Palladium is fixed by Cleidemus, the Attic chronicler. Plutarch reproduces his account of the battle with the Amazons, which as we saw is inspired by the festival Boedromia (pp. 24–5).[10] We should recall and expand our conclusions about the topography. The Amazons had already occupied Athens, and now drew up their line from east to west along the south side of the city, facing the Athenians farther south. The Amazon right wing rested on the Pnyx, the Athenian left on the Museum hill. Here and along much of the line the Athenians at first advanced a long way, retaking ground up to the Peiraic Gate; then they were driven back on the Areopagus. The Amazon left wing was at the 'Amazoneium,' where fallen Amazons were subsequently buried. Other sources locate these burials near the gate to Phalerum, or near the shrine of Ge *olympia*, and so very close to the Olympieium. The Athenian right, which decides the battle, 'attacked from the Palladium and Ardettus and the Lyceium.' The last two points are outside the southeast sector of the city; the Athenian line extended much farther than that of the Amazons. It ran east to Ardettus, then turned sharply north, or even northwest, to the Lyceium.[11] Theseus won because he outflanked the Amazons.

This tactic suits the festival. Theseus as a virtual Polemarch commands on the extreme right, at the Lyceium, which is the Polemarch's domain and the festival setting; before battle is joined, he offers sacrifice to *Phobos* 'Battle-rout' as a personification of the festival business. The Lyceium then is dictated as the end of the line. Perhaps Ardettus is named because the wing should realistically rest on a hill (as do the wings of both armies at the west). The Palladium will be due west of Ardettus, on a line towards the Museum hill. The line crosses the southeast corner of the city, the area of the Olympieium and the 'Amazoneium.' Only here, at the Palladium, did the Athenians directly face the Amazons.

More precisely, the Palladium and the 'Amazoneium' must be sought at the southwest of the Olympieium. The 'Amazoneium,' which was perhaps no more than a stele suggesting a burial, was on the road near the city-gate where Pausanias entered from Phalerum; from this point, we may assume,

---

10 Plut. *Thes.* 27.1–7 (Cleidemus *FGrHist* 323 F 18, in part). At *Thes.* 27.2 Hellanicus is cited for another illustration of the Amazons' hardihood (*FGrHist* 323a F 17); Jacoby gives only the following passage, 27.3–7, to Cleidemus. But 27.1 is inseparable, for it refers to the same battle lines. Robert, *Heldensage* 737, has an impossible notion of the Amazon line: it somehow faces east, with the left wing on the Areopagus.

11 The Lyceium was a large area outside the east wall of Athens, but the exact location and extent remain unknown. Inscriptions that have been posted there have been found in two churches, Sotira Lykodemou and Sotira Kottake, near the southwest corner of the National Gardens: J.P. Lynch, *Aristotle's School* (Berkeley 1972) 16–31, 217; M.H. Jameson, *Archaiognosia* 1 (1980) 225. This is northwest of Ardettus, and due north of the Olympieium.

the procession of 6 Boedromion went out to Artemis' shrine at Agrae. The Palladium as an embodiment of fire from heaven belongs on higher ground. Recent excavation has shown that Peisistratus' temple was built across a ridge running from northeast to southwest.[12] The southwest end of the ridge is a sharp spur of rock: just the place for the Palladium.[13]

As we shall see in a moment, Demophon acquires the Palladium of Troy in a struggle at Phalerum, and the object is carried back to Athens – only one confused source locates the Palladium and the homicide court at Phalerum. Though the story does not impose a particular location, ours fits very nicely.

The Palladium then was close to the Olympieium, and we are led to equate Zeus 'at the Palladium' and Zeus *olympios*. In fact the equation cannot be avoided. All the ancient civic cults of Athens are served by hieratic *genē*. Eleusinian Demeter, Athena *polias*, Zeus *polieus* each has more than one *genos* at his or her disposal.[14] Near the Olympieium, Apollo *pythios* has the *genos* Erysichthonidae, named for Apollo's 'saving' branch, the *eiresiōnē*.[15] A *genos* must be postulated for Zeus *olympios* as well, and the Buzygae meet the requirements exactly.[16] We may recall that Pericles, a thundering orator, was dubbed both 'the Olympian' and 'the Buzyges.'[17] As served by the Buzygae, Zeus also has the epithet *teleios* 'complete': although the epithet lends itself to diverse interpretations, it is appropriate

12 Travlos, *Pictorial Dict.* 289–90, 402, cf. 101 fig. 130, 167 fig. 217, 292 fig. 380.

13 Some remains west of the Olympieium, a stoa and perhaps a court of the early Hellenistic period, have been identified by archaeologists as the lawcourt at the Palladium, but this seems very wishful: A. Andreiomenou, *Deltion* 21 (1966) *Chron.* 81–3; Travlos, *Pictorial Dict.* 412–16 and *Hesperia* 43 (1974) 500–11; O. Alexandri, *Deltion* 27 (1972) *Chron.* 102–4.

14 Eleusinian Demeter: Eumolpidae, Ceryces, Croconidae, Coeronidae, Philleidae. Athena *polias*: Eteobutadae, Praxiergidae. Zeus *polieus*: Thaulonidae, perhaps Centriadae. For the *genē* of Zeus *polieus*, see Deubner, *Att. Feste* 160–70.

15 See *AJP* 105 (1984) 385–93.

16 When Hadrian patronized the cult, priesthoods outside the *genos* were perhaps established for the first time. We find theatre seats of Hadrianic date for 'the priest of Zeus *olympios*' (5025, the most prominent), 'the priest of Olympian Victory' (5027), 'the cleanser, *phaidyntēs*, of Zeus from Pisa' (5064), 'the cleanser of Zeus *olympios* in the city' (5072), and, in the fourteenth row, for 'the god's servants,' *theēkoloi* (5085). Cf. Maass, *Prohedrie, ad locc.*

17 'Olympian': Ar. *Ach.* 530–1; cf. Diod. 12.40.6 (Ephorus *FGrHist* 70 F 196); Quint. 12.10.65; [Luc.] 58 *Demosth. Enc.* 20. 'Buzyges': Ael. Arist. *Or.* 3.51 (Eupol. *Dem.* fr. 103 Kassel and Austin). That Eupolis refers to Pericles is often denied, as by Bourriot, *Nature du genos* 2.1273–4, and indeed by Kassel and Austin, but only because Pericles cannot be a literal Buzyges. Both Aristeides and the scholia are very clear on the matter. Elsewhere in Eupol. *Dem.* 'a Buzyges' or 'the priest of Zeus' is referred to in a different fashion, for his concern with right conduct (fr. 99.107, fr. 113).

in the first instance to the weather-god who brings the grain to ripeness.[18]
The reason why the Buzygae do not use the epithet *'olympios'* is doubtless
that it did not belong to the very earliest nomenclature of cult; it came
somewhat later, most likely with epic poetry.

The Origin of the Festival

Peisistratus' temple was not the first. An earlier temple, itself substantial,
was dismantled to make room, and the new one, though unfinished, must
have sufficed thereafter for the same purposes of cult.[19] This ancient shrine
presupposes an ancient festival; it is wrong to suggest that the Olympieia
originate with Peisistratus.[20] What he did was to enlarge the celebration
in a suitable fashion.

Athens' cavalry were on display at the festival, parading through the
streets and competing in the Hippodrome. However much the program
owes to Peisistratus, we may be sure that some kind of equestrian performance was traditional: the worship of Zeus and Athena regularly calls for
it.[21] If we could see far back, we would find chariots instead of cavalry.
In fact the chariot survives in the ritual of the Olympieia, and also in an
early myth and a later legend that are prompted by the ritual – a myth
about Demophon and a legend about Peisistratus.

This connection between Zeus *olympios* and the cavalry derives from
the seasonal concern that was mentioned at the outset. Clear weather is
needed to ripen the crops. A main event of the festival is a mock combat
in the Hippodrome, full of noise and speed. Trumpets blare, and horsemen wheel and charge. Good entertainment, but also powerful magic. It
is weather magic of the kind perfectly exemplified in a myth of Thes-
saly, the land of magic. Zeus is mocked by King Salmoneus, who flaunts

18 Clytemnestra speaks of Agamemnon as her *anēr teleios*, who brings warmth or coolness
   to the household in due season, even while Zeus governs the weather out of doors; then
   she invokes Zeus *teleios* to fulfil her prayers (Aesch. *Ag.* 969–74). Here the epithet
   plainly evokes weather and marriage at the same time. F. Salviat, *BCH* 88 (1964)
   647–54, expatiates on Zeus *teleios* and Hera *teleia* as deities of marriage, a common
   theme in literature. It is obvious, however, that marriage is a secondary interest for
   both of them. Hera *teleia* brings heifers to maturity at the time for breeding, the
   original *hieros gamos*.

19 For the earlier temple, Travlos, *Pictorial Dict.* 402; Wycherley, *Stones of Athens* 155–6.
   For the condition of Peisistratus' temple, Wycherley 156–60.

20 The suggestion is made in every treatment of the festival: Mommsen, *Feste* 465–8;
   Deubner, *Att. Feste* 177; Parke, *Festivals* 144–5; Simon, *Festivals* 15–16; Kyle,
   Athletics 46.

21 Cf. *RhM* n.s. 128 (1985) 241–53.

and blusters in his speeding, clangorous chariot. Salmoneus' real purpose was not to mock Zeus, but to bring clear still weather.[22] Such was also the purpose of our festival, and the magic was again violent and intimidating.

The Cavalry Parade

The festival began with a cavalry parade. In 318 BC, the horsemen wept and removed their wreaths as they passed somewhere near Athens' prison; for on that very day Phocion was taking poison. The prison has been located outside the southwest corner of the Agora.[23] So the parade followed the Panathenaic Way; as with the Panathenaic procession, the starting-point was the Leocoreium or muster-ground that Peisistratus had marked out at the northwest boundary of the city.

The horsemen presumably went first to the sanctuary of Zeus *olympios*, and then to the Hippodrome at Phalerum where they engaged in contests. The Hippodrome lay very close to the sea, probably in the area of New Phalerum.[24] We shall see in a moment that the Palladium was conveyed for the occasion from the sanctuary to the Hippodrome. After the long parade and the contests, it must have been late in the day when the cavalry and other worshippers returned to the sanctuary of Zeus *olympios* for sacrifice and feasting.[25]

The parade of horsemen wearing wreaths is partly or entirely due to Peisistratus. If there was a parade before, it was shorter. Now the festival parade was perhaps the most impressive of any, after the procession of the Great Panathenaea. It is said that Peisistratus' triumph at Pallene was first broadcast by certain gallant horsemen, and we should ask whether this is history or legend. According to Herodotus, Peisistratus 'mounted his sons on horses and sent them ahead' to reassure those who were fleeing in defeat. According to Polyaenus, Peisistratus told an advance party to wreathe themselves with green sprays and bring word that a settlement had

22 For Salmoneus in the context of weather magic, see S. Eitrem, *Opferritus und Voropfer der Griechen und Römer* (Kristiana 1915) 167–8; W. Fiedler, *Antiker Wetterzauber* (Stuttgart 1931) 7–8, 31.

23 Tears for Phocion: Plut. *Phoc.* 37.1–2. Prison: E. Vanderpool, *Penn. U. Mus. Pap.* 1 (1980) 17–31.

24 W.S. Ferguson, *Hesperia* 7 (1938) 25–6; Kyle, *Athletics* 95–7; Travlos, *Bildlexicon zur Topographie des antiken Attika* (Tübingen 1988) 288. S. Benton, *BSA* 67 (1972) 13–19, does not succeed in showing that the Hippodrome was once at Colonus Hippius.

25 *IG* 2² 1496 lines 82–3 (334–333 BC), 113–14 (333–332): hide-money, respectively, of 671 drachmas and of a sum exceeding 500 drachmas.

been reached (when it had not); the advance party are obviously horsemen, though Polyaenus forgets to say so.[26] These reports cannot both be true; more likely, they were both suggested by the ceremonial horsemen of the Olympieia.

The *Anthippasia*

The principal contest in the Hippodrome, perhaps the only one, was the *anthippasia*, described by Xenophon as an exciting spectacle in which squadrons from the ten *phylai* 'flee' and 'pursue' and charge at each other in pretended combat.[27] Now we hear of a mythical combat very like this, and in the same area, on the shore at Phalerum. The combat is between Athenians and Argives who do not recognize each other; the Argives have put in at Phalerum while returning from Troy; they bring Troy's Palladium, which falls into Athenian hands during the combat. Demophon of Athens 'flees'; the Argives 'pursue'; many are killed. Demophon, moreover, either drives a chariot or rides a horse (the others are not clearly pictured), and he tramples his pursuers, or else an Athenian who gets in the way. Demophon wins possession of the Palladium, and it is set up in Athens.[28] In still other versions the struggle is played out at Troy before the return, and Demophon gives the Palladium 'to an Athenian, called Buzyges, to convey to Athens.'[29]

The myth adverts to other matters besides our festival. Athens' court 'at the Palladium' is now established to deal with involuntary homicide.

26 Hdt. 1.63.2. Polyaenus 1.21.1: παράγγελμα ἔδωκε θαλλῶι στεφανοῦσθαι καὶ μὴ κτείνειν τοὺς ἀπαντῶντας. φράζειν δὲ ὡς ἐσπείσαντο τοῖς πρώτοις.

27 Xen. *Hipparch.* 3.10–13, cf. 1.20. In the third century, perhaps already in the late fourth, the event was also included in the Panathenaic games. For the epigraphic evidence, Vanderpool, *Hesperia* 43 (1974) 311–13; Kyle, *Athletics* 189–90; G.R. Bugh, *The Horsemen of Athens* (Princeton 1988) 59–60.

28 Eustath. *Od.* 1.321, Suda *s.v.* ἐπὶ Παλλαδίωι (Paus. Att. ε 53 Erbse, Phanodemus *FGrHist* 325 F 16, Cleidemus 323 F 20); Poll. 8.118; schol. Aeschin. 2 *De Fals. Leg.* 87; schol. Patm. Dem. 23 *Aristocr.* 27, 71; Harpocr. *s.v.* ἐπὶ Παλλαδίωι; Bekker, *Anecd.* 1.311; Paus. 1.28.8–9. Pausanias speaks of Demophon's 'horse,' as if he were astride; 'chariot' and 'horses' are expressly mentioned only in Bekker, *Anecd.*, but can be inferred for all the parallel accounts. For the myth in general, see Robert, *Heldensage* 1235–7; L. Ziehen, *RE* 18.3 (1949) 176–9 *s.v.* Palladion; Jacoby on Cleidemus *FGrHist* 323 F 20; W. Burkert, *ZRelGeistGesch* 22 (1970) 362–4; U. Kron, *LIMC* 1.1 (1981) 442 *s.v.* Akamas et Demophon.

29 Polyaenus 1.5; Clem. Alex. *Protr.* 4.47.6 (Dionysius of Samos *FGrHist* 15 F 3); Ptol. Chenn. 3.8 p. 24 Chatzis. A contest at Troy is already attested by Macron's cup, mentioned below. Polyaenus says, τὸ μὲν ἀληθινὸν (Παλλάδιον) ἔδωκεν ἀνδρὶ Ἀθηναίωι. καλουμένωι Βουζύγηι. κομίζειν Ἀθήναζε.

In one version the dead Argives are honoured at Phalerum as 'Unknown Gods.' Yet these matters are plainly secondary. The myth is centred on the combat and on possession of the Palladium. Demophon as an Athenian hero was very likely first projected from the festival Olympieia.[30] The name Δημοφῶν, i.e., Δημο-φα-ων, means 'Light-of-the-land,' a good name for the victor. The other Demophon, he of Eleusis, also figures in a ritual combat.[31]

Besides the combat, the myth gives us the Palladium and a virtual priest of Zeus, Buzyges the confidant of Demophon. These items also belong to the festival. Philochorus and ephebic inscriptions speak of a procession that brought the Palladium from Athens to Phalerum, and of another that brought it back again late in the day. The ceremony has never been properly explained. It cannot be the festival Plynteria, the usual opinion until it was refuted.[32] It cannot be a rite of expiation, otherwise unheard of, which signals the opening of the homicide court in late autumn.[33] And it cannot be a commemorative rite re-enacting Athens' evacuation in 480.[34] Instead, it is the Olympieia.

According to Philochorus, the magistrates called *nomophylakes* 'would arrange the procession for Pallas, whenever the wooden image was conveyed to the sea.'[35] In the later Hellenistic period, the corps of ephebes are often commended for escorting 'Pallas' to Phalerum, and then back again

30 Athens' Palladium was linked with Troy's at an early date, and in stories which have not survived. On a cup of Macron, 490–480 BC, Diomedes and Odysseus, each holding a Palladium, are ready to engage, but Demophon and Acamas restrain them: Leningrad B 649 (ARV² 460.13, *LIMC* 1.1 [1981] 437 no. 6 s.v. Akamas et Demophon).

31 Hsch. *s.v.* βαλλητύς; cf. *Hom. H. Cer.* 265–7; Ath. 9.71, 406 D.

32 See W. Burkert, *ZRelGeistGesch* 22 (1970) 358–9. P. Brulé, *La Fille d'Athènes* (Paris 1987) 105–6, is half inclined to reopen the question.

33 According to Burkert, *ZRelGeistGesch* 22 (1970) 356–68, the Palladium is taken to the sea at this time to be purified, and then set up again in Athens to show that the court is open. 'The deed of blood' deducible from the myth is a portentous ox sacrifice like that reported for the cult of Heracles at Lindus. There are several objections. It is hardly credible that the homicide court did not sit from Hecatombaeon to Maemacterion; nor is the procession datable to Maemacterion (n. 37 below). Nothing is said of 'purifying' the Palladium except in a version of schol. Patm. Dem. that is quite unreliable. Our mythical combat does not remotely suggest an ox sacrifice – some other myths are quite explicit. At Athens, moreover, the Dipolieia provide a notorious instance of such a sacrifice; it is barely mentioned by Burkert.

34 So B. Nagy, *Historia* 40 (1991) 288–306. The removal of Athena's statue from the Acropolis was not an event to be commemorated, nor does a true commemoration mimic what was done – this is only an aetiological fancy. Had there been an Athenian festival commemorating the evacuation, we would certainly hear of it in Plutarch. Finally, there can be no doubt that 'Pallas' in the ephebic decrees means the Palladium, just as 'Dionysus' means the statue of Dionysus.

35 Phot., Suda *s.v.* οἱ νομοφύλακες τίνες (Philochorus *FGrHist* 328 F 64b).

by torchlight.[36] The decrees of commendation give no hint of the time of year when this was done.[37] Among the various ceremonial duties of the ephebes, the escorting of the Palladium is always bracketed with a similar activity, the escorting of Dionysus' statue to the theatre. As Dionysus' statue was brought to the theatre to enjoy the plays, we may infer that the Palladium was brought to the Hippodrome to enjoy the combat. Or in terms of magic, to register its effect.

The Palladium was conveyed in a chariot. In a very late ephebic inscription 'the charioteer of Pallas' is named beside other officials.[38] Demophon carries off the Palladium now as a charioteer, now as a horseman. In reality the charioteer was Buzyges, the priest of Zeus 'at the Palladium'; one version of the myth is prosaic enough to say so. We are told that the ephebes of 107–106 BC went in company 'with the members of the genos,' scil. the Buzygae.[39]

Such was the festival which Peisistratus endowed. Afterwards, observers read off Peisistratus' career from the festival business. Why do horsemen parade? Because Peisistratus' coming was first announced by horsemen wreathed in fronds or by his own sons riding ahead. Why does the priest convey the Palladium in a chariot? Because Peisistratus gained power (in the connected story, it was the second or third time) by dressing a woman in armour to look like Athena, and getting her to strike a pose while they rode together in a chariot.[40] 'The silliest affair' on record, says Herodotus, inviting his readers to feel superior. And perhaps we should, when we perceive that the silliness is only another routine aetiology.[41]

---

36 *IG* 2² 1006 lines 11–12, 75–6 (123–122 BC); 1008 lines 9–10 (119–118); *Hesperia* 16 (1947) 170–2 no. 67 line 19 (117–116); 1011 lines 10–11 (107/6). Pélékidis, *Éphébie* 251 n. 3, proposes to restore this occasion in a fragmentary decree, but for no good reason.

37 Burkert, *ZRelGeistGesch* 22 (1970) 359, says that 'the Pallas-procession is constantly named between the Mysteries in the autumn and the Dionysia in the spring,' so that it must fall between these limits, arguably in Maemacterion. The premise is false; the only 'constant' association is with the Dionysia, those of Poseideon as well as those of Elaphebolion. The Mysteries, coming soon after the enrolment of the ephebes, are generally mentioned at the outset; but then the list proceeds by categories, and it is clear in every case that the escorting of the Palladium is a new category.

38 *IG* 2² 2245 line 299 (probably 256 AD): ἡνίοχος Παλλάδος. For the date, Follet, *Athènes* 331–3.

39 *IG* 2² 1011 lines 10–11: συνεξήγαγον δὲ καὶ τὴν Παλλάδα μετὰ τῶν γεννητῶν κτλ.

40 Hdt. 1.60.3–5; [Arist.] *Ath.* 14.4; Ath. 13.89, 609 C-D (Cleidemus *FGrHist* 323 F 15); etc.

41 The explanation favoured nowadays is that Peisistratus was acting out a supposed ritual or was giving expression to a deep pattern that underlies many rituals or customs. See W.R. Connor, *JHS* 107 (1987) 40–50. This is a curious reversal of ancient aetiology: where once a great event was deduced from social custom, now social custom is deduced from a great event.

PART TWO

Sparta

6

The Gymnopaediae and the Enrolment of Citizens

Synopsis

'If there is any festival the Spartans care about,' says Pausanias, 'it is the Gymnopaediae' (3.11.9). He doubtless thinks not only of the artificial splendours of his own day, but also of those famous moments of Spartan history for which the Gymnopaediae supply the background: the humiliation of Demaratus after the kingship is taken from him; the suspension of the festival when Argos is seized by enemies; above all, the report of the catastrophe of Leuctra, while the festival goes on. Not surprisingly, details of the program are sparse and uncertain. Yet enough survives so that we can assign the festival to a common type, a festival of Apollo at the new year in which the young men are enrolled as adult warriors. The Spartan version is of special interest, since Sparta, of all Greek cities, is a community of warriors.

A festival addressed to a particular god at a particular season will show a common pattern in many parts of Greece. This is not to say that the pattern suffices by itself for a reconstruction of any given instance. Rather, such details as we have should be considered in the light of the pattern.

Sparta has three important festivals addressed to Apollo: Gymnopaediae, Carneia, Hyacinthia. The festival Carneia was nearly universal in Dorian cities. The festival Hyacinthia was fairly widespread, to judge from the month name Hyacinthius *vel sim.*; although the month name is likely to be much more restricted than the festival, it occurs often enough in Crete and the Dorian islands. As for the Γυμνοπαιδίαι, the name, meaning 'Naked Sports' (from παιδιά, 'sport' or 'play'), appears to be unique to Sparta; this endearing term has replaced an earlier festival name of the usual kind, i.e., a name describing the ritual. That name was very likely

Ἑκατόμβη, a vanished festival which gives the month name Hecatombeus. The Gymnopaediae fall at a time which is marked elsewhere by festivals of Apollo, roughly the month of July. In calendars which begin round the summer solstice, this is the first month of the year. The first quarter is the occasion for the first public gathering of the year; it is a festival of Apollo, god of civic reunions.

The festival pattern is clearly seen at Athens, in the Apolline festival Hecatombaea, which gives the name of Athens' first month. Let us recall the main points. The aetiological myth tells of Theseus' arrival and reception at Athens. Theseus, an ideal young man, is now enrolled as a member of the Athenian community; the mythical event stands for a general custom, of enrolling a whole age class of young men. Like Theseus, the young men shear their hair, take up sword and sandals, and manhandle the sacrificial victim. After the sacrifice, they are presented to the assembly of adult citizens; all join together in singing paeans and eating and drinking.

The Spartan festival follows the pattern. The young men dance in the agora for Apollo *pythaeus*. Artemis and Leto are honoured too, deities of child rearing who represent the stage now left behind. There are also dancing competitions in the theatre, while the whole community watches. Other age groups, boys and men, engage in both the worship and the contests. But the young men, the age class about to be enrolled as adults, are to the fore. They dance naked, and a choral refrain calls attention to their nakedness and the evidence of physical maturity – hence the festival name. Physical maturity was always a condition for enrolment as a citizen, but only at Sparta was the demonstration so forthright. We are not told that the young men took up their arms at the festival, or that there was any exhibition of strength, as in manhandling the victims. But the music and songs, which included paeans, were renowned for their stirring military quality.

The picture just given is not the one familiar from modern accounts.[1] The Gymnopaediae are said to be an agonistic festival without any deep roots; indeed the notion is abroad that the festival was deliberately created as an element of the Spartan discipline. The notion rests on a *datum* of

1 Nilsson, *Gr. Feste* 140–2; F. Bölte, *RE* 3 A 2 (1929) 1365 *s.v.* Sparta, and *RhM* n.s. 78 (1929) 124–32; L. Ziehen, *RE* 3 A 2 (1929) 1460–1, 1509–10 *s.v.* Sparta; H. Jeanmaire, *Couroi et Courètes* (Lille 1939) 531–7; H.T. Wade-Gery, *CQ* 43 (1949) 79–81; Martin, *Agora* 204–6, 234–5; Jacoby on Sosibius *FGrHist* 595 F 5, Anon. 596 F 41; W. den Boer, *Laconian Studies* (Amsterdam 1954) 221–7; A. Brelich, *Guerri, agoni e culti nella grecia arcaica* (Bonn 1961) 30–4, and *Paides e parthenoi* (Rome 1969) 139–40, 171–3, 188–91; C. Calame, *Les Choeurs de jeunes filles en Grèce archaïque* (Rome 1977) 1.123–4, 352–4.

an especially worthless kind, a foundation date, 668–667, handed down by the chronographers; also on one of Plato's compliments to Spartan education, to the effect that the Gymnopaediae call for extreme exertion in the hot sun. The foundation date evokes that putative landmark of early Greek history, the battle of Hysiae in 669–668; our festival is seen as a consequence of Hysiae.[2] This reconstruction is easily refuted; but that is best done at the end, apropos of evidence for certain changes, but small ones, in the festival program.

Let us consider in turn the calendar date; the month Hecatombeus and the new year at Sparta; the performances in the agora and in the theatre; the warlike songs; the three age groups; the commemoration of Thyrea; the foundation date.

The Calendar Date

The festival went on for several days, three or more, at the hottest time of year, which in Greece is the month of July.[3] It coincides with two notable events: in 417 the Argive democrats rose up as the festival began, and in 371 the news of Leuctra reached Sparta as the festival was ending.[4] Both events serve to date the Gymnopaediae.

For Leuctra, Plutarch gives us a calendar date, or rather two of them, in different parts of his work: 5 Hippodromius in the Boeotian calendar, the month corresponding to Hecatombaeon; and 5 Hecatombaeon in the

2 The secular interpretation, as we may call it, has steadily gained ground. Nilsson all but passed over the Gymnopaediae 'because its importance lies in the agonistic domain.' Then Bölte reduced it to 'a simple rite of harsh, almost fierce, severity.' Finally, Wade-Gery made it into a military drill, 'instituted in the hour of defeat,' 'to train for a reversal of the defeat'; and this view has not to my knowledge been challenged.

3 Xen. *Hell.* 6.4.16: 'the last day' implies a duration of three days or more. Pl. *Leg.* 1, 633 C: 'contending with the force of the heat.' Bölte, *RhM* n.s. 78 (1929) 127–8, gives some truly intimidating details of July heat at Sparta. His purpose is the same as Plato's, to represent the dances of the Gymnopaediae as a terrible ordeal. At *Leg.* 1, 633 B, the Spartan interlocutor recommends several grim exercises which the young undergo at Sparta: hand-to-hand combat, snatching a prize amid a rain of blows, the protracted labours of the *krypteia*. 'Furthermore, *even at the Gymnopaediae, ἔτι δὲ κἀν ταῖς Γυμνοπαιδίαις,* we have severe tests of endurance for those contending with the force of the heat.' And there is much, much more, he says, *πάμπολλα ἕτερα,* beyond my power to mention. Plato's whimsicality has misled both the scholiast and many moderns. Everywhere in Greece July is about the commonest time for agonistic festivals, and the dances of the Gymnopaediae cannot have been unusually taxing.

4 The revolution at Argos: Thuc. 5.82.2–3. The news of Leuctra: Xen. *loc. cit.*; Plut. *Ages.* 29.3–7.

Athenian calendar.⁵ The strict agreement between the two dates raises a difficulty. We know very well that at this period the Athenian calendar of months was subject to frequent and irregular manipulation by the archons; it is therefore unlikely that an Athenian date will ever agree exactly, or even very nearly, with a date in another local calendar. In any case we can hardly suppose that Plutarch found the two dates independently recorded; historians rarely give calendar dates for battles – Plutarch himself is our principal source for such dates. On the other hand, Plutarch might be tempted to equate the two calendars, if it served his purpose; and we shall see in a moment that it did. So we must decide which date is primary. The question is important here because, if the Athenian date is primary, it means very little to us; but we have not the same reason to distrust the Boeotian calendar.

The Boeotian date belongs to a general review of dates for victory and defeat in Greek and Roman history. The review is meant to illustrate a topic which interested Plutarch, and which he also treated, though in a different fashion, in his commentary on the *Works and Days*: scil., whether particular days of the month should be classified as either lucky or unlucky. He has therefore been at pains to collect the material. Moreover, he says that this Boeotian date was doubly significant, for Leuctra and for a much earlier victory at Ceressus, when the Thessalians were overthrown. Now we know from many passages of Plutarch how he usually obtained his dates for historical and legendary events, especially battles: he relied on commemorative festivals.⁶ It may be that, even apart from legendary instances, he was at times misled; but in the fourth century and later, some cherished victories were undoubtedly commemorated on the

---

5 Plut. *Cam.* 19.4; *Ages.* 28.7.
6 A few Athenian instances are assembled at *De Glor. Ath.* 7, 349 E–350 A; others are found everywhere in the *Lives* and in the historical or antiquarian essays. Plutarch did not write a separate work on commemorative festivals, as some have thought; such a work would only duplicate *in extenso* the *Lives* and the essays. The book περὶ ἡμερῶν treated birthdays, as we see from the excerpt at *Quaest. Conv.* 8.1.1, 717 B–C. It is cited once only in all the notices of battle dates, for the date of Salamis (Plut. *Cam.* 19.6 = fr. 142 Sandbach) – because this date was Euripides' birthday. The discussion of unlucky days cited just before this is shown by the context to be the commentary on the *Works and Days* (Plut. *Cam.* 19.3 = fr. 100 Sandbach). W.K. Pritchett, *The Greek State at War* 3 (Berkeley 1979) 168–86, would throw doubt on some commemorative rites, saying, e.g., that when Plutarch associates Mantineia II with 12 Scirophorion, which is also the Scira, 'this statement implies nothing about any religious rites or ceremonies commemorating the battle' (p. 170); but he seems not to ask himself how Plutarch knew of the association. According to Pritchett, 'we do have one very revealing example' of how Plutarch deduced a battle date, namely, Sepeia and the festival Hybristica (p. 184). There are a hundred such examples.

anniversary.[7] If any victory was sure to be so commemorated in Boeotia, it was Leuctra. But the Athenians would not commemorate Leuctra, which disappointed them; nor Ceressus either.

The Athenian date is used to show that Agesilaus, when he called for a reckoning at Leuctra, was governed 'more by passion than by reason.' Leuctra on 5 Hecatombaeon came only twenty days after the peace making at Sparta, which Plutarch dates to 14 Scirophorion, again by the Athenian calendar. The date of a peace treaty (unlike the date of a battle) will be registered in a contemporary document, which may then be used by a historian. Plutarch, we must infer, found this date, 14 Scirophorion, cited by a historian; since he already knew the date of Leuctra, he now had the opportunity to point a lesson. To equate 5 Hippodromius with 5 Hecatombaeon was irresistible. There can be little doubt that the Boeotian date is primary.[8]

Recalling Philippides' run from Athens to Sparta (Hdt. 6.106.1), we infer that the news of Leuctra reached Sparta two days later, on 7 Hippodromius in the Boeotian calendar. Festivals of Apollo typically fall on the seventh of the month,[9] not because seven is a magic number, but because the crisp half-moon appearing at this time is the first phase of the moon that everyone can observe and agree upon, as the signal for a reunion of the whole community. A longer festival may extend to the days before and after. Since the sixth is the holy day of Artemis, Apollo's sister, it will be included if she is; and she was indeed included in the Gymnopaediae (Paus. 3.11.9). It is true that the longest festivals of Apollo span the whole second quarter, like the Carneia and the Apolline Games at Rome. But whatever latitude we allow for the Gymnopaediae, the last day of the festival, when the news arrived, will not be too far off the seventh of a lunar month. The argument supports, or is supported by, the natural assumption that most Greek calendars, such as the Boeotian and the Spartan, ran closely with the moon and hence with each other.

The other event that coincides with the Gymnopaediae is the revolution at Argos. Pausanias tells how the people were inflamed by the outrageous conduct of an oligarchic leader; the details overlap with Diodorus and show that the story comes from Ephorus.[10] It is an aetiology, for the bloodshed

---

7 Cf. E. Badian and J. Buckler, *RhM* n.s. 118 (1975) 229–30.

8 As the relationship of the Athenian and Boeotian calendars at this time remains unknown, so must the interval between the peace making and the battle of Leuctra.
  Unlike Plutarch, Xenophon and Diodorus do not describe Sparta's action as precipitate.

9 W. Schmidt, *Geburtstag im Altertum* (Giessen 1908) 89–94.

10 Paus. 2.20.1–2; cf. Diod. 12.80.2–3. Whereas Thucydides says that the Argive oligarchs came to power at the beginning of spring (5.81.2), Diodorus says that they were

is expiated afterwards by rites of Zeus *meilichios* and by Polycleitus' statue of the god. Nothing more is known of the Argive observance, but Athens had something like it. When Theseus on his approach to Athens arrived at the river Cephisus, he was purified of all the killing he had done at an altar of Zeus *meilichios*.[11] This too is an aetiology, and here the rites are approximately dated by the sequel, Theseus' arrival in Athens, which took place on 8 Hecatombaeon, during the festival Hecatombaea (Plut. *Thes.* 12.2). We may assume that at Argos too the rites of Zeus *meilichios* fell in the early days of Hecatombaeon, or rather of the corresponding Argive month. This is also the date of the revolution, and hence of the first day of the Gymnopaediae.

The Month Hecatombeus and the New Year

The Spartan month corresponding to Hecatombaeon and Hippodromius, the month of the Gymnopaediae, can be identified with some probability. It was not Carneius or Hyacinthius, named for the Carneia and the Hyacinthia; for the Gymnopaediae will not fall in the same month as another important festival of Apollo.[12] Since months, especially summer months, are more likely to be named for festivals of Apollo than for those of any other deity,[13] we should look for yet another month so named. Such a month is Ἐκατομβεύς, attested for Sparta by Hesychius *s.v.* and by an inscription found in the vicinity.[14] The festivals Ἐκατόμβη and Ἐκατόμβαια that give rise to the month names Hecatombeus and Hecatombaeon are undoubtedly Apollo's, even if the festivals of other gods are sometimes so

---

overthrown after eight months. If Diodorus is not prey to some misunderstanding, Ephorus as his source must have counted from a different terminus than Thucydides gives us. It will not do to suggest that the Gymnopaediae might come much later in the year through manipulation of the Spartan calendar; for as we have just seen, the season of the Gymnopaediae was notorious for heat. Cf. A. Andrewes, *HCT* 4.150–1.

11 Plut. *Thes.* 12.1; Paus. 1.37.4. Toepffer, *Att. Gen.* 248–50, disputed the connection with Zeus *meilichios*, but for no good reason.

12 The month name Carneius is attested only for Epidaurus Limera (*IG* 5.1.931 lines 37–8); so it is possible, though not very likely, that the month of the Carneia had another name at Sparta.

13 E.g., Athens and Delos both have five months named for his festivals, and Rhodes has six. The main reason is doubtless that his festivals were the first in the month.

14 *IG* 5.1.511, of Imperial date. It was found 'beside the Eurotas between Sparta and Pharis,' i.e., too close to the city to derive from some outlying community with a different calendar, as suggested by E. Bischoff, *RE* 10.2 (1919) 1578 *s.v.* Kalender, and by L. Ziehen, *RE* 3 A 2 (1929) 1518 *s.v.* Sparta. Nilsson, *Die Entstehung und religiöse Bedeutung des griechischen Kalenders*[2] (Lund 1962) 62, dismisses both instances, Hesychius and the inscription, out of hand.

called or described. Strabo reports that the festival Hecatombaea was once celebrated throughout Laconia.[15]

As we saw above, our festival had some earlier name that was replaced by 'Gymnopaediae.' Now according to Hesychius, it was in the month Hecatombeus that the festival Hyacinthia was celebrated. This cannot be, since the Hyacinthia go with the month Hyacinthius. Spartan festivals are poorly dealt with in the lexica, and Hesychius' entry Γυμνοπαιδία shows confusion between the Hyacinthia and the Gymnopaediae.[16] The same confusion is to be presumed in the entry Ἑκατομβεύς. Finally, the inscription just mentioned comes from a cult of Apollo and records some expenditure or other 'from the sacred revenues of Apollo,' which is dated to the month Hecatombeus; the occasion is no doubt a festival of Apollo falling in this month.[17]

There is reason to think that the Gymnopaediae came round in the first month of the year. Consider Herodotus' tale of how Demaratus was humiliated by his rival at our festival, a humiliation so intense that it drove Demaratus from Sparta into the arms of the Persians (Hdt. 6.67). 'After his deposition from the kingship, Demaratus was serving in an office to which he had been elected,' ἦρχε αἱρεθεὶς ἀρχήν. While he watches the performance in the theatre – sitting near the front, we may suppose, as a magistrate – Leotychides, who is now king instead, sends a servant to

15 Str. 8.4.11, p. 362: 'It is said that [Laconia] was anciently called *hekatompolis* and that for this reason the Hecatombaea were celebrated among them each year.' Despite Nilsson, *Gr. Feste* 138, there is no reason to doubt the reality of the Laconian festival. On Hecatombaea and Hecatombaeon as distinctive of Apollo, Nilsson 174.

16 The first half of this entry is a muddle of the Hyacinthia and the whipping at the altar of Orthia: ephebes run round the altar beating each other, but the altar is 'at the Amyclaeum.' The second half says, 'This is false,' and gives a correct description of the Gymnopaediae. In a similar vein, schol. Pl. *Leg.* 1, 633 C, has boys beating each other at the Gymnopaediae, and brings in the *sphaireis* as well. Apollo *karneios* also comes into it (n. 45 below). All this is the imposture of ignorant grammarians. Jacoby, who prints Hesychius *s.v.* Γυμνοπαιδία as Anon. *FGrHist* 596 F 41, does them too much honour, speaking of a 'polemic' between authorities like Sosibius, and of festival innovations in the Roman period.

17 A likely sequence of summer months at Sparta is Hyacinthius-Hecatombeus-Carneius (or month of the Carneia). The festival Hyacinthia and hence the month Hyacinthius already belong to 'full summer'; cf. Andrewes, *HCT* 5.23. At *IG* 5.1.18 line 8, a festival truce extends from mid Agrianius to early Hyacinthius; Agrianius is named for a Dionysiac festival of spring, and the truce may well span another whole month between these two. The month Carneius at Syracuse, and hence at Corinth, corresponds to Metageitnion (Plut. *Nic.* 28.1), and in general this is the right season for the ritual of the Carneia, which promotes the ripening of the grapes. In 480 BC the Carneia of Sparta fell in mid September; see K.S. Sacks, *CQ*[2] 26 (1976) 245.

bait him. What is it like, Demaratus, to serve in office after ruling as king? Demaratus replies in fury with an ominous threat, wraps his head in his cloak, and leaves the theatre. This is too perfect to be an actual incident. It is a fiction, like the more typical *novelle* that precede and follow – the girl made beautiful by a fairy touch, the wife visited by a demon in the night.[18] The tale is most effective if Demaratus is taunted by his rival just after he has been elected to that office; the office, after all, was invented to make a contrast with his former pre-eminence. The festival Gymnopaediae is chosen as the first great public gathering of the year, when the new magistrates are first seen in their new dignity – but it is a poor dignity beside a king's.[19]

To sum up, the Gymnopaediae resemble the Hecatombaea of Athens as an Apolline festival celebrated near the beginning of the first month of the year. The resemblance extends to the earlier name of the Gymnopaediae, *Hekatombē*.

The Performances in the Agora and in the Theatre

Different sources mention different settings for the Gymnopaediae, the 'agora' and the 'theatre.'[20] Pausanias in touring the agora says that here 'the ephebes perform choral dances for Apollo,' οἱ ἔφηβοι χοροὺς ἱστᾶσι τῶι Ἀπόλλωνι, and that 'this whole place is called "the Dancing-ground,"' Χορός – doubtless meaning the open space of the agora (3.11.9).[21] He also points to statues of Apollo *pythaeus*, Artemis, and Leto. In Hesychius'

18 The second *novella* is analysed in detail by W. Burkert, *MusHelv* 22 (1965) 166–77.
19 The office, unlike the festival, is left unspecified. To suppose that Demaratus was in fact an ephor, and that he was concerned in the festival arrangements, is to spoil the story. Because the occasion is the Gymnopaediae, we see with the mind's eye the immense, crowded theatre. We do not however see Demaratus as a magistrate of a certain kind, because every magistrate is contrasted with a king.
20 No remains have yet been found that can be plausibly assigned to Sparta's agora. Since Pausanias walked west from it to the theatre (3.14.1), it lay on the southwest side of the acropolis hill, perhaps beneath the municipal sports ground where a few soundings were made without result in 1949. Cf. Bölte, *RE* 3 A 2 (1929) 1361, 1365–6; R.V. Nicholls, *BSA* 45 (1950) 289. As for the theatre, we may suppose that it had always been the acropolis slope, at the northwest end, where a monumental building was first installed in the third century BC. The two areas are entirely separate. From the notices of the Gymnopaediae Woodward and others inferred that Sparta's agora and theatre were adjacent and related installations, and this view is still maintained by Martin, *Agora* 233–5, and by Kolb, *Agora* 9, 79–81; it is sufficiently refuted by Bölte.
21 Bölte, *RhM* n.s. 78 (1929) 125 n. 7, thinks that the term ἔφηβοι in Pausanias may, for the sake of *oratio variata*, include παῖδες; but this seems unlikely in a context where the age class is of special interest.

entry Γυμνοπαιδία, a report of ephebes flailing each other round the altar at the Amyclaeum, which is said to be false, is corrected by two observations: that 'they hold festival in the agora,' and that instead of beatings 'there are processions of choral dancers altogether naked,' πρόσοδοι χορῶν γεγυμνωμένων. Since no objection is taken to 'ephebes,' the entry agrees with Pausanias that the dancers in the agora are of this age class. In yet another lexical entry s.v. Γυμνοπαιδία, the agora is the setting for paeans that honour the dead of Thyrea; the entry is one of a series which speak of these paeans, but the setting is not indicated in the rest.[22]

Herodotus, Xenophon, and Plutarch speak of festival crowds and choral competitions in the θέατρον, 'theatre' or 'viewing place.'[23] It is often held that they too mean the agora, which might be a virtual 'theatre' if wooden grandstands were erected for spectators.[24] Though this arrangement has been postulated for other agoras as well,[25] it is most unlikely on general grounds. The agora was in the first instance a large level area for mustering soldiers, as the name indicates. To construct wooden grandstands on the scale required, at the periphery of this area, would be laborious, expensive, and still unsatisfactory. All the more so, when it was easy for spectators to gather on a slope and watch a performance on the ground below. This they did, and the place was called a 'theatre.' Even as a matter of semantics it is hard to believe that quite a different place, the agora or part of it, was also called a 'theatre.'

At Sparta the terminology can hardly be disputed. If there were only Herodotus and Xenophon, we might hesitate. For Plutarch, however, the word 'theatre' means a type of building, as it does for us. Plutarch expatiates on the festival crowd 'in the theatre.'[26] To be sure, he thinks first of Xenophon, and follows him in reporting the conduct of the ephors, who refrained from interrupting the performance. Yet Plutarch also knows contemporary Sparta, with its huge Roman theatre; and like Pausanias, he

22 Phrynichus in Bekker, Anecd. 1.32: Γυμνοπαιδία· ἐν Λακεδαίμονι κατὰ τὴν ἀγορὰν παῖδες γυμνοὶ παιᾶνας ᾖδον εἰς τιμὴν τῶν περὶ Θυρέας. The 'naked boys' can be discounted, as we shall see below.
23 Hdt. 6.67.3; Xen. Hell. 6.4.16; Plut. Ages. 29.3.
24 So Bölte, RE 3 A 2 (1929) 1365 s.v. Sparta; Ziehen, RE 3 A 2 (1929) 1509–10 s.v. Sparta; Martin, Agora 205, 234–5; Kolb, Agora 79–80. Most others, as cited in n. 1, simply assume that the agora was the setting throughout.
25 Most notably, the familiar Agora of Athens: e.g., Martin, Agora 290–1; Wycherley, Testimonia 162; N.G.L. Hammond, GRBS 13 (1972) 399–402; Thompson and Wycherley, Agora of Athens 20, 127–9; Kolb, Agora 26–31, 39–43, 92. It is something else to erect grandstands along the Panathenaic Way for viewing processions and races.
26 'As it happened, the city was conducting a festival and was full of foreigners – for it was the Gymnopaediae – while the choruses competed in the theatre.'

knows the Gymnopaediae as a contemporary festival, saying here that it brought many foreigners to Sparta. He obviously knows of dances in the theatre, just as Pausanias knows of dances in the agora.

The performances in the two places are not described in the same terms. In the agora we have naked ephebes, and dances honouring Apollo *pythaeus*, or processional dances, or paeans for the dead of Thyrea. In the theatre we have competitions, ἀγῶνες, of choral dancers, and Xenophon happens to mention one of the groups who performed: 'the men's chorus,' ὁ ἀνδρικὸς χορός.

The conclusion then, which should not surprise us, is that the festival business of three or more days was not confined to one spot. We might compare the festival Thargelia at Athens, lasting only two days. Choral dancers, both boys and men, performed in tribal competitions in the theatre of Dionysus; but there was also time for a great procession, with basket bearers and every kind of dignitary, to the shrine of Apollo *pythios* in southeast Athens, where sacrifice was offered.[27] At Sparta too Apollo *pythaeus* will require a sacrifice; but Pausanias does not mention a shrine in the agora, only statues. So while the agora served to display the prowess of the naked ephebes, Apollo's shrine lay elsewhere.

The order of events escapes us, as it does with some agonistic festivals far better known. We can only say that the seventh was the proper day for sacrifice and perhaps for the processional dances, and that the last day included competitions.[28]

The Warlike Songs

Sparta was famous for choral performances of military music and song. Sometimes these performances are expressly associated with the Gymnopaediae; nowhere are they expressly associated with any other festival.

In early music [Plutarch] marks two stages of development: the first ascribed to Terpander and occurring at Sparta; the second ascribed to Thaletas and several others, and occurring at Sparta, in Arcadia, and at Argos. The second stage is a military kind of music, performed at the Spartan Gymnopaediae; at the 'displays,' *apodeixeis*, of Arcadian ephebes, which

27 The competitions: J.K. Davies, *JHS* 87 (1967) 34–5. The procession and the sacrifice: W. Peek, *AthMitt* 66 (1941) 181–95 no. 2, 129–128 BC (*LSCG Suppl.* 14).

28 It was the last day, and 'the men's chorus' was performing, says Xenophon. According to Bölte, *RhM* n.s. 78 (1929) 126, 'the men's chorus' indicates that only one such chorus, and hence only one chorus from each of the three age groups, performed on a given day. The inference is too strict. Xenophon may just as well refer to the performance of the whole age group; indeed he could hardly express himself otherwise.

other sources describe as leaping dances in full armour, of the kind some-times called *pyrrhichē;* and at the Argive 'Investitures,' *Endymatia,* in which ephebes receive their arms.[29] Sosibius, in a passage of his work *On Spartan Ritual* which we shall consider (and vindicate) below, gave sev-eral details of the choruses at the Gymnopaediae: *inter alia,* that they 'sing songs of Thaletas and Alcman and the paeans of Dionysodotus the Laco-nian.'[30] The lexica have a number of rather tattered entries *s.v.* Γυμνοπαιδία in which choruses singing 'hymns' or 'paeans' form a constant element; other details fluctuate and are less reliable. Aristoxenus of Tarentum in his works on the dance makes *gymnopaidikē* one of three general categories of choral dancing, beside *pyrrhikē* and *hyporchēmatikē,* corresponding to the three dances of the stage, tragic and satyric and comic. Aristoxenus' terminology is very arbitrary, and *gymnopaidikē* was evidently chosen as an expressive name which lent itself to theorizing; this style of dancing, like the tragic style, is described as 'heavy and solemn.'[31]

Thus far the sources who mention or evoke the Gymnopaediae. A series of notices appearing in Plutarch and the lexica and the paroemiographers – and deriving ultimately from Sosibius, but from the work *On Spartan Manners* – speak of three choruses representing three age groups and singing boastful lines, iambic trimeters, which are quoted. If the occasion is mentioned at all, it is simply 'at the festivals,' ἐν ταῖς ἑορταῖς.[32] Plato in the *Laws* refers allusively to the 'enchanting' songs of 'the three choruses' as a forceful means of inculcating virtue in the young; at an earlier point he mentioned the Gymnopaediae by name, feigning that the competitors were toughened by the heat.[33] The Gymnopaediae are probably evoked in two hexameter lines praising Sparta for its warlike youth and song.[34]

All the songs in question here must have been traditional pieces, re-peated year after year. The three lines of the three choruses are perhaps a refrain that came at intervals. Some songs were ascribed to Thaletas and Alcman, but the ascription was too fanciful to interest Alexandrian editors;

---

29 [Plut.] *De Mus.* 9, 1134 B–C.

30 Ath. 15.22, 678 B-C (Sosibius *FGrHist* 595 F 5).

31 Ath. 14.28, 630 C–E, and 14.29, 631 B–C (Aristoxenus frs. 103, 108 Wehrli). No doubt our festival was also celebrated at Tarentum as a colony of Sparta, but Aristoxenus' details are no more convincing for that.

32 This phrase occurs at Plut. *Lyc.* 21.3; [Plut.] *Inst. Lac.* 15, 238 A. Cf. n. 43 below.

33 Pl. *Leg.* 2, 664 B: φημὶ γὰρ ἅπαντας δεῖν ἐπᾴδειν τρεῖς ὄντας τοὺς χοροὺς κτλ. *Leg.* 1, 633 C: the Gymnopaediae and the heat.

34 Plut. *Lyc.* 21.4; Arr. *Tact.* 44.3 (Page, *PMG* p. 363): 'where the spear of young men thrives, and the clear-voiced Muse, and δίκα εὐρυάγυια, inciter of brave deeds.' The last item may refer to either processional paeans or competitions in the theatre, according as δίκα means 'custom' or 'verdict.'

they did not edit Thaletas at all, and nothing in the surviving scraps of Alcman could possibly derive from the Gymnopaediae.[35] The paeans of Dionysodotus the Laconian, a poet otherwise unknown, are of a different kind from the rest. They must have been composed for the festival at a much later date. The lexica say that hymns or paeans were sung to honour the dead of Thyrea (more of this below); paeans for men rather than gods are a late development,[36] and can be feasibly equated with the paeans of Dionysodotus. It seems rather likely that all these customary songs, early and late, were performed during the worship of Apollo, in the processions of the agora, rather than in the theatre. They do not seem very promising material for competitions, unless we suppose that the crowd of spectators had little taste and much forbearance.

The Three Age Groups

Who then made up the choruses? When the lexica give us 'naked boys,' γυμνοὶ παῖδες, this is but to paraphrase the festival name, and incorrectly. Boys, even naked boys, are not excluded, but neither are they indicated by the name, which means rather 'Naked Sports.' The only good evidence comes from Sosibius, in those two works mentioned above. Unfortunately, both items are difficult to interpret; moreover, current opinion dissevers both from the festival Gymnopaediae. This opinion should be tested. As

35 Note, however, that a papyrus commentary describes Alcman as directing choruses not only of girls but also 'of ephebes': Page, *PMG* 10a = Davies, *PMGF* TA 2 lines 30–4. Thereafter, in fr. 10b, a poem is quoted which names a chorus leader Agesidamus, said by the commentator to be '*ageneios* in point of age.' The chorus address him with flattery, and, says the commentator, go on to speak of his young age, as in the lines quoted next: 'proud and handsome chorus-leaders; for they are themselves young men, νεανίαι, of like age with ourselves, being dear and beardless and unmustachioed.' The chorus who speak are girls of the tribe Dymanes, and the occasion honours the Dioscuri. So we see that choruses of girls and youths bantered each other at the festival Dioscureia (Ar. *Lys.* 1296–1302 also suggests that girls sang at this festival). Alcman wrote for the girls, but, despite the commentator, it is not shown that he also wrote for the youths. A very fragmentary poem, which may or may not be Alcman's, contains the words φοινικέα ... ἀ]ναδήματα in successive lines (Page, *PMG* 162 fr. 2c); but these are 'red hair-bands' rather than palm-leaf crowns.

36 Cf. von Blumenthal, *RE* 18.2 (1942) 2353–4 s.v. Paian; C. Habicht, *Gottmenschentum und griechische Städte*[2] (Munich 1970) index s.v. Paiane. To be sure, it was often a natural development. Paeans for Apollo dwell upon local Apolline 'heroes' like Melampus of Argos, Agemon of Corinth, Theseus of Athens, Euxantius of Ceos, Abderus of Abdera, who represent, at least in part, the kind of achievement admired by the worshippers; so contemporary men of great achievement could be praised in like terms. Whether the development followed this line at the Gymnopaediae is impossible to say.

we have just seen, the songs and choruses of the Gymnopaediae were widely renowned. There is a strong presumption that they were treated by Sosibius, and that his treatment was consulted by later sources.

The passage from *Spartan Ritual* is transmitted in the epitome of Athenaeus which here leaves much to be desired. Athenaeus cited Sosibius for 'Thyreatic' crowns. They are palm-leaf crowns, somehow recalling the battle of Thyrea, worn by chorus leaders 'in this festival, when in fact they celebrate the Gymnopaediae,' ἐν τῆι ἑορτῆι ταύτηι, ὅτε καὶ τὰς Γυμνοπαιδιὰς ἐπιτελοῦσιν. The choruses are then described, with mention of songs by Thaletas and others. The words quoted are a clumsy way to identify the festival, but the epitomator is clumsy. There is no reason, either in the language or in the content of the passage, to suppose that he is wrong, and that the festival is other than the Gymnopaediae.[37]

The 'Thyreatic' crowns worn by chorus leaders may be left aside while we consider the choruses themselves. The passage goes on: χοροὶ δ᾽ εἰσὶν τὸ μὲν πρόσω παίδων, τὸ δ᾽ †ἐξ ἀρίστουτ† ἀνδρῶν, γυμνῶν ὀρχουμένων καὶ ἀιδόντων κτλ. Emendations vary in extent;[38] I obelize only the words that make no sense.[39] The important question is whether the choruses represent two age groups or three. In Greek cities a twofold classification of παῖδες and ἄνδρες is much less common than a threefold classification of boys,

---

37 Ath. 15.22, 678 B-C (Sosibius *FGrHist* 595 F 5). Jacoby brackets the ὅτε clause as intrusive. It is obviously not, as Jacoby says, the words of Sosibius; but the epitomator needs to identify the festival, and he could hardly get it wrong. Jacoby, however, thinks that the 'Thyreatic' crowns as a memorial of Thyrea must have been worn at the festival Parparonia, which is therefore the subject throughout. This is doubly misguided. The Parparonia did not commemorate the battle of Thyrea; it was an ancient local festival, with the hero Othryades as aetiology. The palm-leaf crowns did not really commemorate the battle either; more of this below. Jacoby also thinks, after Bölte, that the wearing of 'Thyreatic' crowns was transferred to the Gymnopaediae from the Parparonia when this festival lapsed. On that view, the ὅτε clause is exactly right for Sosibius; Jacoby has fallen into an inconsequence. Before Jacoby, the ὅτε clause was rejected by S.L. Weber. Nilsson, *Gr. Feste* 141 n. 5, answered Weber by saying, 'With the best will, I can only infer from the καί that the Thyreatic victory festival was connected with the Gymnopaediae, i.e., the competitions.' But καί according to a normal idiom gives an emphasis to the whole clause: 'when in fact they celebrate the Gymnopaediae.' The Gymnopaediae are in full view both before and after the ὅτε clause.

38 ὁ μὲν πρόσω παίδων, ὁ δ᾽ ἑξῆς ἀρίστων ἀνδρῶν Casaubon: <γ᾽>, ὁ μὲν πρόσω παίδων, <ὁ δ᾽ ἐκ δεξιοῦ γερόντων>, ὁ δ᾽ ἐξ ἀριστεροῦ ἀνδρῶν Wyttenbach, Kaibel: τὸ μὲν πρὸς ἔω Wilamowitz.

39 Wilamowitz produces sense by adding one letter, so that we have dances 'at dawn' and 'after breakfast.' Elsewhere this might be divinatory magic, but it is not the way to deal with the epitomator – such fine details would not survive his heavy hand.

youths, and men.⁴⁰ Sparta, to be sure, is a law to itself; yet here too all the evidence suggests that the overall classification was threefold.⁴¹ And there is further reason to think that three age groups took part in the Gymnopaediae.

First, in Sosibius' other work, *On Spartan Manners*, we find three choruses representing three age groups, and singing of military prowess. Admittedly, there is something amiss with one of the age groups, 'old men' beside youths and boys; we shall come to that below. Second, on the evidence of Pausanias and Hesychius, 'ephebes' danced naked during the festival; this is also the implication of Sosibius *On Spartan Manners*, as we shall see. Since our passage speaks of naked dancers, we expect to hear again of that age class; they can hardly be subsumed in either 'boys' or 'men.' We need something like τὸ μὲν πρόσω παίδων, τὸ δ' ὀπίσω ἀνδρῶν, τὸ δὲ μέσον ἐφήβων.⁴²

The other item from Sosibius is handed down in several late versions.⁴³ The fullest of them quote the three lines spoken by the three age groups, as follows. First chorus: 'We once were brave lads,' ἁμές ποκ' ἦμες ἄλκιμοι νεανίαι. Second chorus: 'We are now; if you wish, look well,' ἁμές δέ γ' εἰμές· αἰ δὲ λῆις, αὐγάσδεο. For the last word there is a variant, perhaps an authentic variant in the refrain: 'note the evidence,' πεῖραν λαβέ. Third chorus: 'We shall be far better,' ἁμὲς δέ γ' ἐσσόμεσθα πολλῶι κάρρονες.

The second chorus are youths who have just reached maturity; the third chorus are boys somewhat younger. Who are the first chorus? In the explanatory comments they are called either 'elders,' οἱ πρεσβύτεροι, or 'old men,' οἱ γέροντες, but these comments vary a great deal in their wording, and have no independent authority; they are all deduced from

---

40 Bölte, *RhM* n.s. 78 (1929) 125, desiderates the three age groups which are standard at many agonistic festivals, scil. παῖδες, ἀγένειοι, ἄνδρες. But as we saw, Sosibius may not be speaking of the competitions, or not of them alone. In any case the competitions are for Spartiates, so that the standard categories are irrelevant.

41 The three groups were perhaps over seven, over fourteen, and over twenty. Cf. D.M. MacDowell, *Spartan Law* (Edinburgh 1986) 159–67.

42 The term 'in the front,' τὸ μὲν πρόσω, calls for some balancing term or terms. 'On the right' and 'on the left' will do as well, as in Kaibel's emendation. But if a second group only comes 'next,' ἑξῆς, as Casaubon has it, no prior term is wanted, or none but πρῶτον.

43 The principal sources are cited by Diehl, *Anth. Lyr. Gr.* 2, Carm. Pop. 17, and (more fully) by Page, *PMG* (Carm. Pop.) 870. Sosibius περὶ ἐθῶν, *FGrHist* 595 F 8, is named as the authority only in two paroemiographers. At Poll. 4.107 (Tyrtaeus *test.* 15 Prato), Tyrtaeus is credited with instituting the τριχορία, but the tradition prevailing elsewhere shows that this was not the view of Sosibius.

the lines as quoted.[44] The first line infallibly suggests, to a literary reader, old men reminiscing, a chorus of Nestors as it were. But surely it was spoken by men just a little older than the 'lads,' νεανίαι; for the third line was spoken by boys just a little younger. We have then the same three age groups as before: boys, youths at maturity, and men.

The youths who pronounce themselves 'brave lads' call on the spectators to 'look well,' or 'note the evidence.' This can only mean that they are naked and exhibit all the signs of physical maturity. They are the 'ephebes' who dance naked in the agora.

There is evidence for a somewhat similar ceremony in the cult of Apollo at Patrae (Paus. 7.20.3, 7). Pausanias describes Apollo's sanctuary in the agora, with statues of the god and of three Apolline heroes; the sanctuary of Artemis beside it happens to be linked with Sparta in a tale about the cult statue. Apollo was shown naked but for sandals, with one foot resting on an ox's skull: i.e., as an ephebe who helps with the sacrifice. The three heroes are Πατρεύς, Πρευγένης, Ἀθερίων; 'since Patreus has a boy's age,' says Pausanias, the other two are rendered as boys as well. As the eponym of Patrae, Patreus is more truly an ephebe, a citizen who has just come of age. His companions are named respectively 'Elder-born' and 'Heedless,' the local form of ἀθερίζων, a jesting name for a child. Here too are the three age groups, and naked ephebes.

We may wonder whether boys and men also danced naked. In Athenaeus, the corrupt words about the choruses can be mended, as above, so that 'ephebes' come last. The participles that follow, 'dancing naked and singing songs of Thaletas,' etc., might then refer to the ephebes alone. They might, or they might not; it is a wretched epitome, and an incurable corruption. The question must be left unanswered.

The Commemoration of Thyrea

In last place we should examine the historical associations that are attested or have been inferred for the Gymnopaediae. There are two main items. Eusebius gives a foundation date, 668–667. Sosibius and the lexica say that the battle of Thyrea was commemorated at the festival.

---

44 The former term, which is less definite, is used in the two sources that cite Sosibius (Zen. Prov. 1.82; Anon. Athous in Miller, Mélanges 367); but this is not to say that it goes all the way back to Sosibius. Bölte, RhM n.s. 78 (1929) 125, observed that a chorus of old men is very improbable, which is true; and that the notices of the trichoria must therefore be dissociated from the Gymnopaediae, which does not follow. Rather, the chorus of old men must be ejected from the notices of the trichoria.

To take Thyrea first, the lemma Θυρεατικοί is explained as follows in the epitome of Athenaeus. 'Certain crowns, στέφανοι, are so called at Sparta, as Sosibius says in the work *On Ritual*, stating that they are now named "feathery," being made of palm leaves,' ψιλίνους αὐτοὺς φάσκων νῦν ὀνομάζεσθαι, ὄντας ἐκ φοινίκων. 'He says that they are worn as a memorial, ὑπόμνημα, of the victory at Thyrea by the leaders of the choruses active in this festival,' etc. The passage goes on with details of the choruses and songs, including 'the paeans of Dionysodotus the Laconian.'

The lexica say, s.v. Γυμνοπαιδία, that the choruses at the festival, 'naked boys' if we believe it, sang 'hymns' or 'paeans' in honour of those who fell at Thyrea. It is true that one entry speaks of 'paeans for those who fell at Pylaea.'[45] This, however, is undoubtedly a mistake for 'Thyrea.' The place-name 'Pylaea' is not a likely equivalent for Thermopylae.[46] Nor is it credible that, if the festival commemorated both Thyrea and another battle, all the lexica but one should omit the other battle, and the one lexicon should omit Thyrea.

When we discussed the musical program, it seemed rather likely that the paeans of Dionysodotus and the paeans for the dead of Thyrea were in fact the same. The likelihood now seems even greater, for the lexica will ultimately draw upon Sosibius. The work *On Spartan Ritual* must have dealt at length with that most splendid piece of Spartan ritual, the Gymnopaediae. The discussion did not start with the 'Thyreatic' crowns which captured Athenaeus' interest. In describing the choruses and the songs, Sosibius came finally to the paeans of Dionysodotus, and said that they were added to commemorate Thyrea; and then, no doubt, he said that the crowns worn by the chorus leaders also commemorated Thyrea. Since the battle of Thyrea was forever trumpeted by poets and historians, there is no telling when Dionysodotus composed his paeans, only that it was before Sosibius.

It is widely held that the paeans and the crowns were at first the property of choruses at the agonistic festival Parparonia, and that they were adopted at the Gymnopaediae only when Sparta found it impossible to continue with the Parparonia.[47] Some objections will arise from our

45 Phrynichus s.v. Γυμνοπαιδία in Bekker, *Anecd.* 1.32: εἰς τιμὴν τῶν περὶ Θυρέας. Tim. *Lex.*, Suda s.v. Γυμνοπαιδία: εἰς τιμὴν τῶν ἐν Θυρέαις ἀποθανόντων Σπαρτιατῶν. Etym. Magn. s.v. Γυμνοπαιδία· εἰς τοὺς περὶ Πυλαίαν πέσοντας. In Bekker, *Anecd.* 1.234, we have paeans 'for Apollo *karneios* at his festival,' undoubted confusion. It has led W.F. Otto, *Das Wort der Antike* (Stuttgart 1962) 82, to say that the Gymnopaediae belong to Apollo *karneios*.

46 So Bölte, *RhM* n.s. 78 (1929) 130–1.

47 Ziehen, *RE* 3 A 2 (1929) 1510 s.v. Sparta; Bölte, *RhM* n.s. 78 (1929) 130–2; Wade-Gery, *CQ* 43 (1949) 79–80; Jacoby on Sosibius *FGrHist* 595 F 5.

study of the Parparonia and the Thyreatis. The Parparonia were ancient rites of the mountain Parparus, not a commemoration of any historical victory; there is no reason to think that this festival would end all at once, with a Spartan withdrawal; we do not even know of any moment before the time of Sosibius, say the middle Hellenistic period, when the Thyreatis might have passed decisively from Sparta to Argos. Now we see that for the Gymnopaediae the tradition of 'Thyreatiς' crowns and of commemorative paeans is sound and uniform, and leaves no room for the Parparonia.

We should also ask what the 'Thyreatic' crowns really mean. It is no doubt conceivable that the choruses of the Gymnopaediae took to wearing a new kind of crown at the same time as they began singing paeans for the dead of Thyrea; but the description of the crowns is much against this. They are in truth made of palm leaves, and are called 'feathery' (with a Doric pronunciation) because palm leaves resemble feathers. Palm-leaf crowns were often worn at Spartan festivals. They are probably rendered in sixth-century bronze figurines from Laconian sites outside Sparta itself.[48] They are shown beyond all doubt on an Italiote krater at Tarentum, the name-piece of the Carneia Painter; the two youths who wear them are performing at the Carneia, not the Gymnopaediae, but both are naked, and one is dancing.[49] At Amyclae, where one of the figurines was found, the god Dionysus was honoured with the title 'Feathery,' in a slightly different form;[50] gods take their attributes from their worshippers, and the attribute here was doubtless another feathery crown. The same form of the word, in the plural, receives a cryptic note in Hesychius, 'because of leading the chorus.'[51] Indeed the crowns were so commonplace that their manufacture was a livelihood: 'Feathery-maker,' ψιλινοποιός.[52]

It follows that the palm-leaf crowns of the Gymnopaediae were not at all distinctive. They would be pointless as a later innovation. But once the paeans were added to the program, the chorus leaders were seen in the

---

48 Cf. Wade-Gery, CQ 43 (1949) 80 n. 3; Calame, Choeurs de jeunes filles 1.124 n. 164; P. Cartledge, Sparta and Lakonia (London 1979) 140.

49 Taranto 8263 (CVA Taranto 1, pls. 4–6). The painter indicates the central vein in each leaf.

50 Paus. 3.19.6: Ψίλακα.

51 Hsch. s.v. ψίλακερ. Some other glosses on the feather crowns are collected by Jacoby, n. 103 to Sosibius FGrHist 595 F 5. Wade-Gery, CQ 43 (1949) 80 n. 3, has overshot the mark by adding items in which a dancer is called ψιλός, 'bare,' because he stands at the end of the line and has no partner to cover his flank.

52 IG 5.1.208 line 4; 209 line 24; both of the first century BC.

light of the paeans, and their crowns were taken as emblematic of victory, just as palm fronds are.[53] It may have helped that Thyrea lay on the coast, the region where palm trees grow in Greece.

The Foundation Date

We turn to the foundation date, 668–667.[54] The date is often taken to imply that the festival was founded in the shadow of the defeat at Hysiae, 669–668.[55] Yet the defeat at Hysiae is known only to Pausanias and the Argive source whom he consulted; surely it was invented by that source, and the date was chosen with a view to Thyrea, usually dated to 720–719, just fifty years earlier. But suppose for a moment that the defeat and the date are both authentic. The Spartans then founded the Gymnopaediae straightway, in 668–667. Since this date was, *ex hypothesi*, remembered ever after, our festival, the proudest in the Spartan calendar, was always recognized as marking the defeat. And yet it was also held to commemorate the victory of Thyrea fifty years earlier. These notions defy belief.

The chronographers supply foundation dates for various festivals, but typically they are very much earlier than ours, in the age of heroes. The early dates were excogitated because the festivals had already been traced back to the remotest times, as a matter of local pride. At Sparta, however, we have two great festivals founded at a later period: the Gymnopaediae in 668–667, and the Carneia in 676–672. We may assume that these dates likewise reflect some proud tradition, but one that did not conjure with the age of heroes. After all, it was the Spartan Sosibius, in his role as a chronographer, who gave the foundation date for the Carneia. The passage

---

53 In Herodotus' day it was said that Spartans left their hair unshorn in memory of Thyrea (1.82.8), and it was at the Gymnopaediae that the maturing age class first displayed their adult hairstyle. But it is likely that the custom of wearing long hair had been abandoned long before the paeans were introduced.

54 Euseb. *Can. a.* 668–667; Arm. 665–664.

55 E.g., Andrewes, *CQ* 43 (1949) 77; Wade-Gery, *CQ* 43 (1949) 80–1; G.L. Huxley, *Early Sparta* (London 1962) 54, 72–3; W.G. Forrest, *A History of Sparta 950–192 BC.* (London 1968) 72; Cartledge, *Sparta and Lakonia* 126; A.A. Mosshammer, *The Chronicle of Eusebius and Greek Chronographic Tradition* (Lewisburg, Pa. 1979) 223–5. Andrewes finds a parallel in 'the public funeral instituted at Athens after the disaster at Drabescus,' i.e., in Jacoby's notion of this ceremony. The festival Epitaphia, however, which includes the funeral, is a very old one, and does not commemorate disaster. Jacoby, ns. 109–10 to Sosibius *FGrHist* 595 F 5, thinks of the Gymnopaediae as 'a relatively recent festival,' on the ground that the ephors had charge of it. But in receiving the news of Leuctra, the ephors plainly act as chief magistrates, not as festival organizers. Even if they did have charge of the Gymnopaediae, it means little, for such responsibilities often change.

of Athenaeus which records the foundation date also shows us how it was arrived at: Hellanicus and others said that Terpander was on the scene at this time, and won the very first victory at the Carneia.[56] Sosibius therefore reckoned the date of Terpander as 676–672 (other chronographers have other dates),[57] and made it also the foundation date of the Carneia.

Whereas Terpander organized the first kind of music at Sparta, Thaletas and others organized the second (so [Plutarch], in the passage already mentioned). Now according to Sosibius, Thaletas and Alcman, in that order, composed the songs of the Gymnopaediae. Three dates are handed down for Alcman, on what authority we do not know. The Suda gives 672–668, Eusebius both 658–657 and 609–608.[58] The high date is too early by just a year for the foundation of the Gymnopaediae; the middle date comes ten years after, the low date fifty years after. For Thaletas no date survives. But if Sosibius put him in 668–667, he then had reason to say that the Gymnopaediae were founded in the same year, and that Alcman, also active at the festival, followed at a certain interval, whether it was ten years or fifty.

Our conclusion then is that the festival does not owe its origin or any notable development to the impact of a great event. At a fairly late stage the program was amplified with paeans for the dead of Thyrea; but that was doubtless a sentimental gesture, not a reaction to some contemporary change, such as the loss of the Thyreatis.

---

56 Ath. 14.37, 635 E-F (Hellanicus *FGrHist* 4 F 85; Sosibius 595 F 3).
57 Terpander's date: Marm. Par. *FGrHist* 239 A 34, 645–644; Euseb. *Can. a.* 642–641, Arm. 641–640.
58 Cf. J. Schneider, *REG* 98 (1985) 8–14. Schneider 1–64 reviews all the indications that may have been employed to compute the date of Alcman.

7

Polyandrion Burial and the Fate of the Dioscuri

Synopsis

From the study of festivals we shall turn aside to consider a Spartan military custom: the mass burial of fallen soldiers on the field of battle. Other Greeks preferred to bring home the dead, and from the fifth century onward they were often buried in public cemeteries. The practice is best known at Athens, but there is plenty of scattered evidence to show that it was nearly universal.[1] It is also imprinted in myth; the Greeks at Troy sent home the ashes of the dead, and trouble was taken to recover the bodies of those who fell at Thebes, and to bury them in friendly ground. Exceptions to the practice are mostly due to the fortunes of war; but Marathon and Plataea follow the Spartan example.

In this as in much else Sparta was different. For some Spartans who died in battle, there were individual tombs at home.[2] But the distinctive Spartan custom was to bury the dead in a mass grave on the field; when this could not be done, the bodies were still buried as near the field as possible. The custom is celebrated in myth, in the battle between the Tyndaridae and the Apharetidae. Here we find both a trophy and a burial on the field.

---

1 W.K. Pritchett, *The Greek State at War* 4 (Berkeley 1985) 94–259, offers a collection of material, but it is not arranged or interpreted so as to illustrate the rule and the exceptions. Cf. *EMC* ² (1983) 77–92.

2 Tyrtaeus holds out the promise of an individual tomb: τύμβος (12.29 Bergk/West), κλῆρος καὶ τάφ[ος (23.5). Tombs of individual soldiers are not uncommon in the epigraphic record. Spartan mothers, according to Aelian (*Var. Hist.* 12.21), examined the bodies on the field for honourable wounds in front; bodies so marked they carried home, with a fierce proud look, to family tombs; others were left for the common grave on the field, or buried furtively at home.

Let us consider the myth in general terms; then the trophy; finally, the burial.

The Myth as Aetiology

Our myth is a fairly old one.[3] It gives us, in folk-tale fashion, an impossible dilemma – a contest between warriors so perfectly matched that neither side can overcome the other until Zeus intervenes. The opposing sides are two pairs of marvellous twins, the Tyndaridae and the Apharetidae. The Tyndaridae, alias the Dioscuri, are familiar figures of cult as well as myth, being worshipped by the Dorians as divine warriors who appear in the midst of battle and bring miraculous aid. The Spartan army carried their statues when it marched, and their festival was celebrated in the field as well as at home.[4] The Apharetidae, on the other hand, though equally endowed with warrior qualities, are not heard of apart from this encounter, and the *casus belli* may take different forms, either cattle-reiving or bride-stealing. The Apharetidae were invented for the sake of the story, as a mirror image of the Tyndaridae; the *casus belli* was invented with them.

The end result of the encounter, after Zeus intervenes, is that the Tyndaridae are made immortal; they become those divine warriors, henceforth seen in the sky and worshipped at Therapnae. The battle between the Tyndaridae and the Apharetidae is accordingly a mythical paradigm for all the actual battles in which a Spartan soldier might call upon the Dioscuri.

It has been argued that the story is an aetiology of a different kind, explaining the Spartan festival Dioscureia and especially its athletic contests.[5] During the combat a spear is thrown and later a stone, and the Apharetidae flee and are pursued by Castor; these details are held to prefigure contests in throwing and running. The correspondence is not close enough to be convincing. It does not extend to the more curious features of the combat, as remarked below; and it does not give us any normal program of events for the festival.[6] The argument rests on Pindar's account of the combat in

---

3 Cf. Robert, *Heldensage* 311–19.

4 Statues: Hdt. 5.75.2. Festival: Paus. 4.27.2–3; Polyaenus 2.31.3. A Spartan king when going to war sacrifices Δὶ ἀγήτορι καὶ τοῖς σὺν αὐτῶι, according to the received text of Xenophon: *Lac.* 13.2. The latter phrase is sometimes emended, and Marchant makes it a sacrifice to the Dioscuri: τοῖν σιοῖν [αὐτῶι]. But although Xenophon writes ναὶ τὼ σιώ in reported speech (*Hell.* 4.4.10), it is unlikely that he used the dialect form here.

5 R. Merkelbach in *Le Monde grec ... hommages à C. Préaux* (Brussels 1975) 94–101.

6 Merkelbach 99–100 thinks of foot races and of throwing spear and discus. But throwing a discus does not much resemble the action of Idas, who aims and throws a grave marker uprooted from his father's tomb.

Nemean 10, and on the further supposition, which is hardly tenable, that Pindar celebrates a victory in the Dioscureia.[7] Moreover, we know that Pindar follows the *Cypria* in describing the combat, so that the aetiology is carried back to this source; but it is very hard to see why the epic should refer to such a festival (the context in the *Cypria* is briefly considered below).[8] This interpretation can be set aside.

Our sources agree that the encounter between the Tyndaridae and the Apharetidae was a virtual 'war.' Pindar begins by declaring that the shared immortality of the Dioscuri came about when 'Castor died in war,' φθιμένου ... Κάστορος ἐν πολέμωι – which one might call a lapidary phrase, since ἐν πολέμωι is regularly used on the tombstones of fallen soldiers, both at Sparta and elsewhere. [Apollodorus], who also follows the *Cypria*, speaks of the Tyndaridae as 'marching out,' στρατεύσαντες, to recover their cattle. In the *Cypria* the incident occurred on the very eve of the Trojan War, as we see from Proclus' summary; it is somehow relevant to the Trojan War. Theocritus' account diverges from the *Cypria*, but the combatants go to war in Homeric style, riding up in their chariots and making speeches and duelling with sword and spear. Ovid's account is different again, and very brief; but the weapons and wounds are Homeric, and the combat takes place on open ground chosen for the purpose, *apta area pugnae*.[9] Thus the encounter was always presented as an avowed war and a set battle.

The combat, in whatever version, develops naturally – swordplay first, or thrusting of spears; then flight and pursuit; finally, casting of javelin and stone. But two features are unexpected, and hitherto unexplained. The battle begins at an oak tree and ends at a grave mound: the Tyndaridae

---

7 The poem, in honour of Theaeus of Argos, was sung at the Argive Hecatombaea (22–3), and Pindar mentions first the victories of Theaeus at this festival (24), then his victories elsewhere (25–36), and finally the victories of kinsmen (37–48). As elsewhere in Pindar, the Dioscuri are mentioned for their help (38, 50–1); they also visited the table of one of Theaeus' family – he must have had some role in the Argive Theoxenia (49–50); whereafter, we hear that the Dioscuri are patrons of games at Sparta too (51–4), and finally of their myth (55–90). This is not an intelligible way of saying that Theaeus was victorious at the Spartan Dioscureia.

8 The festival name and the games are not expressly mentioned until the Roman period (*IG* 5.1.559, 602, cf. 658); but we may agree with L. Ziehen, *RE* 3A 2 (1929) 1478 *s.v.* Sparta, that 'there is no reason not to regard them as an old tradition': cf. n. 35 on the Gymnopaediae. As an early indication, Ziehen points to the armed dances which Plato ascribes to the Spartan cult of the Dioscuri (*Leg.* 7, 796 B); these, however, are absent from Merkelbach's aetiology.

9 Pind. *Nem.* 10.59. [Apld.] *Bibl.* 3.11.2.4 (3.136); cf. Tzetz. *Alex.* 511. Procl. *ap.* Phot. *Bibl.* 319 (Davies, *EGF* p. 31; Bernabé, *PEG* p. 40). Theocr. *Id.* 22.141–204. Ov. *Fast.* 5.707–12.

are discovered sitting in the tree, and the Apharetidae are slain beside the mound. These features were prominent in the *Cypria*. Now if the story is an aetiology of battle as the Spartans knew it, the oak and the mound must be typical of battle. It is not that either is a sacred place; the story does not lead up to any cult foundation.

The Trophy

Let us examine the details. Lynceus with his lynx eyes scanned the whole Peloponnesus from the top of Taÿgetus, and saw Castor and Polydeuces sitting inside a hollow oak tree; Idas went up and stabbed Castor right through the bark.[10] Then Lynceus and Idas fled; Polydeuces 'pursued,' and struck Lynceus with a javelin.[11] After Idas too was dealt with (more of this in a moment), Polydeuces returned to the spot where his brother lay dying, i.e., to the oak tree. Here he called on Zeus, who in answer to his prayer gave both the twins a share of immortality.[12] Thus far the *Cypria*. Other accounts omit the oak tree altogether, but the combat still unfolds as before: close combat, flight and pursuit, a final blow or cast.[13]

What does the oak tree mean? In effect it marks the place where, after sharp fighting, the enemy turns and flees; it is also the place where Polydeuces prays to Zeus. Now a trophy, *tropaion*, marks the place where the enemy turns and flees, and it honours Zeus. An oak tree is a good support for a trophy;[14] all the more, if the tree is dead and leafless, as this one is, being 'hollow.' A trophy that Polydeuces reputedly 'set up over Lynceus' was to be seen in Sparta;[15] that of course was a secondary monument, but it shows that a trophy was thought appropriate. We may suppose that in the *Cypria* Polydeuces stripped Lynceus of his arms and hung them on the oak tree as a solace for Castor. Because of Polydeuces' action, Spartan victors ever since have hung the arms of the defeated on a tree: such is the implication of the story.

10 Schol. Pind. *Nem.* 10.114a (*Cypria* fr. 13 Davies, 15 Bernabé): ἔσω κοίλης δρυός. Pind. *Nem.* 10.61–2: δρυὸς ἐν στελέχει. Lycophr. *Alex.* 553–4: κοῖλον ... στύπος φηγοῦ κελαινῆς.

11 Pind. *Nem.* 10.66; [Apld.] *Bibl.* 3.11.2.5 (3.136); Tzetz. *Alex.* 511.

12 Pind. *Nem.* 10.73–90.

13 Theocr. *Id.*. 22.198–204; Ov. *Fast.* 5.709–12.

14 *A.P.* 7.430 (*HE* Dioscorides 31): ποτὶ δρυὶ τᾶιδε. Virg. *Aen.* 11.5: *ingentem quercum decisis undique ramis.*

15 Paus. 3.14.7.

This curious *aition* is evoked in an episode of Messenia's pseudo-history which mocks Spartan pretensions.[16] At the battle of Boar's Tomb, Aristomenes went from one part of the Spartan line to another and routed each in turn, until the Spartans were everywhere flying in disorder from the field, and Aristomenes was everywhere pursuing. But a seer warned him not to pass a wild pear tree at a certain point on the plain, 'for he said that the Dioscuri were sitting on the wild pear tree,' καθέζεσθαι ... ἐπὶ τῆι ἀχράδι. Aristomenes neglected the warning, and passed the tree, and just then lost his shield; while he looked for it, the Spartans escaped.[17] Pausanias' source is the epic poet Rhianus of Crete;[18] when a Hellenistic poet like Rhianus has the Dioscuri sitting in a tree, there can be no doubt that he takes the notion from the *Cypria*. The tree is now associated with a Spartan defeat. It was here that Aristomenes lost his shield, and to this alone the Spartans owe their escape. So we see why Spartan soldiers ever since have hung up arms, especially a shield, upon a tree. Rhianus may or may not have made the aetiology explicit.

The Burial

The combat between Tyndaridae and Apharetidae resumes, after the flight and the pursuit, at the grave mound of Aphareus, father of the one pair of twins; Lycophron situates the mound at or near Amyclae.[19] It is here that Lynceus is killed by Polydeuces (so the *Cypria*), or by Castor (so Theocritus). Idas now pulls up the gravestone and hurls it at Polydeuces;[20]

16 Paus. 4.16.3–5. The episode, regarded as 'Messenian saga,' is set beside the myth of the Tyndaridae by S. Wide, *Lakonische Kulte* (Leipzig 1893) 316–17, who thinks of *Baumkultus*. But this is to ignore the context in both tales, scil. of battle and of battle rout.

17 There is a sequel to the story, in which Aristomenes consults the oracles of Delphi and Lebadeia, recovers the shield, and dedicates it at Lebadeia, where Pausanias saw this impressive object (4.16.7). S. Marinatos in *Essays in Memory of K. Lehmann* (New York 1964) 223–6 speculates on its appearance. The sequel does not affect the sense of the battlefield episode.

18 Some would say that Pausanias knew Rhianus only through a late intermediary: cf. the discussion of Messenian legends below, apropos of the Ithomaea. The question does not matter here.

19 Pind. *Nem.* 10.66: τύμβωι σχεδὸν πατρωίωι. Lycophr. *Alex.* 559: τῶν Ἀμυκλαίων τάφων. Theocr. *Id..* 22.141: τύμβον ... ἀποφθιμένου Ἀφαρῆος. 199: σῆμα πατρός. 207–8: Ἀφαρηίου ... τύμβου. Tzetz. *Alex.* 511, cf. 553: τοῦ Ἀφαρέως τάφου.

20 Pind. *Nem.* 10.67–8: ἁρπάξαντες ἄγαλμ' Ἀίδα, ξεστὸν πέτρον. Lycophr. *Alex.* 559: ἄγαλμα πήλας τῶν Ἀμυκλαίων τάφων. Tzetz. *Alex.* 511: στήληι λιθίνηι. 553: στήλην. Tzetz. *Alex.* 511 copies out [Apld.] from a better exemplar than our mss., which have πέτραι instead of στήληι λιθίνηι.

or else he is about to hurl it at Castor.[21] In the *Cypria* the gravestone strikes Polydeuces and knocks him out; Pindar, however, denies that the missile had any effect. At all events, Zeus now flings a lightning bolt so as to kill Idas.[22] The lightning also consumes the bodies of both brothers. Pindar says that 'they were burned up together all by themselves,' ἅμα δ' ἐκαίοντ' ἐρῆμοι; Lycophron, that the lightning bolts 'will obliterate' them, καταξανοῦσιν.

We have then the main elements of a burial on the field: a grave mound with a stele, and a virtual cremation. The story feigns that the mound and the stele, like the oak tree, already existed on the site before that primordial combat was joined. Thus does it explain why Spartan soldiers ever since have erected a mound and a stele on the field. The *aition* is naïve, but it could not do better. Logic of course requires that Polydeuces should bury Castor, but the Tyndaridae are not available at this point; both are summoned to a different fate. Hyginus, however, preserves a realistic version in which the burial is made just as logic requires (*Fab.* 80): it confirms the sense of the original story.

In Hyginus the fighting again has several stages. First Castor kills Lynceus, and Idas gives up the war in order to bury his brother, *omisit bellum ... coepit fratrem sepelire.* 'As he was placing the bones in the tomb, Castor came and forbade the construction of the monument, saying that he had beaten him as if he were a woman,' *cum ossa eius collocaret in pila, intervenit Castor et prohibere coepit monumentum fieri, quod diceret se eum quasi feminam superasse.* Idas in a fury kills Castor. There is also a variant in which Castor attacks, and is killed, as Idas is heaping up the mound, *alii dicunt quemadmodum aedificabat pilam super, Castorem impulisse et sic interfectum.* Next Polydeuces kills Idas. 'And he recovered his brother's body and consigned it to burial,' *corpusque fratris recuperatum sepulturae dedit.* Then the usual ending: Zeus grants immortality to Polydeuces, and Polydeuces asks to share it with his brother.

Here the *aition* is quite explicit: the winning side recovers and buries the dead. We also see that the losing side has no right to erect a tomb on the field; for when Idas attempted this, Castor stopped him and mocked the slain; or else he renewed the attack. The triumphant burial of Spartan dead is contrasted with the treatment of other dead, who are denied this privilege.

---

21 Theocr. *Id..* 22.207–8: στήλην Ἀφαρηίου ἐξανέχουσαν τύμβου ἀναρρήξας. 210–11: τυκτὴν μάρμαρον.
22 Pind. *Nem.* 10.71–2; Theocr. *Id..* 27.211; Lycophr. *Alex.* 560–1; [Apld.] *Bibl.* 3.11.2.5 (3.137); Tzetz. *Alex.* 511.

Hyginus' *Fabulae* is a miserable work, a blundering abridgement of a muddled compilation; but it often goes back to sources that are otherwise quite lost to us. Here the ultimate source, or rather sources, since a variant is recorded, are probably Hellenistic; for it was then that mythical aetiology truly flourished, both in prose and in poetry, and Sparta of all places was not neglected. Aetiology looks to existing customs, or to those that are well remembered; in so far as the custom is unchanged, a Hellenistic aetiology will be just as revealing as an earlier aetiology.[23] Sometimes it is more revealing, for Hellenistic writers were attentive to curious details. The myths favoured by (say) Callimachus or Apollonius provide a very literal rendering of a given custom. Hyginus now gives us a literal burial of a fallen soldier, as the *Cypria* does not.

The Spartans themselves thought that the combat should issue in a burial. When the story was first told, the setting was only a notional landscape with an oak tree and a grave mound. But later the memorials could be seen on the ground. In the agora of Sparta, 'near' the ancient assembly place called *Skias*, Pausanias saw a 'grave-monument,' μνῆμα, of Castor, together with a 'shrine,' ἱερόν; also 'beside the *Skias*' was a 'tomb,' τάφος, of Idas and Lynceus (3.13.1).[24] The two terms, μνῆμα and τάφος, are merely an elegant variation. Elsewhere in Sparta, near the racecourse, *Dromos*, that was used for the exercises of young Spartiates, Pausanias saw a 'trophy'; 'they say that Polydeuces set it up over Lynceus' (3.14.7). The separation of trophy and tombs is faithful to the story; for the trophy marks the spot where the pursuit of the Apharetidae began, and the tombs mark the spot where the fighting ended. We may suppose that the sources of Hyginus had an eye on these Spartan monuments. In one respect, however, they differ from the monuments; or at least one of the sources differed. In Hyginus only Castor is properly buried on the field. The Spartans, on the other hand, allowed that the Apharetidae were buried at about the same place. We should ask why this opinion was just as congenial as the other.

In later sources Aphareus and his sons are associated with Messenia, so that the fight between Apharetidae and Tyndaridae prefigures the wars between Messenia and Sparta. Whether this association goes back to the *Cypria* does not appear;[25] in any case the combat was always

23 For the principle, *EMC* ² 10 (1991) 73.

24 The *pila, τὴν πεῖλαν*, which was constructed for the Dioscuri by a priest and priestess under Trajan or Hadrian (*IG* 5.1.233), seems to be a 'pier' of some kind on the Eurotas bank: A.J.S. Spawforth, *BSA* 80 (1985) 203–4, and, with P. Cartledge, *Hellenistic and Roman Sparta* (London 1989) 135, 256 n. 18.

25 It is often said that Aphareus is the eponym of Messenian Φαραί, and that he and his sons derive from local cult: e.g., Robert, *Heldensage* 311, after Wilamowitz.

thought of as occurring at or near Sparta.[26] It is likely, as was said, that the Apharetidae were created for the sake of the story. If so, the name Ἀφαρητιάδαι will be transparent, and since a leading quality of these warlike twins is swiftness, it very likely comes from ἄφαρ; the Apharetidae are then 'sons of Swift.' In the *Cypria* Lynceus goes swiftly on swift feet up Taÿgetus, αἶψα ... ποσὶν ταχέεσσι πεποιθώς. In Pindar the Apharetidae come swiftly on swift feet to the oak tree, λαιψηροῖς δὲ πόδεσσιν ἄφαρ ἐξικέσθαν.[27] We may wonder if the *Cypria* played upon the name.

Now the Dioscuri like the Apharetidae are ideally swift. Statues of the Dioscuri stood at the starting line of the *Dromos*, with the title ἀφετήριοι, 'starters of the race.' Beyond the finish-line, as it seems – 'as you go on from the *Dromos'* – was a shrine of the Dioscuri and the Charites, worshipped no doubt as bestowers of victory in the race.[28] The swiftness of the Dioscuri was displayed in the pursuit that led from the *Dromos* and the trophy to the *Skias* and the tombs. The Apharetidae are indeed a mirror image of the Dioscuri, and from this point of view they too are appropriately honoured with a tomb. The *Dromos* and the *Skias* were chosen for the trophy and the tombs because both places were used by the Spartan army: racing was a military exercise, and the assembly was of warriors, in early days of warriors under arms.

The army is also concerned in the other localization of the combat, at or near Amyclae. In Lycophron the pre-existing tomb, obviously the tomb of Aphareus as in the *Cypria*, is called 'Amyclaean.'[29] The tomb is doubtless at a certain distance from the scene of the initial fighting, which

---

The Apharetidae and Pharae are conjoined at Lycophr. *Alex.* 552 and, probably, at Steph. Byz. *s.v.* Φαραί (Ἀφαρητιάδαι Xylander, Φηρητιάδαι Pinedo). But the connection must be secondary. The epic place-name is Φηραί; in the *Cypria* sons of the eponym would not be called Ἀφαρητιάδαι, but *Φηρητιάδαι. Pherecydes is another early source who may or may not have spoken of Messenia: Philodem. *De Piet.* N 247 Vᵃ 23 + 242 Vᵃ 24 + 247 Vᵇ 1 (*Cypria* fr. 14 Davies; Pherecydes *FGrHist* 3 F 165 *corr.*).

26 At Hyg. *Astr.* 2.22 the Apharetidae are said to 'besiege' Sparta.

27 Schol. Pind. *Nem.* 10.114a (*Cypria* fr. 13 Davies, 15 Bernabé) lines 1–2. Pind. *Nem.* 10.63–4.

28 Paus. 3.14.6–7.

29 Lycophr. *Alex.* 559. Tzetzes is vapouring when he asserts, on *Alex.* 553, that 'Amyclus was king of Pherae, and he built an enormous tomb.' Aphareus also had a grave monument, μνῆμα, in the Spartan agora, but it was inside the old Ephors' quarters, together with a grave monument of Epimenides (Paus. 3.11.11). Whatever the significance of this monument, it did not mark the site of the combat. On the old Ephors' quarters, see N.M. Kennell, *AJA* 91 (1987) 421–2.

is the Cnecion crossing, Κνηκιῶν πόρος.[30] The Cnecion then is one of the rivers flowing into the Eurotas from the west, just above or below Amyclae. [Aristotle] was right to say, apropos of the Great Rhetra, that the Cnecion is 'a river,' evidently an unimportant one; but others were wrong to identify it with the chief tributary of the Eurotas north of Sparta, the Oenus.[31] It is named in the Rhetra as an extreme limit of Spartiate territory, and was so understood by Plutarch (*Pel.* 17.13). The river was once a frontier at which the Spartan army performed its 'rites of crossing,' διαβατήρια; for the river name is formed from the genitive plural of κνήκια, 'rites of the tawny one,' i.e., the goat.[32] If in the Rhetra the assembly must always meet 'between' the two limits named (*Lyc.* 6.2), it is reasonable to infer that sometimes it met just at the one limit or the other. On this showing the 'Cnecion crossing,' like the *Skias*, was a muster-ground of the Spartan army; so the tomb of Aphareus was sought and found nearby. No doubt the oak-tree trophy was to be seen here too. Pausanias speaks of a trophy set up by the Dorians over the Amyclaeans, evidently of venerable aspect (3.2.6); this may be the same trophy, as viewed by those who preferred to situate the combat of the twins at Sparta.

In short, our myth explains and glorifies the Spartan custom of burial on the field.[33] It is obvious that the myth originates at Sparta and was current there before the *Cypria* took it up, probably near the end of the sixth century;[34] so the custom is at least as old as this. The *Cypria* recounted the myth just after Helen was abducted from Sparta, and just before Menelaus was informed of this by Iris – whereupon 'he takes counsel with his brother concerning the expedition to Troy' (so Proclus' summary). Why was the

---

30 Lycophr. *Alex.* 550.

31 Plut. *Lyc.* 6.4 ([Arist.] fr. 536 Rose³). Cf. F. Bölte, *RE* 3A 2 (1929) 1372 *s.v.* Sparta, and *RE* 17.2 (1937) 2280–1 *s.v.* Oinus 1.

32 Κνηκιῶν, like the names of Attic and Ionic months, e.g., Ἑκατομβαιών, is an adjective form that supplants the genitive plural of a neuter substantive, κνηκίων or Ἑκατομβαίων, in denoting the river or the month *of* the κνήκια or the Ἑκατόμβαια. For κνηκός or κνήκων 'goat,' see Gow on Theocr. 3.5. For the διαβατήρια, Xen. *Lac.* 13.2–3; H. Popp, *Die Einwirkung von Vorzeichen, Opfern und Festen auf die Kriegführung der Griechen* (Würzburg 1957) 42–6; M.H. Jameson in *Hoplites: The Classical Greek Battle Experience*, ed. V.D. Hanson (London 1991) 202–3.

33 Other military customs are likewise traced to the Dioscuri. Armed dances were invented by Castor or by the pair: K. Latte, *De Saltationibus Graecorum* (Giessen 1913) 29–30. After capturing Aphidna, they dedicate the spoils at the shrine of Athena *chalkioikos* – even though it is allowed that the existing temple and statue are very much later (Paus. 3.17.2).

34 M. Davies, *Glotta* 67 (1989) 93–4, 97–100, gives linguistic reasons for dating the *Cypria* 'shortly before 500.'

myth recounted at all? Why was it recounted at this critical point? It must be that the Spartan custom was recognized as quite distinctive in Greece, and yet seemingly akin to the practice of the Trojan War; for tradition always said that several of the leading Greek heroes, Protesilaus and Achilles and Ajax and others, were buried on the field, beneath the mounds of the Trojan plain. The *Cypria* evidently dwelt upon the burial of the dead. Proclus says that after the very first engagement at Troy, in which Protesilaus is killed by Hector and Cycnus by Achilles, 'they take up the bodies,' καὶ τοὺς νεκροὺς ἀναιροῦνται.

PART THREE

Argos

8

The Parparonia and
the Battle of Thyrea

Synopsis

The agonistic festival Parparonia is known from the victory list of the
Spartan Damonon and his son, conjecturally dated to the early fourth century, which mentions both horse-races and foot races, and from Hesychius,
who speaks of 'Parparus' as the setting of games and dances. Parparus is
also named by Choeroboscus as the 'place at which Argives and Spartans
fought over Thyrea.' And since it appears in Pliny's list of the mountains
of the Argolid, Parparus must be Mount Zavitsa, which runs east from
Parthenius to the sea and closes the plain of Thyrea on the north. The
place-name is probably used as the name of a person in a votive inscription found in the vicinity, of which more below.[1]

It is evident that the festival Parparonia and the battle of Thyrea, or
battle of the champions, are somehow connected. Since Sparta won the
battle, at least by her own account, which became the vulgate, and since
the Thyreatis was afterwards in Spartan hands, it has always been assumed
that this is in origin a Spartan festival. But the assumption is ill considered.
There is every reason to suppose that the festival antedates the Spartan
occupation and was formerly conducted either by Argos or by the local
people.

The usual notion of the Spartan festival is that it was founded to
commemorate the Spartan victory. We have met a similar notion of the

---

1 IG 5.1.213 lines 44–9, 62–4 (L. Moretti, Iscrizione agonistiche greche [Rome 1953]
  16): Παρπαρόνια ἐνίκε κτλ. For the date, see L.H. Jeffery, BSA 83 (1988) 179–81. Hsch.
  s.v. Πάρπαρος· ἐν ὧι ἀγὼν ἤγετο καὶ χοροὶ ἵσταντο. Choerob. in Gramm. Gr. 4.1.297:
  Πάρπαρος· τόπος ἐν ὧι περὶ Θυρεῶν ἐμαχέσαντο Ἀργεῖοι καὶ Λακεδαιμόνιοι. Plin. Hist.
  Nat. 4.17: montes Artemisius, Apesantus, Asterion, Parparus. The 'Parparus' inscription: n. 50 below.

Gymnopaediae, one of Sparta's most renowned festivals, scil. that it was founded to bolster morale after the Spartan defeat at Hysiae. On this reckoning the two festivals mark important stages of Sparta's development, at an interval of about 120 years, in 669–668 and in ca. 547. It is further held that after Sparta lost the Thyreatis, the Parparonia lapsed and some of its observances were transferred to the Gymnopaediae.[2] These notions should be discarded. The Gymnopaediae were an age-old festival of Apollo which had its counterpart in every Greek city at the same season. The battle of Hysiae was an Argive tradition, and probably a very late one, and of no account at Sparta. Furthermore, and this will soon emerge from our examination of the battle of Thyrea, the relationship that Argives envisaged between the battles of Hysiae and Thyrea was the reverse of modern doctrine: Hysiae was a riposte to Thyrea after half a century. Finally, the festivals Gymnopaediae and Parparonia have no affinity whatever, being addressed to different deities at different times in different places.

Another view of the festival and the battle has been expressed from time to time. Details of the battle are thought to be legendary, perhaps inspired by choral songs at Sparta; or the battle is described as a 'ritual war.'[3] These suggestions have not been clearly worked out, and even if they were accepted in principle, they might still leave room for a historical battle. Yet they point in the right direction. They should prompt us to ask whether the battle is not from the start an aetiological legend. Admittedly, almost nothing is known about the ritual of the Parparonia. We can see, however, that the festival is of the same type as the Ithomaea of Messenia; both are festivals of Zeus conducted beside a mountain. The Ithomaea are associated with the exploits of Aristomenes, the Parparonia with the battle of Thyrea.

2 F. Bölte, *RhM* n.s. 78 (1929) 130–2, and *RE* 18.4 (1949) 1872–3 *s.v.* Parparos; V. Ehrenberg, *RE* 3A 2 (1929) 1380 *s.v.* Sparta; L. Ziehen, *RE* 3A 2 (1929) 1510, 1516 *s.v.* Sparta; A. Andrewes, *CQ* 43 (1949) 77; H.T. Wade-Gery, *CQ* 43 (1949) 79–81; Jacoby on Sosibius *FGrHist* 595 F 5; G.L. Huxley, *Early Sparta* (London 1962) 50, 72–3, 126–7; P. Cartledge, *Sparta and Lakonia* (London 1979) 126, 140; A.A. Mosshammer, *The Chronicle of Eusebius and Greek Chronographic Tradition* (Lewisburg, Pa. 1979) 223–4.

3 Legends inspired by choral songs: Ehrenberg, *RE* 18.2 (1942) 1872 *s.v.* Othryadas. 'Ritual war' or the like: A. Brelich, *Guerre, agoni e culti nella Grecia arcaica* (Bonn 1961) 22–34; Moretti, *Ricerche sulle leghe greche* (Rome 1962) 10–12, 27–33; C. Calame, *Les Choeurs de jeunes filles en Grèce archaïque* (Rome 1977) 1.353; J. Christien and T. Spyropoulos, *BCH* 109 (1985) 459. These writers differ widely, however, in assessing the ritual and legendary elements (they might not like to be lumped together in this note). And most are ready to credit a historical battle as well, or even two or more battles.

The reputed battle site, which is also the festival site, was marked by some kind of tomb. Pausanias took it as a burial of the champions in *polyandrion* style, but earlier tradition makes it the tomb of Othryades. Though Sparta and Argos had contrary versions of the battle, both asserting victory, they agreed that the outcome turned on the death of Othryades. Othryades is a hero projected from the festival, and his death is a myth of a familiar type explaining how the festival arose. It was only in the fifth century that the myth became a legend, the contest of champions, explaining in turn how the Thyreatis passed into Spartan hands.

We shall consider first the evidence for the battle and for Sparta's occupation of the Thyreatis: Herodotus on the battle; other sources on the battle; the *'kenearion'* inscription; tombs at Sparta for the dead of Thyrea; the early history of the Thyreatis; Cleomenes' attack on Argos. Then the Parparonia: the festival name and site; Pausanias' burial site; the 'Parparus' inscription; the tomb of Othryades; the champion Perilaus; the monument seen by Pausanias; the festival aetiology; other stories about the battle of Thyrea. (See map 6.)

Herodotus on the Battle of Thyrea

Conflicting dates are handed down for many persons and events of early Greece. Yet the dates seldom differ as much as do those of the battle of Thyrea. Herodotus thinks of it as occurring just at the time when Croesus was unexpectedly besieged by Cyrus: Sparta, though absorbed in the struggle for Thyrea, made ready to help him. But another authority, probably Ephorus, put the battle soon after the end of the First Messenian War, in the time of the Spartan kings Theopompus and Polydorus.[4] The implied dates are nearly two hundred years apart. It is, however, the same battle, or rather the same sequence of battles – a contest of champions, which is indecisive, followed by an engagement between the full levies of both cities; and it has the same result, to establish Spartan control over the disputed area for a long time.

Herodotus is the earlier and better source; and the date he implies is hardly more than two generations before his own lifetime. Most scholars accept his version without further ado. The battle of Thyrea, he says, took place while Sardis was under siege by the Persians. From reading modern works, one might suppose that the intent as well as the effect of Herodotus' account is to supply an approximate date for the battle, 'in

---

4 The time of Croesus: Hdt. 1.82–3. The time of Theopompus and Polydorus: Plut. *Apophth. Lac.* 231 E; Paus. 3.7.5, cf. 2.38.5, 3.3.4, 10.9.12.

c. 547.' But this is a poor way of rendering his emphasis. Messengers of Croesus set off at speed to call for help, and one of them came to Sparta; 'at this very time,' κατ' αὐτὸν τοῦτον τὸν χρόνον, 'a conflict had arisen with the Argives,' etc. (1.82.1). The contest of champions and the general engagement are recounted. Then Herodotus resumes, 'while such troubles were upon them,' τοιούτων ... ἐνεστεώτων πρηγμάτων, 'the Sardian herald arrived to ask help for Croesus against the siege. They none the less, on hearing the herald's news, hastened to bring help; and they were already mustered, and the ships were ready, when a second message came, that the Lydian stronghold had fallen and Croesus was taken alive' (1.83).

Before this sudden turn, Herodotus has shown us a dramatic process, the rise of Lydia as a great Oriental power; all the more dramatic when set beside the rise of Sparta (1.65–70). Down to this period Sparta was nothing – she was the most disordered state in Greece, as we see from the oracle addressed to Lycurgus, and from the dispensation that followed; she was impotent even against her nearest neighbour Tegea, as we see from the oracle and battle of the fetters. But when Croesus looked for allies, Sparta was just emerging, as we see from the oracle and incident of the smithy. The battle of Thyrea set the seal on Sparta's power, for until then Argos had controlled the whole east coast of the Peloponnesus, as far as Cythera (1.82.2). And it came at the very moment that Lydia was overthrown. It could have come at no other time.

Such is Herodotus' date or context. Though almost universally endorsed in modern books, it was a venture that was not repeated by ancient writers. An altogether different date or context became current later. Our sources are Plutarch and Pausanias and late chronography.

Other Sources on the Battle of Thyrea

'When the Argives, after the combat of the three hundred, had again been beaten with their full levy in a pitched battle, his allies urged Polydorus not to lose the opportunity,' etc. (Plut. Apophth. Lac. 231 E). The anecdote that follows is jejune, but it starts from a received account in which the battle of Thyrea, unfolding just as in Herodotus, takes place in the reign of the Spartan king Polydorus; we see that Polydorus himself commanded the Spartan side in the general engagement.

Pausanias, who recounts the lineage of the two royal houses in succession, does not mention Thyrea when he comes to Polydorus as a member of the first house; for his narrative is selective, and Polydorus' reign is notable for domestic events (3.3.2–3). The battle of Thyrea is recorded instead under the reign of Polydorus' colleague Theopompus; yet Theopompus himself did not take part, being very old and distressed by the death of his son (3.7.5). It follows that the Spartan commander was the other king, Polydorus. Pausanias' battle, described as 'the contest about the so-called Thyreatic territory between Sparta and Argos,' is undoubtedly the battle we hear of elsewhere. It is a Spartan victory, and a decisive one; Pausanias has already noted that in the reign of Polydorus' son, Sparta had no trouble from Argos (3.3.4). It makes an end to an earlier period in which all 'Cynuria' belongs to Argos – though Sparta intervenes at will, for this is a frankly chauvinist account; the Cynurians themselves are Argives, descended from Perseus (3.2.2–3, 7.2). It also comes just after the First Messenian War, in which Messenia is annexed by Sparta. It is a virtual *akmē* of Spartan power.

The battle of Thyrea finds a place in the chronographers. It is dated to 720–719 by Eusebius (719–718 in the Armenian version); to 735–734 by Solinus (*Collect.* 7.9). The different dates derive from different systems of computing Spartan kings, but express the same result: the battle of Thyrea follows the First Messenian War by an interval of one Olympiad.[5] The chronographers drew on the same vulgate account as did Plutarch and Pausanias. It was probably established by Ephorus.

Thus far the tradition of the battle of Thyrea. It is uniform in asserting that the battle was a turning-point. Before it, the area was always Argive; after it, the area was always Spartan. And the area that changes hands appears to be, both in Herodotus and in Pausanias, the eastern coast of the Peloponnesus from the plain of Thyrea to Cythera, so-called 'Cynuria.'

We should also glance at the battle of Hysiae, more fully dealt with elsewhere. This was a victory of Argos over Sparta at another strategic place. Pausanias, and he alone among ancient writers, mentions it in his tour of the Argolid (2.24.7), and also supplies a date, both by Olympiad and by Athenian archon, which he says that he has just ascertained: 669–668 BC. His manner of speaking makes it very likely that he first learned of this battle either from an Argive informant or from a book of Argive history. In any case the date comes from a late source. Such a source could not fail to be cognizant of the date of the battle of Thyrea, 720–719 BC according to the usual system. The Spartan victory is reversed by an Argive victory after fifty years. Since it was agreed that the effect of the Spartan victory was somewhat lasting, fifty years is about the minimum interval that an Argive chauvinist might assert.

Thus Herodotus and the later vulgate discredit each other. One might attempt to save Herodotus by supposing that the victory was authentically

5 Jacoby, *Apollodors Chronik* (Berlin 1902) 129 n. 7; Mosshammer, *Chronicle of Eusebius* 204–8; J. Schneider, *REG* 98 (1985) 20, 27–8.

remembered as occurring in the context of other affairs. Perhaps the Spartans were proud of fighting in Thyrea at a time when they were also heavily engaged in preparations to help Croesus. But if so, why was the connection afterwards forgotten? Or why was it neglected by the writer, Ephorus or another, who set down the other version? Relations between Sparta and Persia were not a topic which ceased to be of interest after Herodotus. Surely the connection can be attributed to Herodotus himself. As we saw, the battle of Thyrea and the messages from Sardis are bound together in his narrative so as to form a climax: together, they conclude the tale of Sparta's rise and Croesus' fall. Herodotus' Spartan informants will have applauded this connection. But it was not a Spartan tradition.

Given both the differences and the similarities between Herodotus and the later vulgate, the only reasonable conclusion is that the Spartan tradition of the battle did not include a date. Instead the battle was spoken of as a paradigm of hard-fought but conclusive victory. In other words, it was a popular legend which historians situated in time according to their own lights.

Legends of course may still go back to real events, even if we have no means of distinguishing the reality. Yet we shall find that all the details of the battle have the appearance of aetiology.

The 'Kenearion' Inscription

A local inscription has been much discussed of late as evidence for either the battle of champions or some other battle between Argos and Sparta, and even as a reference point in the topography of the Thyreatis. We must examine it, but only to declare it out of play. The inscription is of eight lines in large letters on a block or stele of limestone, evidently a public installation of some kind.[6] It was found high up on the south side of Zavitsa; the letter forms are Argive, probably of the late fifth century. The misunderstanding that has arisen is partly due to the vagaries of publication; the text was divulged in two instalments. Soon after its discovery the block

---

6 The first half of the text: K.A. Rhomaios, *Praktika* 1950.237; *SEG* 13.266; K.I. Kalitsis, *ArchEph* 1960 [1965] Chron. 6 n. 10, 1965 [1967] Chron. 16–18; L.H. Jeffery, *The Local Scripts of Archaic Greece* (Oxford 1961) 171 no. 50; W.K. Pritchett, *Studies in Ancient Greek Topography* 3 (Berkeley 1980) 110–18; *SEG* 30.379; C. Clairmont, *Patrios Nomos: Public Burial in Athens* (BAR S 161, 1983) 1.245 no. 84. The full text: P.B. Phaklaris, *Archaia Kynouria* (Salonica 1985) 100–101, pl. 70, and *Horos* 5 (1987) 101–19; C. Kritzas, *BCH* 109 (1985) 710–13; *SEG* 35.295; Pritchett, *Topogr.* 6 (Berkeley 1989) 79–83, pls. 156–8. Cf. Ernst Meyer, *KlP* 4 (1972) 528 s.v. Parparos; LSJ *Suppl. s.v.* κενεάριον; Cartledge, *Sparta and Lakonia* 189; Pritchett, *The Greek State at War* 4 (Berkeley 1985) 160–1, 251.

was smashed to pieces by a shepherd in search of treasure, and some pieces disappeared. The original editor decided to publish only the first half of the text, evidently mistrusting the sense of the rest. But a copy which was made before the stone was broken (and which was available to the original editor) has now been published. It agrees with the pieces still remaining, and can be accepted without reserve. The first half of the inscription did not really lend itself to the interpretation of the original editor and of all who followed him; and the second half explodes this interpretation.[7] It is still upheld, however, more determinedly than ever.[8]

The full text runs as follows.

[μεδ]εὶς
[ἀδι]κείτο
[τὸ κ]ενε-
[άρ]ιον·
[τὸν] ὀχε-
[τὸν {ο}] μὲ
[ἀδικε-]
[ίτο.]

The first half has been taken to mean, 'Let no one harm *the cenotaph.*' It is suggested that the Argives erected a cenotaph, though belatedly, on the battlefield of Thyrea; or else on the site of some unrecorded battle. As to the battle of champions, Pausanias thought he saw an actual burial of both Spartans and Argives, not a cenotaph. In general, cenotaphs were not erected on the field except as a last resort, when the bodies could not be found.[9] Now that the second half gives us a 'conduit' or 'water channel,' ὀχετός, and another interdiction, 'Let him not harm the conduit,' it is suggested that the conduit ran beside a road and past the cenotaph.[10]

7 So Kritzas. His demonstration should have sufficed, even though he did not find quite the right meaning; but since Pritchett attempts to refute him on linguistic grounds, it seems worthwhile to explain the morphology of κενεάριον.
8 So Phaklaris and Pritchett and also F.E. and J.E. Winters, EMC² 9 (1990) 232. Phaklaris and the Winters, however, do not think that the battle commemorated by the 'cenotaph' helps to situate the battle of champions.
9 Cf. Xen. Anab. 6.4.9, on Arcadian mercenaries killed near Calpe: a large mound serves as cenotaph for the missing, and other mounds cover the bodies that were found. Pritchett, Gr. State at War 4.160–1, 251, thinks that our stone marks the site of a battle which Argos commemorated with a cenotaph on the field, while removing the bodies for burial at home. One would like to hear more of this practice.
10 Perhaps I have not done full justice to Pritchett's argument. Apart from the question of meaning, he seems to me to misconceive or disregard both the location and the

Even when the first half stood alone, the form κενεάριον invited us to look for a meaning other than 'cenotaph.' The form κενήριον, which is used with this meaning mainly in poetry, was often understood, anciently and since, as a compound of κενός and ἠρίον, 'empty mound.' That etymology looks rather fanciful (a built tomb may be literally 'empty,' but not an earthen mound), and κενεάριον now proves it so. This cannot be the Doric form of a compound of ἠρίον, for ἠρίον occurs with -η- both in Doric inscriptions and in Theocritus (a fact which favours a derivation from ἔρα 'earth').[11] Instead κενεάριον is the noun formed from the adjective κενέαρος, glossed by Hesychius as κενός, ἐλαφρός. The form κενέαρος stands to κενεός as νεαρός to νέος. The contracted form of νεαρός is νηρός; a contracted form of κενέαρος would be *κένηρος. Both κενεάριον and κενήριον are nouns referring to something 'empty.' It is not surprising that one form of the noun should take on the special meaning 'cenotaph,' a tomb without a body. Nor is it surprising that elsewhere, in the dialect of Argos or the Thyreatis, the other form should take on a special meaning that has to do with the conveyance of water.

It remains to determine this meaning. Some kind of 'cavity,' i.e., a cistern or a basin, has been suggested.[12] But we should be guided rather by a close verbal parallel that occurs in the rules for the Mysteries of Andania. It is for the agoranomos to look to the provision of water at the festival, and to ensure that no one interferes – to ensure, first of all, ὅπως ... μηθεὶς κακοποιεῖ μήτε [τὸ β]ήλημα μήτε τοὺς ὀχετούς, 'that no one damage either the β]ήλημα or the conduits.' Though the first letter of the word is not preserved on the stone, it is restored with certainty from Hesychius s.v., who defines it as a sluice, a suitable meaning for a concrete noun formed from ϝειλέω 'compress.'[13] But this is also a suitable meaning for κενεάριον, since the effect of a sluice is to 'empty' a conduit.

---

date of this inscription. In any case, it is not so much an argument as a polemic, a genre in which Pritchett is well practised. Anyone who disputes the meaning 'cenotaph' can expect to hear himself derided as ignorant, presumptuous, and confused. This is good fun. But after we see that no one but Pritchett knows Greek or the rules of epigraphy, we encounter with some surprise the conjectural supplement which he offers for the second half of the inscription: Topogr. 6.80. The supplement is of two words, put together with the help, as he tells us, of Veitch's Greek Verbs. Much more help was needed; for the two words are ungrammatical nonsense.

11 SIG³ 11 = Jeffery, Local Scripts 271, 277 no. 33 (a Selinuntine tomb at Delphi); IG 12.1.168 (Rhodes); Theocr. Id. 2.13.

12 So Kritzas, BCH 109 (1985) 713.

13 IG 5.1.1390 lines 103–4 (SIG³ 736, LSCG 65). Hsch. βήλημα: κώλυμα, φράγμα ἐν ποταμῶι· Λάκωνες. Cf. Frisk, Gr. etym. Wörterb. s.vv. βήλημα, εἰλέω 1.

The inscription then forbids one to damage either 'the sluice' or 'the conduit.' The language, two clauses without a connective, is no worse than in many another inscription. We might say in colloquial English, 'No one harm the sluice, no one harm the conduit.' In Greek it is natural to juxtapose the two objects, and to vary the negative as between μηδείς and μή.

The most remarkable circumstance in the discovery of this inscription has not yet been mentioned. The road construction that turned up the stone also turned up an ancient water channel, which was no doubt supplied by the nearby spring Spartino. Whether the channel was contemporary with the stone does not appear; but we may assume that this was a lasting arrangement. So the inscription is concerned with the conveyance of water from the spring, and has no bearing on the battle of Thyrea.

It might conceivably pertain to the sanctuary of Zeus Parparōnios (for this was somewhere on the mountain, as we shall see) and to the part of the festival Parparonia that was celebrated at the sanctuary. This is only a possibility, however; nothing more can be said unless new evidence comes to light.

Tombs at Sparta for the Dead of Thyrea

Two or three epigrams in the *Anthology* are meant for the tombs of individual Spartans who died at Thyrea. They are of course literary exercises, not authentic epitaphs; yet verisimilitude is a requirement of the genre. Given Pausanias' report of a *polyandrion* burial, epigrams for individual tombs are unexpected. When epigrammatists write on famous battles, they mostly look to the monuments on the field, e.g., to the tombs or the lion monument of Thermopylae. Of all the epigrams that celebrate Thyrea, only one, ascribed to 'Simonides,' envisages a *polyandrion* burial; we shall come to it below.

Let us consider the epigrams for individual tombs. Chaeremon praises Cleuas for 'cutting off' Thyrea, the term used by Herodotus: 'Cleuas son of Etymoclas, you couched your spear for Thyrea, and met your death while cutting off disputed land.'[14] Damagetus says that Gyllis killed three of the enemy; a surviving epitaph at Sparta says that its subject killed one of the enemy. 'O Spartans, this tomb holds your warlike Gyllis, who died for Thyrea; he slew three men of the Argives, and spoke this word, "May

---

14 *A.P.* 7.720 (*HE* Chaeremon 2), ἀμφίλογον γᾶν ἀποτεμνόμενος. Herodotus uses the term twice to describe the conflict: ἀποταμόμενοι ἔσχον, of the Spartans; τῆι σφετέρηι ἀποταμνομένηι, of the Argives (1.82.2–3).

I die having wrought worthily of Sparta."'[15] Finally, Dioscorides gives us a six-line epigram on Thrasybulus, who took seven wounds in front from the Argives and was brought home on his shield to Pitane and burned on a pyre and buried by his father.[16] Though the occasion is not made explicit, Thyrea is almost certainly intended; Dioscorides also writes on Othryades.

These notional tombs are at Sparta, not on the battlefield; for such is the way with individual burials. And there must have been actual tombs like these, commemorating soldiers who died at Thyrea. But although the inscriptions on the tombs might name the battle site,[17] they would not describe the fighting in terms that would identify a particular battle. There was fighting in the Thyreatis in the time of Cleomenes I and in 424 and 414, and doubtless later too;[18] Spartans will have died there at different times, to be commemorated in much the same fashion. Thus the actual tombs which we postulate at Sparta give no support to the tradition of that great battle.

The Early History of the Thyreatis

In Herodotus, and so far as we can see in the later version too, the battle of Thyrea unfolds as follows. The Spartans occupy the Thyreatis, and the Argives march out against them. The two armies first meet in strength, then agree on a contest of champions; during the contest the rest withdraw, but afterwards the full levies engage on the same site. Modern accounts do not as a rule insist on these details; it is simply a battle between the hoplite armies of Argos and Sparta. But the plain of Thyrea is not a feasible place for a hoplite battle.

Let us briefly recall the actual fighting that is attested here; there is no need to go into detail. In an episode examined below, Cleomenes I 'killed' someone in the Thyreatis, and embarked his army on Aeginetan and Sicyonian ships for an invasion of the Argolid. In 424 the Athenians landed on the coast and captured Thyrea a short way inland; but it was not

---

15 A.P. 7.432 (HE Damagetus 3), ἄνδρας ὃς Ἀργείων τρεῖς ἔκτανε. Cf. IG 5.1.721.3–4, seemingly from the battle of Tanagra, ἄνδρα | ηελών (i.e., εἰλών).

16 A.P. 7.229 (HE Dioscorides 30); cf. Aus. Epigr. 43 Peiper. As the poet's epigrams include three on Sparta, he may be one with Dioscorides, or Dioscurides, the writer on Spartan institutions (FGrHist 594). Jacoby at FGrHist 594 prints the Spartan epigrams in small type, as F 9–11, and leaves the question open; it is not considered by Gow and Page.

17 Cf., e.g., IG 5.1.721.7, ἐν Ταν]άγραι; 723.1, εἷλε Κόρινθος; 1124 (Geronthrae), ἐν Μαντινέαι.

18 The time of Cleomenes I: Steph. Byz. s.v. Ἀνθάνα; cf. Hdt. 6.76.2, 92.1. 424 and 414: Thuc. 4.56.2–57.3, 6.95.1; Paus. 10.9.12. Later times: cf. Paus. 2.20.1, 7.11.1.

defended by the Spartan garrison, who had withdrawn to higher ground. In 414 the Argives invaded and plundered the district. It is sometimes held that they invaded it again in 369, in concert with Epameinondas; but Sparta was the main target of Epameinondas' army, and the Argive contingent too must have followed a more direct route.[19]

No hoplite battle was fought on these occasions, and none could have been. The overland routes leading to the plain of Thyrea are difficult, from either Sparta or Argos; once an army was in the field, the other side could not deploy against it.[20] That great battle was fought, we are told, after the Spartans had seized the Thyreatis, 'had cut it off.' How then did the Argive army reach the plain? By the mountain road across Zavitsa, or by the coastal road called Anigraea, or by the sea? To mention any of these alternatives is to reject it.[21] The Argives could not enter the plain if it was already occupied in force.

If the battle of Thyrea is stricken from the record, how and when did the Thyreatis come into Spartan hands? All sources agree that it formerly belonged to Argos; according to Herodotus, the 'Cynurians' were Argive *perioikoi*.[22] Herodotus asserts that Argos controlled the whole east coast as far as Malea, and all the islands as far as Cythera, a realm that somewhat resembles Agamemnon's in the *Iliad* (2.108). We may well hesitate to follow him, and yet suppose that possession of the Thyreatis was the authentic element that gave colour to the rest. Pausanias too, in his early history of Sparta, says that the 'Cynurians' are Argives, descended from Cynurus son of Perseus. Philostephanus gave out the eponym of Anthene

19 424 and 414: n. 18 above. That Argos seized the Thyreatis in 370–369 is maintained by Bölte, *RE* 2A 2 (1929) 1303–4 s.v. Sparta, and *RE* 18.4 (1949) 1873 s.v. Parparos; Cartledge, *Sparta and Lakonia* 297, and again *Agesilaos* (Baltimore 1987) 234. This view is rejected on good grounds by Christien and Spyropoulos, *BCH* 109 (1985) 463–4. For the invasion route, see J. Buckler, *The Theban Hegemony* (Cambridge, Mass. 1980) 78–9, 293–4.

20 The battle of Plataea was fought after Mardonius waited for the Greek army to cross Cithaeron; for the plain of Thebes was the ground he chose as favourable to his cavalry (Hdt. 9.13.3, cf. 19.3). The Spartans, however, would not wait until the Argives could join battle on equal terms. The contest of champions was arranged only when the two armies had already met, so as to avoid a more costly engagement.

21 That either armies or champions might engage on a ridge or slope of Zavitsa is a notion that need not be re-examined in the cold light of day, since the purported evidence, the 'cenotaph' inscription, has been discounted.

22 Hdt. 8.73.3. In this passage Christien and Spyropoulos, *BCH* 109 (1985) 459 n. 23, think of emending Ὀρνεῆται to Ὀρειῆται, not unfeasibly. For the *perioikoi*, M. Wörrle, *Untersuchungen zur Verfassungsgeschichte von Argos* (Erlangen 1974) 106–13; A. Andrewes in E.M. Craik, ed., *'Owls to Athens.' Essays Presented to Sir Kenneth Dover* (Oxford 1990) 171–8. All other notices refer to the sequel of Sepeia.

as Anthes son of Poseidon, a figure otherwise known as an eponym and ruler at Calaureia and Troezen, and an eponym and founder at Halicarnassus.[23]

Another item of Argive nomenclature has not been noticed. In Pausanias' day the three villages of the Thyreatis included Νηρίς as well as Anthene and Eva. Callimachus used the name for 'an Argive mountain,' one that stood above a long river valley with a frightening torrent called Charadrus.[24] Details like these are precious to topographers, who have always looked for the village Neris beneath a steep mountain and beside a long dangerous river.[25] But Neris the mountain belongs elsewhere. For the name has appeared once more, in the form Νῆρις, in a papyrus fragment of Euphorion, and the scholiast describes it as a place 'at which the Heracleidae encamped during their expedition to Argos.'[26] Now we hear very little about the route of the Heracleidae after they entered the Peloponnesus, save that they passed through Arcadia without disturbing the inhabitants.[27] In some accounts, however, they clearly make for Sparta or Amyclae as the centre of resistance.[28] It is likely that they skirted the plain of Argos on the way south, then turned back from Sparta. But they would not go by way of the Thyreatis. It is safe to assume that they followed the main road north and struck at Argos by the shortest route, from Mantineia past Oenoe. And just here is a long valley with a dangerous torrent, now the Xerias, but anciently Charadrus. The steep mountain at its western end is therefore Neris.[29] Our hopes of situating the village Neris are dashed,

---

23 Paus. 3.2.2. Steph. Byz. s.v. Ἀνθάνα. For Anthas at Troezen and Halicarnassus, *Phoenix* 36 (1982) 21–3.

24 Schol. Stat. *Theb.* 4.46 (Callim. fr. 684); Stat. *ibid.*

25 Pritchett, *Topogr.* 3.122–3, and 6.92–4; Christien and Spyropoulos, *BCH* 109 (1985) 457; J.E. and F.E. Winter, *EMC²* 9 (1990) 237–8.

26 Euphorion, *Suppl. Hell.* fr. 430.24, 31–5, cf. Callim. fr. 457. In Euphorion the name seems to come in a passage where Argive rivers run with milk, a Dionysiac miracle, and the scholiast is puzzled to hear of Neris as a river. Perhaps Euphorion said that Neris was flecked with milk: i.e., the mountain was flecked as with spume, for Charadrus, unlike other Argive rivers, is a rushing torrent.

27 Cf. Robert, *Heldensage* 661–4; F. Prinz, *Gründungsmythen und Sagenchronologie* (Munich 1979) 299–313.

28 Pind. *Pyth.* 1.65–6, 5.69–72, *Isthm.* 7.12–15; schol. Pind. *Pyth.* 1.121c, 5.92, 101b (Ephorus *FGrHist* 70 F 16), *Isthm.* 7.18a, b, c. The capital of Teisamenus' realm can be regarded as Sparta rather than Argos, as it is several times by Pausanias.

29 The resemblance is uncanny between Statius' description of Charadrus and Neris and Frazer's description of the Xerias valley and torrent and the 'steep mountain' that looms up at the end (*Pausanias* 3.215–16) – though Frazer himself did not perceive it, writing before the papyrus discovery, and assuming that Neris and Charadrus were in the Thyreatis (*Pausanias* 3.309). The river even has the same reputation now as then.

but we learn that the toponym is distinctive of both the Argolid and the Thyreatis.

The plain of Thyrea is linked by nature with the plain of Argos: the routes by land are difficult, but by sea it is a short passage between sandy shores. For Sparta, however, the Thyreatis had no attraction as an outlet to the sea; the Spartan plain opens on the sea at the south. Did Sparta value the Thyreatis for its agricultural land and produce? The hoplite battle, did we believe it, would suggest that Sparta coveted this territory. Yet the Thyreatis was never incorporated into the Spartan system. Thucydides says that the Spartans 'had the use of it,' νεμόμενοι δὲ αὐτήν, but that in 431 they 'gave the Aeginetans Thyrea to occupy and the land to use,' τοῖς Αἰγινήταις ... ἔδοσαν Θυρέαν οἰκεῖν καὶ τὴν γῆν νέμεσθαι. So the district had neither perioecic communities nor helots; the working of the land was not a primary concern.[30] The reason why Sparta seized the Thyreatis must lie elsewhere.

Cleomenes' Attack on Argos

Thyrea was the embarkation point when Cleomenes invaded the Argolid and inflicted an overwhelming defeat at Sepeia near Tiryns. Though all the details of this campaign are again ensnarled in aetiology, it is easy to see that his success was mainly due to surprise. Cleomenes had at first advanced by land, as far as the river Erasinus, but withdrew after a sacrifice proved unfavourable (Hdt. 6.76.1). It was unfavourable, we may be sure, because the Argives were visibly ready for him: 'even so,' said Cleomenes, 'the Argives will have no joy of it,' Ἀργείους μέντοι οὐδ' ὡς χαιρήσειν. Yet when he sailed from Thyrea, the attack was unexpected; for he was able to land at Nauplia and to deploy before the Argive army came up (Hdt. 6.76.2–77.1). How could this be unexpected? He had just advanced and withdrawn by the land route; an attack by sea was the obvious next step – provided that the Thyreatis was already in Spartan hands. Cleomenes' success should indicate to us that he now seized the Thyreatis for the first time.

According to Statius, the mountain is terrified by the spates, *quaeque pavet longa spumantem valle Charadron Neris*. According to Frazer, the spates are 'much dreaded' by the natives, and the danger is remarked by good authorities.

30 Christien and Spyropoulos, *BCH* 109 (1985) 459–61, hold that Cleomenes tried, and failed, to obtain from Argos 'a treaty which would have allowed the exploitation of the Thyreatis'; thereafter, 'the Spartiates gave up hope of exploiting the region, including the plain, on their own account.' This ingenious hypothesis does not go very far towards explaining the conduct of Cleomenes.

Herodotus does not hint at this, saying only that 'after withdrawing, he led his army down to Thyrea, sacrificed a bull to the sea, and brought them on ships to the district of Tiryns and to Nauplia' (6.76.2). The Spartan seizure of the Thyreatis has been narrated by Herodotus in its place, a perfect place it was, the very moment when Croesus was overthrown. But Stephanus' entry for Ἀνθάνα refers to hostilities by Cleomenes. There was someone at, or from, Anthene, 'whom Cleomenes the brother of Leonidas killed and flayed, writing the oracles on his skin so as to keep them safe,' ὃν Κλεομένης ὁ Λεωνίδου ἀδελφὸς ἀνελὼν καὶ ἐκδείρας ἔγραψεν τοὺς χρησμοὺς ὧδε τηρεῖσθαι. Who this person was we do not know: something has dropped out in the manuscripts, and the relative clause is absurdly attached to the eponym of Anthene, Anthes son of Poseidon.[31] The lacuna is of a common kind, words omitted between one name and the next, and the second name as well. It does not impair the sense of what is left. Cleomenes killed a prominent person at or from Anthene.

The flaw in the text, and the bizarre tale about writing oracles on the skin, no doubt explain why the passage is seldom attended to. There have been two attempts at interpretation. It is suggested that Anthene joined in the colonizing expedition led by Dorieus, and therefore offended Cleomenes; but this depends entirely on a conjecture in Pausanias that cannot be upheld.[32] It is suggested too that Cleomenes' action was to desecrate a tomb of the hero Anthes; but this cannot be extracted from

31 Steph. Byz. s.v. Ἀνθάνα. *Excidisse videtur*: ἐκ ταύτης ἐγένετο [ὁ δεῖνα] Meineke. Or perhaps, ἀφ' οὗ ἐγένετο [ὁ δεῖνα]. The missing person was said either to come from Anthene or to be descended from Anthes.

32 E. Lobel, *CQ* 21 (1927) 50, emends Paus. 3.16.4 so that men of Anthene sail with Dorieus to Sicily, to be honoured afterwards at Sparta. He is followed by Huxley, *Early Sparta* 79; W.G. Forrest, *A History of Sparta* (London 1968) 86; and Cartledge, *Sparta and Lakonia* 145–6. Pausanias points to a hero shrine of Chilon and to another monument beside it, for men who sailed with Dorieus, but their name or nature is concealed by a corruption: †Ἀθηναίων ρω† mss: Ἀνθηνέων ἡρίον Lobel. There are at least four objections. It is unlikely that men of Anthene could be at all prominent in Dorieus' expedition; unlikely again that their death in Sicily would be commemorated at Sparta by a 'mound' (an empty mound?); unlikely once more that these stout fellows would go unmentioned in the excursus on Dorieus which immediately follows; and unlikely in the last degree that Pausanias' text is to be restored by a slight alteration of letters, for Ἀθηναίων appears to have intruded quite unwarrantably, doubtless as a gloss written *in rasura*. Though Pausanias' exact words are beyond recovery, the context plainly requires another hero shrine like Chilon's, but for all the eminent Spartiates who sailed with Dorieus. *Lege*, e.g., <ἀνδρῶν ἐπιφανεστέ>ρω<ν>, as a description of Dorieus' company, and suppose that a scribe was reminded of that most famous phrase, ἀνδρῶν γὰρ ἐπιφανῶν πᾶσα γῆ τάφος (Thuc. 2.43.3); hence 'Athenians.'

Stephanus.[33] The most straightforward inference is that Cleomenes was opposed when he suddenly entered the Thyreatis on his way to Argos.

As for writing oracles on someone's skin, we should recall a Spartan tradition about Epimenides, probably recorded by Sosibius. Epimenides' body, which was preserved at Sparta (thus Sosibius), had been discovered after death to be tattooed with oracles; 'the Epimenidean hide,' τὸ Ἐπιμενίδειον δέρμα, became proverbial for secret lore.[34] The two stories perhaps imply a collection of important documents inscribed on leather. At all events, a tale about oracles fits Cleomenes. For he tampered with the Pythia, it is said, in order to discredit his colleague Demaratus; he invoked the Delphic oracle in assailing the Peisistratids at Athens, and again in attacking Argos, or after he attacked and withdrew; another Delphic utterance, a strange one in verse, predicted an Argive defeat at this time. One implication of our tale is that Cleomenes manipulated oracles in some other quarter besides Delphi.[35] But in the absence of his victim's name, it is futile to attempt to fill out the story.

So Sparta seized the Thyreatis not in the time of Theopompus or Croesus, but in the early fifth century, and not for its own sake, but as a means of harming her principal enemy. It could always be used to invade or threaten Argos. In the peace negotiations of 420, Argos was determined either to have the district returned at once or to provide a means of contesting it in future. She did not get it back for a long time. There is no good reason to suppose that Argive control was re-established after Leuctra, or even that it was secure after Philip's dispensation of 338. The Thyreatis must have been a prize in the undoubted conflicts between Argos and Sparta during the Hellenistic period. In Pausanias' day the Argives 'had recovered it by virtue of an arbitration,' ἀνασώσασθαι δίκηι νικήσαντες (2.38.5), not it seems a landmark decision of the remoter past, but a result of Roman organization.

For Thyrea the early days were the happiest. The festival Parparonia,

---

33 So A. Griffiths in *Classical Sparta. Techniques behind her Success*, ed. A. Powell (London 1988) 62–71. Though ἀνελών is elsewhere used of 'recovering' a soldier's body, it cannot mean 'disinter.' Nor does Griffiths tell us what remains in the hero's tomb were suitable for flaying and writing on.

34 Diog. Laert. 1.115 (Sosibius *FGrHist* 595 F 15, cf. Epimenides *Vorsokr* 3 A 1, *FGrHist* 457 T 1); Suda s.v. Ἐπιμενίδης (*Vorsokr* 3 A 2, *FGrHist* 457 T 2); Diogen. *Prov.* 8.28 (*FGrHist* 457 T 5b); cf. Paus. 3.11.11 (*FGrHist* 314 Anhang F 3a, 457 T 5c).

35 D.M. Leahy, *Phoenix* 12 (1958) 155, associates both 'the Epimenidean hide' and the skin of the Anthenian with the oracle of Epimenides predicting a Spartan defeat at Orchomenus (Theopompus *FGrHist* 115 F 69), and this in turn with Cleomenes' Arcadian intrigue.

to which we now turn, shows that the district shared in the aristocratic culture of the Archaic period.

The Festival Name and Site

Whereas the place-name is given as Πάρπαρος, the festival name Παρπαρώνια is formed from a noun Παρπάρων. The place-name Παρπάρων and the ethnic Παρπαρώνιος, with the variant Περπερηνή, are also attested for a city and 'territory,' χώριον, in Mysia. The Athenian tribute-quota lists of the years 451–440 register the Παρπαριῶται or Παρπάριοι as one of many small communities in Caria.[36] No doubt the underlying term denotes a mountain in all cases, so that Πάρπαρος and Παρπάρων are equivalent forms; near the first Παρπάρων there is also Πάρνων. Παρπαρώνια are 'rites of (the mountain) Parparon.'

Such a name belongs to a rather small class of festival names. It is true that agonistic festivals are often referred to, at least in a catalogue of victories, by a locative phrase such as (ἐν) Πυθοῖ, Νεμέαι, Σεκυῶνι. Some of the most renowned of festivals are even named from the place where they were celebrated: Πύθια, Νέμεα, Ἴσθμια. But lesser festivals are not so named, because the place-name had no resonance of its own. There is however a distinct class of festival names formed from mountain names: Ἰθωμαῖα from Ἰθώμη, Λυκαῖα from Λύκαιον, and Ὀλύμπια from Ὄλυμπος (though here the mountain is only an article of belief). The reason for this nomenclature is that the mountain setting is especially significant for the rite. In the same fashion the festival name Ἑκαλεῖα or Ἑκαλήσια is formed from the place-name Ἑκάλη, meaning 'far place,' a place set apart for ritual;[37] it too was on a mountain, Pentelicus. These are all festivals of Zeus, the god who is quite typically worshipped on a mountain. We may infer that the Parparonia are a festival of Zeus.[38]

36 The place in Mysia: Steph. Byz. s.v. Παρπάρων (Apollodorus FGrHist 244 F 7a, Androtion FGrHist 324 F 15); cf. W. Ruge, RE 19.1 (1937) 890–2 s.v. Perperene. In Caria: IG 1³ 262 ιι 8 (451–450), etc.; also Androtion, as it seems; cf. Meyer, RE Suppl. 12 (1970) 1007–8 s.v. Parparos 2; R.T. Marchese, The Lower Maeander Flood Plain (BAR 5 292, 1986) 1.107, 134.

37 Cf. Hsch. ἑκαλία· πόρρωθεν, and ἑκάλλιθμος· ἱερός, ἀφειμένος. Ἑκαλήσια (or the epithet Ἑκαλήσιος) is formed from the locative Ἑκαλῆσι, 'at the far place,' just as Διάσια is formed from *Διᾶσι, 'at the rites of Zeus' (scil., in the district Agrae); this morphology likewise shows the importance of the ritual setting. The old woman Hecale and her story are projected from the rite; there is nothing to suggest that she was a figure of cult.

38 Jacoby, n. 105 on Sosibius, suggests Apollo as the god of the Parparonia, pointing to Πασπάριος Ἀπόλλων (Hsch.) and 'the later connection with the Gymnopaediae.' Wilamowitz, Glaube² 1.104–5, leaves the question open.

The inference is confirmed by the story of the battle. Othryades, the last surviving Spartan, calls on Zeus as he sets up his trophy (as in several sources cited below). To be sure, trophies as a rule belong to Zeus, and especially Spartan trophies; but we shall see that the outcome of the battle, in both the Spartan and the Argive versions, was itself suggested by the festival. The very name Ὀθρυάδης evokes the mountain setting. Besides the mountain name Ὄθρυς, note the glosses ὄθρυν and ὀθρυόεν in Hesychius, said to mean 'mountain' and 'rugged,' 'steep,' respectively.[39] As the name occurs nowhere else, it is undoubtedly significant.

The sanctuary of Zeus and the facilities for the games can be located only by conjecture. If we look to the Ithomaea and the Lycaea as similar agonistic festivals, we find that the altar and sanctuary of Zeus are at the very summit of the mountain, whereas the stadium and hippodrome are on level ground far below. Probably then our altar and sanctuary were on or near the peak of Zavitsa, which rises to 974 m not far from the sea; otherwise on the ridge that extends towards the west. The stadium and hippodrome must be sought in the plain below.

Pausanias' Burial Site

When Pausanias comes to the Thyreatis, he reports the burial mounds of both the Argive and the Spartan champions (2.38.5). Since the battle is assigned to the same place, Parparus, as the festival, the location of the mounds should be considered here. Pausanias' itinerary fixes the general area. From Lerna he journeys south along the coast, traversing the seaward slope of Mount Zavitsa by 'the road called Anigraea, narrow and very difficult,' until he reaches the plain of Thyrea, described as an olive-growing region (2.38.4). As the plain opens 'on the left,' ἐν ἀριστερᾶι, he goes inland, ἰόντι δὲ ἄνω πρὸς τὴν ἤπειρον, and first remarks the 'place,' χωρίον, where the battle was fought, and the burials.[40] 'Going on from the tombs,' ἀπὸ δὲ τῶν πολυανδρίων ἰόντι, he names the three 'villages,' κῶμαι,

---

39 The word is perhaps a differentiated form of ὀφρῦς: Frisk, *Gr. etym. Wörterb. s.v.* Ὄθρυς.

40 The text needs to be quoted in full at the point where Pausanias reaches the plain and turns inland, because a word has dropped out, and (as we shall see) some large hypotheses have butted in. After one traverses Anigraea, ἔστιν ἐν ἀριστερᾶι μὲν καθήκουσα ἐπὶ θάλασσαν καὶ δένδρα, ἐλαίας μάλιστα, ἀγαθὴ τρέφειν γῆ· ἰόντι δὲ ἄνω πρὸς τὴν ἤπειρον ... αὐτῆς χωρίον ἐστίν, ἔνθα δὴ ἐμαχέσαντο κτλ. The antecedent of αὐτῆς is the long phrase with γῆ, i.e., the plain. Editors now print Bursian's <ἀπ'> αὐτῆς, so that Pausanias goes inland *from the plain.* On this reading, one might prefer to situate the burials just beyond the coastal plain, as at Loukou (n. 41). But <δι'> αὐτῆς, *through the plain,* will do just as well.

of Anthene, Neris, and Eva, which are said to lie beneath Mount Parnon (2.38.7).

The burials are either in the coastal plain or in the uplands behind, but nearer than any of the villages to the northeast corner of the plain where Pausanias turned inland.[41] They are close to the foot of Mount Zavitsa and the presumed site of the stadium and hippodrome. Since the plain has a deep alluvial layer,[42] we can hardly expect to recognize any of these remains on the ground. As to the villages, the location of all three is quite uncertain,[43] but no reasonable solution will affect the burial site.

It is true that a lacuna has sometimes been posited in the text of Pausanias, inasmuch as Thyrea itself goes unmentioned, though known from earlier sources as the chief town of the Thyreatis.[44] The inference is unnecessary and even improbable. Elsewhere Pausanias refers to 'Thyrea' as a familiar name; these notices are far from proving that Thyrea still existed in his day.[45] We may easily suppose that the town-site had been abandoned, and that nothing was left to see. Pausanias' text is coherent as it stands,[46] and he speaks of Eva as 'the largest of the villages' and of its local hero, Polemocrates, as held in honour 'by the neighbours,' παρὰ τῶν

41 Bölte put the battle, without reference to the festival, either at Loukou or a little farther east. 'In the scrub woodland at Moní Lukú': Bölte, RE 18.4 (1949) 1873 s.v. Parparos. 'In the coastal plain east of the monastery Moní Lukú': Bölte apud Ehrenberg, RE 18.2 (1942) s.v. Othryadas. That is, he interprets Pausanias straightforwardly (cf. n. 40). More recently, the battle site has been sought in other quarters – high up on Mount Zavitsa (Kalitsis, Pritchett), or at Xerokambi at the southwest corner of the Thyreatis (Phaklaris, J.E. and F.E. Winter). These odd locations are solely due to the 'kenearion' and 'Parparus' inscriptions.

42 'The archaeological level in the plain is likely to lie at a depth of several metres': Christien and Spyropoulos, BCH 109 (1985) 455 n. 2.

43 Since Eva was in later days the chief settlement in the district, the discovery at Helleniko of a tile with this name, Εὐατᾶν, falls short of proving that the site was Eva. See Phaklaris, Archaia Kynouria (Salonica 1985) 120–1, 234–5, and Horos 5 (1987) 110. The coordinates for Neris have been sharply changed by Euphorion's mention of the name, as we saw above.

44 E.g., R.A. Tomlinson, Argos and the Argolid (London 1972) 46. In the passage quoted in n. 40, Musurus inserted Θυρέα in place of αὐτῆς, so that Thyrea is the 'place' where the battle was fought. Once a popular remedy, this is now rightly rejected. It does not help to smuggle in the name by whatever means, without a description of the site.

45 8.3.3: the sons of Lycaon are eponyms of many places in Arcadia and even of 'Thyrea in the Argolid and the so-called Thyreatic Gulf.' 8.54.4: 'the straight road to both Thyrea and the villages of the Thyreatis.' Why mention the villages unless 'Thyrea' by itself was a doubtful indication? 10.9.12: 'the contest over so-called Thyrea,' ὑπὲρ τῆς καλουμένης Θυρέας. At 3.7.5 Pausanias has 'the contest about the so-called Thyreatic territory,' περὶ τῆς Θυρεάτιδος καλουμένης χώρας; but there is no reason to emend either phrase.

46 I.e., as coherent as the rule in his mss.; cf. n. 40 above. The place-names Ἀνθήνη and Πάρνων (this a hapax) must be restored by a slight correction of letters.

προσοίκων (2.38.6). If Pausanias also had the town of Thyrea to describe, these details would be out of scale.

The hypothetical lacuna plays a part in some recent work on the topography of the Thyreatis.[47] And it is a larger lacuna than anyone had guessed before, one that conceals a major route. Pausanias, it is held, did not turn inland at the end of the Anigraea – here the lacuna begins – but continued to skirt the coast until he came to the site called Haghios Andreas, near the southeast corner of the plain. This was Thyrea, and he described it. Then he retraced his steps along the coast: back across the edge of the plain, back over the rough and narrow Anigraea, back a little farther still, to Lerna. Finally, he struck inland in a southwesterly direction and climbed over Zavitsa by a mountain path. On the col of Zavitsa – and here the lacuna ends – he found the battle site and the burials. On the south side of Zavitsa he passed through the villages of Anthene and Neris; Eva was farther on, at the west side of the plain.

Even if we could credit this lacuna and these perambulations, the text we have would be incomprehensible. Pausanias, we are told, proceeds south along the coast – but the plain of Thyrea 'reaches to the sea on the left.'[48] Anthene and Neris, we are told, are on the south side of Zavitsa – but Mount Parnon is 'above' them.[49] Our present concern is with the reputed battle site. It has been sought on the col of Zavitsa: this dictates the whole notion of Pausanias' mountain route. Now both the contest of champions and the general engagement that followed were always thought of as hoplite battles, fought on ground chosen for the purpose. It is disconcerting to be told that this was a mountain top. The sole warrant is the *kenearion* inscription – which we have disposed of.

To sum up, the received text of Pausanias is our best guide to the festival site. The true significance of the burial mounds will be discussed below.

The 'Parparus' Inscription

Another local inscription has been thought to bear on the festival Parparonia. It consists of three or four words engraved on the back and sides of

47 The lacuna: Pritchett, *Topogr.* 6.91–101. The topography of the district: *id.*, *Topogr.* 3.102–42; *Topogr.* 4 (Berkeley 1982) 64–79; *Topogr.* 6.79–106. Pritchett's lacuna is disputed by J.E. and F.E. Winter, *EMC*[2] 9 (1990) 230–3; but they are inclined to posit another lacuna farther on (p. 236).

48 The lacuna is placed after the sentence ending with γῆ, and in the next sentence ἐκ Λέρνης is substituted for αὐτῆς; cf. n. 40 above.

49 'Mount Parnon rises above the villages,' ἀνατείνει δὲ ὑπὲρ τὰς κώμας ὄρος Πάρνων. Or 'beyond' them: despite Pritchett, *Topogr.* 6.93 n. 5, it is all the same.

a miniature bronze bull.[50] The word on the back is not in doubt: ἀνέθεκε, 'dedicated.' The words on the sides appear to be proper names. The name on the right flank is plausibly read as Ἑλικίς, a woman's name for which good parallels exist.[51] It is the word or words on the left flank that are in dispute. The transcription ΠΑΡΠΑΟ of the original editor has recently been interpreted as πὰρ Πάο (gen.), 'from Paos.'[52] 'Paos' vel sim. is a small town in northwest Arcadia, remote indeed from the Thyreatis.[53] The phrase takes the place of an ethnic adjective, and the meaning will be 'Helikis dedicated (the object), from Paos.' This interpretation can be fairly called far-fetched.

The reading of the letters is not straightforward. The engraver reached the end of the flank with ΠΑΡΠΑ, and he placed the Ο directly beneath the Α. And there is something more to the Α – a loop attached to the right leg, which makes a virtual Ρ: ΠΑΡΠΑΡΟ. Since the engraver was very short of space, this reading is at least as defensible as the other.[54] And it is hard to resist, given the toponym Πάρπαρος in the near vicinity.

The meaning is another matter. A dative Παρπάρο(ι) has been suggested, so that the dedication is addressed to Πάρπαρος.[55] An eponymous hero who is also a figure of cult is no doubt conceivable, but he is far from being implied by the festival Παρπαρώνια, which honours a deity, Zeus if we are right, with the epithet Παρπαρώνιος. The omission of Ι in the dative form is also surprising, for the engraver could easily have managed this letter after Ο.

50 E. Protonotariou-Deïlaki, Deltion 26 (1971) Chron. 84, pl. 70B; Phaklaris, Archaia Kynouria 226–8, pl. 156B, and Horos 5 (1987) 115–17; Kritzas, BCH 109 (1985) 714–15; L. Dubois, REG 100 (1987) 414 no. 621; SEG 35.302; Pritchett, Topogr. 6.21, pl. 38.

51 So Kritzas, conformably with the transcription of Protonotariou-Deïlaki. As we saw apropos of Poseidon helikōnios, the word means 'black.' Phaklaris at first preferred a man's name hενίκις (which is unparalleled), but this is now given up.

52 So Kritzas, followed by Dubois. Dubois indeed prefers the dative case, πὰρ Πάο(ι), normal in Arcadian: but the verb form is not Arcadian, and the omission of Ι (as in the interpretation to be considered next) is not so inconsequential as he thinks.

53 The name of the town is variously given as Πάος, Παῖον, and Παῖοι or Παῖα; only the last (ἐμ Παίοις) occurs on stone, in a list of Delphic thearodokoi. Cf. Ernst Meyer, RE 18.2 (1942) 2398–2400 s.v. Paion 1.

54 So Phaklaris. Kritzas' objections are not compelling. 'Ligatures,' he says, are not used in Archaic inscriptions: but we are dealing with makeshift, not convention. And the loop looks too deliberate to be a saut of the burin.

55 So Phaklaris, followed by Pritchett and by J.E. and F.E. Winter, EMC² 9 (1990) 231–2. Christien and Spyropoulos, BCH 109 (1985) 456 n. 8, 459, speak of an offering 'to ΠΑΡΠΑΟ' and of 'the cult of ΠΑΡΠΑΟ' (and refer to the transcription of Protonotariou-Deïlaki).

The reading ΠΑΡΠΑΡΟ might represent either a feminine nominative Παρπαρώ or a masculine genitive Παρπάρω. The former is not wanted, since Ἐλικίς is on hand already, but the latter will do as the woman's father. Personal names often come from place-names, and it happens that in Asia Minor we have the personal names Πέρπερος and Περπέρης,[56] which doubtless come from the other form of the toponym, as in Περπερηνή. Ever since the first publication the words have been read in the order right flank, back, left flank. But they can just as well be read in the order right flank, left flank, back: Ἐλικὶς | Παρπάρω | ἀνέθεκε, 'Helikis daughter of Parparos dedicated (the object).'

Πάρπαρος then is a man named after the mountain. Neither the name nor the offering helps us to locate the festival. The bull was found in the district of Xerokambi on the west side of the plain of Thyrea, and here are also 'the foundations of a building probably belonging to a sanctuary.'[57] But any facilities for the Parparonia should be much closer to the foot of Zavitsa. Such bulls were a staple form of dedication. One very similar, bearing Apollo's name, came from the ruins of a temple on Mount Elias near Tyrus, on the coast south of the plain of Thyrea.[58]

The Tomb of Othryades

The name 'Othryades' points to the mountain setting of the cult. But this transparent figure has a story, first told by Herodotus. It is also the subject of three epigrams in the *Anthology*, by Dioscorides and Nicander and 'Simonides.' No doubt there once were many more, for the name Othryades was a byword like Thermopylae, and his trophy can be compared with the rescue of a legionary eagle. A prose version appears in two very late and derivative sources, Theseus and 'Chrysermus' (in [Plutarch's] *Parallela Minora*). In 'Chrysermus,' as also in Strabo and a scholiast, Othryades has become a Spartan general.[59]

---

56 Πέρπερος brother of Ἐπαφρᾶς and son of Ἀπολλωνία: SEG 34.1236, Silandus in Lydia, Imperial period. M. Aurelius Περπέρης: CIG 2.3189, 3195, Smyrna.

57 So Kritzas. Phaklaris, *Horos* 5 (1987) 101–19, regards this as the site of both the festival and the battle.

58 IG 5.1.1518; Jeffery, *Local Scripts* 200 no. 40. The photograph in IG (provided by the excavator, Rhomaios) leaves no doubt that the two bulls were produced by the same workshop.

59 A.P. 7.430 (HE Dioscorides 31); A.P. 7.526 (HE Nicander 2); A.P. 7.431 (HE 'Simonides' 5, FGE 'Simonides' 65) lines 5–8. Othryades and Thermopylae in the same breath: A.P. 11.141.3–4 (Lucilius). Trophy and eagle: A.P. 7.741.1 (GP Crinagoras 21.1). Theseus FGrHist 453 F 2; 'Chrysermus of Corinth' FGrHist 287 F 2a. Str. 8.6.17,

The epigrams are intended for a monument of Othryades on the battlefield. Othryades was also represented in a statue group at Argos, in
combat with an Argive champion, this too the subject of epigrams. The
story and the monuments of Othryades are revealing for the origin of the
legend. Indeed Othryades *is* the legend, in large measure.

The story differs somewhat as between Herodotus and the later sources.
The later version is this. Othryades was the last man left alive on the
field, for the two Argive survivors had gone home. He stripped the enemy
dead, and set up an Argive shield as a trophy, and inscribed it with his
own blood to proclaim the Spartan victory. Then he expired. The form of
words which he inscribed varies in the sources; it is evident that no set
form was handed down; but Zeus is usually invoked.[60] In Theseus and
'Chrysermus' the blood comes from the wounds he has suffered, and they
cause his death. In Nicander he kills himself with his sword, a suicide as in
Herodotus, after inscribing the trophy by whatever means. In Dioscorides'
ten-line epigram, which takes the form of a dialogue between the two
Argive survivors after they return to the field, Othryades is discovered
lying beside the trophy, at the point of death – σπαίρει, 'he is gasping.' It
is the fresh blood upon the trophy that draws attention to his fate. If we
regard the story realistically, as Dioscorides appears to do, we shall reflect
that the trophy was set up and inscribed some time after the battle, on
the following day no doubt, and that fresh blood was needed to inscribe
it, blood that was still flowing. Perhaps Othryades was sometimes thought
to have inflicted a fatal wound upon himself, the last of many wounds it
might be, in order to obtain fresh blood.

Let us compare this with the simpler version of Herodotus. 'Othryades
stripped the bodies of the Argives and brought over the arms to his own
camp and remained at his post'; the Spartans claim the victory because
'their man stayed on the field and stripped the bodies of the other side'
(1.82.5–6). Afterwards – after the general engagement, in which 'many'
fell – it is mentioned by the way that Othryades killed himself at Thyrea,
being ashamed to go home to Sparta as the sole survivor of the champions (1.82.8). The usual view is that this is the original version, and that
the trophy inscribed with Othryades' blood is a later embroidery.[61] But

---

p. 376; schol. Stat. *Theb.* 4.48. For a full treatment of the later sources, P. Kohlmann,
RhM n.s. 29 (1874) 463–80, and 31 (1876) 300–2.

60 In [Plut.] *Parall. Min.* 3A, 'Chrysermus of Corinth,' Othryades' inscription is said to
be precisely Διὶ τροπαιούχωι, but this detail is worthless, occurring also in the Roman
parallel, from 'Aristeides of Miletus.'

61 So Jacoby on 'Chrysermus of Corinth' *FGrHist* 287 F 2; Gow and Page on *HE*
Dioscorides 31 and Nicander 2. Yet Gow and Page are strangely inadvertent, asserting

the opposite development is much more likely: that Herodotus was told everything about Othryades, and kept only those details that seemed of practical consequence, the stripping and removal of the arms. Trophies, though Herodotus never mentions them, were a constant feature of warfare in his day; and to remain on the field, as Othryades does, is a strict condition for erecting a trophy. The Athenians once put up a trophy after an undoubted victory, but they had meanwhile left the field; so the trophy was unwarranted, and the enemy pulled it down (Thuc. 8.24.1). The story of Othryades teaches the same lesson, but Herodotus thought the lesson unimportant. We should also note that Othryades' subsequent death is far better motivated if it is caused by wounds and if his blood has been used to inscribe the trophy.

The epigrams on Othryades look to some monument on the field, but not, it seems, to a *polyandrion* burial. What monument was this? We might think first of a marble trophy, a reproduction of the ephemeral trophy set up by Othryades. After all, marble trophies were erected on some famous battlefields of historical times; and they were also to be seen, at least in later times, at some mythical battle sites. Yet the epigrams are chiefly concerned, not with any aspect of the trophy that might have been perpetuated, but with the blood of Othryades, with his wounding and death. In Dioscorides' epigram, the fullest, the Argive survivors are dismayed by 'the fresh drops of Othryades' blood' and by the gasping, prostrate form. In 'Simonides' 'the valiant blood of Othryades' is evidence of the Spartan victory; it does not matter that Argives have escaped alive; 'at Sparta it is not dying, but fleeing, that is death.' Nicander like Herodotus thinks of the suicide as heroic. The monument to which the epigrams refer is the tomb of Othryades.

The Champion Perilaus

The Argives did not dispute that the contest of champions took place, only that the Spartans won. Indeed they believed so firmly in this contest that they hoped for a resumption in the future, whenever a challenge should be issued by either side.[62] A statue group seen by Pausanias in the theatre of Argos represented the Argive Perilaus killing Othryades (2.20.7). Here

---

that Othryades' death was not mentioned at all by Herodotus, and that the suicide may be Nicander's idea. They also suggest, most unconvincingly, that a sixth-century trophy is anachronistic.

62 Thuc. 5.41.2–3. Sparta's attitude is at first surprisingly aloof: 'a piece of silliness,' μωρία. Perhaps it was not really Sparta's attitude, but Thucydides' attribution of τὸ δέον as he conceived it.

is the same contest, but a different outcome. Whereas the Spartan version names Alcenor and Chromius as the two Argive survivors (Hdt. 1.82.4), the Argive version speaks of Perilaus as prevailing at the last.[63] In the time of Pausanias the Spartan version had long been famous, and it was respected by Pausanias' informants in so far as they gave out Perilaus as 'son of Alcenor.' But Perilaus (or Perilas, or Perillus) is a rather prominent Argive name, borne by a tyrant and occurring in the epigraphic record; 'this Perilaus,' the slayer of Othryades, 'had still earlier won a victory at Nemea in wrestling' (Paus. 2.20.7).

About 'this Perilaus' different guesses might be entertained.[64] Perhaps a real Perilaus was recorded or remembered as a Nemean victor of early days. Perhaps a family who favoured this name, and went in for sports, invented a like-named ancestor. Perhaps a real Perilaus was buried in a grave that recorded his death in the Thyreatis; for Spartan soldiers were buried in graves that recorded this detail. We might even suppose that a real Perilaus was known both as a Nemean victor and as having died in the Thyreatis. Yet wherever Perilaus comes from, surely he did not provide any authentic date or context for the battle. The story in Pausanias shows once again how arbitrary any date or context was.

It will not be fortuitous that the man whom Argos exalted as the slayer of Othryades was also celebrated as a wrestler. Wrestling above other sports was regarded as a preparation for war. Marathon, Thermopylae, and Leuctra were all virtual wrestling matches.[65] At Argos wrestling was featured in the festival Sthenia: the matches were conducted to the music of pipes, and took place in the centre of the Agora, at the reputed tomb of Danaus, otherwise known as 'The wrestling-ground,' πάλινθος.[66] Zeus sthenios, who gives his name to the festival, is also associated with the coming of age of Theseus, for the place at which Theseus heroically acquired his sandals and sword was marked by an altar of this deity (Paus. 2.32.7). Theseus' prowess was especially displayed in wrestling.[67] So Perilaus embodies

---

63 M.T. Mitsos, *Argolikē Prosōpographia* (Athens 1952) s.v. ΠΕΡΙΛΑΟΣ[1], seeks to reconcile the different reports: Perilaus must have killed Othryades in the general engagement that followed the combat of champions, 'unless the group in the theatre derives from another period and refers to other like-named persons.' But in the Spartan version Othryades dies alone, of his wounds or as a suicide.

64 We may not, however, identify our Perilaus with the tyrant, as suggested by Jeffery, *Archaic Greece* (London 1976) 139, 144 n. 4. For Pausanias, who is our only source for both, clearly thinks of them as different persons (2.20.7, 23.7).

65 Plut. *Quaest. Conv.* 2.5.2, 639 F; Philostr. *Gymn.* 11.

66 Str. 8.6.9, p. 371; Plut. *De Mus.* 26, 1140 C; cf. Paus. 2.20.6.

67 The place where Theseus wrestled Cercyon of Eleusis was called παλαίστρα Κερκυόνος (Paus. 1.39.3; schol. Luc. *Jup. Trag.* 21), a counterpart to πάλινθος at Argos.

the ideal of every young Argive, victory in wrestling and victory on the field.

The Argive version no less than the Spartan is known to epigrammatists; two of them plainly write for the statue group in the theatre. The earlier is Chaeremon, who also wrote for a tomb at Sparta deriving from the battle.[68] 'Equal strength of hand we had, and equal arms we joined, and Thyrea was the prize of the spear. We both, ἄμφω, with equal readiness gave up our home-coming, and leave the report of our death to birds of prey.' The lines are spoken by two champions, one from either side. All the champions save these are dead. And when these two die, birds of prey will gather round the field to indicate the outcome. We now learn that Perilaus fell dead after killing Othryades; he must have been wounded by a previous stroke. There can be no doubt that the Argive version is in view. The Spartans always said that after the battle Othryades was left alone on the field. Only the Argives said that the battle ended in single combat between the last two champions.

The later epigram is by Gaetulicus, arguably the poet Cornelius Lentulus Gaetulicus:[69] 'These two swords,' δισσά ... τάδε φάσγανα, 'fierce Ares drew forth, out of three hundred Argives and Spartans, when we sustained a battle with none to report it, the one man falling on the other, and Thyrea was the prize of the spear.' That is, amid the larger contest of champions, Ares caused us two men to draw swords and fight a duel. Chaeremon was the model for Gaetulicus, who even repeats a phrase verbatim, the phrase about Thyrea. At the same time Gaetulicus is more explicit – the two men fight with swords, and they fall together – so that he either had independent knowledge of the monument, or had other models too, which have not survived. Neither supposition is difficult.

Such is the Argive version of the contest of champions. Although victory now rests with the Argives, the action is much the same as before. The outcome still turns on the death of Othryades. Though the names of the Argive combatants differ as between the Argive and the Spartan

---

68 *A.P.* 7.721 (*HE* Chaeremon 3). The opening words are corrupt (I omit them in translating), but probably identified the combatants as Argive and Spartan.

69 *A.P.* 7.244 (*FGE* Gaetulicus 5). Page discusses the identity of Gaetulicus. The sense of the epigram has not been grasped at all by commentators, not even by Page, who envisages 'the dedication of an unspecified number of swords, some Argive and some Spartan, taken from the battlefield.' The objections to this are manifold. The parallels for such a meaning of δισσά, '[swords] of two kinds,' are not very close; a dedication would include only the arms of the vanquished, and shields, not swords, are the preferred item; here the soldiers are seen together with the swords ('when we sustained a battle ... the one man falling on the other'). In any case Chaeremon as the model dictates the interpretation of Gaetulicus.

versions, Othryades is constant. And he dies with the last stroke, whether it is dealt by an Argive or by his own hand.

The Monument Seen by Pausanias

When Pausanias came to the battle site, he thought he saw a burial of all the champions. 'Over the dead the tombs were here heaped up,' τοῖς μὲν ἀποθανοῦσιν ἐχώσθησαν ἐνταῦθα οἱ τάφοι (2.38.5); afterwards, he goes on to the villages from τὰ πολυάνδρια. Perhaps we should imagine two mounds close together. The language, however, is as vague as it could be; Pausanias does not say, as he does of some other mounds, that they were large or small, or marked with gravestones, or planted with trees, or adjoined by something else.

Another question arises. These mounds were heaped over the champions. Thereafter, says Pausanias, the full levies joined battle, and Sparta won (historians, both Herodotus and the later version examined above, always give this sequence). Now the Spartan custom was to bury the dead on the field, and many more died in the general engagement than in the contest of champions; for that is the point of the story. Where then is the burial that followed this general engagement? The question is nearly idle if we are satisfied that both events, the general engagement as well as the contest of champions, are legendary. But it should be asked quite earnestly by all those for whom the battle of Thyrea is a great historical event. The only answer is that the mounds seen by Pausanias were not distinctly marked.

The epigrammatists mainly extol the tomb of Othryades. But 'Simonides' begins as if writing for the Spartan three hundred, and ends as if writing for Othryades alone.[70] The first half of this eight-line epigram commemorates the champions – 'These three hundred,' etc. – and might serve for their tomb. The second half, however, is about the exploit of Othryades. Thus the same mound might be regarded as either a *polyandrion* burial or the tomb of Othryades. This was only possible if the mound was unmarked. In later times the festival site must have fallen into decay.

In Pausanias' time the Thyreatis was a backwater, and the very town of Thyrea had disappeared. Faced with an unmarked mound, Pausanias did not hesitate. Everywhere in Greece, not only at Athens, Pausanias is intent on recording *polyandrion* burials; understandably so, for he would impress upon his readers the warlike spirit of Greeks in the old days, and no kind

70 A.P. 7.431 (HE 'Simonides' 5, FGE 'Simonides' 65).

of monument was better suited to the purpose. And hardly any battle of Greek history was more famous than Thyrea.

The Festival Aetiology

Othryades is the leading figure in the story, right from its first appearance in Herodotus. He has monuments at Argos and at the festival site. The statue group at Argos is plainly secondary, but the tomb of Othryades must be early, being presupposed in both the Spartan and the Argive versions of the contest. The Argives, who believed as devoutly as the Spartans in the contest of champions, also pointed to the battle site with solemn pride. For the Argives, the tomb of Othryades showed that he was the last to die – struck down by the Argive Perilaus. For the Spartans likewise, the tomb of Othryades showed that he was the last to die – having inscribed a trophy with his blood.

Othryades' name evokes the mountain setting, as does the festival name, Parparonia. Although the festival was addressed to Zeus, it also needs a 'hero.' Every agonistic festival of early times has its hero. For in Greek belief such a festival originates with the death, and often the burial, of some remarkable person. The games, they said, began as funeral games; or, if the person was not entitled to a proper funeral, if he was a child or a monster for example, they began as expiation for his death. All the agonistic festivals of which we are sufficiently informed are said to have arisen at someone's death. The great Panhellenic festivals and the obscurest local festivals are alike in this respect. The main difference is in how far back in time the person lived; lists were compiled showing the chronological sequence of festival origins.

Somewhere at the festival site a memorial of the person, often a grave, was displayed; often, but not always, he had an altar and sacrifice. These arrangements belong by definition to a 'hero,' a person of long ago who is still held in honour. Heroes are therefore exceedingly diverse; sometimes they are projections of ritual, sometimes figures of local legend. Theories exist about the character and origin of 'hero cult,' but for our purpose no general theory is required. It was natural to conduct games at the festivals of the gods, and natural to conduct them at funerals; both customs are widely paralleled. What is distinctive about the Greeks is their penchant for aetiology, which led them to assimilate the one kind of games to the other, and to evolve a class of 'heroes' as the common ground.

This class includes Othryades. As a formidable warrior who dies in combat, he makes a very typical 'hero.' Spartans and Argives have different views of Othryades, but this is now easily explained. The Argive view came first. When the festival was in their hands, they spoke of Othryades as an enemy overthrown, and no doubt his death somehow decided possession of the Thyreatis; it is like (*si parva licet componere magnis*) Apollo killing Python. When Sparta seized the district, Othryades too was appropriated, and became a Spartan champion whose death was tantamount to a Spartan victory, since he inscribed a trophy with his blood.

Other Stories about the Battle of Thyrea

Both Spartans and Argives held that the battle of Thyrea was commemorated among them in the most fundamental way, in the way they respectively wore their hair (Hdt. 1.82.7–8). After the battle, says Herodotus, the Argives 'sheared their heads,' and from then on they wore their hair short, though they had always worn it long before. The Spartans adopted the opposite custom, of wearing their hair long, though they had always worn it short before. Argive women also gave up wearing gold ornaments.

We see that short hair could be taken as a sign of mourning or renunciation, long hair as a sign of pride (and we also know that this interpretation is bogus, since long hair was the earlier custom, which Sparta always retained, and short hair was the later fashion, which Argos shared with other Greeks). This does not quite explain why the signs of pride or mourning are associated with the battle of Thyrea. We must remember too that every Greek adopted the customary hairstyle of his community at the moment when he came of age, when he left the youths and joined the men. The transition was signalled by a haircut and by a public festival at which members of the eligible age group were accepted as mature. In early Greece both the haircut and the festival had a military flavour, for a mature man was a warrior.

The Spartan festival Gymnopaediae 'Naked Sports' was so called because the young men went naked to display their physical maturity. As we saw, this festival commemorates the battle of Thyrea with two observances, more and less explicit, both adventitious. First, the choruses sing paeans in honour of the fallen soldiers. But these paeans do not belong to the ancient repertory of festival songs, which are ascribed, fancifully of course, to Thaletas and Alcman; they were probably composed by one Dionysodotus, and perhaps as late as the Hellenistic period. Second, the leaders of the choruses wear palm-leaf crowns called 'Thyreatic.' But these palm-leaf crowns are an age-old custom, and had nothing to do with Thyrea, until they were reinterpreted as symbolizing victory. The paeans then are a late addition, and so is the significance attached to the crowns. In Herodotus' day observers merely pointed to the young men sporting with long hair (but newly shorn in front, if the Spartans were like the Abantes and the early Athenians), and spoke of Thyrea.

The Argive festival was called the Ἐνδυμάτια, 'Investitures,' because the young men were invested with a warrior's arms.[71] All we know is that it was rather like the Gymnopaediae and like dress parades, *apodeixeis*, in Arcadia; and that paeans were sung. The festival setting is not reported, but perhaps the young men received their arms in the theatre, at least in later days, as did Athenian ephebes.[72] If so, it was a good place to exhibit that statue group, the combat of two champions. At all events, observers again pointed to the young men on parade, but now with hair cut short, and spoke of Thyrea.

When girls came of age at Argos, the transition was solemnized in the sanctuary of Hera – a famous custom, reflected *per contrariam* in the myth of the daughters of Proetus.[73] For these flighty girls refused to grow up or to honour Hera; they boasted of their own wealth and mocked the goddess's poverty; in one account they removed the gold from her statue, leaving the old *xoanon* quite bare. We infer that Argive girls on coming of age surrendered their girlish finery and thereafter dressed more plainly; in particular, they renounced gold ornaments. Observers pointed to the girls emerging from the sanctuary, and spoke of Thyrea.

In the battle of the champions, the three hundred on either side are probably the graduating youths of the three Dorian *phylai*. As an agonistic festival of Zeus, the Parparonia resemble the Ithomaea of Messenia. At the Ithomaea, as we shall see, the young men had a special part to play in the great sacrifice of rams, up to one hundred rams: they manhandled the victims at the altar. The feat is duly reflected in the legends of the Messenian wars. No doubt Argive youths were active in the ritual and the games of the Parparonia until the festival was closed to them by the Spartan occupation. Pausanias refers to this age class as the target of Spartan intervention. In the time of Echestratus son of Agis, the Spartans expelled all 'Cynurians who had come of age,' Κυνουρέας τοὺς ἐν τῇ ἡλικίαι, on the uniquely sanctimonious ground that they were harrying the Argives, their kinsmen (3.2.2). At an earlier stage, the battle of the champions was invented by festival observers.

---

71 [Plut.] *De Mus.* 9, 1134 C.
72 [Arist.] *Ath.* 42.4: at the beginning of their second year, the ephebes give a display in the theatre and, presumably at the same time, receive spear and shield. At an earlier date, a panoply is presented to war orphans in the theatre, but it is during the Dionysia (Aeschin. 3 *Ctes.* 154; etc.); also in a Rhodian law of 305 BC (Diod. 20.84.3).
73 See *TAPA* 113 (1983) 158.

9

A Festival of Cenchreae and the Battle of Hysiae

Synopsis

Pausanias informs us of the battle of Hysiae, a victory of Argos over Sparta, and dates it exactly, to 669–668 BC, and points to a monument, a burial of the Argive dead at Cenchreae (2.24.7). His report consists of just three sentences, which also include a notice of the town of Hysiae. Perhaps no secular Greek text of equal length has enjoyed equal authority. For the battle of Hysiae figures in almost every modern account as the first dated battle of Greek history, and as a leading episode in the long-drawn struggle, as it is thought to be, between Argos and Sparta, and sometimes as a turning-point in the development of Spartan society. It has indeed been questioned, on the reasonable ground that it is mentioned nowhere else in ancient literature.[1] But the objection has been ignored or swept aside.[2] Books, articles, and chapters on early Sparta which agree in nothing else agree on the importance of Hysiae.

The grounds for suspicion should first be stated, or restated. Then we should consider an important fact of life at Cenchreae that has not been noticed: an agonistic festival was once conducted at this upland site. Such a festival always has its myth of origin. The myth here was very likely the slaying of the hero or monster Argus. If so, the myth may well account for the monument seen by Pausanias. This explanation cannot be presented

---

1 T. Kelly, *AJP* 91 (1970) 31–42, and *A History of Argos* (Minneapolis 1976) 86–7.
2 About the largest concessions that I have seen are by P. Cartledge, *JHS* 97 (1977) 25 n. 104, and J. Ducat, *REG* 96 (1983) 200, both resisting Kelly. Cartledge: 'there is [however] nothing sacrosanct about the traditional date of 669 BC.' Ducat: 'it is evident that that one must refrain from building too many arguments upon it.'

as a certainty: our knowledge of Cenchreae is too limited. But it may still seem more probable than the battle. (See map 6.)

The Battle of Hysiae

During his tour of the Argolid, Pausanias took the road leading southwest from the plain of Argos to the plain of Tegea, an upland road that passes between the higher reaches of Mounts Artemisius and Parthenius. Once this had been an important route, but in Pausanias' day there was almost nothing to be seen (2.24.7). He names Cenchreae, but says nothing about it save that it was next to a landmark called Τροχός or Τρόχος, and that the burial of Argive soldiers was here. It is not clear whether Cenchreae was then an inhabited town. 'How the place, χωρίον, got its name they do not say, οὐ λέγουσι, unless it too was named for Peirene's son Cenchrias.' Pausanias recalls this figure of Corinthian myth only because he could get no local information. Hysiae, a larger town farther on, was a field of ruins, ἐρείπια.

Amid this desolation the only monument, besides Τροχός or Τρόχος, is the burial. At Cenchreae, Pausanias says of the battle, 'I ascertained that this contest occurred,' τὸν δὲ ἀγῶνα τοῦτον συμβάντα εὕρισκον, in the year 669–668: the date is given both by Athenian archon and by Olympiad, the serial number and the year number and the victor.[3] Then, at Hysiae, 'and here they say the Spartan defeat took place,' καὶ τὸ πταῖσμα Λακεδαιμονίοις ἐνταῦθα γενέσθαι λέγουσιν.

'I ascertained,' 'they say.' This is not how Pausanias usually speaks of the great events of history. When he is not recounting a stretch of history ex professo, he will refer to events offhandedly; for he is widely read, and sometimes his memory plays him false on details. We must infer that Pausanias first learned of the battle of Hysiae from an Argive informant, either at these sites or when he set forth from Argos. As for the date, perhaps he learned it at the same time, or perhaps he looked it up afterwards in a book: if so, it was not a general work, such as Pausanias had read before, but a specialist work on the history of Argos. Presumably this source, whether book or person, expressed the date as he does, by archon and by Olympiad; for there is no real indication that Pausanias added dates from a table of his own. But even if he did add part of the date, archon or

3 Though the serial number of the Olympiad, the twenty-seventh, has dropped out of the mss., it is dictated by other evidence. Cf. T.J. Cadoux, *JHS* 68 (1948) 90; L. Moretti, *Olympionikai* (*MemLinc* 8.8.2, 1957) 63 no. 36. The name Εὐρύβοτος for the Athenian victor is branded as 'suspect' by Rocha-Pereira, after Hitzig; but Kirchner observed that this is indeed the Attic form (*PA* 5959, cf. 5960).

Olympiad, even if he converted some different system of reckoning, his source still dated the battle exactly. It was a very late source, a learned person or a specialist work.[4]

This source did not hold the view of Hysiae that is current nowadays, *viz.* that it was the first direct encounter between Argos and Sparta, that henceforth Sparta trained to do better, that long afterwards Sparta triumphed at Thyrea. Ancient writers from the fourth century onwards put the battle of Thyrea just after the First Messenian War; when this battle was dated exactly, the year was 720–719. Pausanias' source asserted that Hysiae was an Argive counterstroke, just fifty years later.

Modern accounts often bring Hysiae into relation with Pheidon.[5] Two dates for Pheidon are handed down, one by the chronographers, ca. 790,[6] and the other by Pausanias himself in his tour of Elis. Pheidon, says Pausanias, helped the Pisatans to celebrate the Olympic festival in the year 748, the eighth Olympiad (6.22.3). Let Pausanias give way to emendation: make it the *twenty*-eighth Olympiad, the year 668.[7] On this showing, Pausanias' Argive source thinks of Hysiae as a victory of Pheidon – for if this source knows of any date in Argive history, he knows of Pheidon's. The tyrant Pheidon is also well known to Pausanias himself (*ibid.*). Why then does Pausanias, having just been instructed by his Argive source about the battle of Hysiae, omit the most significant detail, that it was a victory of Pheidon?

4 Kelly (n. 1 above) thinks that whereas Pausanias heard of the battle from local informants, he took the date from an Athenian source. It is misguided, however, to suppose that such a source is implied by the archon date. Nor does Kelly strengthen his case by suggesting that Pausanias confused an Athenian attack on Boeotian Hysiae with a Spartan attack on Argive Hysiae.

5 So A. Andrewes, *CQ* 43 (1949) 70–8; followed by, e.g., E. Will, *Korinthiaka* (Paris 1955) 346–51; Moretti, *Ricerche sulle leghe greche* (Rome 1962) 12–14; R.A. Tomlinson, *Argos and the Argolid* (London 1972) 79–84; L.H. Jeffery, *Archaic Greece* (London 1976) 134–6; R. Sealey, *A History of the Greek City States ca. 700–338 BC* (Berkeley 1976) 41–3; N.G.L. Hammond, *CAH*² 3.3.325.

6 Marm. Par. *FGrHist* 239 A 30–1; Euseb. *Can. a.* 797–796. Marm. Par. A 30–1 must be reversed to make sense; for the supporting evidence, and for Ephorus as the source of both entries, see Jacoby *ad loc.*, and more fully *Das Marmor Parium* (Berlin 1904) 93–4, 158–62.

7 Two further grounds are offered for the emendation. First, the foundation date of the Spartan Gymnopaediae is given as 669 or 665, as if it might be a consequence of Hysiae; this notion is considered elsewhere. Second, in other sources we find a long-drawn Pisatan occupation, or more than one occupation, at various dates from 672 onward; Africanus has a first Pisatan occupation in this very year, 668. But these sources never speak of Pheidon as well; and Pausanias, unemended, has a Pisatan occupation in 644 and further trouble in 588 and a later year. Another brief occupation in 668 does not do much to bring him into line.

Even if the omission could be credited, the emended date could not. The transmitted date, 748, is conformable with Ephorus, who said of Pheidon, when he intervened at Olympia, that he was tenth in line from Temenus. Ephorus spoke of Temenus at the starting-point of his history, the return of the Heracleidae, and this starting-point of Ephorus is expressly dated to the year 1069, 735 years before Alexander's crossing.[8] Ten generations from 1069 bring us within the range of the two attested dates, ca. 790 and 748. The chronographers' date for Pheidon, ca. 790, is undoubtedly an inference from Ephorus, for the language of the Parian Marble agrees quite strikingly with the language of the Ephoran excerpts in Strabo. There can be little doubt that Pausanias' date is also an inference from Ephorus, but in a different system. Such then was the normal range for Pheidon's date. It was impossible for Pausanias' Argive source to associate Pheidon with Hysiae.

Pheidon aside, a battle at Hysiae, in Argive territory, could only come about through Spartan aggression. And to reach Hysiae the Spartans must pass Tegea. Shall we suppose that Tegea was then allied with Sparta? Or that Tegea was ignored by Sparta? It is more natural to suppose that Tegea, as a powerful neighbour, always opposed Sparta, and blocked any advance in this direction, until an understanding was reached in the mid sixth century.[9] Herodotus thought so, in his account of Sparta's rise; later historians thought so, when they reported more than one Spartan defeat at Tegea, and as early as king Charillus, fifth in line from Eurypon; and legend says so too, when Hyllus son of Heracles is slain by Echemus king of Tegea. The battle of Hysiae is, however, true to much later conditions. In 417 the Spartans marched to Argos, and when the city did not come over as expected, they seized Hysiae instead, and slaughtered all the free inhabitants (Thuc. 5.83.1–2). Pausanias' Argive source must have remembered this occasion, and perhaps others like it.

The only impediment to dismissing Hysiae as an outright fiction is those graves at Cenchreae. 'And there are *polyandrion* graves here,' καὶ πολυάνδρια ἐνταῦθά ἐστιν, says Pausanias, 'of Argives who defeated the Spartans in battle round Hysiae.' He is just as vague as at Thyrea, where the evidence of earlier sources makes it hard to believe that he saw a true *polyandrion* burial. Furthermore, the burial is not on the battlefield, at the town of Hysiae, but several miles away, at the smaller town of

8 Ephorus *FGrHist* 70 T 10, F 115, 223. Cf. G.L. Huxley, *BCH* 82 (1958) 588–601.
9 The unlikeliness of a Spartan advance past Tegea is drawn out by D.M. Leahy, *Phoenix* 12 (1958) 159–60, albeit for the purpose of commending a reconstruction of the battle of the fetters that is far too hypothetical.

Cenchreae.[10] This is doubly surprising. First, what we know otherwise of Argive burials, both historical and legendary, indicates that Argos like most cities preferred to bring home the dead. Second, had the Argives chosen for once to bury their dead on the battlefield, like the Spartans, they could easily have done so, for this was an Argive victory in Argive territory.

A burial there was, or a reputed burial, at Cenchreae. But surely it has been misunderstood or misrepresented.

A Festival of Cenchreae

Pausanias says that Cenchreae, i.e., the town site, lies on the road to Tegea, 'at the right' of a certain landmark, ἐν δεξιᾶι τοῦ ὀνομαζομένου Τροχοῦ. The last word is so accented in the manuscripts, and is so printed by many editors. 'The so-called *Wheel*'? The site of Cenchreae is agreed,[11] and topographers have looked hard for some natural feature, for trace of some construction, for anything that might be called the *Wheel*. They have not found it, and can hardly guess what it might be.[12] To describe the quandary is to see that it is misconceived. Pausanias would not leave his readers in the dark about the *Wheel*, strange work of nature or of man. The term must be self-explanatory. Siebelis set matters right with a change of accent: Τρόχου, 'Running place,' 'Racecourse.' This is a much less common word; its accent has been misplaced in authors whose manuscripts are far better than those of Pausanias.[13]

10 It should be said in passing that the graves at Cenchreae, whatever form they took, were undoubtedly distinct from the ruined 'pyramid' that still exists in the Kiveri valley, also on the road to Tegea, but much nearer to Argos. L.E. Lord, *AJA* 43 (1939) 78–84, showed that this structure, like some others in the Argolid, must have served as strongly fortified quarters for a garrison which patrolled the area. Pausanias' graves are still from time to time identified with the 'pyramid'; indeed they were by Lord himself, but offhandedly. There is no reason for it.

11 W.K. Pritchett, *Studies in Ancient Greek Topography* 3 (Berkeley 1980) 54–74, with a compendium of travellers' notes and opinions.

12 Cf. Tomlinson, *Argos and the Argolid* 37, 265 n. 35, also quoting Frazer: perhaps the road itself, 'because of its many windings'; perhaps 'a circular enclosure, or a tower of circular plan, now completely lost.'

13 See, e.g., Pearson on Soph. *Ant.* 1065; W.H.S. Jones on Hp. *Vict.*, Loeb vol. 4, 378 n.4, 428 n.6. Grammarians and scholia are at pains to distinguish the words. Note in passing that the word is wrongly accented, and misinterpreted as 'hoop,' in the epitaph published by C. Marek, *EpigrAnat* 6 (1985) 137 no. 12 (*SEG* 35.1327) and discussed by C.P. Jones, *EMC*² 9 (1990) 53–63. The subject is practised in all athletic activities, 'wrestling, javelin, pancratium, discus, *running*, jump': τρόχου, not τροχοῦ.

It is sometimes said that τρόχος denotes a circular racetrack, as if it were again a virtual 'wheel.'[14] The Greeks, however, did not use circular tracks, but always raced in a straight line, then back again for extra laps.[15] The two nouns formed from τρέχω both express the notion of running, not of circularity, for a wheel too 'runs.' We may still ask why the landmark was called τρόχος rather than δρόμος, the usual term for any racetrack. The answer must be that τρόχος was the Argive term. The Argive hero Τροχίλος proves it so. He invented the chariot and founded the agonistic festival Heraea, the most renowned of Argive festivals.[16] Trochilus is thus a counterpart of the Athenian hero Erichthonius, who invented the chariot and founded the agonistic festival Panathenaea. Pausanias himself mentions Trochilus in illustration of Argos' claim to surpass Athens in ancientry and the favour of the gods; for Trochilus comes as 'hierophant' from Argos to Eleusis and fathers a line of Eleusinian heroes, including Triptolemus (Paus. 1.14.2). Although Pausanias does not say so, here too Trochilus is an exponent of chariot racing; for we may assume that Triptolemus grew up to found the Eleusinia, which in Athenian tradition was sometimes reckoned the oldest agonistic festival of all, older than the Panathenaea.[17] The hero's name, like the name τροχίλος for the plover, comes from the word for 'race,' not the word for 'wheel.'[18]

14 LSJ s.v. τρόχος I 1, 'circular race'; the passages cited do not indicate any circular shape or motion. J. de Romilly, Le Monde grec ... hommages à C. Préaux (Brussels 1975) 144, in a paper dealing with 'cycles and circles,' quotes fragments of tragedy with the word accented thus, τρόχος, but this is doubtless inadvertent, since one of them is afterwards quoted again, p. 151, with τροχός (though from a different edition, as if it were a different instance). Pritchett, Topogr. 3.66, looked round Cenchreae for 'a small, oval race-course'; why oval, one does not see (it is the wrong shape for a wheel as well).

15 This prepossession for racing in a straight line is clearly seen in Xenophon, Anab. 4.8.25–8. Dracontius of Sparta, a hard man from a hard school, arranged for games, including a horserace, to be conducted on very rough terrain. But the horses still ran straight down a steep slope to the sea, then struggled straight up the slope.

16 Tert. De Spect. 9; schol. Arat. Phaen. 161; Hyg. Astr. 2.13; Euseb. Can. a. 1569–1568. Cf. Jacoby, Das Marmor Parium (Berlin 1904) 47. Trochilus like his mother Callithyia may belong to Tiryns, not Argos, in the first instance.

17 Arist. Panath. 362; schol. ibid., 3.323 Dindorf ([Arist.] Peplus fr. 637 Rose³).

18 Robert, Heldensage 254 n. 3, derives it from τροχός 'wheel.' F. Graf, Eleusis und die orphische Dichtung Athens (Berlin 1974) 158 n. 2, thinks that Trochilus qua hierophant takes his name from the bird; but as we just saw, the role of hierophant is secondary. We might compare the hero Εὐρυγύης or Εὐρύγυος at Athens, the personification of 'the wide way' on which funeral games were conducted, originally perhaps the Phalerum road, later the Academy road: Hsch. s.v. ἐπ' Εὐρυγύηι ἀγών (Amelesagoras FGrHist 330

Pausanias then points to 'the so-called Racecourse.' A suitable piece of ground had once been used for races, and was still so called. It was a clear landmark on a mountain road. A racecourse presupposes an agonistic festival.[19]

No cult or festival of Cenchreae is directly attested, except perhaps a cult of Asclepius.[20] But a famous episode in the myth of Io, the slaying of Argus by Hermes, takes place at Cenchreae. Like other elements of the myth, this is undoubtedly a ritual *aition*, and the background is most likely an agonistic festival of Hermes.[21]

In *Prometheus Vinctus* the maiden Io is summoned by insistent dreams to Lerna, to its 'deep meadow' and its 'pastures and stalls,' so that Zeus can have his way with her. When in due course she is expelled from home, she rushes in cow form to 'the spring of Lerna,' there presumably to mate. And the impulse takes her farther, to 'the fresh stream of Cenchreae.' Argus, meanwhile, the ever-watchful cowherd, follows close upon her tracks, until he is suddenly killed. Then the gadfly comes, and drives her across the world. Io's narrative, brief and excited though it is, indicates that Argus was killed at Cenchreae. Outside the myth of Io, the watchful cowherd is better spoken of. Argus killed the bull that ravaged Arcadia, and also a satyr who reived Arcadian herds. This is a very old tradition, for Argus' costume, so variously rendered in later art and literature, was at first the hide of the Arcadian bull. The story belongs to a setting where Argive pasture land meets Arcadian, i.e., the road to Tegea.[22]

F 2; [Hes.] *Cat.* fr. 146 Merkelbach-West); Hdn. καθ. προσωιδία ed. Hunger, *JbOest-ByzGes* 16 (1967) 17 ([Hes.] fr. 145a). Or the hero Δόλιχος, though he is the race rather than the track.

19 Pritchett, *Topogr.* 3.66, thinks of a racetrack as a workaday fixture in any Greek community. But the instances he mentions, Athens and Corinth, are not quite parallel with Cenchreae; and in any case the racetracks there were likewise meant for festivals.

20 An altar at Rhodes, inscribed 'in very fine lettering of the end of the fourth century,' is dedicated 'to Asclepius at Cenchreae in Argos,' Ἀσκληπιῶι τῶι ἐν Κεγχρεαῖς ταῖς ἐν Ἄργει, and to Hygieia (*IG* 12.1.26). On the face of it, this testifies to a renowned cult of Asclepius at Cenchreae. But it seems more likely that 'Argos' is the Rhodian deme, and that 'Cenchreae' is a place within the deme, perhaps the modern Σκληπιανός. See D. Morelli, *I Culti in Rhodi* (Pisa 1959) 115–16.

21 W. Burkert, *Homo Necans* (Berlin 1972) 181–9, interprets the slaying of Argus as a portentous ox sacrifice preliminary to the Argive festival Heraea. This sequence is held to resemble Athens' Dipolieia and Panathenaea, and to mark the turning of the year. But there is in fact nothing to suggest that the Heraea were a new year's festival; cf. P. Charneux, *BCH* 114 (1990) 399 n. 28.

22 *Prom. Vinct.* 652–4, 673–82; cf. Ov. *Met.* 1.597. Bull and satyr killed by Argus: [Apld.] *Bibl.* 2.1.2.2–3 (2.4). Bull's hide costume: Apld. *ibid.*; schol. Eur. *Phoen.* 1116 (Dionysius

We should consider the significance of the myth and of the festival which inspires it. The gods and their festivals are concerned with man's staple livelihoods, chiefly with the different kinds of agriculture and stock breeding. Hera and Zeus are concerned with cattle breeding; festivals of Hera which mark the seasonal routine, especially the mating of the animals, give rise to myths like Io's. The roles of Argus and of Hermes represent another aspect of cattle breeding, the procurement of hides for leather making.

Hermes as a pastoral god has more to do as a rule with sheep and goats: the smaller animals are more extensively pastured. But the best hides for leather are from cattle that are pastured in the mountains, for wind and weather toughen the skin. Therefore Hermes in the *Homeric Hymn* drives the cattle far afield, up hill and down dale, and when he slaughters them, he takes particular care with the hides – afterwards Apollo marvels at his handiwork.[23] As for Argus, the bull's hide he wears is emblematic of his calling (like the costume of any god or hero). The reason why he is so vigilant, as he follows his charge through upland pastures, is that the animal must be guarded against thorns and tangles and flies, in order to ensure the quality of the hide. The worst threat is gadflies; their larvae cause warbles, swellings that disfigure the hide. Hera was cruel when she sent the gadfly after Argus' death; but she was cruel before, since Argus was tending Io for the leather trade. Ἀργός takes his name, 'Glistening,' from the appearance of a hide that is soaked in oil.[24] The two operations needed for harness leather, stretching and soaking in oil, are described in a simile of the *Iliad* (17.389–93). From them Hermes gets his ancient epithets, διάκτορος ἀργειφόντης, 'he who stretches it, he who makes it glisten.'[25]

---

of Samos *FGrHist* 15 F 1); bf. amphora, London B 164 = *ABV* 148.2; rf. hydria, Boston 08.417 = *ARV*² 579.84; rf. krater, Ruvo, Jatta 1498 = *ARV*² 1409.9.

23 Hermes drives the cattle far over the mountains: *H. Merc.* 94–5, cf. 491–2, 556–7, 567. He stretches the hides on a rock, a practice that continues still: 124–6. Apollo admires the treatment of the hides: 403–5. Hermes also uses oxhide to make the lyre: 49–50.

24 The use of oil is further intimated when Argus tethers Io to a sacred olive tree at the Heraeum of Mycenae ([Apld.] *Bibl.* 2.1.3.4 [2.6]; Plin. *Hist. Nat.* 16.239; cf. bf. amphora, Munich 573 Jahn; rf. stamnos, Vienna 3729 = *ARV*² 288.1). This must be a secondary version, since the point of recruiting Argus is that Io was out to pasture; it was a local tale that was told of the actual tree.

25 In the *Iliad* the men 'stand apart,' διαστάντες, as they hold and pull the hide. Since διάκτορος is plainly an agent noun of διάγω, the meaning of the verb must be 'pull apart,' 'stretch.' The first element of ἀργειφόντης is an σ- stem of ἀργός, seen in many other compounds, e.g., ἀργεσ-τής; the second element is φαίνω, 'make (it) appear,' as

Thus the myth of Argus derives from a festival of Hermes that promoted leather making. [26] Cenchreae, in good mountain pasture not far from Argos, was the place for such a festival. At the festival site there was some memorial of Argus, no doubt a grave. But in Pausanias' day the festival was long forgotten; the very town of Cenchreae may have disappeared. It was easy to regard the monument of Argus as a monument to other heroes, Argive soldiers who fell in battle. So it was at Thyrea: the monument of Othryades became a mass burial of the champions.

---

in ἱερο-φάντης. The spelling -φόντης is Aeolic, and Hermes is especially prominent in Aeolis.

26 Yet another deity of cattle breeding, the rival of Hera, is Heracles. At his festival on Oeta the prizes were oxhides: schol. *Il.* 22.159. Like Argus, Heracles was effective in repelling noxious insects, both flies and locusts, the latter destructive of summer pasture.

PART FOUR

Messenia and Phigaleia

10

The Ithomaea and the Messenian Wars

Synopsis

The festival of Zeus at Mount Ithome is mentioned in the legends of the early Messenian wars, and on closer inspection it emerges that the festival business has helped to shape the legends. In speaking of the Messenian wars, I shall use the term 'legend' loosely, to include not only popular tales about the past, but also mere fictions of literary origin; for here the two things are hard to distinguish. Almost everyone agrees that these legends, even when they are popular tales, have no value as a record of events. To demonstrate the aetiological element is not to overturn a cherished certitude. All the same, the correspondence between the festival and the legends is interesting for its own sake, as a kind of social history. It can be worked out rather fully, and throws some light on the parallel case of the festival and legends of Thyrea, where the festival business remains unknown.

The sacrifice at the festival was famous, under the picturesque name 'Hundred-slaughter,' ἑκατομφόνια. A great many rams, ideally one hundred, are led to the mountain altar. Bronze tripods as numerous as the victims are also carried up to receive the meat, which is consumed as stew on the following days. Messenian youths who have just come of age lay hold of each victim by the horns and wrestle it to the altar.

Such a rite might well evoke a war. In the First Messenian War, as told by Myron of Priene, three hundred Spartans, including King Theopompus, are taken alive by Aristomenes; he slays them all at the altar. The number three hundred points to the respective contributions of three Dorian *phylai*, as in the tale of Thyrea. Later, when the Messenians lose the war, it is because they are unable to perform the ritual. Victory is promised by the

Delphic oracle to the side that first sets up one hundred bronze tripods beside the altar; the Spartans manage it more nearly than the Messenians. And when the Messenian king attempts to sacrifice, all the rams break free and dash themselves against the altar, dying untowardly. In the Second Messenian War, as told by Rhianus of Crete, Aristomenes wins three great victories, and each time conducts the 'Hundred-slaughter' sacrifice – with animal victims, but attesting that he has killed one hundred Spartans.

The correspondence between the ritual and the narrative is so obvious because Myron and Rhianus follow the Hellenistic fashion of literal and pedestrian aetiology. They know the ritual at first hand; it was handed down without change from the Archaic period. In earlier days, however, the worshippers were not warriors but hunters, the way of life in rural Messenia.

First the festival and the 'Hundred-slaughter' sacrifice; then the legends of victory and defeat; next Aristomenes and his chosen band; finally, warfare and hunting as two related spheres promoted by the festival.

The Festival and the 'Hundred-slaughter' Sacrifice

The cult of Zeus on the mountain peak was an ancient one, a congener of other mountain cults of the weather god; after 369, it became the chief cult of the city of Messene.[1] The priest appears in the heading of documents as the yearly eponym, and the officials who conducted the festival Ithomaea are named beside him in several agonistic inscriptions. Whereas sacrifice was offered at an altar on the mountain top, the festival competition no doubt took place on level ground near the city.[2] The statue of Zeus by Hageladas was renowned; since there was no temple in the sanctuary, it

---

1 Cf. Nilsson, *Gr. Feste* 32; Adler, *RE* 15.2 (1916) 2304–5 s.v. Ithomatas; Fimmen, *RE* 15.2 (1916) 2306–7 s.v. Ithome 1; A.B. Cook, *Zeus* (Cambridge 1914–40) 2.741–3, 3.1153; W. Otto, *De Sacris Messeniorum* (Halle 1933) 18–27; Ernst Meyer, *RE Suppl.* 15 (1978) 149–50, 154 s.v. Messene 3, 287 s.v. Messenien; H. Schwabl, *RE Suppl.* 15 (1978) 1087 s.v. Zeus.

2 A musical competition was remembered from the distant past, and is implied by Eumelus' hymn (Paus. 4.33.2). It has been suggested that this competition took place on the peak in an area now occupied by a paved threshing floor, and used for dances at the peasant festival of the Panaghia: Frazer, *Pausanias* 3.437; Meyer, *RE Suppl.* 15 (1978) 150 s.v. Messene 3. Yet we might expect Pausanias to have mentioned this, for the athletic contests of the festival as he knew it will have taken place in the stadium southwest of Mavromati. The ἀγών and the ἀγωνοθέτης are mentioned in several inscriptions close to Pausanias' own day (*ArchEph* 1965, 116–21 lines 22–3, ὁ ἀγὼν τῶν Ἰθωμαίων; *IG* 5.1.1427 lines 11–12, 1467 line 2, 1468 lines 8–9, 1469 line 2, *Ergon* 1969, 105–6, ὁ ἀγωνοθέτης, second in importance to the priest). It is clear that even the

was kept for safety in the house of the priest, again in the city. As depicted on coins, the statue was of Zeus striding forward with a thunderbolt in his raised right hand, and an eagle perched on his extended left hand.[3] On some coins a tripod stands before him, or is shown on the reverse; tripods are a sacrificial emblem occurring in other cults of Zeus, as at Olympia, Dodona, and Mount Ida. Here the tripod intimates that the statue has been placed in the sanctuary to receive the annual sacrifice.

The original form of sacrifice became a byword – the ἑκατομφόνια, or 'Hundred-slaughter,' i.e., the slaughter of a hundred animal victims.[4] It is always spoken of in a legendary context, as a thank-offering made by Aristomenes; neither Plutarch nor Pausanias knew it as a contemporary practice. There can be no doubt, however, that details of the sacrifice were authentically remembered. We shall examine the details below: the victims were rams, and the meat was cooked in tripods as numerous as the victims.

A sacrifice called ἑκατομφόνια is also attested for the town Biennus or Biannus in Crete, but here it was addressed to Ares, who on the evidence of Hellenistic inscriptions was the principal deity of the town.[5] Of the two *aitia* which Stephanus offers for the name Biennus, the one recalls the 'violence,' βία, done to Ares by the twins Otus and Ephialtes.[6] The story explains the sacrifice as well as the name, and we shall see below how it did so. It is not surprising in itself that the same form of ritual should be used both for Ares and for Zeus in his warlike aspect; there is a complication, however. We learn from the same entry in Stephanus that Biennus was renowned for its cult of Zeus, possibly on the neighbouring Mount Hierus.[7] According to the other *aition* one of the Curetes was named 'Biennus.' The Curetes as attendants of Zeus recur at Ithome, and like Aristomenes and his companions in arms, they personify the youthful

---

early festival was partly conducted on lower ground, for there Pausanias saw a 'Ritual depository' furnished with 'ancient tripods': the significance of this is discussed below.

3 Head, *HN*[2] 431–3; fuller references in Otto, *De Sacr. Mess.* 26–7.

4 Plut. *Sept. Sap. Conv.* 16, 159 E, *Quaest. Conv.* 4.1.1, 660 F, *Rom.* 25.4; Paus. 4.19.3; Polyaenus 2.31.2; cf. Clem. Alex. *Protr.* 3.42.1; Euseb. *Praep. Ev.* 4.16, p. 157 C. Cf. P. Stengel, *RE* 7.2 (1912) 2790 s.v. Ἑκατομφόνια.

5 Steph. Byz. s.v. Βίεννος; *ICret* 1 VI 1.11 (201 BC), 2.24 (*post* ca. *a.* 170 BC). Cf. R.F. Willetts, *Cretan Cults and Festivals* (London 1962) 286.

6 The cult of Biennus or another like it may stand behind a myth recorded by Sallust, that Otus was buried in Crete and gave his name to *Otii campi*: Serv. *Aen.* 3.578 (Sall. *Hist.* fr. 3.13 Maurenbrecher); cf. Plin. *Hist. Nat.* 7.73.

7 Cf. Müller on Anon. *Stad. Maris Magni* 320, *GGM* 1.505–6; Cook, *Zeus* 1.623; H. Verbruggen, *Le Zeus crétois* (Paris 1981) 134, and *Sources Pertaining to the Cult of Zeus on Crete* (Louvain 1985) 13. The mountain setting would help to attract the myths of the Curetes and of Otus and Ephialtes.

age class who had a prominent part in the ritual. Otus and Ephialtes too are warlike youths. Even so, it is easy to suppose that the youths of Biennus were active in both cults, of Zeus and of Ares. But we must still confront the mythographer Fulgentius.

Fulgentius offers yet another instance of the term ἑκατομφόνια, citing Diophantus of Sparta in his book *On the Worship of the Gods*, and representing it as a human sacrifice to 'Mars' both at Athens and, it seems, on Lemnos, in token of killing a hundred enemies.[8] The citation is plainly false (Diophantus takes a bow in another work of Fulgentius, there with fourteen books of *Antiquities*),[9] and the localities, Athens and Lemnos, can be set aside. Moreover, it seems almost certain that the term was known to Fulgentius from the legend of Aristomenes, for different versions of Aristomenes' sacrifice (attributable to Rhianus of Crete and Myron of Priene, respectively) say either that he killed a hundred enemies or that he sacrificed his captives at the altar. Yet Aristomenes' sacrifice is always addressed to Zeus. Three possibilities must be reckoned with. Either Fulgentius knew only of Aristomenes' sacrifice to Zeus, and himself substituted Mars as a lurid and plausible name; or he knew also of a like-named sacrifice to Ares in a different quarter, presumably the one at Biennus; or he knew of an account of Aristomenes in which Zeus of Ithome was replaced by Ares or Mars.

Finally, a promised sacrifice of one hundred men is handed down as an explanation of the proverbial phrase, an old one, Θετταλῶν σόφισμα, which was seemingly applied to any shifty trick in fighting (cf. Eur. *Phoen.* 1407–8). A Thessalian inquired of the Delphic oracle and was warned that the enemy might make a vow more generous and effective than his own; to forestall this, he vowed to sacrifice 'a hecatomb of men,' ἑκατόμβην ἀνδρῶν, to Apollo; after he won, he declined to fulfil the vow on the ground that it

---

8 Fulg. *Expos. Serm. Ant.* 5, p. 112, 17 Helm: *Diofontus Lacedemonius, qui de sacris deorum scripsit, ait aput Athenas Marti solere sacrificare sacrum, quod ecatonpefoneuma appellatur; si quis enim centum hostes interfecisset, Marti de homine sacrificabat aput insulam Blemnon. Athenas: Itomas* Schäfer. *Blemnon aut Blennon: Lemnon* Müller: *Biennum* Schäfer. Schäfer's corrections are quite arbitrary.

9 *Mitologiae* p. 15, 21 Helm: *Diophantus Lacedaemonum auctor, 14 libri antiquitatum.* Skutsch, *RE* 7.1 (1910) 219 *s.v.* Fulgentius 3, notes the parallel citations of Diophantus, and describes Fulgentius as 'a *Schwindler* ... like Ptolemaeus Chennus ... or Virgilius Grammaticus.' The passage about the 'Hundred-slaughter' was printed as a fragment of Diophantus – otherwise known as the author of a work on the Black Sea – by Müller, *FHG* 4.497, and by A. Tresp, *Die Fragmente der griechischen Kultschriftsteller* (Giessen 1914) 175–6; it is omitted by Jacoby, *FGrHist* 805. L.R. Farnell, *Cults of the Greek States* 5 (Oxford 1909) 405, 412, includes Diophantus among the rather sparse testimonies for the worship of Ares.

was unseemly.[10] This elaborate and amusing explanation is obviously very late. The Thessalian's name appears to be corrupt wherever it occurs; even if we restore it as Αἶατος, the Thessalian Heraclid who invaded Boeotia, we may still assume that it was only a suitable name adopted for the purpose.[11] The story is the invention of a grammarian who knew of the Messenian ἑκατομφόνια, probably in the version of Myron, which ascribed to Aristomenes an actual sacrifice of one hundred men.

To sum up, ἑκατομφόνια is a striking term and a striking custom, which we find at two places only, on Mount Ithome and at Biennus. The difference between this term and ἑκατόμβη is partly that the victims are not specified as oxen, but also that the sacrifice is described as an act of murder, φόνος. In the Athenian rite called βουφόνια the most precious of victims, a plough ox, was struck suddenly with an axe.[12] In our rite the victims were manhandled at the altar. This is the implication of an anecdote about Philip V, when he considered whether to seize and garrison Ithome.[13] He went up to the sanctuary, sacrificed an ox, and asked his companions, Demetrius the Pharian and Aratus, to read the entrails and so decide what he should do. Demetrius answered in figurative language. 'Grasp both horns to hold down the ox'; i.e., secure both Ithome and Acrocorinth in order to control Greece. The answer was apt because the sacrificial victim was so treated. In the legend of the First Messenian War, as we shall see in a moment, disaster is portended when the victims break loose.

Just when the 'Hundred-slaughter' became imprinted in the legends of early Messenian wars is hard to tell. The original rite was doubtless revived after 369. Conceivably, it went on even during the fifth century; for although the perioecic communities of Messenia were not very near, hunting was always feasible in the region of Ithome, and the ritual was of interest to hunters. But the old ways were certainly cherished by the Messenians of the *diaspora*. Hageladas made the statue of Zeus for those of Naupactus (Paus. 4.33.2). And it must have been Messenians abroad

10 Suda *s.v.* Θετταλῶν σόφισμα; Eustath. 331.20 (Paus. Attic. Θ 12 Erbse); Zenob. 4.29; etc. Only Zenobius gives Apollo the epithet καταιβάσιος, but it is doubtless part of the original story.

11 Cf. Steph. Byz. *s.v.* Δώριον (Charax *FGrHist* 103 F 6); Polyaenus 8.44. Αἰάτῳ was K.O. Müller's correction of Eustathius; *alii alia.*

12 Cf., e.g., Porph. *De Abst.* 2.29–31 (Theophr. *De Piet.* fr. 18 Pötscher); Ael. *Var. Hist.* 8.3; Paus. 1.28.10.

13 Plb. 7.12.1–3; Str. 8.4.8, p. 361; Plut. *Arat.* 50.3–6. In the event Philip accepts Aratus' advice, to resist the opportunity and rely on goodwill; Walbank on Polybius therefore supposes that the anecdote was told by Aratus, though not in his *Memoirs*, which ended at an earlier juncture. This seems rather unlikely, for Demetrius' trenchant words have the effect of commending the other course.

who preserved the old processional hymn for a Messenian choir on Delos, with its prominent mention of Zeus of Ithome – if indeed the hymn was what Pausanias took it to be, the only surviving poem of Eumelus of Corinth. Yet the two lines he quotes are no sufficient test, and when we remember that Eumelus was a magnet for pseudepigraphy, and Messenia for pseudo-history, the confidence of modern editors and commentators seems misplaced.[14] It may well be that the hymn was composed at a later date without intent to deceive. For when Messenian refugees settled at Naupactus in ca. 460, they kept their attachment to Zeus of Ithome, as we see from Hageladas' statue, but became devoted allies of Athens; this was the time, and there was hardly any other, for Messenians to join in the celebration of Apollo's festival on Delos.[15] On this reckoning, the hymn is even better evidence that Messenians abroad actively maintained the traditions of Ithome.

The Legends of Victory and Defeat

We turn to the legends of early Messenian wars in Pausanias. For the First Messenian War, he avowedly follows Myron of Priene; for the Second, Rhianus of Crete.[16] The legends of both wars are considerably indebted to the cult on Ithome. The doubts that have been raised about Pausanias' sources do not matter here, though my own conviction is that Pausanias has drawn directly on Myron and Rhianus, as he says he did, while omitting the role which Myron gave to Aristomenes.[17] The legendary content will

14 Paus. 4.4.1, 33.2, 5.19.10 (PMG fr. 696). F. Kiechle, *Helikon* 6 (1966) 514–16, holds that the Aeolic forms in the hymn reflect an Aeolic substrate in Messenia; he is followed by Meyer, *RE Suppl.* 15 (1978) 234 s.v. Messenien. But the forms come rather from the traditions of lyric poetry, and are widely paralleled down to the late Hellenistic period.

15 Though Athens again conducted the Delia in the fourth century, there is no sign that it had any following among other Greeks; and Athens and Messene were no more than occasional allies. C.M. Bowra, *CQ*[2] 13 (1963) 152–3, who thinks of the choir as appealing for support of the Messenian cause, suggests (after A. Andrewes) that it was sent by Messenian exiles in Euboea, just before they joined in the foundation of Rhegium. Now this is to discard Pausanias' account of how and when the choir was sent (4.4.1). Once that is done, there is little reason to follow Pausanias in other details, such as the early date or the ascription to Eumelus.

16 Myron *FGrHist* 106; Rhianus *FGrHist* 265. Rhianus' birthplace was perhaps Lebena rather than the notional 'Bene,' for the ethnic form appears only in Stephanus, the Suda, and a suspect passage of Pausanias: K.J. Rigsby, *BCH* 99 (1986) 350–5.

17 Admittedly, it continues to be generally held that Pausanias followed a local antiquarian writer of Roman times: e.g., Meyer, *RE Suppl.* 15 (1978) 240–53. But the antiquarian bias is probably due to Pausanias himself; for his account of Andania, see *GRBS* 29 (1988) 239–54. As to the content of Rhianus' work, J. Schneider, *REG* 98 (1985) 30–55, has recently subjected Jacoby's hypothesis, and also Wade-Gery's, to searching

be the same even if Pausanias drew rather on an intermediary source close to his own time, a source who had made over Myron and Rhianus, and even if Rhianus' subject was in fact a Third Messenian War.

The first war, after two battles at Stenyclerus, is fought round Ithome, where the whole population of Messenia takes refuge (Paus. 4.9–13). This notion of the war is of course inspired by the fifth-century siege of Ithome and by the site of the later city at the mountain foot. But it also looks to the festival of Zeus. In the last year of the war, a Delphic oracle promises victory 'to those who first set up for Zeus of Ithome one hundred tripods round his altar' (4.12.7). One hundred tripods are the apparatus of a large-scale sacrifice; we recall the tripod shown on coins together with Hageladas' statue. Both sides vie to fulfill the oracle, but neither does so in a satisfactory manner. Instead of bronze tripods, the Spartans set up tripods of baked clay, the Messenians tripods of wood (4.12.8–10). Acting first, the Spartans win the war; but their tripods being of clay, victory is not conclusive, and a second war will soon break out.

After the tripods, i.e., the preparation for sacrifice, we hear of the animal victims, which provide an omen of Messenian defeat. 'And as Aristodemus is about to sacrifice the victims to Zeus of Ithome, the rams of their own accord and with great force dash their horns against the altar and die from the blow' (4.13.1). When the sacrifice is properly conducted, the animals are restrained by strength of arm, by gripping their horns; in the anecdote mentioned above, this was an image for controlling Greece.

In the second war, Aristomenes thrice offered to Zeus of Ithome 'the sacrifice which they call "Hundred-slaughter"; it had been a custom from the most ancient times, and was traditionally offered by those Messenians who killed a hundred enemy warriors' (4.19.3). Aristomenes offered the first sacrifice after the battle of Boar's Tomb, and the second after surprising a Corinthian force at night, and the third after some 'later raids.' The raids are not described by Pausanias, but there is room for them in the further course of the war. Plutarch and Polyaenus likewise refer to the three successive sacrifices, without adding details. To be sure, Polyaenus makes it appear that Aristomenes was already known for the three sacrifices at the time when he was captured by the Spartans and thrown down a precipice, a time before the last two occasions in Pausanias; but Polyaenus is speaking offhandedly.[18]

---

criticism; the story that Pausanias tells proves to be much more self-coherent than either hypothesis.

18 Plut. *Sept. Sap. Conv.* 16, 159 E, *Quaest. Conv.* 4.1.1, 660 F, *Rom.* 25.4; Polyaenus 2.31.2. Kiechle, *Messenische Studien* (Kallmünz 1959) 104, infers quite unnecessarily

Clement, echoed by Eusebius, has a different version.[19] 'Aristomenes of Messenia slaughtered three hundred men for Zeus of Ithome,' τῶι Ἰθωμήτηι Διὶ τριακοσίους ἀπέσφαξεν, 'thinking such and so many hecatombs a fine offering indeed; among them was even the Spartan king Theopompus, a noble victim.' Though Clement ironizes, he assuredly did not invent this version. It is a version in which Aristomenes fights in the First Messenian War, the time of the Spartan king Theopompus, and Theopompus himself dies at the hands of Aristomenes.

Now according to Pausanias this is exactly the version of Myron of Priene. Myron wrote of the First Messenian War, and brought Aristomenes on stage, and – the ultimate falsehood, in Pausanias' view – 'he feigned that Aristomenes killed Theopompus the king of Sparta,' πεποίηκε γὰρ ὡς ἀποκτείνειε Θεόπομπον τῶν Λακεδαιμονίων τὸν βασιλέα Ἀριστομένης, 'a little before the death of Aristodemus; but we know that Theopompus fought out the war to the end and did not die beforehand, either in consequence of battle or in any other way,' οὔτε μάχης γιγνομένης οὔτε ἄλλως προαποθανόντα (4.6.3–4). Plutarch too, in a glancing reference, mentions different views, Messenian and Spartan, as to whether Theopompus was killed by Aristomenes, or only wounded; it is natural to suppose that the 'Messenian' view – or better say 'pro-Messenian' – is Myron's.[20] We have then in Clement an unattributed fragment of Myron of Priene, which also goes some way towards confirming that Pausanias knew Myron at first hand.

It is possible to situate the fragment within Pausanias' account of the First Messenian War, an account which follows Myron while removing Aristomenes. Myron, as we just saw, had Theopompus killed by Aristomenes 'a little before the death of Aristodemus,' the second of two Messenian kings who wage war. Aristodemus kills himself in despair after a series of untoward oracles and omens (Paus. 4.12.4–13.4). They unfold during the last year or two of Aristodemus' reign of almost seven years (4.13.4); within this sequence, there is no room for

---

that Polyaenus knew a Messenian tradition in which Aristomenes was captured near the end of the war.

19 Clem. Alex. *Protr.* 3.42.1; Euseb. *Praep. Ev.* 4.16, p. 157 C.

20 Plut. *Agis* 21.4. 'Whereas the Messenians say that Theopompus fell by the hand of Aristomenes,' ὑπ' Ἀριστομένους πεσεῖν, 'the Spartans deny it, and say that he was only wounded. There is a controversy about it,' ἀλλὰ ταῦτα μὲν ἔχει τινὰς ἀμφιβολίας. According to Kiechle, *Mess. Stud.* 103–4, Plutarch refers not to Myron but to 'a Messenian popular tradition.' Yet if Plutarch knew of Myron at all, we must grant that this brief notice of the 'controversy' is inexact. And it was bound to be, for Plutarch only means to mention, in passing, the possibility that one other Spartan king before Cleombrotus I (and Leonidas) was killed in battle. To do this, he will simply speak of 'Messenian' and 'Spartan' views, and of death or wounding.

the killing of Theopompus, or rather for the capture and sacrifice of a full three hundred Spartans, with the king among them. But just before this sequence, 'in the fifth year of Archidemus' reign,' Messenians and Spartans and all their respective allies fight a pitched battle by consent (4.11.1), and the battle ends in a Spartan rout, and at this point it is the Spartans who despair, 'because many outstanding men had died in the battle' (4.12.1). The Messenian commander is Aristodemus (4.11.2), but on the Spartan side no commander is named, though we might expect to hear of Theopompus, since he has commanded in every previous engagement (4.7.7–9, 8.8–9, 10.3). It is obvious that Pausanias has omitted mention of Theopompus because he was now captured and sacrificed by Aristomenes.

Thus in Myron's version of the First Messenian War the chief Messenian success is signalled by a spectacular sacrifice to Zeus of Ithome, by the 'Hundred-slaughter' in which three hundred Spartan captives, including Theopompus, were led to the altar. The ensuing Messenian decline is accompanied by bungled sacrifice – by tripods of clay or wood, by bolting victims. In Rhianus' version of the Second Messenian War (if such it is), Aristomenes' greatest exploits are each commemorated by sacrifice to Zeus of Ithome, by the 'Hundred-slaughter' which attests the slaying of one hundred enemy warriors. It is true that other aetiologies, notably in the cult of Artemis, have also contributed to the story.[21] But the cult and festival of Zeus are at the centre.

Aristomenes and His Chosen Band

Aristomenes himself and his chosen band of warriors represent the age class that was prominent at the festival. Aristomenes in Rhianus is like Achilles in Homer (Paus. 4.6.3); we recall that Achilles was the youngest of warriors as well as the best. The Messenians began the second war at the urging of Aristomenes and other youths who had just come to maturity (4.14.6–8). Aristomenes was accompanied in his exploits by a body of picked youths of his own age (4.16.3, 8, 18.1). This age class often figures in legend. The Partheniae of Sparta were youths who threatened defiance just as they came of age; the threat is expressly linked with the festival Hyacinthia. Once at Argos, when the young men came of age, they freed their city from the rule of slaves.[22]

21 Legends concerning Artemis: Paus. 3.2.6, 7.4, 4.13.1, 31.3; Str. 8.4.9, p. 362. Concerning Hera: Paus. 4.12.6. Concerning the Dioscuri: Paus. 4.16.5, 27.1–3.
22 The Partheniae and the Hyacinthia: Str. 6.3.2, p. 278 (Antiochus FGrHist 555 F 13). The young men of Argos: Hdt. 6.83.1.

The Curetes too appear at Ithome, as the mythical projection of the same young men. They stole away the infant Zeus for his own safety, and he was bathed by local nymphs, Ithome and Neda; this was said to explain the name of an abundant spring – Clepsydra 'Steal-water' – which supplied both the sanctuary and the city.²³ And the Curetes are found again at Biennus, together with our other instance of the sacrifice called 'Hundred-slaughter'; so are the youthful twins Otus and Ephialtes, of whom more below.

The youths whom Aristomenes had 'about him' at first numbered eighty (4.16.3), so that the total with the leader is eighty-one. Later he raised the number to three hundred (4.18.1). These figures are likely to be significant. The first, eighty-one, is attested for certain celebrants of the Spartan Carneia, as described by Demetrius of Scepsis: they occupied nine tents in groups of nine, and did everything in response to trumpet signals, giving the appearance of military discipline.²⁴ As multiples of three, both figures presumably derive from the early system of three Dorian *phylai*. It is true that after 369 Messenia was organized on a system of five *phylai* that was carried back in legend to early days. But at Sparta too the original system had been superseded, at least for practical purposes, even in the fifth century. If in the Hellenistic period the Spartan Carneia still retained a vestige of it, we may readily suppose that the Messenian festival did so at the time when the stories of Aristomenes were first told.

Whether we follow Myron or Rhianus, it is Aristomenes who offers sacrifice to Zeus. At the real-life festival the young men whom Aristomenes represents were called upon to display their strength by man-handling the sacrificial victims. This was a widespread custom; in the commonest form, as at Athens, the young men lifted up an ox at the altar while its throat was cut. Theseus as a model youth subdues the Marathonian bull – seizing its horns, and roping it, and dragging it along.²⁵ At Ithome the usual victims were rams, as we see from the sacrifice of Aristodemus that went wrong; they were numerous, ideally one hundred, and no doubt each of them was held by a young man. Afterwards the meat was cooked in tripods; since an oracle calls for a hundred of these, each victim must have been cooked separately.

23 Paus. 4.33.1, cf. 31.6. In the city of Messene, the Curetes were associated with a place of sacrifice of a kind called *megaron*; here animals and birds were thrown whole into the fire, a rite which doubtless belongs to Artemis *laphria*, worshipped nearby (Paus. 4.31.7, 9). Youths are to the fore in the cult and myths of Artemis as well. Moreover, Artemis *laphria* like Zeus of Ithome was a patron of the hunt, an age-old way of life round Ithome; so she was readily adopted by the Messenians of Naupactus.

24 Ath. 4.19, 141 E-F (Demetrius fr. 1 Gaede).

25 Cf. H. Herter, *RE Suppl.* 13 (1973) 1083–90 s.v. Theseus 1.

At Biennus in Crete the local form of ἑκατομφόνια was explained by the strange old myth of Otus and Ephialtes binding Ares. According to Stephanus, 'they say that it was here that [Ares] was bound by Otus and Ephialtes the sons of Poseidon, and up to this very day the so-called "Hundred-slaughter" is sacrificed to Ares,' καὶ μέχρι καὶ νῦν τὰ καλούμενα ἑκατομφόνια θύεται τῶι Ἄρει.[26] The myth can now be recognized as a sacrificial *aition*. Otus and Ephialtes are boisterous youths who are just coming of age – had they reached their full growth, they would have overthrown the gods (*Od.* 11.307–20). Like other youths, like Theseus for example, they bind their victim with a rope (*Il.* 5.386). It is an act of warlike prowess; so the victim is called Ares. The same act on the part of Messenian youths made some observers think of Aristomenes killing Spartans. After being bound by the twins, Ares 'was confined in a bronze jar,' χαλκέωι δ' ἐν κεράμωι δέδετο (*Il.* 5.387): i.e., the victim is placed in a cauldron. After thirteen months Ares was released by Hermes: i.e., at the next yearly festival the business is entrusted to other youths.[27]

Tripod cauldrons were commonly used for cooking in early days. The reason why they are so prominent at Ithome (and in the myth of Otus and Ephialtes) is doubtless that the meat was boiled and then kept for some time in the cauldrons, to be reheated at need and served as stew. This was the practice at the Olympic festival; the sacrifices at the altar of Zeus produced a large quantity of meat which was boiled in tripod cauldrons and served to victors and officials for days afterwards at the Prytaneium. It was also the practice, on a much smaller scale, at the festival of the hero Aleximachus at Aegiale on Amorgos; on the first day the boiled meat was offered to the hero and on the second awarded to the victors.[28] We can see why the same thing was done at Ithome. In the 'Hundred-slaughter' a great many animals were sacrificed at the altar of Zeus; the meat could not possibly be consumed within the sanctuary on the mountain peak. Instead it was brought down in cauldrons to the mountain foot and consumed at leisure. Somewhere in the city of Messene, Pausanias saw a place called ἱεροθέσιον, which might be rendered 'Ritual depository' (4.32.1); within it

26 Steph. Byz. *s.v.* Βίεννος.
27 In such myths the names of the principals are often kennings for the animal victims: Pelops 'Dark-face' is a black ram; Oedipus 'Swell-foot' is a pig with knobbly hocks. So with Ὠτος and Ἐφιάλτης, respectively, 'Horned,' i.e., a ram (the word otherwise denotes the horned owl), and 'Mounter,' i.e., a frisky male animal.
28 Olympia: Hdt. 1.59.1; Paus. 5.13.8, 11, 15.9, 12. Aegiale: *IG* 12.7.515 (excerpted as *LSCG Suppl.* 61) 77–8, 80. At Olympia, Herodotus shows us that the meat was boiled, Pausanias that it was consumed in the Prytaneium. For the boiling of sacrificial victims, F. Puttkammer, *Quo modo Graeci victimarum carnes distribuerint* (Königsberg 1912) 64 n. 2, gives us only the rite at Aegiale and another at Athens, addressed to the Horae.

were 'ancient tripods,' of the kind known to Homer; we infer that these tripods were once used for the annual sacrifice on Ithome. The oracle calling for a hundred tripods to be set up round the altar presupposes that the sanctuary itself is not furnished with tripods, that they must be fetched from another quarter.

Warfare and Hunting

From at least the fifth century, for the Messenians of the *diaspora* and then for the new state centred on Ithome, the festival of Zeus and the great sacrifice evoked the struggle against Sparta; and the story grew of how a heroic youth named Ἀριστομένης, 'Best in might,' slew Spartans like victims at the sacrifice, or even *as* victims at the sacrifice. It is natural that when young men come of age, their festival exercises and displays should be seen as an image of war; for most communities, war was a large part of adult life. But Ithome was not a settlement site in the beginning, and indeed Stenyclerus, the upper Messenian plain, had no early settlement of consequence.[29] Despite the legends of the Messenian wars, warfare can hardly have been a normal or staple enterprise for Messenians of say the eighth or seventh centuries BC – at least in this area, which is the focus of the legends. The legends, however, allow us to glimpse another form of livelihood more suited to the area, namely hunting. Even in later days hunters must have been well represented at the festival.

The Spartan infiltrator who contrives to fulfil the oracle of the tripods is an ordinary man, not a noble, and he comes in the guise of a hunter, ἀνὴρ θηρευτής, carrying nets, δίκτυα, and a game bag, πήρα, in which the clay tripods, evidently miniatures, are concealed (Paus. 4.12.9). A little before this, we have that pitched battle in which Pausanias will not allow Theopompus to be taken captive; the battle is decided, however, not by the hoplite ranks, but by a large body of light-armed Messenians, and also Arcadians, who skirmish with the Spartans; their strange costume is described in some detail (4.11.3–7). Light-armed troops they are called, and a few of them are slingers or archers, and have either breastplates or shields. But after conceding this much to verisimilitude, Myron described the others, who wear only skins of goats or sheep, or the hides of wild animals, those of wolf and bear especially, and who carry only javelins or spears. They are virtual hunters.

In the second war, Aristomenes is a hunter of Spartans. He was greeted one day, as he returned to Andania, with a song that runs, 'Into the mid

29 Cf. Meyer, *RE Suppl.* 15 (1978) 137 *s.v.* Messene 3, 185–94 *s.v.* Messenien.

Stenyclerian plain, and up to the top of the mountain, Aristomenes pursued, εἵπετο, the Spartans' (4.16.6). The song, says Pausanias, 'is still sung to this day,' presumably by the women, as it was then; and since the women at the same time pelted Aristomenes with ribbons and flowers, we may suppose that this gesture too still continues, and honours a hunter returning with his kill. Aristomenes also figures in a dream as a lion that is subdued by wolves and then gets free. The girl who dreamed, and who brought about the fulfilment of the dream, was given in marriage to Aristomenes' son just as he came of age, 'when his eighteenth year was not yet past' (4.19.6).

These picturesque details are taken from the youthful hunters who joined in the festival on Ithome. In early days the festival was chiefly theirs, and the "Hundred-slaughter" was a thank-offering for the hunting season of spring and summer. Hunting and warfare are similar and related activities; it was easy for a festival that celebrates the hunt to become a festival that celebrates war. The same development can be seen elsewhere. At Athens, Artemis *agrotera* was once a deity of the hunt, as her epithet plainly tells us. But the festival Boedromia, in which, as often, she is worshipped beside Apollo, is a festival of war, as the name plainly tells us; the festival, moreover, is about as old as the office of Polemarch, who had charge of it (pp. 22–5 above). The ritual includes an offering of goats to Artemis which was once a thank-offering for the hunt; but it came to signify the kill at Marathon instead.[30]

30 Ar. *Eq.* 660–1; schol. *ad loc.*; Xen. *Anab.* 3.2.12; Plut. *De Herod. Mal.* 26, 862 A; Ael. *Var. Hist.* 2.25.

11

A Festival of Heroes
and the Ordeal of
Phigaleia

Synopsis

The town of Phigaleia is small and remote, but great events, if we believe them, were once enacted there. Pausanias has a historical excursus on Phigaleia, unparalleled at other small towns of Arcadia. The town was first besieged and captured by the Spartans, then liberated by a band of Oresthasian champions, who all laid down their lives. The Oresthasians were buried in a tomb in the agora, one of the few but striking Phigaleian monuments noticed by Pausanias; and sacrifice was offered each year as to heroes.

Modern writers have not questioned these events, nor their ostensible commemoration in the tomb and hero cult of the agora. They should have, for everything about the story makes it suspect, not least the tomb and hero cult. Long before Pausanias, Phigaleia's festival of heroes was described by the antiquarian writer Harmodius of Lepreum, but he did not regard it as a commemoration of fallen soldiers. Pausanias' tale of invading Spartans is not the only one. In Polyaenus, the perfidious enemy march into the city disguised as friends. This is a patent aetiology of an armed procession.

History as we know it from better sources gives a different picture of relations between Phigaleia and Sparta. In the period before Leuctra, Phigaleia was a strategic outpost of Spartan domination, firmly held by oligarchs. After Leuctra it was attached to the Arcadian regime round Megalopolis, i.e., the district of Oresthis. Patriotic literature celebrated the new order and also transformed the past. Phigaleia's connection with Sparta was remembered as involuntary.

A list of pan-Arcadian kings was perhaps first created at this time; Phigaleia and Oresthis were joined together by means of eponyms. Thereafter the list was often varied and expanded. Pausanias' list is the latest and fullest of all and gives special prominence to Phigaleia. It is from the same late source that Pausanias draws his sensational account of Phigaleian cults, including the cult of heroes in the agora.

We shall consider the following points: the stories of Spartan aggression; Pausanias' source on Phigaleia, and the strange lore of Eurynome and Black Demeter; the Arcadian king list; Phigaleia and Sparta; Phigaleia and Oresthis; the hero cult in the agora; a local festival of Apollo.

The Stories of Spartan Aggression

Pausanias' story runs as follows (8.39.3–5, 41.1). 'The Spartans, when they attacked Arcadia, invaded Phigaleia too with an army.' The inhabitants got away, and the town was taken. 'The capture of Phigaleia and the flight of Phigaleians from it took place' in the year 659–658, a date expressed in two systems, by Athenian archon and by Olympiad. Phigaleia was then held by the Spartans until the Delphic oracle revealed the only means by which it could ever be recovered. One hundred picked men from Oresthasium must join the Phigaleians and give their lives in the struggle. This was done, and the liberation is commemorated by the grave of the Oresthasians in the agora and by a yearly sacrifice in their honour.

The ordeal of Phigaleia is similar to the battle of Hysiae in being reported by no one but Pausanias, and also in being dated with such punctilio. Like the battle of Hysiae, it is uniformly accepted, though of course the prophetic details are left aside. But the date, 659–658, is more often discounted. This date, it is held, merely implies a connection with the Second Messenian War, as conventionally situated in the time of the poet Tyrtaeus. After all, the Arcadians sided with the Messenians, and Phigaleia is very close to Hira, the last Messenian stronghold. If then the Messenian wars are reconstructed, as they sometimes are, so that the fighting round Hira falls in ca. 600 or in ca. 500, these events will come at the same time, or shortly after.[1]

1 Pausanias' date accepted: G.L. Huxley, *Early Sparta* (London 1962) 57–8; W.G. Forrest, *History of Sparta 950--192 BC* (London 1968) 71, and *CAH*² 3.3.310; L.H. Jeffery, *Archaic Greece* (London 1976) 171. Ca. 600 preferred: D.M. Leahy, *Phoenix* 12 (1958) 164; H.T. Wade-Gery in *Ancient Society and Institutions: Studies Presented to V. Ehrenberg* (Oxford 1966) 296–7; M. Jost, *Sanctuaires et cultes d' Arcadie* (Paris 1985) 539. Ca. 500 preferred: F. Hiller von Gaetringen, *IG* 5.2 p. 106; Ernst Meyer, *RE* 19.2 (1938) 2081–2 *s.v.* Phigaleia, and *RE* 18.1 (1939) 1016 *s.v.* Oresthasion. It is no doubt by inadvertence that F. Pfister, *Der Reliquienkult im Altertum* (Giessen 1909–12) 1.319, dates the event to 'the middle of the sixth century.'

This is worse than the argument which associates Pheidon with Hysiae. There, we start from Pausanias' date, 668–667, and reach out to collar Pheidon – even though Pausanias himself has a different date for Pheidon and does not think of him in this context. Here, even the date must be discarded before the hypothetical connection can be made. And again it is Pausanias himself who forbids the connection by his silence. He is our fullest source for the Second Messenian War, for the role of the Arcadians therein, for the siege of Hira; he even mentions the marriage of Aristomenes' sister to a man of Phigaleia. All this in Book 4, in the history of Messenia. When he comes to the history of Arcadia in Book 8, he reminds us once more of the alliance between Arcadia and Messenia, and of the treachery of the Arcadian king.[2] Nowhere does he intimate that Phigaleia was concerned in the fighting. Had she been, he might perhaps pass it over in his general account of Messenia or of Arcadia. But he could hardly do so in his tour of Phigaleia, while narrating the chief events of Phigaleian history.

The Spartans are said to have invaded Phigaleia 'when they attacked Arcadia,' ἡνίκα 'Αρκάσιν ἐπεχείρησαν, i.e., sometime during the endless hostilities between these neighbouring peoples. This is not a definite occasion, a sequel (say) to the Second Messenian War, but the most general context that could be evoked. As a rule the hostilities of early days are played out at Tegea in southeast Arcadia. Epimenides, however, was able to predict a Spartan defeat at Orchomenus, an event about as likely in itself as the invasion of Phigaleia.[3] Since this event is handed down in perfect isolation, we are free to speculate that it was somehow associated with the Messenian wars, in which the wicked king of Orchomenus has a certain prominence. Nothing in all this suggests a context for Phigaleia.

Polyaenus has a circumstantial story of how the Spartans captured Phigaleia: after laying siege to the town, they disguised themselves as a relief force from Argos and were admitted at the city gate (6.27.2). Pausanias, on the other hand, says that the Phigaleians either escaped or were allowed to depart – perhaps he found the alternatives in his source, or perhaps he is expanding the story. In either case the circumstances are different, and it is accordingly supposed that Polyaenus describes a later incident, possibly from the years after the Peace of Nicias, when Argos and Phigaleia might

---

2 The marriage: Paus. 4.24.1; cf. Rhianus *FGrHist* 265 F 40. Arcadians in the Second Messenian War: Paus. 4.15.1, 7, 17.2–3, 6–8, 22.1–23.1, 8.5.13–6.1.

3 Diog. Laert. 1.115 (Epimenides *Vorsokr* 3 A 1, Theopompus *FGrHist* 115 F 69). Leahy, *Phoenix* 12 (1958) 141–65, builds a massive edifice of conjecture.

have been allied.[4] Now it is quite conceivable that Polyaenus' source gave an altogether different date or context from Pausanias. But the two stories are broadly similar in so far as Phigaleia, a walled city, is under siege and is overcome with difficulty or by deceit. Moreover, in Polyaenus as in Pausanias a Phigaleian custom stands in the background – Polyaenus' story is clearly an *aition* of a procession under arms (more of this below). Both stories provide an explanation of how Phigaleia came under Spartan control, but either explanation is wholly fictitious. There was a time, as we shall see, when Phigaleia had need of some excuse for having formerly submitted to Sparta.

Pausanias' Source

As with Hysiae, so for the ordeal of Phigaleia it is obvious that Pausanias has consulted a special authority. Some events of early Arcadian history are familiar to him from his general reading. There is the famous ambush and capture of a Spartan army under King Charillus, referred to several times in Book 8 and once in Book 3, on Laconia. There is another Spartan defeat at Tegea, just as thorough, caused by a surprise attack in cold weather. There is the treachery of that Arcadian king, referred to in both Book 8 and Book 4. None of these other events is precisely dated. Moreover, they are all known from other sources, sometimes in more than one version.[5]

The nature of this special authority is much clearer at Phigaleia than at Hysiae. Pausanias consulted the authority for other matters too, for curious unverifiable details about the rural sanctuaries of Phigaleia. The authority described two fantastic hybrid statues, of Eurynome and of Black Demeter, which Pausanias did not see; he also explained how the features of Demeter's statue had been faithfully preserved from the distant past; he even adorned the tale with a Delphic oracle. That it is the same authority throughout, for the rural sanctuaries and for the cult of heroes in the agora, can scarcely be doubted. We should examine briefly those other blocks of material, about Eurynome and Black Demeter.

The shrine of Eurynome at the confluence of the Neda and the Lymax was 'hard to reach because of the rough terrain,' and was in any case kept

---

4 Hiller von Gaertringen, *IG* 5.2 p. 106; Meyer, *RE* 19.2 (1938) 2082 *s.v.* Phigaleia. Polyaenus, says Meyer, describes a 'fortified' city; but so does Pausanias. Hiller remarks that the preceding strategem in Polyaenus is the battle of Aegospotami, 405 BC (6.27.1); but this can hardly signify, if the capture of Phigaleia is assigned to a distinctly earlier date, 'c. a. 418?' as Hiller has it.

5 Spartan army ambushed: Paus. 3.7.3, 8.5.9, 45.3, 47.2, 4, 48.4–5; cf. Hdt. 1.66; Deinias *FGrHist* 306 F 4. Spartan army surprised in cold weather: Paus. 8.53.9–10; cf. Polyaenus 1.8.

closed at all times but the day of festival, which did not coincide with Pausanias' visit (8.41.4–6). So he did not see the statue of Eurynome; presumably he did not even make an excursion to the site.[6] Now whereas 'the people of Phigaleia,' ὁ μὲν τῶν Φιγαλέων δῆμος , say of Eurynome that this name is an epithet of Artemis, 'those of them who have absorbed ancient traditions,' ὅσοι δὲ αὐτῶν παρειλήφασιν ὑπομνήματα ἀρχαῖα, describe her as a daughter of Ocean renowned in literature. The description of the statue which 'I heard from the Phigaleians,' τῶν Φιγαλέων δ' ἤκουσα, is, as Pausanias remarks, appropriate to a daughter of Ocean but not at all to Artemis.

In the long account of Black Demeter, worshipped at a mountain cave, we find the same distinction between ordinary local informants and a more privileged source (8.42.1–7, 11–13). Outside the cave, Pausanias saw the altar where, at festival time, certain offerings were made by certain officiants; but inside, there were only marks on the roof that suggested a rockfall.[7] The fantastic statue which Pausanias had heard of, which indeed had brought him to Phigaleia, was not to be seen, and 'most' of the Phigaleians, οἱ πολλοί, did not even know that it had once existed (8.42.12). Among the people he met, only one old man, the oldest of all, τῶν δὲ ἐντυχόντων ἡμῖν ... ὁ πρεσβύτατος, happened to recall that 'three generations before his own time' rocks fell from the roof and smashed and buried the statue (8.42.13). The statue, however, has already been described, and so has an earlier rendering of the same figure, on the authority of 'the Phigaleians,' φασὶν οἱ Φιγαλεῖς (8.42.3, cf. 42.1). Since no living Phigaleian, except perhaps the gaffer, knew anything about it, we see that this phrase, 'the Phigaleians say,' denotes a book about Phigaleia. The same book was obviously used for Eurynome.

It is true that the material about Eurynome and Black Demeter is different in kind from the story of Phigaleia's ordeal. The Phigaleians, we are told, chose outlandish forms in which to represent the two deities. Eurynome was a woman down to the thighs, a fish below, entwined with golden chains. Demeter was a woman dressed in a long black robe, sitting on a rock, but with a horse's head, and snakes and other beasts growing out of the head, and a dolphin placed on one of her hands, and a dove on the other. Yet these peculiar statues, like the story of Phigaleia's ordeal, are bound up with actual cults of Phigaleia. Moreover, the description is veristic – Eurynome was an ancient statue of wood, a *xoanon*, and so was

6 The directions which he gives are obscure or conflicting, so that the location of the shrine is disputed: Meyer, RE 19.2 (1938) 2072–3 s.v. Phigaleia.

7 A cave that was found recently on a mountain southwest of Phigaleia satisfies Pausanias' indications quite strikingly, even in the appearance of a rockfall from the roof: F.A. Cooper, *Journal of Field Archaeology* 8 (1981) 133–4.

Black Demeter to begin with, but afterwards, when the original had long disappeared, Onatas rendered the same figure in bronze, working from a painting or a copy that had come to light, but guided even more by dreams. Indeed the statue of Demeter has a long history. The wooden statue was mysteriously burnt, a bad omen, in the reign of Simus, the fifth king of Arcadia after the Dorian invasion (Paus. 8.5.8). The worship was then neglected until famine struck and Delphi issued a ten-line oracle. The oracle, horrendous but jejune, has plainly been contrived for the sake of the story – like the other oracle, which is not quoted, calling for one hundred Oresthasians to sacrifice themselves.

The source for Phigaleia's ordeal was a late one, dating the event by archon list and Olympiad.[8] The source for Eurynome and Black Demeter was just as late, as we can see from the language of the oracle, full of grandiloquent epithets.[9] There is also a strong suspicion that this source has contributed to the lower reaches of the long list of Arcadian kings which forms the general history of Arcadia. The list includes the note about the burning of Demeter's statue in the reign of Simus; and the previous ruler, Simus' father, is 'Phialus' the eponym of Phigaleia in its later pronunciation (Paus. 8.5.7, 39.2). He is the second such eponym, for 'Phigalus' was named long before at the proper place in the stemma, as a son of Lycaon (Paus. 8.3.1–2). It is said of Phialus that 'he deprived Lycaon's son Phigalus of his honour as founder by changing the city's name to Phialia, after himself; yet this name did not exclusively prevail.' The spelling 'Phialia' is found from the third century onwards, but the other continues beside it until Imperial times.[10] The rather trivial device of the second eponym is likely to be late.[11]

We may therefore suppose that Pausanias drew on the same late source for both the story of Phigaleia's ordeal and the lore of Eurynome and Black Demeter. Some moderns believe and uphold this lore, even or especially the statues.[12] They are well-meaning but misguided. It does not help to

8 J.E. Fontenrose, *The Delphic Oracle* (Berkeley 1978) 297, thought it 'probable' that Pausanias drew on Ariaethus of Tegea (*FGrHist* 316); but he gave no reason, and I see none.

9 'The late Hellenistic or Roman period': H.W. Parke and D.E.W. Wormell, *The Delphic Oracle* (Oxford 1956) 1.323–4, 2.200–1.

10 Meyer, *RE* 19.2 (1938) 2065–7 *s.v.* Phigaleia.

11 It is 'a quite childish grammatical hair-splitting': Hiller von Gaertingen, *Klio* 21 (1926) 8.

12 Those who believe in Onatas' statue are numerous and unequivocal, and include every recent authority on Classical sculpture: e.g., J. Dörig, *Onatas of Aegina* (Leiden 1977) 8–9; L. Beschi, *LIMC* 4.1 (1988) 849 no. 11, *add. s.v.* Demeter. Yet they seem indifferent to the extraordinary consequences of their belief. As we saw (n. 7 above), the cave of Black Demeter now appears to be located (another candidate was previously

expatiate on other 'theriomorphic' traces in Arcadia, for as Pausanias lets us see, it was just these that gave a handle to the fiction: the account of Black Demeter begins by differentiating Phigaleian belief from Thelpusan (8.42.1). The animal guises at Lycosura were undoubtedly known to Pausanias' source, and probably to Pausanias himself. Here the officiants put on animal masks and foot-pieces as they paraded to the altar where live animals were cruelly dismembered. The several species include horse and mule; indeed these are rather prominent among the relief figures on Damophon's statue.[13]

Pausanias then is candid, after a fashion, in reporting the facts. He tells us what he saw and heard at Phigaleia, and also what he did not see or hear. A thoughtful reader will not be gulled; Pausanias himself was not gulled. He was aware, however, that there is a very large class of readers, and of listeners and observers too, who actively want to be deceived, for whom delusion is one of life's chief pleasures. He wrote with them in mind, as do many other ancient authors.[14]

Coming from such a source, the story of Phigaleia's ordeal deserves no credit. There is in principle the possibility that an authentic event has been quite wilfully embroidered. Yet as we saw, none of the details can be regarded as a likely starting-point.

The Arcadian King List

In Pausanias' story Phigaleia is recovered when a band of Oresthasians lay down their lives, to be commemorated with a grave and festival in the agora. Oresthasium, also called Oresthis, was a district in the plain of Megalopolis, afterwards included in the great city: a strategic area athwart an important route.[15] That Oresthasians should play a role at Phigaleia is unexpected; shall we therefore say that it cannot be pure invention? There is, however, another link between Phigaleia and Oresthasium, just as explicit, but a thing of pure invention.

The father of Phialus in the Arcadian king list is Bucolion (Paus. 8.3.2, 5.7, 39.2); he is another eponym, like the majority of names. The place

---

offered), and it is remote and undisturbed. Would not a little digging produce the rarest and strangest of works by an ancient master?

13 Animal guises: Jost, *Cultes d' Arcadie* 328–9, 332–3, and pl. 45 (but the bear-headed figures on a vase at Brauron should not be cited as a parallel, for this is the myth of Callisto and Arcas). Sacrifice: Paus. 8.37.8.

14 Wilamowitz, *Glaube*[2] 1.395–6, cf. 216–17, analysed the passages correctly, but he should not have vilified Pausanias as a helpless dupe, who 'fell into the trap,' 'was caught in the snare,' and so on. Cf. D. Fehling, *CR*[2] 38 (1988) 19.

15 Meyer, *RE* 18.1 (1939) 1014–16 s.v. Oresthasion; A. Andrewes, *HCT* 4.91–3.

Bucolion of which he is the eponym was a settlement in Oresthasium.[16] Phigaleia obviously owed a debt to Oresthasium, a debt which is acknowledged in different fashions by the king list and by the story of Oresthasian champions.

It is important to observe that this Arcadian king list, the longest of any king list in Greece, has been constructed from quite disparate elements.[17] Eponyms are introduced at several stages. In a simpler conception of the list, such as we find in [Apollodorus], the eponyms can all be reckoned sons of Lycaon; and [Apollodorus] differs greatly from Pausanias in his tally of these sons – indeed he includes Bucolion, but not Phi(g)alus.[18] In Pausanias the names in the last part of the list, after the Dorian invasion, show a prepossession for the region of Megalopolis. Cypselus, reigning at the time of the invasion, is the eponym of Cypsela, a town on the west side of the plain;[19] Hicetas, the next to last king, is the eponym of Hiceteia, a place between Lycosura and Megalopolis;[20] and of course there is Bucolion. It is very likely that these names go back to the time when Megalopolis was newly founded and her claims were being pressed. But the last part of the list has other elements too, and at least one connection with Megalopolis has been dropped. The wicked kings ruling at the time of the First and Second Messenian Wars belong to Orchomenus, which was often at odds with other Arcadians; but elsewhere in Pausanias they belong to Trapezus, where resistance to Megalopolis was fiercest.[21]

16 The sequence of events at Thucydides 4.134.1–2 serves to locate Bucolion rather closely. Mantineia and Tegea fight a battle 'at Laodiceium in Oresthis,' just south of the site of Megalopolis. As the battle is drawn, both sides erect a trophy. But whereas the Tegeans do so at once, encamping on the field, 'the Mantineians withdrew to Bucolion and erected theirs afterwards.' Bucolion is no more than a few stades from Laodiceium.

17 For the king list, see Hiller von Gaertringen, IG 5.2 pp. xxix–xxx, and Klio 21 (1926) 1–13; C. Callmer, Studien zur Geschichte Arkadiens (Lund 1943) 59–67; Jacoby on FGrHist IIIb § X, Arkadien; R. Drews, Basileus (New Haven 1983) 71–4; Carlier, Royauté 405–7. Strange to say, both Drews and Carlier conclude that Arcadia at large was once ruled by such a dynasty. This seems unlikely in the last degree, when we consider how limited and unavailing was every later attempt to unite that land of mountains. Hiller and Jacoby are completely sceptical about the tradition, and rightly so. Hiller's analysis has much to commend it, though as Jacoby says, he oversimplifies. Jacoby also objects that Hellanicus, who wrote on Arcadia and mentioned Cepheus (FGrHist 4 F 37), must have had a predominating role. Possibly; but our single testimony does not prove or even suggest that Hellanicus' work on Arcadia was important and authoritative; or if it was, that the backbone was a pan-Arcadian king list.

18 [Apld.] Bibl. 3.7.8.1–3 (3.96–7).

19 Thuc. 5.33.1; Ath. 13.90 (Nicias FGrHist 318 F 1).

20 Hicetas: Paus. 4.17.2, 8.5.13. Hiceteia: IG 5.2.444 line 12.

21 Orchomenus: Paus. 8.5.11–13, 13.5. Trapezus: 4.17.2–7, 22.1–7. Other sources show that Orchomenus was the original seat of the wicked kings, or king, so that the propaganda

We saw above that the king list includes a note about the burning of Demeter's statue; the note is due to Pausanias' source for Phigaleia, and likewise that mincing eponym 'Phialus.' There is reason to think that the source for Phigaleia supplied the final redaction of the whole king list. At the end of the list Pausanias says, 'The foregoing genealogy of the kings was furnished me by the Arcadians in response to my inquiry,' τὰ μὲν δὴ ἐς τοὺς βασιλέας πολυπραγμονήσαντί μοι κατὰ ταῦτα ἐγενεαλόγησαν οἱ Ἀρκάδες (8.6.1). This is an emphatic statement, but the emphasis is, despite appearances, on the authenticity of the list rather than on the means of obtaining it. Authenticity was guaranteed by independent inquiry; Herodotus always professes to have made independent inquiries, and Herodotus was Pausanias' model. Whatever we think about Herodotus' inquiries, six centuries later the local exponents of oral tradition had disappeared, and that gaffer at Phigaleia was a poor substitute. For Pausanias, such a statement is a literary convention. Nor does he hide it. The strange details of Eurynome and Black Demeter are recounted with the phrases, 'I heard from the Phigaleians,' and 'the Phigaleians say.' Yet Pausanias at once proceeds to tell us that nothing of the sort was known to anyone at Phigaleia. Those phrases are in effect contrasted with real inquiries on the spot.

It follows that the Arcadian king list, like the details of Eurynome and Black Demeter, was drawn from a book, probably the same book, to judge from 'Phialus' and the note about the statue. Such a late source need not be responsible for linking the eponyms of Phigaleia and Bucolion. We shall see below that this affiliation suits the fourth century, when the king list was expanded in favour of Megalopolis.

Phigaleia and Sparta

The stories we have examined are suspect on every count. That gallant struggle so long ago, in 659–658, is another little-known episode, like the battle of Hysiae, which Pausanias took from a specialist source; and his source at Phigaleia was particularly unreliable. The hero cult in the agora, far from confirming the story, suggests that it can only be an aetiology. As for the previous capture of Phigaleia by the Spartans, the ruse or 'strategem' of Polyaenus is an aetiology as plain as day. But apart from

---

for Megalopolis merely introduced a variant. It first appears in Ephorus (Nicolaus *FGrHist* 90 F 31 ~ Ephorus *FGrHist* 70 F 116). Cf. Hiller von Gaertringen, *RE* 2.1 (1896) 938–9 *s.v.* Aristokrates 1, and *Klio* 21 (1926) 7, 12; Meyer, *RE* 6 A 2 (1937) 2213–14 *s.v.* Trapezus 1; Jacoby, n. 4 to *FGrHist* IIIb § X, *Arkadien;* Carlier, *Royauté* 406–7. Jacoby is somewhat captious, asserting for example that Ephorus will depend on Hellanicus.

all details, there remains the notion that Phigaleia once fell into Spartan hands and was freed by Oresthasians. We should examine the relations between these places to see how the notion arose.

To believe that Phigaleia and Sparta were somehow embroiled in early days, we must first believe in the siege of Messenian rebels on Mount Hira; for Phigaleia is too small and too remote to be otherwise concerned in the Messenian Wars. But then it is embarrassing that Pausanias, our chief authority for the siege of Hira, does not mention it while recounting the capture and liberation of Phigaleia. Clearly the connection was not indicated by his source. Elsewhere in Pausanias Phigaleia comes into the legends of the Messenian wars, but only as a reflection of much later circumstances.

Aristomenes' sister, it is alleged, married a Phigaleian. Since a member of this Phigaleian family was prominent in the early fourth century, and others later, it is all but certain that the allegation is coeval with the prominence of the family. Ties of marriage are also alleged between Aristomenes and families of Lepreum, Heraea, and Rhodes, ties that are obviously and admittedly fictitious. If the Phigaleian is married to a sister who is named, and the others to daughters who are not, this does not suggest that the Phigaleian tie is authentic, or even that it is prior.[22] After 369 Phigaleia undoubtedly had very close relations with Messenia, closer than the other places did. Harmodius of Lepreum, in his book *On the Customs of Phigaleia*, said that Phigaleians grew accustomed to sojourn in Messenia, and became too fond of drink.[23] The liberation of Messenia and the founding of Messene meant that Phigaleia for the first time had a large powerful neighbour; it is understandable that she anxiously asserted a long-standing friendship.

We should also reflect that whatever may have passed between Phigaleians and Spartans in early days, there was certainly much contact later, from at least the late fifth century; and unless we suppose that Phigaleia had written records to the same extent as much larger cities, the later contacts must have superseded the early memories. In the years before Leuctra Phigaleia, like many another town in the Peloponnesus, was ruled by pro-Spartan oligarchs (Diod. 15.40.2). Spartan influence at Phigaleia will go back to the time when Sparta began to intervene against Elis on behalf of Lepreum and the Triphylians. She did so during the Peloponnesian War

---

22 Marriage ties: Rhianus *FGrHist* 265 F 40; Paus. 4.24.1–3. Phigaleian family: Paus. 6.6.1; *Inscr. Olymp.* 161; *SIG*³ 472 lines 7, 9. Cf. Wade-Gery in *Ancient Society and Institutions* 292–5.

23 Ath. 10.59, 442 B (Harmodius *FGrHist* 319 F 2).

and in the early fourth century; in 421 some emancipated helots were settled at Lepreum.[24] Phigaleia was not necessarily involved in any fighting. When Sparta attacked Elis from the south rather than the east, the obvious route was through northern Messenia and along the coast.[25] But since Phigaleia lay right between Messenia and Triphylia, she was bound to feel some pressure. And she somehow prospered from Sparta's interest in the region; the great Doric temple at Bassae was built towards the end of the century, an extraordinary undertaking for a small town.

Under the year 375–374 Diodorus describes how fighting broke out in many cities, 'especially those of the Peloponnesus,' between democrats who had just come to power and oligarchs who had previously relied on Spartan support (15.40). His examples are Phigaleia, Corinth, Megara, Sicyon, and Phlius. Since this is Diodorus, the date is as likely to be wrong as right; if such conditions are wide-spread, they must be a consequence of Leuctra.[26] Phigaleia is the leading instance, though it is not, for other purposes, a town to be mentioned in the same breath as Corinth, Megara, Sicyon, and Phlius. Phigaleia must have been a most notorious Spartan redoubt.

'First,' says Diodorus, 'the exiles from Phigaleia rallied and occupied so-called Heraea, a fortified place. From here they set out and slipped into Phigaleia, and as the festival Dionysia happened to be under way, they fell unexpectedly on those who were sitting in the theatre, and after killing many, but also persuading not a few to join them in their desperate resolve,' οὐκ ὀλίγους δὲ καὶ συναπονοήσασθαι πείσαντες, 'they withdrew to Sparta.' The reason why the oligarchs, after seizing Phigaleia, did not hold it was doubtless that they were threatened by the united Arcadians of Megalopolis.[27] Few Phigaleians can have been left in the town. For the oligarchic faction killed 'many,' and then went off to Sparta, and so did 'not a few' who, in the conditions they foresaw, chose to follow the oligarchs.

Two statues from the Phigaleian sanctuaries on Cotilius, a colossal bronze of Apollo and a marble one of Pan, were now installed at

24 Cf. Ehrenberg, *RE* 16.2 (1935) 2396–7 *s.v.* Neodamodeis; Bölte, *RE* 7 A 1 (1939) 197–9 *s.v.* Triphylia; Andrewes, *HCT* 4.27.

25 For the route, Meyer, *RE* 16.2 (1935) 2171 *s.v.* Neda.

26 In the paragraph before, Diodorus recounts the rising power of Thebes, down to and including the great victory of Leuctra; 'but we shall treat of this more fully a little later,' etc.

27 According to Strabo, Arcadian Heraea was strengthened by the synoecism of nine villages 'either by Cleombrotus or by Cleomenes' (8.3.2, 337); Cleombrotus died at Leuctra and was succeeded by Cleomenes. The synoecism may be somehow related to the intrusion of Phigaleian oligarchs or to their predicament later. Cf. Hiller von Gaertringen, *IG* 5.2 p. 103.

Megalopolis (Paus. 8.30.2–4).[28] The Apollo, a statue 'worth seeing,' is described by Pausanias as 'a contribution to the adornment of Megalopolis.' Moderns often speak to the same effect, as if Phigaleia gave the statues freely, in an outpouring of goodwill. The motivation is implausible. Cities were jealous of their sanctuaries; and although a result of founding Megalopolis was to vacate or diminish many rural sanctuaries, this can hardly have been welcomed by the towns that remained, chiefly Phigaleia. More likely, the statues were removed to punish Phigaleia. Since these works no doubt derived from the prosperity which Phigaleia had enjoyed under Spartan tutelage, the punishment was condign.

Phigaleia and Oresthis

When Megalopolis was founded, most settlements in southwestern Arcadia were either abandoned or reduced. The list does not extend to Phigaleia; it lay a little farther off, and was moreover a strategic site, guarding the approach to Arcadia from this direction.[29] But if Phigaleia was to be maintained at all, it would need to be reinforced. As we have just seen, it was much weakened by civil strife, and a considerable faction had taken refuge with the Spartans. So whereas many people were brought into Megalopolis, it is likely that a few were sent the other way, to Phigaleia. And whereas the efforts to unify Arcadia were resented and opposed by some on the periphery, it is likely that dwellers in the plain of Megalopolis were entirely in favour, for they had always suffered from Spartan encroachment. The main district near the centre of the plain was Oresthasium/Oresthis, often named as a staging point for Spartan armies. If there was ever a time when a body of Oresthasians came to Phigaleia, it was surely in the early or mid 360s.

From the moment that it arose, the new conformation of the Peloponnesus was celebrated in vehement patriotic literature which reconstructed the past in the light of the present. For Messenia much survives, but for Arcadia little but the king list. As we saw, the eponyms after the Dorian invasion are mainly focused on the plain of Megalopolis. Another item is undoubtedly that stratagem of Polyaenus. It was not to be denied that Phigaleia had once sided with Sparta. On the new outlook, this could only

28 L. Deubner, *RhM* n.s. 59 (1904) 476 = *Kleine Schriften* (Königstein 1982) 46, showed that the statue of Pan must come from Bassae.

29 Cooper, *AAA* 5 (1972) 363, describes a watch-tower near Phigaleia which overlooks the coastal plain and the lower Neda. Like similar towers in the wall of Phigaleia, it is assigned to the first half of the fourth century.

happen under duress. Polyaenus gives us a tale of Spartan trickery; there are several such in the legends of the Messenian wars. He must have had the strategem from some mainstream historian, perhaps Ephorus.

The king list signals Phigaleia's debt to Oresthasium by making Phi(g)alus the son of Bucolion. Did patriotic literature also give the Oresthasians a more immediate role, as soldiers who freed Phigaleia from Spartan domination? If so, it can hardly have identified these soldiers with the heroes worshipped in the agora. For any historical Oresthasians came to stay, and the reputed burial of champions does not explain or even allow this fact. So for a long time the matter rested well short of the version which we find in Pausanias. That version is taken from a writer whose penchant was for reinterpreting ancient cults and providing pedigrees replete with Delphic oracles.

The Hero Cult in the Agora

Having recounted the ordeal of Phigaleia as an introduction to the site, Pausanias comes afterwards to the agora and the commemorative monument and custom, the *polyandrion* tomb and the hero cult conducted there (8.41.1). These things should put us on our guard at once. It is typical of ancient writers to say that a given monument or custom testifies to some great event, when in fact the event has been deduced from the monument or custom as its *raison d'être*. If, moreover, the event is so intrinsically improbable as this one, a hundred picked men sacrificing themselves at the instance of the Delphic oracle, and if the source is so late and fanciful as that book on Phigaleia, we should be doubly on our guard.

The custom is worth considering. 'They sacrifice to them as heroes,' ὡς ἥρωσιν αὐτοῖς ἐναγίζουσιν. In this form of sacrifice, the animal is slaughtered so that the blood runs into the earth, often into a pit; the usual victim, at least for soldier-heroes like ours, is an ox or bull.[30] It is true that such a sacrifice might be performed for men who really did die in battle; it was performed, for example, in Athens' public cemetery at the festival Epitaphia, and on the field of Plataea at the annual grave service.[31] But it was more commonly performed for legendary heroes; the bull

---

30 Pfister, *Reliquienkult* 2.466–80; S. Eitrem, *RE* 8.1 (1912) 1123–4 *s.v.* Heros; P. Stengel, *Die griechischen Kultusaltertümer*[3] (Munich 1920) 138–44.

31 Athens: [Arist.] *Ath.* 58.1 (*lege* καὶ τοῖς τετελευτηκόσιν ... ἐναγίσματα ποιεῖ); Heliod. *Aeth.* 1.17.5. Plataea: Plut. *Arist.* 21.3, 5. A similar sacrifice at Megara: *IG* 7.53 (Peek, *GVI* 9; Page, *FGE* 'Simonides' 16) line 13. Another on Thasos: J. Pouilloux, *Recherches sur l'histoire et les cultes de Thasos* 1 (Paris 1954) 371–2 no. 141 (*LSCG Suppl.* 64; *Nouv. choix d'inscr. gr.* 19) lines 10–11.

sacrifice for Aristomenes at Messene is described by Pausanias and receives attention in a document of the Augustan period.[32] The blood was for the heroes to drink: the Polemarch at Athens and the archon at Plataea called on those 'brave men' to come and drink. The lifeblood spouting from a large animal makes a substantial drink, but it was needed, especially for a plurality of legendary heroes. At Zancle in Sicily the officiants called on the nameless founder-hero to bring two or more companions; for 'ox's blood is shed in plenty.'[33]

At Phigaleia the sacrifice is avowedly made for one hundred picked men of old; it was therefore on a large scale. Harmodius mentions our sacrifice as an instance of the robust Phigaleian way of taking food and drink. He describes such customs in general, as seen in daily life; but two festivals are singled out. The one is the festival of Dionysus, the chief deity of Phigaleia; the other is the sacrifice for 'the heroes.' 'Whenever they sacrifice to the heroes, a great ox sacrifice takes place,' ὅταν δὲ τοῖς ἥρωσι θύωσι, βουθυσία μεγάλη γίνεται, 'and they all feast together with their slaves. At the feast the children eat together with their fathers, sitting naked on stones.'[34] There can be no doubt that our sacrifice is in view. Harmodius' term is θύειν rather than ἐναγίζειν because he thinks of the feast enjoyed by the worshippers, not of the blood offered to the heroes. The oxen which provide blood for a hundred heroes will provide abundant meat for a public feast. In a town the size of Phigaleia there can hardly have been more than one festival addressed to a group of 'heroes' and featuring 'a great ox sacrifice.' The Phigaleians had a reputation as trenchermen; though Harmodius traced it to the influence of Messenia, our hero cult must have already set them on the path.

It is possible that the cult is referred to in a very fragmentary inscription, among 'sacrifices in the agora';[35] but we learn nothing more. Harmodius' picture is of a hearty meal and general good fellowship; masters and slaves, parents and children dine together. Such companionable feasts

32 Paus. 4.32.3. L. Migeotte, BCH 109 (1985) 597–607 lines 13–14, a contribution of money εἰς ἐναγισμὸν Ἀριστομέ|νει ταύρου.

33 πάρεστι δὲ καὶ δύ' ἄγεσθαι | καὶ πλέας· οὐκ ὀλίγως αἶμα βοὸς χέχυται (Callim. Aet. Bk. 2, fr. 43.82–3).

34 Ath. 4.31, 149 C (Harmodius FGrHist 319 F 1). Cf. Pfister, Reliquienkult 2.478, 486 n. 104; Eitrem, RE 8.1 (1912) 1126 s.v. Heros; Hiller von Gaertringen, IG 5.2 p. 107; Meyer, RE 19.2 (1938) 2084 s.v. Phigaleia; Jost, Cultes d'Arcadie 538. Meyer and Jost identify Harmodius' heroes with the Oresthasians; Pfister, Eitrem, and Hiller do not, nor Jacoby ad loc.

35 IG 5.2.421 line 7: καὶ θυ[σ]ίαι ἐν ἀγορᾶι θε[οῖς]. The stone is lost, and editors do not suggest a date.

were distinctive of Arcadia at large, and were also described by Hecataeus and Theopompus, quoted in the same passage of Athenaeus as Harmodius.[36] And there is something similar in Sosibius' account of the Laconian festival Προμάχεια, seemingly 'the rites of champions'; it too is quoted by Athenaeus, though not for any element of food or drink.[37] The celebrants included country people, 'those from the *chōra*,' and 'the children from the *agōgē*.' As others have remarked, a festival in which country people are prominent, whether *perioikoi* or helots, may well originate among the pre-Dorian inhabitants of Laconia, and so among kinsmen of the Arcadians.

Harmodius had no reason to say who 'the heroes' were. Did those jolly Phigaleians really think that they were honouring one hundred picked men from Oresthasium? It is legitimate to ask whether a large civic festival of a standard kind is likely to have grown up around a burial. There may be a better explanation.

Hero cults are found in the agora of every Greek city,[38] but the 'heroes' are exceedingly diverse. Most of course are mythical figures, but they range from the merest eponyms, who were doubtless invented on the spot, to solid figures of legend, who were recruited from some other quarter. A hero shrine is naturally regarded as a tomb, and sometimes there was an effort to make it literally so by fetching the hero's bones. Translation stories are attached to the cults of Orestes at Sparta, of Arcas at Mantineia, of Aristomenes at Messene, of Theseus at Athens (this last in the 'old agora' east of the Acropolis). Such instances are historical in so far as a pretence of obtaining the bones was put forth at a given moment. Finally, there are tombs of historical persons, of Euchidas at Plataea, of Themistocles at Magnesia, of Brasidas at Amphipolis. These historical tombs were not always invested with cult – nor were the mythical tombs – but they belong

---

36 Ath. 4.31, 148 F (Hecataeus *FGrHist* 1 F 9); Ath. 4.31, 149 D (Theopompus *FGrHist* 115 F 215).

37 Ath. 15.15, 674 A–B (Sosibius *FGrHist* 595 F 4). Cf. S. Wide, *Lakonische Kulte* (Leipzig 1893) 349 n. 1, 356; Nilsson, *Gr. Feste* 470; Höfer, *ML* 3.2 (1902–9) 3030 *s.v.* Promachos 9; L. Ziehen, *RE* 3A 2 (1929) 1516–17 *s.v.* Sparta; M.C. van der Kolf, *RE* 23.1 (1957) 641 *s.v.* Promacheia; G. Radke, *RE* 23.1 (1957) 642–3 *s.v.* Promachos 2; R. Parker in *Classical Sparta: Techniques behind her Success*, ed. A. Powell (London 1988) 145–6.

38 E. Rohde, *Psyche*[2] (Eng. tr., 1925) 1.127–30, 148–9; Pfister, *Reliquienkult* 2.445–9; Martin, *Agora* 194–201; Kolb, *Agora* 5–8, 31–4, 43–4; I. Malkin, *Religion and Colonization in Ancient Greece* (Leiden 1987) 189–266. Martin gives separate lists of hero cults and of burials (195 n. 2, 200–1 n. 5), but the distinction fails at every point. Kolb's thesis is that the agora as a meeting-place originates in the cult of heroes and chthonian deities, among whom he reckons Dionysus; objections are raised by R. Seaford, *CR*[2] 33 (1983) 288–9, and by W. Schuller, *Gnomon* 57 (1985) 363–5.

to the category of heroes installed in the agora. In the Archaic period it is often doubtful whether a person, or a burial, is historical or legendary: consider Battus at Cyrene, Orsippus at Megara, Cleomachus at Eretria. If we were disposed to believe that a band of Oresthasians were buried in the agora of Phigaleia in the mid seventh century, or even at any time in the Archaic period, it might well be the earliest burial of historical persons – it is almost the largest burial asserted for any agora.[39] But all these uncertainties only go to show that the main problem, the problem of origins, lies elsewhere.

Scholars have always tackled the problem of origins by asking which instance, or which kind of instance, comes first. It is, however, futile to debate any single instance, since there is no contemporary evidence earlier than the fifth century. Some maintain that the general practice owes much to colonies abroad, where the cult of founders was perhaps the first distinctive local cult.[40] But even if the practice spread because it was a fashion of the times, there is still the question of why it first began.[41] Why bury someone in the agora? Why feign that someone, a hero, is buried in the agora? One sees that in early days, when settlements were small, burials were made much closer to the centre; and that in later days, as burial was hedged with more and more restrictions, a grave within the settlement, and especially one near the centre, was for the most part unusual and honorific. But the agora, the muster-ground of citizen-soldiers, was never the obvious place for burial: not at the beginning, and not as a later development.[42]

The Greeks were therefore wrong in their belief that the hero cults of the agora arose from the burial of great men. Though actual bones were fetched, and actual burials made, all the instances are secondary to the belief. Yet the belief was universal: from the very start, something was done in every agora that gave rise to the belief that great men were buried here. Elsewhere we have dealt with another *locus* of hero cult, those festivals of the gods at which games were conducted; there the belief arose because games were common to funerals as well. Games, however, are but seldom attached to the hero cults of the agora; as a rule they are secondary,

---

39 The largest of all will be the purported grave of the Megarian dead from the battle of Plataea (*IG* 7.53); Megarian losses were very heavy (Hdt. 9.69.2).

40 Martin, *Agora* 198; Malkin, *Religion and Colonization* 266.

41 Scholars concerned with the archaeology of the agora, e.g., Martin, *Agora* 194–6, often speak as if it were self-evident that the agora will be the setting for burials, real or imaginary, of important persons. But it is not self-evident.

42 The burials in and round the familiar Agora of Athens were made at a time when the main settlement and its agora lay elsewhere, east and south of the Acropolis.

like the actual burials. The general custom that is shared by the hero cults of the agora was described at the outset: the slaughter of oxen or bulls and the shedding of their blood.

This ritual act was regarded as a means of refreshing the heroes, but of course it is a species of the large genus of ritual acts which we call animal 'sacrifice.' The term 'sacrifice' or *Opfer*, though always adopted in modern discussion, is a fatal misnomer. There is no such general term in Greek, or in the languages of other ancient peoples who treat animals in the same way.[43] Moreover, in normal usage 'sacrifice' and *Opfer* imply a recipient, a god honoured by the rite; but the gods themselves are doubtless projected from ritual, as the most ancient form of aetiology. It is better to speak simply of the magic use of animals. We must remember that live animals are the most potent item, for either public or private purposes, in the whole cabinet of *materia magica* (but private magic with more modest means makes do chiefly with birds, bats, and puppies).[44] Magic consists of actions as well as materials, and live animals can be subjected to many expressive actions. Demeter's pig was slit open and buried; Dionysus' goat was cut to pieces, then strewn about; other animals were burnt to ashes, hung in trees, sunk in water sources, and so on. Since burning is the most efficacious of actions, it was natural that it should become the typical use, called θυσία in Greek, but only for a small select portion of the animal, so that the rest was available as food.

The oxen or bulls of professed hero cult are brought to the centre of the community, the agora; they are used to soak the earth with blood. The centre is a part that stands for the whole, and all the members of the community may be on hand, adults and children, masters and slaves; for all will benefit from this fertilizing action. Like any magic, the rite originates not in conscious belief but in the urgent desire for important results, a desire that can only issue in suitable action. Actions like this one are very widely attested. In early Rome, where the magic use of animals was much more restricted than in Greece, the *mundus* at the foot of the Capitol was opened at intervals in late summer and autumn, the time for ploughing and sowing, and greens and fruits which were then in season were placed within.[45]

---

43 Cf. J. Casabona, *Recherches sur le vocabulaire des sacrifices en grec* (Aix-en-Provence 1966); E. Benveniste, *Le Vocabulaire des institutions indo-européennes* (Paris 1969) 2.223–31; R. de Vaux, *Ancient Israel* (Eng. tr., 1961) 2.415–46.

44 For the magic use of animals, *EMC*[2] 9 (1990) 432–4, and *Ancient Economy in Mythology*, ed. M. Silver (Savage, Md. 1991) 15–16. For Demeter's pig and Dionysus' goat, *GRBS* 29 (1988) 219–22.

45 The sources are given by A. Degrassi, *Inscriptiones Italiae* (Rome 1963) 13.2 p. 502, commentary on Aug. 24. F. Coarelli, *Il foro romano: periodo arcaico* (Rome 1983) 207–25, has shown reason to equate the *mundus* with the existing *umbilicus Romae*.

Ritual precedes and begets belief. Greeks who shed the blood of oxen in the agora believed that they were feeding buried heroes. After all, food was brought to actual graves, and especially liquids like water, milk, wine, oil, and honey, which were all poured on the ground or into tubes inserted in the ground.[46] As each community grew up in the Dark Age or the Archaic period, the local hero acquired his name. At Phigaleia the shedding of blood was so profuse that it seemed to be intended for a large company of heroes. We may wonder whether their very number caused them to remain, for most observers, nameless and mysterious. Nameless heroes there were;[47] and to judge from Zancle, the mystery might arise just because the blood-letting was greater than any single founder-hero needed.[48] On this view Harmodius' 'heroes' had no other name that was generally acknowledged, and the door was open to that intriguing writer who also discoursed of Eurynome and Black Demeter in a fashion that no ordinary Phigaleian could understand.

A Festival of Apollo

We conclude that the story of those hundred Oresthasians is the *aition* of a pre-existing hero cult. Now as a chapter of Phigaleian history, the *aition* starts from a definite assumption, namely, that Phigaleia had been captured and was tightly held by the enemy, Sparta. This assumption prepares us for the Delphic oracle and some marvellous remedy. Pausanias, as we saw, was vague about the circumstances of the capture, saying only that the

---

The *mundus* has several aetiologies, all very feeble by Greek standards; in one it is a grave.

46 The blood of oxen or of any animal was no part of the liquid offerings at actual graves, no more than it was part of one's ordinary diet; or not until a much later time, when every deceased person was called a 'hero' and might be honoured with something like hero cult. In this as in other respects, modern accounts often confuse grave service and hero cult, asserting that blood was offered to the dead as well as water, milk, and the rest: e.g., W. Burkert, *Griechische Religion* (Stuttgart 1977) 299, where the sources cited in n. 42 plainly refer to hero cult, not grave service. Bull's blood was so exclusively the drink of heroes, the mighty dead, that it was fabled to cause instant death if drunk by any living man, such as Psammenitus or Themistocles. To say that it choked one by congealing is only a later rationalization.

47 Rohde, *Psyche*[2] (Eng. tr.) 1.126–7, 147–8; Pfister, *Reliquienkult* 2.463–5; Nilsson, *Gesch. der gr. Rel.*[2] 1.188.

48 Callimachus gives us both the invocation that was used at Zancle – 'come and bring two or more besides' (n. 33 above) – and a story of how two leaders quarrelled over the honour of being founder. Malkin, *Religion and Colonization* 197–200, assumes that the quarrel as well as the leaders are historical, and finds the invocation inconsequent: 'why not "one more"?' But the invocation is the primary *datum*, and it shows, if this be needed, that the story is only a routine fiction.

Spartans 'defeated the natives in battle and sat down to besiege the city; as the fortification wall was in danger of being taken, the Phigaleians fled, or else the Spartans allowed them to depart under truce' (8.39.3). Polyaenus tells us that the Spartans laid siege to Phigaleia and finally captured it by a trick (6.27.2). On a literal reading, we have two distinct occasions on which Phigaleia was besieged and captured by the Spartans. But Pausanias and Polyaenus are both equally delusive; we cannot rely on either, much less on both. Pausanias, or possibly his source, gives a vague summation. Polyaenus gives us another picturesque *aition*, as the previous chapter of Phigaleian history.

Polyaenus' strategem survives only in a late paraphrase, as follows.[49] 'The Phigaleians while besieged sent a herald summoning the Argives to alliance. The Spartans got hold of him, changed their dress to look like Argives, and advanced as if by the route leading from Argos,' Ἀργείων σχῆμα μεταμφιασάμενοι ἐφέροντο ὡς ἀπὸ τῆς ἐξ Ἀργείων ἀπαγούσης ὁδοῦ. 'When the Phigaleians saw them, they thought the alliance had come, and opened the gates and admitted them.'

Like so many of the strange deceptions narrated by later Greek historians, and then excerpted as 'strategems,' this is not a credible story. An invading army could not disguise itself completely as a relief force of friends. Yet the details are circumstantial: there is a herald, and there is a body of men dressed like Argive soldiers, and marching along the road as if from Argos, and entering the gates of Phigaleia. We must assume that such a scene was actually before the eye: it was a ceremonial procession, and it was said, as ceremonies often are, to be the re-enactment of something that once happened, something important – the capture of Phigaleia by the Spartans.

How can a processioner look very much like an Argive soldier, and not at all like a Spartan? By far the most conspicuous and distinctive element in a soldier's appearance is his shield; therefore the procession was of men carrying shields. It is harder to say how the distinction between Argive and Spartan shields was conceived. All hoplite soldiers carried a large round shield, which was usually painted with either an individual device or a national emblem, such as Λ for 'Lacedaemon'; whether or not the shields at Phigaleia bore any emblems, the *aition* might well assume that they had once been the means of disguise. The Argives were, however, famous for the colour of their shields, painted

49 The epitome of Polyaenus preserves fifteen strategems lost from the original work: Melber, *praef.* xix–xx. This one is told in the epitomator's own words; but whatever may have been omitted, it is clear that nothing has been added.

white;[50] conceivably the shields at Phigaleia were white. It is also true that, whereas the standard round shield is called 'Argive,' as the standard helmet is called 'Corinthian,' because reputedly invented at Argos, we do hear of shields called 'Laconian,' for whatever reason, and a surviving Spartan shield from those captured on Pylus is not quite round but somewhat oval;[51] perhaps then the standard round shield was enough to suggest Argive friends rather than Spartan enemies. The precise distinction is of little consequence. There can be no doubt that the processioners carried shields.

Now on the site of Phigaleia, which has not been excavated, one of the visible remains is a large square block, probably a metope, with a hoplite shield sculpted in high relief.[52] It lies in the area where the monumental remains are thickest; for this reason the area has been thought to be the agora, and the metope has been thought to belong to the tomb of the heroes, the sole monument in the agora mentioned by Pausanias, apart from the statue of an athlete. These are only conjectures. We might say with a little more confidence that the shield metope is likely to come from a building close to the destination of the shield procession.

There is the question too whether the processioners carrying shields were the citizens at large, those of an age for active service, or rather young men of the age group just enrolled as adults, and newly furnished with their arms. After the Archaic period, it was perhaps not very common for a citizen army to turn out for dress parades at festivals, because it was too dangerous. Archaic Athens supplies the chief examples, a hoplite muster at the Synoecia and a hoplite parade at the Great Panathenaea; but (as we have seen) both customs were amended in due course.[53] The processioners at Phigaleia were more probably young men. Such *apodeixeis*, 'displays' of discipline or prowess, were staged by the young in every city, but those

---

50 Aesch. *Sept.* 90–1: ὁ λεύκασπις ... λαός. Soph. *Ant.* 106–7: ὁ λεύκασπις ... φώς. Eur. *Phoen.* 1099: λεύκασπις ... στρατός.

51 In their inventory of 368–367, Athens' Treasurers of Athena register ἀσπίδες Λακωνικαί, worth a quarter of a talent, as conserved in 'the old temple,' among many other articles of bronze: *IG* 2² 1425.397. In a small fragment of an inventory from the end of the fifth century, [ἀσπίδε]ς Λακον[ικαί] is one of two restorations proposed by Woodward, but the other is just as well supported by parallels: *IG* 1³ 413.2. The shield from Pylus: Thompson and Wycherley, *Agora of Athens* 92–3, and pl. 49d.

52 Jost, *Cultes d' Arcadie* 87–8, and pl. 20.3.

53 If we believe, with Aristotle, that Archaic tyrants made a practice of confiscating all arms in private hands, it follows that any armed parades were also suspended, both for citizens at large and for young men. But in the two cases distinctly reported, of Peisistratus and of Aristodemus of Cumae, the confiscation is but an *aition* of ceremonial observances. The case of Peisistratus has been discussed above, apropos of the Panathenaea.

of Arcadia were the most renowned, and took the form of armed dances as well as marches. [Plutarch] mentions the *apodeixeis* of Arcadia beside the 'Naked Sports' of Sparta and the 'Investitures' of Argos to exemplify the kind of martial music that was traced back to very early poets. Polybius as an Arcadian was proud of the military aspect of Arcadian upbringing; the dances performed by the young were called *'men's* dances,' i.e., warrior dances. Xenophon admired the armed dances of Arcadian mercenaries who kept up their youthful accomplishments.[54] Such dances are also imprinted in legend, in the joyful leaping of Nestor after he has killed or knocked down the Arcadian champion Ereuthalion; Nestor was then in the prime of youth.[55]

At Phigaleia the procession was led by a herald from a point outside the city up to the southeast gate. It was hereabouts that Pausanias saw the shrine of Saviour Artemis, from which, he says, processions started – i.e., outward processions to rural sanctuaries, and inward processions to city shrines.[56] The shield procession must have started from a shrine in the country, and the line of march shows which it was. The bogus relief force appeared to come from Argos, and not from a quarter where Spartans might be lurking. The usual approach to Phigaleia, followed by Pausanias, was from the east, through the upper valley of the Neda; Argives too would normally come this way. But now it was held by invading Spartans; so the putative Argives came instead from the northeast, along the road from Bassae. The starting-point must be the temple at Bassae, and the destination some cognate shrine in the city. A festival of Apollo, then. If it was also the first such festival of the year, like the Gymnopaediae at Sparta or the Hecatombaea at Athens, this was just the time for enrolling young men as citizens.

---

54 [Plut.] *De Mus.* 9, 1134 C, τὰ περὶ τὰς ἀποδείξεις τὰς ἐν 'Ἀρκαδίαι (the word should not be printed as 'Ἀποδείξεις, for unlike 'Gymnopaediae' and 'Endymatia' it can hardly be a name). Plb. 4.20.9, οἱ δὲ νεανίσκοι (χορεύουσι ἀγῶνας) τοὺς τῶν ἀνδρῶν λεγομένους. Xen. *Anab.* 6.1.11, the Arcadians danced in armour ὥσπερ ἐν ταῖς πρὸς τοὺς θεοὺς προσόδοις, i.e., as in their former *apodeixeis.*

55 Schol., Eustath. *Il.* 4.319 (Ariaethus *FGrHist* 316 F 7); cf. *Il.* 4.318–21, 7.132–57; schol. *Il.* 7.135 (Pherecydes *FGrHist* 3 F 159). The sense of the legend was explained by F. Vian, *La Guerre des géants* (Paris 1952) 242.

56 For the gate and the shrine, see Jost, *Cultes d'Arcadie* 84, 86, 88.

MAPS

Maps will help the reader to follow the argument at certain points. But whereas the argument only says that a given item (a shrine or other public building) is to be sought on this side or that, a map must somehow show it. I have therefore invented a good many locations, especially on maps 1 and 3. The intention is honest, even if the appearance is not. My thanks to Emily Robertson for executing these maps.

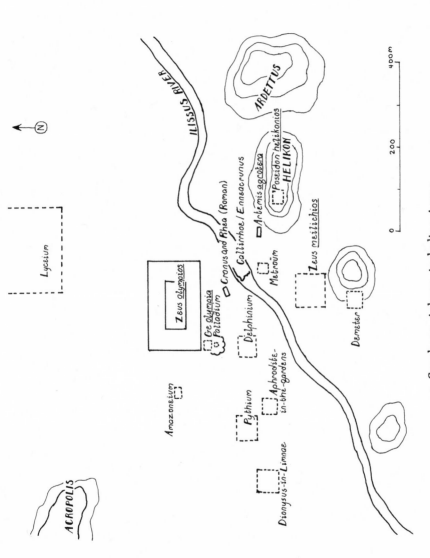

1. Southeast Athens, including Agrae

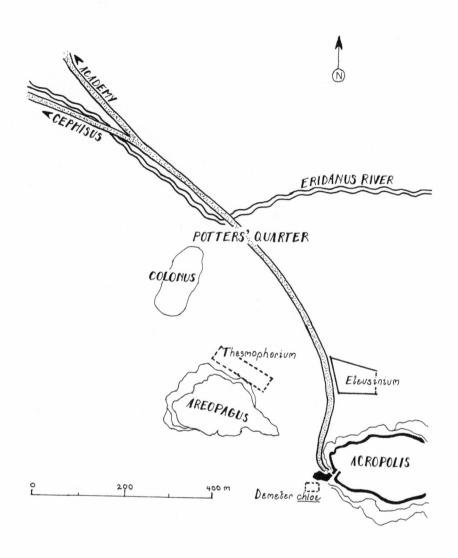

2. Northwest Athens, with Shrines of Demeter

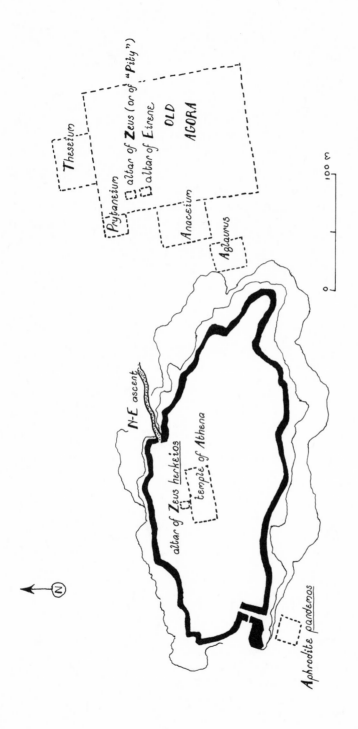

3. The Acropolis and the Old Agora

4. Attica, with Philochorus' 'Twelve Cities'

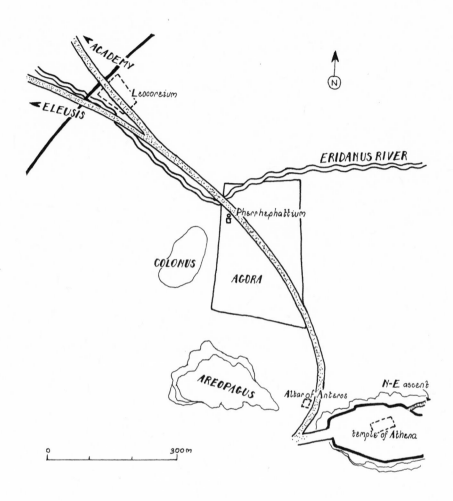

5. Northwest Athens, with the Route of the Panathenaic Procession

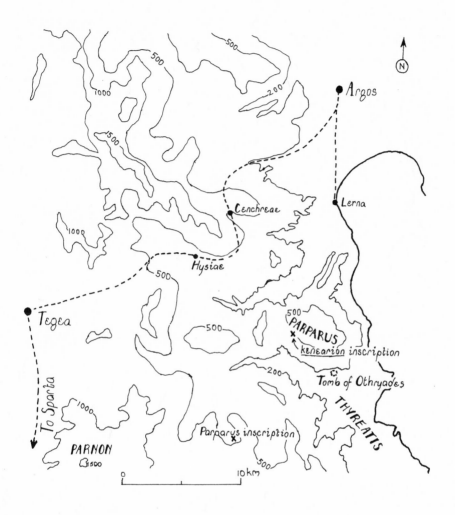

6. The Thyreatis; Cenchreae

INDEX OF SOURCES

Authors

Inscriptions

INDEX OF GREEK WORDS

INDEX OF
DEITIES, HEROES, SHRINES, FESTIVALS

GENERAL INDEX

Phoenix Supplementary Volumes